Innovations in Education

Reformers and Their Critics

Fourth Edition

John Martin Rich

The University of Texas at Austin

Allyn and Bacon, Inc.
Boston   London   Sydney   Toronto

Production Coordinator: Helyn Pultz
Production Services: Kailyard—Editing, Writing, Design
Compositor: A & B Typesetters, Inc.

Library of Congress Cataloging in Publication Data
Main entry under title:

Innovations in education.

   Includes bibliographies and index.
   1. Education—Addresses, essays, lectures. 2. Educational innovations—Addresses, essays, lectures. I. Rich, John Martin.
LB41.I4818   1985   370   84-6230
ISBN 0-205-08206-8

Printed in the United States of America

10 9 8 7 6 5 4 3

89 88 87 86 85

Contents

Preface

Education today is in a state of ferment. We hear about the loss of confidence in public education, the enrollment growth in private schools, retrenchment, tuition tax credits, back-to-basics, and the impending technological revolution in education. In light of these and other significant developments, a number of reformers have offered ideas for extricating education from the morass in which it finds itself. These writers are distinguished by their ability to break with tradition and the conventional modes of perceiving educational problems and situations. They have advanced some bold and imaginative proposals for transforming education.

All too frequently the proposals of these reformers are either accepted so uncritically that their ideas become dogmas rather than possible ways of liberating thought and action, or else they are rejected out of hand. In this book, selections by reformers are followed by those of their critics to overcome this problem. In this way readers can gain a balance of viewpoints, weigh reformers' strengths and weaknesses, and use the material to help develop their own positions.

There is considerable interest today in promising innovations and alternatives in education. They exhibit possibilities for new curricular and instructional patterns as well as a break with traditional forms of school organization and financial support. Both the pros and cons of these innovations and alternatives are presented here.

Thus the book consists of two parts. Part I contains representative selections by today's leading educational reformers. Part II is composed of selections, both pro and con, on the latest and most prominent educational innovations. The innovations presented may include but are not restricted to those advocated by the specific reformers in Part I. Introductions precede the main parts, laying the background for the ideas that follow. Readers may find it useful to read over the discussion questions and activities before reading the selections.

The fourth edition features changes in both parts of the book. In Part I, some new reformers and critics are introduced, more representative or up-to-date selections by earlier reformers are provided whenever appropriate, and some reformers who once were prominent but have faded have been deleted. New innovations and alternatives in Part II include managing retrenchment, microcomputers in education, experiential education and learning, tuition tax credits, and private schools. Other features include new selections for some of the reformers and innovations retained from the third edition, updated suggested readings and biographies, and new introductions, discussion questions, and activities wherever needed. Additionally, the introductions to Parts I and II have been greatly expanded and an annotated appendix of research sources for papers has been added. The numerous teaching methodologies currently in use have not been included but have been left for methods courses.

I wish to extend thanks to George Blanco for his help on bilingual education and to Arthur Brown, Bruce S. Cooper, Harold G. Shane, and Donna Logsdon for their constructive comments on the book as a whole. Susanne F. Canavan and Hiram G. Howard of Allyn and Bacon served as connecting links to the publishing world, Marian Morse and Pattie Rose efficiently handled the manuscript typing, and Rosemary Brandt quickly typed the permission letters. I have also been encouraged to undertake this edition by favorable informal feedback by the many who successfully used the book in their classes and by the reactions of my own students.

While preparing this edition I have been impressed by the great ferment in education. I hope the reader, too, will be caught up in the intellectual excitement of contrasting ideas and the vigorous search for solutions to today's most pressing educational problems.

PART I

Educational Reformers and Their Critics

Education today is under criticism. Many citizens believe that discipline in schools is far too lax; others believe that schools should return to the basics and fundamentals. Some students are concerned that schools and colleges do not adequately prepare them for the world of work; others find schools to be basically alienating institutions that deny them the freedom to learn as they choose. A number of reformers have joined this criticism with a more penetrating analysis of greater scope that seeks to locate the roots of the malaise. These reformers view many educational practices as anachronistic and dehumanizing and attempt to show how these conditions can be overcome and new ways of educating can be initiated.

Enrollments have declined in some school districts and funding has been shifted to other needed community services. Many agree that taxes are too high, with some communities even defeating school bond issues. Citizens are demanding that schools become more accountable and that both teachers and students demonstrate requisite competencies.

How should the dissatisfaction toward public education be handled? Reformers have addressed themselves to a wide range of problems and have offered a number of startling recommendations for reconceptualizing, restructuring, and revitalizing education. The essays in this anthology provide viewpoints that should inform, stimulate thought, and encourage the readers to reason carefully in order to clarify their own thinking about the topics addressed. If, in fact, readers are able to accept neither the reformers' nor the critics' positions, then it is their task to explore beyond what is provided here. (The suggested readings and discussion questions and activities should help.)

THE TASKS OF EDUCATIONAL REFORM

Generally one thinks the purpose of reform is to amend what is defective, vicious, corrupt, or depraved. It also aims to remove an abuse, a wrong, or errors, and to make changes for the better. Reform, which means to correct, rectify, amend, and remedy by making something right which is wrong, also implies changing something to eliminate imperfections or effect a new form of character, as in changing a policy within an institution.

The two characteristic types of reform are programmatic and systemic. *Programmatic reform* refers to curricula and programs that are used in or influence organized instruction; it also is associated with innovation. An *innovation* is any new idea, method or device that, in contrast to change, is deliberately introduced for some purpose. One could be an innovator but not a reformer, but every programmatic reformer is an innovator and much more, since he or she goes beyond merely introducing one or more innovations by developing an organized plan for change that may embody various innovations organized to achieve new goals. Thus both the scope and intent of programmatic reform differs from innovation.

Systemic reform pertains to authority relationships and the distribution and allocation of power and resources that control the educational system as a whole. It is often carried out beyond the school, drawing upon social and political forces with which reformers need to be aligned; it calls for a redistribution of power and resources. There has been considerable programmatic reform during this century but a dearth of systemic reform—which is generally understandable because of its threat to the educational power structure.

To perceive what is needed, reformers must be highly sensitive to abuses and imperfections and be dissatisfied and restless once they are uncovered; then they must develop a broad view and a bold vision of what is possible and seek to disseminate new ideas widely in hopes that the proposed reform will be implemented. While it is heartening to have strong organizational support, access to the media, and generous financial backing, few reformers can initially boast of such advantages. Some reformers may feel that their task has been completed once they write and speak to the widest possible audience. Others may go further by setting up learning experiments (Skinner), teaching in public or private schools (Holt), counseling students (Rogers), working with prospective teachers (Adler), raising funds to support reform programs (Jackson), teaching adults literacy skills (Freire), or setting up a free school (Neill).

THE CONTINUITY OF EDUCATIONAL REFORM

Today's educational reform is part of a process that began many years ago. Of course current reform has some distinctive features, but it is indebted to a long and colorful history that can only be ignored at our peril. While today's reformers may wear flashy new shoes, they still stand on the shoulders of great thinkers of the past.

Many of the earliest reformers' ideas were associated with a movement or an educational philosophy; therefore it may be helpful to see how each reformer relates to these broader patterns. Our survey will selectively focus on twentieth-century American educators but will relate them to European antecedents.

Sense Realism. Early European educational philosophy had an affect on twentieth-century American education by its opposition to formalism and abstraction in instruction, its deductive approach, its emphasis on rote learning, and its reliance upon the teacher's authority and the written word. In opposition to this prevailing system were Wolfang Ratich (1571–1635), John Amos Comenius (1592–1670), and Johann Heinrich Pestalozzi (1746–1827), who developed different principles of instruction sometimes known as *sense realism*.

Things should be studied before words because words and language itself are more abstract, according to the sense realism theory. For example, in a science demonstration, a thing or experiment would be shown first and then an explanation would follow. Everything was to be learned by an inductive process that Francis Bacon (1561–1626) had advocated. The young, said Comenius, should see real and useful things that can make an impression on the senses and the imagination. If the thing is not available, a representation should be used. Books should have pictures, diagrams, charts; and many pictures should be hung in the classroom. Too often students in traditional schools were required to learn by rote and therefore would not have necessarily understood the material committed to memory; thus rote learning was discouraged by sense realists.

Nature, said Pestalozzi, makes no sudden leaps but unfolds gradually. Consequently, every instructional act should be a small, scarcely perceptible addition to what the learner already knows. Material should become more complex only as the learner's intellectual abilities mature. Each step must be well mastered before the next step is taken. Objects are indispensable, Pestalozzi believed, and must precede pictures. The picture comes later and aids the child in making the transition to drawing, reading, and writing. The child does not just wait passively to receive objects of nature but takes an active role in analyzing and abstracting the qualities of the object. Instruction should proceed from the known to the unknown, from the concrete to the abstract, or from the particular to the general.

Twentieth-century progressives in Europe and America took up the principles of sense realism and combined them with their own ideas. Sense realism, however, was far more suited to elementary than to advanced instruction. It did not develop a sophisticated theory of how the mind works or explain the operations of higher cognitive processes. Nevertheless it was a salutary corrective and an important advance over the inflexible and authoritarian instructional practices of the period.

Romanticism. Sweeping across Western Europe and Russia in the late eighteenth and early nineteenth centuries, *romanticism* became a broad movement that greatly influenced poetry, prose, painting, architecture, music, education, and the tenor of thought. It sought a simpler life, elevated feelings and emotions over intellect, empathized and identified with the poor and downtrodden, deified the child, expressed a love of animals and the beauties of nature, and contrasted these charms to the corruptions and cruelties of urban life. Jean Jacques Rousseau (1712–1778), the leading French romantic, was a highly influential figure in political and educational thought, whose ideas also influenced literary sensibility. Rousseau believed that man is born free yet everywhere he is in the chains of corrupt institutions. One approach to removing these chains was to educate the child close to nature by removing him from organized social life. Thus Emile, Rousseau's imaginary pupil, would grow up naturally by letting the laws of nature unfold and not having to perform tasks before readiness was evident. Rousseau attacked the notion of original sin and depravity by declaring that the child is born good. He recognized different stages of growth, explaining how the tutor would relate to Emile at each stage, and the different materials and activities that would be appropriate to introduce in light of the child's naturally unfolding inner development. The program would emphasize activities and experiences, deemphasize book learning, seek to avoid bad habits and instill good ones, and restrict desires so that they are in proportion to the ability to fulfill them. By the time of late adolescence, Emile would have acquired the requisite abilities to return to the larger society, learn from it, but not be corrupted by it.

Child-Centered Progressivism. *Progressivism* was both a movement and a philosophy for educating the child that developed in America and Western Europe during the early part of this century. It was based on placing the child centerstage in the educational process, emphasizing the child's needs and interests, striving to develop "the whole child"—not just the child's mind but the emotional, moral, social, and physical characteristics as well. Such educators as Francis W. Parker (1837–1902) adapted curriculum to the needs of individual learners and emphasized more active learning and less dependence on textbooks. William Heard Kilpatrick (1871–1965) opposed a curriculum composed of disparate subjects and instead promoted the use of student projects. For child-centered progressives, the teacher was no longer a taskmaster or authority figure but one who helped guide meaningful learning activities. The subject matter curriculum, which represents the way scholars organize knowledge, is not consonant with the way the child learns; consequently, programs were based more on the student's needs and interests and on valuable experiences and activities.

The child-centered progressives were influenced by sense realism and romanticism. Learning activities were usually approached inductively and were based upon concrete experiences before any generalizations were drawn. Progressive classrooms usually had many sensory objects—children's drawings, photographs of historical figures, bulletin boards, science displays, with live animals in some instances. Progressives believed in first-hand experiences that included frequent field trips.

As for romanticism, child-centered progressives held that the child was born basically good and therefore there is no need to place many restrictions on the child's self-expression. Although they did not educate the child away from society, they did believe in nature study and readiness for learning. Some progressives were more permissive with children than Rousseau advocated, and the teacher was more of an organizer of learning activities than a fount of knowledge. Pupil-teacher planning was promoted as not only a democratic procedure but one that would improve learning outcomes.

Child-centered progressivism was criticized by essentialists and other groups. *Essentialism* believes that the goals of education are to develop the mind and prepare people for citizenship responsibilities by having them study essential knowledge embodied in a subject curriculum that is taught by a knowledgeable teacher who expects students to respect authority and exhibit disciplined behavior. Essentialists charged progressives with neglecting basic knowledge, failing to discipline students properly, insufficiently developing their minds, and not preparing them adequately for citizenship responsibilities. Essentialism also rejected romanticism and the romantic view of the child.

Dewey's Pragmatism. Although John Dewey (1859–1952) was also considered a progressive as well as a pragmatist, he was not child-centered and criticized this branch of the movement for alleged excesses. Dewey claimed that one cannot develop a philosophy merely by doing just the opposite of what one is against. In other words, since the traditional teacher was usually authoritarian, the child-centered educator became permissive and laissez-faire; in opposition to subject matter developed in advance and neatly laid out in compartments, were substituted the techniques of teacher-pupil planning and reliance on first-hand experience; and in opposition to external discipline free activity was used.

Dewey sought to find the relationship between organized bodies of knowledge and the emerging interests and curiosities of the children. He agreed with child-centered educators that one should begin with children's interests, but differed from these educators by stating that one should connect these interests to what they ought to become interested in. The generic method of education, for Dewey, was the scientific method, which he believed could be applied to all areas of human inquiry by teaching problem-solving. Reflective thinking or problem-solving begins with an indeterminate situation where puzzlement arises, the problem is then defined, and an hypothesis is advanced to guide observation and the collection of data. The hypothesis is then elaborated and sometimes transformed to deal with the problem more expeditiously and effectively, and finally the hypothesis is tested by overt and imaginative action and is either accepted or rejected. If accepted, an indeterminate situation has been made more determinate; whereas if rejected, a new hypothesis will need to be introduced, elaborated, and tested.

Dewey's pragmatism related to his reflective thinking process. Rather than "truth," Dewey preferred the term, "warranted assertibility," to refer to the end result of having hypotheses successfully tested. Once one reaches the final stage of the reflective thinking process and accepts the original hypothesis as fulfilling the conditions of the situation, and once it has been subject to public verification, one is warranted in asserting the statement. *Pragmatism,* in other words, holds that ideas must be referred to their consequences for their truth and meaning. Ideas become instruments for solving problems, attaining goals, and anticipating future experiences.

For Dewey, life is development and development is growth. Because the characteristics of life are growth, education is one with growth. Additionally, since growth is relative to nothing but further growth, education is not subordinate to anything except more education. Education, Dewey says, is a continuous reorganization, reconstruction, and transformation or experience that adds to the meaning of experience and improves the ability to deal with subsequent experience.

Although Dewey achieved a wide following, his ideas were criticized by many different groups and divergent philosophies. Most prominent were those who rejected his pragmatism because it renounced absolute truths and values. Some held that there are some truths that remain true for all times and places, and these are the truths that should constitute the curriculum. And one cannot be considered an educated person until having wrestled with these ideas. Moreover, in contrast to Dewey's emphasis on the educative process, critics insisted on concentrating more on assuring specific learning outcomes that are measurable. More recently, a group of reformers, referred to as romantic naturalists (though they may have had some affinities with progressivism), rejected Dewey's conviction that schools can be sufficiently improved to become fully educative institutions.

Romantic Naturalists. The *romantic naturalists* of the late 1960s and early 1970s shared some beliefs with the early progressives. Like the progressives, they believed that the child rather than the subject matter should be the focal point—the child's needs interests, and concerns. They also objected to practices that stifled initiative, creativity, and freedom to develop, and sought to make the classroom a place where children were free to move about question, and explore their interests.

But whereas the progressives believed that enlightenment and human progress could be provided by extending the benefits of a more responsive public education to all youth, such romantic naturalists as John Holt, Herbert Kohl, Jonathan Kozol, and the early writings of Neil Postman and Charles Weingartner generally held that school systems have become highly bureaucratic institutions that establish unwarranted constraints over youth, stifling their creativity and alienating them from schools. Some urged open classrooms and free schools; others offered different alternatives.

Paul Goodman, for instance, while seeing a need for compulsory education in the primary grades, opposed its extension to the high school. He recommends that the funds for compulsory secondary education be turned over to youth to establish their own learning communities and enable them to be free to experiment with their own life styles and seek their self-identity. The funds could also be used to promote apprenticeship programs. Ivan Illich goes further by recommending that compulsory schooling be abolished, the whole system be dismantled, and society be deschooled. He proposes instead informal learning arrangements in the larger society that would be based on natural interest and curiosity and entered into voluntarily. Thus the faith that Dewey and the progressives had in innovative organized schooling was, from Illich's viewpoint, seriously misguided.

Although the romantic naturalists have concentrated on how the student can overcome alienating learning conditions, they have made less of a contribution to curriculum theory. How the organizational and administrative structure can be transformed so that their ideas could be effectively implemented is seldom discussed. Thus they have rarely concentrated on the power structure and how it can be changed. Even Illich's deschooled society offers no assurance that the kinds of learning networks envisioned will be successful because the larger society itself remains essentially unchanged. Romantic naturalists also fall into Rousseau's trap in their belief in the basic goodness and natural curiosity of the child who, once freed from restrictions, will blossom naturally. But what is known about child development today suggests that far more structure and guidance are needed than the romantic naturalists would provide, if the child is to develop healthily and become an educated person.

Humanistic Education. *Humanistic education* was a movement of the 1970s that had more in common with early progressive education than did the views of the romantic naturalists. Humanistic education advocated the principles of treating the student as a person and integrating cognitive learning and affective experience.

Rational beings are people and must not be treated merely as means but also as ends in themselves. Thus the teacher would endeavor to gain an empathetic understanding of the students' feelings and values, and an understanding of how students perceive their schooling. Teachers should become more concerned with the personal development of each student than with acquiring bodies of knowledge. Teachers should seek to understand students as whole persons and avoid labeling them, since those who use labels apply a label to a behavior pattern and then posit the label as the cause of the behavior. Moreover labeling may legitimize mistreatment and set children apart from one another. Thus such labels as "slow learner," "delinquent," "troublemaker," and others may prove self-defeating.

Humanistic educators agree that the affective side of education has been generally neglected by schools, more emphasis should be placed on it, and it should be more fully integrated with cognitive learning. The affective domain includes values, attitudes, feelings, and emotions. Many programs in values education have been developed to enable students to develop greater awareness of their values and to think more critically and constructively about them so that their decisions will be better informed (see Part II on cognitive moral development and values clarification).

Numerous objections, however, have been raised against humanistic education. It is charged that such programs are likely to neglect the study of organized subject matter and the basics. There is concern by some parents that their children may be indoctrinated or inculcated with a set of values different from their own, and they insist that such matters should be the responsibility of the home. Some educators claim that most teachers are not adequately prepared to handle affective education programs. Moreover, it is suggested that such programs are difficult to evaluate. Even some of the basic concepts in humanistic education are difficult to agree upon and are extremely complex. Nevertheless, despite these criticisms, the ideals of the early progressives of educating the "whole child" were carried forward effectively by some exceptional humanistic educators such as Carl Rogers (see selection in Part I).

Freudianism. Sigmund Freud (1856–1939), Austrian neurologist and father of psychoanalysis, had a vast influence on modern thought with his theory of psychoneurosis and his stress on the role of sexuality in human development. Freud believed that there are basic sex and aggressive drives and stated a hard determinism in which early childhood greatly influenced the structure of personality in adulthood. His psychoanalysis sought the roots of neuroses by unearthing from the unconscious repressed wishes and desires of childhood.

Freud's influence on education, though important, was indirect and diffuse. Psychoanalytic theory offered the notion of *sublimation*, which held that the gratification of instinctual impulses, usually of a sexual or aggressive nature, could be achieved by substituting socially accepted behavior for expression of the prohibited drives. Teachers were to recognize unconscious motivation and seek to sublimate the child's repressed desires into socially useful channels. Teachers must also understand their own unconscious in order to improve the way they relate to students.

One example of Freud's ideas in education was Margaret Naumberg's Children's School in New York City in 1915. She thought the child should be weaned from egocentrism but found the task of doing so much more complex than most educators had imagined. Conventional education, she believed, only dealt with symptoms of the basic drives and therefore frequently led to further repression. Thus she sought to bring the child's unconscious to the surface of consciousness by permitting greater freedom, especially in the arts, which she thought would bring out the child's inner life. Children would also have to relinquish their dependence on textbooks and teachers and begin to develop independence of thought and action. Other examples of Freudian ideas in education are A. S. Neill's Summerhill.

Freud's theory has been criticized as not being scientific: it is not falsifiable and is unamenable to other canons of scientific experimentation and testing. Although Freud believed that his stages of psychosexual development and other findings were universal, they appear to be not only culturally relative but relative to certain social classes within a culture. Psychoanalysis itself has proven to be an extremely costly, time-consuming process that has a rather poor record of overcoming patients' psychoneuroses. Moreover, hardly any teachers have the technical preparation to apply Freudian techniques properly. Even if more teachers or guidance counselors developed such skills, one could still seriously question whether the application of psychotherapy is a purpose of schooling.

Reconstructionism. A new educational philosophy emerged during the 1930s under the leadership of George S. Counts and Harold Rugg, and was later brought to fruition by Theodore Brameld. *Reconstructionism* recognized that progressivism had made certain advances over traditional education in teacher-pupil relations and teaching methodology, but it charged that progressivism had become fixated on the child and thereby had failed to develop long-range, compelling goals for a society undergoing great social, political, and economic transformations. The crises that gave reconstructionism its urgency were the great depression of the 1930s and the earliest dangers of nuclear annihilation in the 1950s. The reconstructionists urged that a new social order be built that would fulfill basic democratic values and harmonize the underlying forces of the modern world. They put forth such ideas as: working people should control institutions and resources if the world is to become democratic. The aim should be the development of an international democracy or world government in which all nations will participate.

An education for a reconstructed society must recognize the interdependence of the world's population (as in cases of ecological and economic problems). Thus students need to study the realities of the modern world and recognize that they live in a global village. The teacher, therefore, critically examines the cultural heritage, explores controversial issues, provides a vision of a new and better world, and enlists students' efforts to promote programs of cultural renewal. The teacher attempts to convince students of the validity of reconstructionist beliefs but employs democratic procedures in doing so.

Although reconstructionism undergirds its beliefs and proposals by drawing upon findings from the social and behavioral sciences, the established empirical conclusions from these disciplines may well be insufficient to use in developing a planned international world order. Thus many of their assertions lack sufficient scientific backing. Reconstructionists have also been accused of indoctrinating students. While Brameld denied the charge, Counts insisted that it is not whether "imposition" will take place but the source from which it will come. Rather than have ruling groups or classes impose ideas on society, teachers, according to Counts, should take the lead in helping to build a new social order. But, one can ask, is this an appropriate goal for education? Reconstructionism does demand a commitment of the educator who in turn tries to bring about strong student commitment. It therefore assumes—probably erroneously—that a consensus can be reached on guiding ideals, goals, and values. In contrast, followers of Dewey would claim that students should be taught to use the scientific method but be free to arrive at their own conclusions.

TYPES OF REFORMERS

As an analogy, let us imagine a situation where five experts are called in to examine a complex machine that fails to operate properly. After examining the machine *A* and *B* think the breakdown is minor, whereas *C, D,* and *E* consider it serious and of major proportions. *A* says that the machine is a good one and all that is needed is a workable part, which he promptly installs. *B* agrees with *A* that it is a good machine and that the breakdown stems from a defective part; however, *B* believes that the part itself is obsolescent and therefore invents a new type of part that he claims will work more efficiently. *C, D,* and *E* agree with one another that the entire machine is obsolescent; they disagree, however, over what should be done about it. *C* points out extensive changes in the machine that will make it more effective; whereas *D* argues that the machine should be replaced by one that is different and much better. *E*, on the other hand, contends that all such machines can be abolished and society instead can have individuals and voluntary groups design a device that is not a machine but will provide genuine benefits.

Applying these five types to innovators and reformers, we can distinguish two types of establishment educators: a conventional and an innovative one. They share the view that the system should be both maintained and improved, but established educators place greater emphasis on maintenance. In the previous illustration, Individual *A* is a *conventional establishment educator* who believes that schools are basically good and when things go wrong they can be rectified by rearranging and reorganizing some aspect of the system. *B* shares with *A* a belief in the value of the system; however, *B* is an *innovative establishment educator* who believes that when problems arise innovations should be introduced and effectively implemented. Critics of the reformers would most likely be conventional establishment educators or innovative establishment educators. Some critics, however, may be neither educators nor key establishment members; but they are supportive of the establishment and essentially endorse the same position as *A* or *B*. They could be called *conventional critic* (Type A) or *innovative critic* (Type B). Many of the authors in Part II are innovative establishment educators or innovative critics.

Types *C, D,* and *E* are reformers. They all believe that drastic changes are needed and they seek to correct abuses; however, they disagree as to what should be done. Type *C* could be called a *system reformer*, one who believes that the school system is salvageable but that extensive and drastic changes may need to be made before it can truly provide quality education. *D* believes that public schools are too defective to offer a quality education and are unlikely to overcome their endemic weaknesses in the near future. *D* is an *options reformer;* she or he has left the public school to develop options, such as free schools, outside public education. Finally, reformer *E* is a *deschooler*, who usually argues that compulsory schooling should be abolished, support for formal systems be withdrawn, and learning should take place in informal networks within the community.

You may wish to keep these different types in mind while reading the selections in Part I to see whether doing so promotes better understanding of reformers and critics.

REFORM RATIONALES

Reformers may appeal to one or more of the following rationales to justify their arguments: (1) quality; (2) quantity; (3) equity; (4) rights; (5) decision-making; (6) restoration. Reforms that appeal to quality refer either to the outcomes of education or the process. An outcome criterion would focus on desirable outcomes amenable to behavioral formulation and measurement (competency testing, for instance). On the other hand, some reformers appeal to the worthwhileness of the educational process itself and the excitement and stimulation students find in learning (Summerhill and open education).

An appeal to quantity calls for larger appropriations, greater and more extensive facilities, more specialists. Such appeals were made during the post–World War II period of high birth rates and the later Sputnik era that appropriated more funds for training scientists and engineers in order to surpass the Russians in the space race. It is also seen today in the demand for higher teacher salaries.

Appeals to equity argue for reform on grounds that fairer and more equal distribution of educational resources and more equal access are needed. Such arguments are characteristic of the school desegregation movement and recent school financial reform proposals (such as the Serrano case in California).

A rationale that appeals to rights usually claims that certain fundamental rights have been denied and a need exists to rectify injustices and protect rights. Examples are arguments to eliminate corporal punishment, enact school dress codes, and protect children's rights.

Those arguments appealing to decision-making allege that certain community groups have been denied a voice in decisions about public education, consequently, reforms are demanded to make decision-making more widely shared. The community control movement, in which minorities seek power to make key decisions in neighborhood schools, is a case in point.

Finally, an appeal to restoration is based on the conviction that present standards and programs are inferior to those of the past. This argument is similar to the quality appeal except that it primarily seeks to restore neglected standards rather than invent new ones. The back-to-basics movement is an example.

Thus, depending on the case, reformers appeal to a rationale of quality, quantity, equity, rights, decision-making, or restoration. Deliberations about educational reform are likely to be improved by greater attention to the concept of reform and the rationale of reform arguments.

1
The Paideia Proposal

Since the philosophy of perennialism underlies Adler's educational proposals, a word about that philosophy is in order. Adler holds that there are absolute truths and values that are knowable, many of which are expressed in the *Great Books of the Western World*. The ultimate ends of education are the same for all persons at all times and everywhere; these ends are absolute and universal principles. The ultimate ends are the first principles, and the means in general are the secondary principles.

The problems of education are both theoretical and practical. A theoretical question is one that inquires about the nature of things, as in educational science and history. A practical question asks what should be done. Practical questions have three levels: the first and most specific is practice that deals with particular cases; the second is policy that pertains to a class of cases in which rules can be formulated; and the third is the principles that deal with universals or all cases (the realm of educational philosophy).

Education, for Adler, is a process by which the abilities of humans are perfected through artistically developed good habits. Education is a cooperative enterprise and no person can completely educate himself or herself. In other words, the infant is dependent upon adults—learning skills are initially acquired from others.

Adler envisions the goals of schooling to be the same for all students. This rests on his view of human nature: human beings are essentially rational creatures and rationality is not only a distinguishing trait (from animals) but also one of their best traits. Rationality needs systematic attention and cultivation; this can best be done under a plan of systematic schooling.

Adler's Paideia Proposal provides a more tangible grounding for his educational thought in a specific curriculum. His curriculum consists of three divisions: the first is devoted to acquiring knowledge in three subject areas; the second is designed to develop intellectual skills of learning; and the third is devoted to enlarging the understanding of ideas and values. Different methods of instruction are employed in each division.

The Paideia Proposal: Rediscovering the Essence of Education

Mortimer Adler

Mortimer Jerome Adler (b. 1902) was awarded the Ph.D. by Columbia University and taught at that institution, the University of Chicago, and was a visiting lecturer at St. John's College. It was at the University of Chicago, in conjunction with Robert Maynard Hutchins, that he developed the Great Books program. Professor Adler has been Director of the Institute of Philosophical Research since 1952. Since 1966 he has served as Director of Editorial Planning of the 15th edition of Encyclopedia Britannica *and has been Chairman of the Board of Editors since 1974. Since 1945 he has been Associate Editor of the* Great Books of the Western World *and in 1952 developed its Syntopicon. Professor Adler is author and co-author of more than thirty books, ranging from religious to scientific studies. Philosophically, he is one of the leading perennialists.*

In the first 80 years of this century, we have met the obligation imposed on us by the principle of equal educational opportunity, but only in a quantitative sense. Now, as we approach the end of the century, we must achieve equality in qualitative terms.

This means a completely one-track system of schooling. It means, at the basic level, giving all the young the same kind of schooling, whether or not they are college bound.

We are aware that children, although equal in their common humanity and fundamental human rights, are unequal as individuals, differing in their capacity to learn. In addition, the homes and environments from which they come to school are unequal — either predisposing the child for schooling or doing the opposite.

Consequently, the Paideia Proposal, faithful to the principle of equal educational opportunity, includes the suggestion that inequalities due to environmental factors must be overcome by some form of preschool preparation — at least one year for all and two or even three for some. [See definition and list of participants on page 20.] We know that to make such preschool tutelage compulsory at the public expense would be tantamount to increasing the duration of compulsory schooling from 12 years to 13, 14, or 15 years. Nevertheless, we think that this preschool adjunct to the 12 years of compulsory basic schooling is so important that some way must be found to make it available for all and to see that all use it to advantage.

From Mortimer Adler, "The Paideia Proposal: Rediscovering the Essence of Education." Reprinted, with permission, from The American School Board Journal, *July, pp. 17–20. Copyright 1982, the National School Boards Association. All rights reserved.*

THE ESSENTIALS OF BASIC SCHOOLING

The objectives of basic schooling should be the same for the whole school population. In our current two-track or multitrack system, the learning objectives are not the same for all. And even when the objectives aimed at those on the upper track are correct, the course of study now provided does not adequately realize these correct objectives. On all tracks in our current system, we fail to cultivate proficiency in the common tasks of learning, and we especially fail to develop sufficiently the indispensable skills of learning.

The uniform objectives of basic schooling should be threefold. They should correspond to three aspects of the common future to which all the children are destined: (1) Our society provides all children ample opportunity for personal development. Given such opportunity, each individual is under a moral obligation to make the most of himself and his life. Basic schooling must facilitate this accomplishment. (2) All the children will become, when of age, full-fledged citizens with suffrage and other political responsibilities. Basic schooling must do everything it can to make them good citizens, able to perform the duties of citizenship with all the trained intelligence that each is able to achieve. (3) When they are grown, all (or certainly most) of the children will engage in some form of work to earn a living. Basic schooling must prepare them for earning a living, but not by training them for this or that specific job while they are still in school.

To achieve these three objectives, the character of basic schooling must be general and liberal. It should have a single, required, 12-year course of study for all, with no electives except one — an elective choice with regard to a second language, to be selected from such modern languages as French, German, Italian, Spanish, Russian, and Chinese. The elimination of all electives, with this one exception, excludes what *should* be excluded — all forms of specialization, including particularized job training.

In its final form, the Paideia Proposal will detail this required course of study, but I will summarize the curriculum here in its bare outline. It consists of three main columns of teaching and learning, running through the 12 years and progressing, of course, from the simple to the more complex, from the less difficult to the more difficult, as the students grow older. Understand: The three columns (see chart below) represent three distinct modes of teaching and learning. They do not represent a series of courses. A specific course or class may employ more than one mode of teaching and learning, but all three modes are essential to the overall course of study.

The first column is devoted to acquiring knowledge in three subject areas: (A) language, literature, and the fine arts; (B) mathematics and natural science; (C) history, geography, and social studies.

The second column is devoted to developing the intellectual skills of learning. These include all the language skills necessary for thought and communication — the skills of reading, writing, speaking, listening. They also include mathematical and scientific skills; the skills of observing, measuring, estimating, and calculating; and skills in the use of the computer and of other scientific instruments. Together, these skills make it possible to think clearly and critically. They once were called the liberal arts — the intellectual skills indispensable to being competent as a learner.

The third column is devoted to enlarging the understanding of ideas and values. The materials of the third column are books (*not* textbooks), and other products of human artistry. These materials include books of every variety — historical, scientific, and philosophical as well as poems, stories, and essays — and also in-

The Paideia Curriculum

	Column One	Column Two	Column Three
Goals	Acquisition of Organized Knowledge	Development of Intellectual Skills and Skills of Learning	Improved Understanding of Ideas and Values
	by means of	by means of	by means of
Means	Didactic Instruction, Lecturing, and Textbooks	Coaching, Exercises, and Supervised Practice	Maieutic or Socratic Questioning and Active Participation
	in these three subject areas	in these operations	in these activities
Subject Areas, Operations, and Activities	Language, Literature, and Fine Arts Mathematics and Natural Science History, Geography, and Social Studies	Reading, Writing, Speaking, Listening, Calculating, Problem Solving, Observing, Measuring, Estimating, Exercising Critical Judgment	Discussion of Books (Not Textbooks) and Other Works of Art Involvement in Music, Drama, and Visual Arts

The three columns do not correspond to separate courses, nor is one kind of teaching and learning necessarily confined to any one class.

dividual pieces of music, visual art, dramatic productions, dance productions, film or television productions. Music and works of visual art can be used in seminars in which ideas are discussed; but as with poetry and fiction, they also are to be experienced aesthetically, to be enjoyed and admired for their excellence. In this connection, exercises in the composition of poetry, music, and visual works and in the production of dramatic works should be used to develop the appreciation of excellence.

The three columns represent three different kinds of learning on the part of the student and three different kinds of instruction on the part of teachers.

In the first column, the students are engaged in acquiring information and organized knowledge about nature, man, and human society. The method of instruction here, using textbooks and manuals, is didactic. The teacher lectures, invites responses from the students, monitors the acquisition of knowledge, and tests that acquisition in various ways.

In the second column, the students are engaged in developing habits of performance, which is all that is involved in the development of an art or skill. Art, skill, or technique is nothing more than a cultivated, habitual ability to do a certain kind of thing well, whether that is swimming and dancing, or reading and writing. Here, students are acquiring linguistic, mathematical, scientific, and historical *know-how* in contrast to what they acquire in the first column, which is *know-that* with respect to language, literature, and the fine arts, mathematics and science, history, geography, and social studies. Here, the method of instruction cannot be didactic or monitorial; it cannot be dependent on textbooks. It must be coaching, the same kind used in the gym to develop bodily skills; only here it is used by a different kind of coach in the classroom to develop intellectual skills.

In the third column, students are engaged in a process of enlightenment, the process whereby they develop their understanding of the basic and controlling ideas in all fields of subject matter and come to appreciate better all the human values embodied in works of art. Here, students move progressively from understanding less to understanding more—understanding better what they already know and appreciating more what they already have experienced. Here, the method of instruction cannot be either didactic or coaching. It must be the Socratic, or maieutic, method of questioning and discussing. It should not occur in an ordinary classroom with the students sitting in rows and the teacher in front of the class, but in a seminar room, with the students sitting around a table and the teacher sitting with them as an equal, even though a little older and wiser.

Of these three main elements in the required curriculum, the third column is completely innovative. Nothing like this is done in our schools, and because it is completely absent from the ordinary curriculum of basic schooling, the students never have the experience of having their minds addressed in a challenging way or of being asked to think about important ideas, to express their thoughts to defend their opinions in a reasonable fashion.

The only thing that is innovative about the second column is the insistence that the method of instruction here must be coaching carried on either with one student at a time or with very small groups of students. Nothing else can be effective in the development of a skill, be it bodily or intellectual. The absence of such individualized coaching in our schools explains why most

of the students cannot read well, write well, speak well, listen well, or perform well any of the other basic intellectual operations.

The three columns are closely interconnected and integrated, but the middle column—the one concerned with linguistic, mathematical, and scientific skills—is central. It both supports and is supported by the other two columns. All the intellectual skills with which it is concerned must be exercised in the study of the three basic subject-matters and in acquiring knowledge about them, and these intellectual skills must be exercised in the seminars devoted to the discussion of books and other things.

In addition to the three main columns in the curriculum, ascending through the 12 years of basic schooling, there are three adjuncts: One is 12 years of physical training, accompanied by instruction in bodily care and hygiene. The second, running through something less than 12 years, is the development of basic manual skills, such as cooking, sewing, carpentry, and the operation of all kinds of machines. The third, reserved for the last year or two, is an introduction to the whole world of work—the range of occupations in which human beings earn their livings. This is not particularized job training. It is the very opposite. It aims at a broad understanding of what is involved in working for a living and of the various ways in which that can be done. If, at the end of 12 years, students wish training for specific jobs, they should get that in two-year community or junior colleges, or on the job itself, or in technical institutes of one sort or another.

Everything that has not been specifically mentioned as occupying the time of the school day should be reserved for after-hours and have the status of extracurricular activities.

Please, note: The required course of study just described is as important for what it *displaces* as for what it introduces. It displaces a multitude of elective courses, especially those offered in our secondary schools, most of which make little or no contribution to general, liberal education. It eliminates all narrowly specialized job training, which now abounds in our schools. It throws out of the curriculum and into the category of optional extracurricular activities a variety of things that have little or no educational value.

If it did not call for all these displacements, there would not be enough time in the school day or year to accomplish everything that is essential to the general, liberal learning that must be the content of basic schooling.

THE QUINTESSENTIAL ELEMENT

So far, I have set forth the bare essentials of the Paideia Proposal with regard to basic schooling. I have not yet mentioned the quintessential element—the *sine qua non*—without which nothing else can possibly come to fruition, no matter how sound it might be in principle. The heart of the matter is the quality of learning and the quality of teaching that occupies the school day, not to mention the quality of the homework after school.

First, the learning must be active. It must use the whole mind, not just the memory. It must be learning by discovery, in which the student, never the teacher, is the primary agent. Learning by discovery, which is the only genuine learning, may be either unaided or aided. It is unaided only for geniuses. For most students, discovery must be aided.

Here is where teachers come in—as aids in the process of learning by discovery not as knowers who attempt to put the knowledge they have into the minds of their students. The quality of the teaching, in short, depends crucially upon how the teacher conceives his role in the process of learning, and that must be as an aid to the student's process of discovery.

I am prepared for the questions that must be agitating you by now: How and where will we get the teachers who can perform as teachers

should? How will we be able to staff the program with teachers so trained that they will be competent to provide the quality of instruction required for the quality of learning desired?

The first part of our answer to these questions is negative: We *cannot* get the teachers we need for the Paideia program from schools of education *as they are now constituted*. As teachers are now trained for teaching, they simply will not do. The ideal—an impracticable ideal— would be to ask for teachers who are, themselves, truly educated human beings. But truly educated human beings are too rare. Even if we could draft all who are now alive, there still would be far too few to staff our schools.

Well, then, what can we look for? Look for teachers who are actively engaged in the process of *becoming* educated human beings, who are themselves deeply motivated to develop their own minds. Assuming this is not too much to ask for the present, how should teachers be schooled and trained in the future? First, they should have the same kind of basic schooling that is recommended in the Paideia Proposal. Second, they should have additional schooling, at the college and even the university level, in which the same kind of general, liberal learning is carried on at advanced levels—more deeply, broadly, and intensively than it can be done in the first 12 years of schooling. Third, they must be given something analogous to the clinical experience in the training of physicians. They must engage in practice-teaching under supervision, which is another way of saying that they must be *coached* in the arts of teaching, not just given didactic instruction in educational psychology and in pedagogy. Finally, and most important of all, they must learn how to teach well by being exposed to the performances of those who are masters of the arts involved in teaching.

It is by watching a good teacher at work that they will be able to perceive what is involved in the process of assisting others to learn by discovery. Perceiving it, they must then try to emulate what they observe, and through this process, they slowly will become good teachers themselves.

The Paideia Proposal recognizes the need for three different kinds of institutions at the collegiate level: The two-year community or junior college should offer a wide choice of electives that give students some training in one or another specialized field, mainly those fields of study that have something to do with earning a living. The four-year college also should offer a wide variety of electives, to be chosen by students who aim at the various professional or technical occupations that require advanced study. Those elective majors chosen by students should be accompanied, for all students, by one required minor, in which the kind of general and liberal learning that was begun at the level of basic schooling is continued at a higher level in the four years of college. And we should have still a third type of collegiate institution — a four-year college in which general, liberal learning at a higher level constitutes a required course of study that is to be taken by all students. *It is this third type of college, by the way, that should be attended by all who plan to become teachers in our basic schools.*

At the university level, there should be a continuation of general, liberal learning at a still higher level to accompany intensive specialization in this or that field of science or scholarship, this or that learned profession. Our insistence on the continuation of general, liberal learning at all the higher levels of schooling stems from our concern with the worst cultural disease that is rampant in our society — *the barbarism of specialization.*

There is no question that our technologically advanced industrial society needs specialists of all sorts. There is no question that the advancement of knowledge in all fields of science and scholarship, and in all the learned professions, needs intense specialization. But for the sake of preserving and enhancing our cul-

tural traditions, as well as for the health of science and scholarship, we need specialists who also are generalists — generally cultivated human beings, not just good plumbers. We need truly educated human beings who can perform their special tasks better precisely because they have general cultivation as well as intensely specialized training.

Changes indeed are needed in higher education, but those improvements cannot reasonably be expected unless improvement in basic schooling makes that possible.

THE FUTURE OF OUR FREE INSTITUTIONS

I already have declared as emphatically as I know how that the quality of human ife in our society depends on the quality of the schooling we give our young people, both basic and advanced. But a marked elevation in the quality of human life is not the only reason improving the quality of schooling is so necessary — not the only reason we must move heaven and earth to stop the deterioration of our schools and turn them in the opposite direction. The other reason is to safeguard the future of our free institutions.

They cannot prosper, they may not even survive, unless we do something to rescue our schools from their current deplorable deterioration. Democracy, in the full sense of that term, came into existence only in this century and only in a few countries on earth, among which the United States is an outstanding example. But democracy came into existence in this century only in its initial conditions, all of which hold out promises for the future that remain to be fulfilled. Unless we do something about improving the quality of basic schooling for all and the quality of advanced schooling for some, there is little chance that those promises ever will be fulfilled. And if they are not, our free institutions are doomed to decay and wither away.

We face many insistently urgent problems. Our prosperity and even our survival depend on the solution of those problems—the threat of nuclear war, the exhaustion of essential resources and of supplies of energy, the pollution or spoilage of the environment, the spiraling of inflation accompanied by the spread of unemployment.

To solve these problems, we need resourceful and innovative leadership. For that to arise and be effective, an educated populace is needed. Trained intelligence—not only on the part of leaders, but also on the part of followers—holds the key to the solution of the problems our society faces. Achieving peace, prosperity, and plenty could put us on the threshold of an early paradise. But a much better educational system than now exists also is needed, for that alone can carry us across the threshold. Without it, a poorly schooled population will not be able to put to good use the opportunities afforded by the achievement of the general welfare. Those who are not schooled to enjoy society can only despoil its institutions and corrupt themselves.

HERE'S WHAT PAIDEIA MEANS

The Greek word Paideia (pronounced PIE-day-uh) means general, humanistic learning—the learning that should be the common possession of all human beings. That is why we adopted *paideia* as the name for our project and our proposals.

The Paideia group has spent more than two years thinking about what must be done to rescue our schools from the anything-but-innocuous desuetude into which they have fallen. My summary of the Paideia Proposal in the accompanying article must necessarily omit many details. But I have tried to describe the essentials of our proposals for the reform of basic schooling.

The other participants in the Paideia Project include the following:

Jacques Barzun, formerly provost of Columbia University, currently literary adviser of Charles Scribner's Sons;

Otto Bird, formerly head of the program of general studies, University of Notre Dame;

Leon Botstein, president of Bard College, Annandale-on-Hudson, N.Y.;

Ernest Boyer, president of the Carnegie Foundation for the Advancement of Teaching, Washington, D.C.;

Nicholas Caputi, principal of Skyline High School, Oakland, Calif.;

Douglass Cater, senior fellow of the Aspen (Colorado) Institute for Humanistic Studies;

Donald Cowan, formerly president of University of Dallas, and currently fellow of the Dallas Institute for Humanities and Culture;

Alonzo Crim, superintendent of schools, Atlanta;

Clifton Fadiman, director of the Council for Basic Education, Washington, D.C.;

Richard Hunt, director of program, Andrew W. Mellon Faculty Fellowships in the Humanities, Harvard University;

Ruth Love, superintendent of schools, Chicago;

James Nelson, director of the Wye Institute, Queenstown, Md.;

James O'Toole, professor of management in the Graduate School of Business

The Paideia Proposal: Noble Ambitions, False Leads, And Symbolic Politics

Willis D. Hawley _____

Willis D. Hawley is dean of George Peabody College for Teachers at Vanderbilt University in Nashville.

Any idea that has the support of both Mortimer Adler and Albert Shanker is an idea worth engaging and, some would say, worrying about. *The Paideia Proposal* enjoys the endorsement not only of these two luminaries but of people as diverse in background and commitments as Benjamin Mays, William Friday, Theodore Sizer, Ruth Love, Jacques Barzun, Alonzo Crim, Ernest Boyer, Clifton Fadiman, and Gus Tyler.* It has been the focus of national news magazines and TV talk shows. Bookstores in many parts of the country report that the attractive 84-page "manifesto" is already sold out.

Interest in the Paideia group's proposal

From Willis D. Hawley, "The Paideia Proposal: Noble Ambitions, False Leads, and Symbolic Politics."
Reprinted with permission from EDUCATION WEEK, Volume II, Number 12 (November 24, 1982).

---

*Benjamin Mays, president emeritus, Atlanta Board of Education; William Friday, president, University of North Carolina; Theodore R. Sizer, chairman, "A Study of High Schools" and former headmaster, Phillips Academy, Andover; Ruth B. Love, superintendent of schools, Chicago; Jacques Barzun, former provost of Columbia University, author, and critic; Alonzo Crim, superintendent, Atlanta Public Schools; Ernest L. Boyer, president, Carnegie Foundation for the Advancement of Teaching; Clifton Fadiman, author and critic; Gus Tyler, assistant president, International Ladies Garment Workers Union.

seems traceable to the growing national concern that our schools are not preparing our young people for the challenges of what Daniel J. Boorstin calls "the technological republic" and that this failure, especially when compared to the achievements of other nations, threatens our economic prosperity and even our national security.

The Paideia proposal eloquently urges on us a single-track core curriculum for elementary and secondary schools and certain strategies for teaching those subjects. There is much to admire in the proposal. There is no question that we need to change the curriculum of American schools to make it more rigorous and to ensure attention to more advanced mathematics, science, and language competencies. And, it is surely time that we ask more of youngsters than we are asking and that we insist that the gaps in achievement among and within most schools be reduced dramatically. It is easy to identify with Mr. Adler and his colleagues in the Paideia group when they assert that we should insist on education of superior quality for all Americans, regardless of their social background.

As a call to renewed interest in the quality of our schools, as a stimulant to re-examine what is being taught, and as a challenge to expect more of our schools and of our young people, the Paideia proposal contributes much to the growing demand for educational change. But as a guide to action, which it purports to be, the proposal leads us down primrose paths and away from the main roads we need to travel if we are to secure, as almost all now agree we must, higher quality education for all the nation's youngsters.

The Paideia Proposal is not a blueprint for a new structure within which we can bring about meaningful change in the effectiveness of our schools. Rather, it is an artist's rendering that pays little attention either to the terrain upon which the new structure will be built or to the practical problems of financing and construction.

Mr. Adler is impatient with those who

charge that the proposal is impractical. He has been quoted as saying ". . . I don't see why our group, having come up with the proposal, should solve all the practical problems." Nice work, if you can get it. But one reason one might want to engage practicalities is that they often suggest important shortcomings of an idea. Educational reformers are well acquainted with windmills, and the lesson of past reform efforts is that the search for "a solution" or "an approach" is futile. If only it were as simple as deciding what it would be nice for everyone to know (which is, according to the Paideia proposal, *everything* except vocational skills).

But the key to improving our schools is not curriculum reform. Americans have always sought a quick and simple fix to what they have perceived to be the problems of schools. However, meaningful changes will require that we undertake the complicated jobs of improving teaching, dealing with diversity, and ensuring effective management of resources. Better curricula will help, to be sure, but they are not *the* answer.

The inadequacies of our schools mirror the characteristics of our society. Dramatic inequalities of income, racial and social class discrimination, chronic unemployment in some sectors, and the historically low status of education are the causes, not the products, of schools' shortcomings.

The Paideia group's proposal fails us for at least three reasons: the idea of a core curriculum is not only impractical but educationally unsound; its attention to evidence about learning and school effectiveness seems nonexistent; and its emphasis on curriculum as the vehicle for change puts the cart before the horse and seems likely to direct attention away from more promising but more complicated solutions.

The single-track core curriculum proposed by Mr. Adler and his colleagues insists that all children learn the same things in schools. For example, all children are expected to know calculus. The first question is: Can all children learn—and become proficient in—the same subjects? It is one thing to say, as many scholars and educators now do, that almost all children can be expected to acquire certain knowledge and skills and to demonstrate reasonably high levels of achievement. It's quite another to neglect the reality that successful efforts to do this require heavy emphasis on a limited number of subjects and the adaptation of the pace and content of learning to the capabilities of students. Never mind that teachers do not know many of the things that the Paideia proposal says students need to learn. Let me assert that a majority of the nation's brightest college students—or philosophers—could not employ calculus to solve a problem if their lives depended on it. Fortunately, few of us are in such mortal danger or ever will be. The Paideia group wants everyone to learn everything—our language, a foreign language, literature, fine arts, mathematics, natural science, history, geography, and social studies. On top of this, students will take 12 years of physical education as well as industrial arts; they will be involved in drama, music, and the visual arts; and they'll learn how to exercise critical and moral judgments. Let him or her among us . . . cast the first stone.

The second problem with the idea of a core curriculum is that it assumes that all students learn in the same way. What people can learn— even if they have the same capabilities—is related to what they want to learn and to differences in the ways they acquire, process, and integrate information. These differences in interest and "learning style" are affected not only by what goes on in schools, but by differences in genes and in home and community environments.

Third, the Paideia group's heavy emphasis on a core curriculum ascribes more importance to *what* one learns than to the acquisition of an ability to learn and a love of learning. In a society where the average person may change occu-

pations five times and where the ability to use new information may be the most important determinant of success, our concept of what it means to be an educated person will need to change. It will be more important to be a learner than to be learned.

In dealing with the teaching and learning process, the Paideia proposal imagines that one can divide the things to be learned into three classes and for each of these a particular pedagogical approach is most appropriate. No evidence is offered to support this important assertion. Research on effective teaching suggests that good teachers have a broad repertoire of teaching skills and that while teaching a given subject the teachers easily move from one to another in meeting the needs of their students.

Those who study how children learn will be surprised to find that lectures and description are strongly recommended teaching styles and that the group advocates "coaching" as the major way to ensure that children develop their intellectual skills.

To accept fully the argument of the Paideia group, educators would need to overlook much of the recent research on effective teaching and effective schools because that research directs the quest better education to concerns largely unaddressed in the proposal.

The history of American education is replete with efforts to find, as the Stanford University scholar David Tyack has put it, the "one best system." We want desperately to make the big play that will, in itself, turn the game around. Whether it is desegregation, open classrooms, technology, or curriculum reform, we persist in searching for *the* solution. In many ways, curriculum reform is the most attractive strategy for change. It is easily explained, can be imposed from above (seemingly), is hard to argue against, and, if properly articulated, holds out hopes for great change. Everyone knows that a better cake can be had through a better recipe. But experience indicates that curriculum reform is illusory. The distance between mandating a curriculum and student learning is great indeed. The "new math," for example, stumbled on teacher incapacity and parental ignorance. The results of the more recent legislatively imposed requirements that economics (especially free enterprise) be taught in schools should provide no sense of security to those who worry about the collapse of our economy or the triumph of democratic socialism.

Curriculum reform is not only difficult to achieve at the classroom level, but the imposition of new structures lulls us into a sense of false security. As Soviet educators know, if people see everyone taking physics courses, they are less likely to ask whether students are learning about physics. And, as university professors know, if the curriculum is rigorous, the blame for student failure can be assigned to students.

The point here is the argument of Murry Edleman (professor of political science at the University of Wisconsin) that many public changes in structures can be thought of as symbolic politics. They create the illusion of real change, which, in turn, dampens the fires of reform and induces quiescence. The Paideia proposal is patent medicine in this sense. Unfortunately, the formula that will improve the health of the body education is more complicated and, probably, more difficult to sell.

At best, this critique may seem like overkill to many. The goals of the Paideia group are noble ones, after all, and the proposal will surely encourage us to rethink what we are doing. Isn't it all right to set high goals and let others worry about whether it can really work? No, it is not.

First, to pursue the holy grail with no certainty of its powers and without a reasonably good map is not likely to be productive. Such a quest, instead, is likely to be frustrating and to engage energies that could be better spent on the pursuit of more promising ways to improve American education.

Second, we have substantially increased our knowledge about effective teaching and effective schools, and it seems important to pursue the directions suggested by this relatively recent research. Some school systems are now engaging successfully in such pursuits though they are certainly less dramatic than the steps the Paideia group would have us take.

Third, a major obstacle to securing an educational system that produces high academic achievement among all youngsters is the social and economic inequality that distinguishes the United States from most other industrialized nations. The relationship between family income and academic performance is powerful. The Paideia proposal takes note of this fact by urging a system of preschool education, but it does not emphasize this strategy nor does it recognize that persistent efforts to expand publicly supported, early-childhood programs, which now serve less than one-third of the children who are legally eligible for (much less need) such services, have been unsuccessful. Nor does the Paideia proposal grapple with the fact that differences in the wealth of the haves and the have nots is growing and that the proportion of school children from families *below* the median income is rising. It is not enough to hold high hopes.

A growing body of knowledge about teaching and learning suggests directions for change that can increase the academic achievement of students from different backgrounds. A strategy for change must be of many parts. A core curriculum, much less one taught in specified ways, does not emerge from the accumulated knowledge as a strategy that has worked or is likely to work in the United States.

Instead, the research tells us, among other things, that student learning is fostered by engaging students in intensive success-bringing learning experiences, by using interactive teaching strategies, by refocusing the principal's efforts on instructional support, by restructuring decision making at the school level, by adapting the curriculum to student needs while insisting on high performance and steady progress, by creating school climates that emphasize academic achievement, by promoting change from the bottom up, and by encouraging stability in interpersonal contacts and curricula.

This is not an exhaustive list of promising strategies for school improvement. And, to be sure, we need to know more. But now that we are beginning both to understand systematically how to meet effectively the very diverse needs of students and to have the ability to learn more, it is time to put that knowledge and capacity to work.

There is in the land a sense that the improve-ment of our schools is not only necessary but possible. But failure to recognize that low achievement is critically related to poverty, to racial, class, and ethnic discrimination, and to the prospect of unemployment upon graduation is a form of national self-delusion. Changes in our educational system could improve the education of almost all children. But even if we make substantial progress in what and how we teach, the fundamental inequalities of income, status, and opportunities created by our economic, political, and social systems make it very unlikely that we will achieve equal outcomes for all.

DISCUSSION QUESTIONS AND ACTIVITIES

1. Is Adler warranted in advocating the same goals for all students?

2. "Our society," he says, "provides all children ample opportunity for personal development." Is that an accurate statement?

3. Basic schooling must prepare students for earning a living but not by preparing them for a specific job while in school. What reasons does Adler offer for this provision? Are his reasons adequate?

4. Examine the three broad divisions of the curriculum. What features do you consider unnecessary? What needs to be added? Should this curriculum be required for all students?

5. Adler's curriculum displaces many elective courses presently found in schools, specialized job training, and optional extracurricular activities. These activities, he insists, have little or no educational value, especially in contributing to a general, liberal education. Explain why you agree or disagree with this proposal.

6. Where would Adler find qualified teachers to staff his program? Are persons of the preparation he describes likely to be best qualified for such positions?

7. Willis D. Hawley claims that the key to school improvement is not curriculum reform. What, then, is the key?

8. Review and evaluate the three reasons Hawley gives for his assertion that a core curriculum is not only impractical but educationally unsound.

9. Hawley charges that the Paideia Proposal pays more attention to what students learn than to acquiring an ability to learn or gaining a love of learning. Is this accurate?

10. What recent findings from research about teaching and learning does the Paideia Proposal neglect?

11. Make a survey of present school systems for programs similar to the Paideia Proposal and evaluate their success.

12. Look at the recent history of education in America for similar programs. Trace and appraise their progress.

13. Organize a classroom debate of the Paideia Proposal and the perennialist philosophy on which it rests.

SUGGESTED READINGS

Principal Educational Works of Mortimer J. Adler

Adler has written more than 30 books and numerous articles. Listed below are his more important publications about education. See *Books in Print* for his other works.

A General Introduction to the Great Books and to a Liberal Education. Chicago: Encyclopedia Britannica, 1954. (with Peter Wolff)

"In Defense of the Philosophy of Education." In *Forty-first Yearbook of the National Society for the Study of Education*, Part 1, ed. Nelson B. Henry. Chicago: University of Chicago Press, 1942, pp. 197–249.

How to Read a Book, rev. ed. New York: Simon and Schuster, 1972 (with Charles van Doren).

The Paideia Proposal. New York: Macmillan, 1982

Philosopher at Large: An Intellectual Autobiography. New York: Macmillan, 1977.

Reforming Education in America. Boulder, Col.: Westview Press, 1977.

The Revolution in Education. Chicago: University of Chicago Press, 1958.

Works about Mortimer J. Adler's Educational Philosophy

Brameld, Theodore. *Patterns of Educational Philosophy,* Part 4, New York: Holt, Rinehart and Winston, 1971.

Childs, John L. *Education and Morals.* New York: Appleton-Century-Crofts, 1950, ch. 5.

Chu, Don-Chean. *Philosophical Foundations of American Education.* Dubuque, Iowa: Kendall, Hunt, 1971, ch. 3.

Hook, Sidney. *Education for Modern Man,* enlarged ed. New York: Knopf, 1963, ch. 3.

O'Neill, William F. *Educational Ideologies.* Santa Monica, Cal.: Goodyear Publishing, 1981, ch. 5.

Pratte, Richard. *Contemporary Theories of Education.* Scranton, Pa.: Intext, 1971, ch. 6.

2
Home Instruction

John Holt urged in his first two books — *How Children Fail* (1964) and *How Children Learn* (1966) — that children should be helped to make sense of the world around them in ways that most interest them. They should have the freedom to live and think about life for its own sake. Schools, he said, should become a smorgasbord of artistic, intellectual, creative, and athletic activities from which children take whatever they want and as much as they desire.

At first Holt did not question compulsory school attendance. But by 1968 he became convinced that the changes needed in schools and in teacher-pupil relations could not occur so long as schooling was compulsory. During the 1970s he focused more on educational resources than educational institutions by pointing to the many resources in the community: mini-libraries in storefronts, multilith presses, bulletin boards, tape recorders, photographic equipment, language tapes and texts, toys, games, puzzles, etc. Communities, he believed, could become places where it is much easier for people to share what they know, ask questions, and have their curiosity satisfied.

Since the 1970s, Holt has insisted that children should have basically the same rights as adults, and that compulsory school attendance is a gross violation of civil liberties. Young people should have the right to decide about their own education and whether they want to attend school or learn elsewhere.

He also claims that many adults dislike and distrust children. For these adults, life is hard and jobs are painful and monotonous; yet they persist anyway because of the work ethic. Thus schools are boring and regimented because that is what people want them to be.

Holt's advocacy of home instruction for concerned and able parents stems from criticisms of the educational system and his convictions that home instruction offers significant advantages over organized schooling. Home instruction, a young movement found in the United States and other countries, is promoted by various newsletters and magazines. A 1981 survey of the National Committee for Citizens in Education shows that 38 states allow home schooling. In some states, parents must demonstrate that they are offering equivalent instruction to public schools before being granted approval.

Holt's selection explains home instruction and answers criticism about it.

Though John Egerton recognizes many weaknesses in public schools, he wants to improve them and therefore strongly objects to Holt's recent failure to try to make schools more effective.

Schools and Home Schoolers: A Fruitful Partnership

John Holt

John Holt (b. 1923) is a widely-read author who has had a notable influence on parents who are dissatisfied with organized schooling. He is a Yale graduate, held various positions with the World Federalists USA, taught high school for four years in Carbondale, Colorado, two years in Boston, and elementary school for six years in Cambridge, Massachusetts. Since 1969 he has been an author and lecturer on educational reform and is President of Holt Associates in Boston. Mr. Holt has been a visiting lecturer at Harvard Graduate School of Education and the University of California at Berkeley. He has contributed numerous articles to magazines and is the author of many widely-read books, the first of which was How Children Fail. *He is editor and publisher of the magazine,* Growing Without Schooling.

In September 1978 Elaine Mahoney, whose two daughters attended public school in Barnstable, Massachusetts, decided to take the girls out of school and teach them herself (or rather, allow and help them to learn), at home and in as much of the world around the home as she could make accessible to them. She was, of course, by no means the first person to do so. For much of history this is what everyone did. Even since the beginning of universal compulsory schooling, a number of parents, because of geographical isolation (still often the case in Alaska) or personal conviction, have always chosen to teach their own children.

What was most significant here was not that the school board allowed Mahoney to teach her children at home (many other school boards have done so) but that it invited her children to use the schools and their staff members and equipment as part of their learning resources. In other words, the Mahoney girls could come to school as part-time volunteers, to use the library or take a special class, to go on a field trip, use a lab or shop, or take part in such activities as music, drama, and sports. The *Cape Cod Times* reported on 22 June 1979, "The school committee has made it possible for the Mahoney children to attend special programs offered in Cape schools in order to round out their education and to provide opportunities for them to socialize with their peers. In the past year [the girls] have attended school workshops in solar energy, woodcarving, beekeeping, jazz, and arts and crafts. . . ."

This pattern of cooperation between schools and what we have come to call home schoolers exists in a small but increasing number of school districts in different parts of the U.S.

From John Holt, "Schools and Home Schoolers: A Fruitful Partnership," Phi Delta Kappan *64 (February 1983): 391–94. Reprinted by permission of the author.*

In one district two children eagerly attend school one day each week to take part in a creative art class. A number of school districts have offered to supply parents with the textbooks and materials used in their regular classes, and one district provided a family with $200 a year to buy books and materials of their own choosing. Some children go to school for half the day only; others go for one or two full days a week. The oldest daughter of the Kinmonts, one of the most active home-schooling families in Utah, attends a regular drama class at her local high school. In June 1982 the president of the Utah Home Education Association wrote the superintendent of a large school district asking him how home-taught children might take part in district band and orchestra programs; the superintendent promptly took steps to make participation by home-schooled children possible.

Although such patterns of cooperation are occurring more frequently, they still seem to be more the exception than the rule. Most school districts, faced with a family that wishes to teach its own children, tend to respond with grudging tolerance, echoing the words of one superintendent: "We don't approve of it, but it's your right." These superintendents—and there are many of them—forbid home-taught children to use any school facilities; some have refused to tell families even what texts and materials the schools are using. Some school districts—probably fewer than formerly—respond to requests to teach children at home by threatening to take the families to court and even to deprive them of their children.

I contend that it would be in the interest of schools everywhere—even in the most narrowly conceived terms (e.g., budgets, jobs, etc.)—to follow the example of the Barnstable School District and cooperate fully with home schoolers rather than oppose them. First, it is simply not realistic for school departments and districts to perceive home schooling (as many seem to) as some kind of threat, either in the short or long run. True, the number of home-schooling families has grown rapidly in recent years and, if the legal situation does not change for the worse, is likely to continue to grow. But the actual number of families who have chosen not to send their children to school is hardly more than ten or fifteen thousand. Even if present rates of growth continue for a generation, it is most unlikely that more than 5% or perhaps 10% of families in the U.S. will choose to teach their own children. Most children will remain in public or private schools for as far into the future as anyone dare look.

A county district attorney in Minnesota, testifying before the education committee of the state house of representatives, cogently expressed the reasons why schools are unwise to pursue and prosecute home-schooling families. He said, in effect, it costs us a lot of time and energy to take these cases through the courts; we get a lot of terrible publicity; we lose many more cases than we win; and even when we win we don't gain anything, for the family usually just moves to another school district, or perhaps out of state, and we or someone else has the whole thing to do all over again. His remarks are true everywhere. Prosecuting these cases wastes a lot of the schools' and the courts' time, energy, and money—so much that district attorneys in some states simply refuse to prosecute them. Families do indeed win far more often than they lose. I cannot think of one well-prepared case (unfortunately, not all are well prepared) in recent years in which the family has lost. Since the press and other media have been generally sympathetic to home schooling, these cases almost always bring the schools much unfavorable publicity. And of those families who, because of poorly prepared cases, *do* lose in court, very few knuckle under and send their children back to public school. Most simply move to another jurisdiction or find another way to teach their children.

My point is that schools would be wise not merely to refrain from opposing home schoolers but to cooperate with them as fully as possible. For one thing, such cooperation might well bring schools some good publicity, and that would be a welcome change. About two years ago I spoke on a local television talk show about the Mahoneys' home schooling and their happy relationship with the Barnstable schools. Shortly thereafter, Barnstable school officials began to receive queries by mail and by phone from parents and school officials across Massachusetts and even from neighboring states. The Barnstable school district was naturally delighted to be the center of so much admiring attention and to help break new and important ground in education.

But a far more important reason for cooperating with the home-schooling movement is that it is likely to yield important ideas and methods that might help schools solve many of their most serious and intractable problems. To be sure, some of these problems have their origins outside the schools and can hardly be affected by anything schools do. But others have their origins in the schools themselves, in the way they are organized and in their fundamental assumptions. U.S. schools are burdened by a set of assumptions: first, assumptions about children; second, about learning; and finally, about teaching and the relationship between teaching and learning. These assumptions shape everything schools do, and I believe them to be a root cause of the schools' frustrations and failures.

Schools tend to assume that children are not much interested in learning, are not much good at it, and are unlikely to learn anything useful and important unless adults tell them what to learn, tell them when and how to learn it, check up on them to make sure they are learning it, and reward or penalize ("reinforce") them according to whether they seem to be learning it or not. These assumptions about children are often unconscious, and, indeed, school people often *say* the very opposite. Moreover, these assumptions about children are not supported by re-

search or experience. They are rooted in popular Calvinist assumptions about the inherent badness of children and in the deep need of many adults to credit themselves for anything good that children may do. No one with eyes and ears open and a mind in working order can long remain in the company of babies or young children without observing that they are in fact voracious, tireless, and skillful learners and that they *create* learning out of their experiences in much the same way that scientists create it out of theirs.

Concerning learning, teaching, and the relationship between them, schools tend to operate according to the following seven assumptions:

- The act of learning is inherently passive, difficult, painful, and dull—mostly memorizing uninteresting facts because one is forced or paid to do so.

- Learning is and can only be the result of teaching; nothing is learned unless it is first taught; children learn only when (and only because) adults teach them.

- Teaching is a mysterious and difficult activity that can best be carried out by specially trained and licensed people.

- Teaching consists mainly of dividing the material to be learned into the largest possible number of the smallest possible units of information and presenting them to children in a predetermined sequence, with an appropriate schedule of rewards and penalties.

- When trained and licensed people carry out these procedures and children do not learn (or soon forget what they are taught), it can only mean that something is wrong with the children.

- By definition, all problems of learning can only lie in the child, his or her family, social class, etc.; none can ever be blamed on the school, its teachers, or its methods.

- Therefore, an important part of teaching consists of diagnosing the many neurological, environmental, and psychological disorders of children — the supposed causes of their failure to learn — and prescribing and carrying out various treatments (rarely cures) for these disorders.

Of course, many people in education do not share these assumptions, and some oppose them passionately. Over the years I have met many such people — classroom teachers, administrators, professors of education. Yet, even at the height of supposed change in education, they have always felt themselves to be members of a small and hard-pressed minority, usually misunderstood, distrusted, or even despised by most of their colleagues, often in danger of losing their jobs. Never, anywhere, have such people said to me, "Around here *we* are *in charge.*" Instead, they talk mostly in terms of surviving. The effective and controlling assumptions of education and everywhere are the ones I have named.

One serious consequence of the prevalence of these assumptions, grounded more in folklore than in experience or research, is that they can scarcely be tested with a large enough population and over a long enough period to produce meaningful results. However, many small-scale experiences, in homes and in schools, have shown that, when children are allowed to decide when they will begin the exciting task of learning to read and are allowed to work out for themselves the problems of doing so (with no more help or checking than they ask for), the great majority of them learn to read much more quickly, enthusiastically, and efficiently than most children in conventional schools. But not in the foreseeable future can we expect a school district to duplicate this experience with more than a tiny fraction of its pupils — if any at all.

Similarly, many experiences in homes and schools (even in the penal institution for boys described by Daniel Fader in *Hooked on Books*) have shown that, when children who can read at least a little are given access to a large and varied selection of books, told to read what they like, and given plenty of time without interruption, checking, testing, or competitive grading, not only does their reading skill improve but they come to love reading. Yet even those schools that have tried such programs on a small scale and found them successful have rarely applied them more widely. A number of schools in various parts of the U.S. have begun to devote a short time each day to "sustained silent reading," but even these schools rarely allow more than 10 minutes a day for this work. To give even as much as a single hour per day to silent reading (thus taking time away from reading *instruction*) would strike most educators as a dangerously radical experiment.

Not in the foreseeable future can we imagine a school district saying to its students, "You can read anything you like, and as much as you like, and we aren't going to grade you on it." Or, "You can study whatever you want, and we don't care what grade you're in." Or, "If you're working on some project, take as much time as you need to finish it." If educational experiments such as these are ever to be undertaken on a large scale (as they should be), it is not likely to be in schools as we know them. Nor are we likely to see large-scale and long-term research conducted to find out whether frequent testing actually helps children learn or only hinders them, or whether other methods of evaluating learning might not be better than the standardized testing now almost universally used. We are equally unlikely to see any research that questions or examines any other standard assumptions and practices in education.

There is only one place where this kind of research is likely to be carried out on a large enough scale and for a long enough time to yield significant results. That place is in the homes of families who are teaching their own children.

This is the main reason why the home-schooling movement is so important to schools. It is — in effect, though certainly not by design — a laboratory for the intensive and long-range study of children's learning and of the ways in which friendly and concerned adults can help them learn. It is a research project, done at no cost, of a kind for which neither the public schools nor the government could afford to pay.

Even if our public institutions could afford such research, it would not be as good as that now taking place in homes. The idea that conducting research requires "professional distance" — according to the many teachers and student-teachers I have asked, still the prevailing opinion taught in many schools of education — ignores the value of flexibility of curriculum and schedule, and above all the closeness, the intimacy, the emotional warmth, and the security of those homes in which parents elect to teach their own children.

The absence of professional distance makes those homes effective environments not only for children's learning but also for the training of the parent/teachers themselves. All teachers who learn to teach well learn to do so mostly from their students, who show by their responses when teaching has been helpful and when it has not. But even the most attentive, perceptive, and thoughtful classroom teachers could never elicit from their students the amount and intensity of feed back that home-schooling parents typically get from their children, because parents know and understand their children so much better.

Some people might argue that this family activity could not properly be called research, that it would not be significant because it would be haphazard and uncontrolled. Careful sampling and other matters of research protocol may indeed be necessary if we want to know what large numbers of people are doing, but these procedures are worthless if we want to learn what people might be capable of doing. It

took only one person, Roger Bannister, to prove that the four-minute mile was possible. That no one else had done it was beside the point. Not only did he show that it could be done; he showed that, if you wanted to find how to do it, he — not the average runner — was the one to ask. So far, the home-schooling movement may not have generated statistically impressive numbers of success stories, but, if it is not legally prevented from growing, it is sure to do so. Meanwhile, as it grows, it gives more and more encouragement and support to those people within the schools who are trying to make fundamental changes.

But the home-schooling movement provides more than just encouragement to those who seek change in the schools; it also provides much useful information. There is a great deal of internal communication within the home-schooling movement. As people who teach their own children discover new ways to help their children learn (sometimes finding that the children don't need help at all), they tell this to others. When home schoolers have problems, they ask other home schoolers for help; when they solve their own problems, they share their solutions. If they live near enough to each other, they usually meet informally, sometimes as often as once a month. At these gatherings, home schoolers and their children get acquainted, share ideas and experiences, and often plan and carry out group projects. Since the bond between them is a strong one, many home schoolers become close friends; indeed, many people in the home-schooling movement liken it to being a member of a very large but close family.

Much of this communication between friends and colleagues is printed in the magazine I publish, *Growing Without Schooling*. Admittedly, some of this information is of interest mainly to parents, but much of it could be of immediate use to classroom teachers and others working in schools. The very first issue of

Growing Without Schooling contained a short article titled "A Studying Trick," which described a trick that I invented as a student that greatly improved my studying efficiency and would probably do the same for most students. And subsequent issues have contained many suggestions and reports about the learning and teaching of the so-called "basics."

Growing Without Schooling is only one of three national magazines devoted to home schooling, although it has the largest circulation and is the only one that might be called international (we have many readers and correspondents in Canada, Great Britain, and other countries). There are also at least a dozen state, regional, or other newsletters—all well-edited and informative. All of this activity adds up to a substantial, growing, and extremely useful network of communication and support.

As far as I know, there is nothing in public education that is comparable to this network. Certainly a great number of educational magazines exist, but most of these are written *by* the editors and writers *for* the teachers. None that I have seen are open forums in which teachers can talk freely to one another, especially about their problems and failures. Nothing would do more to improve the morale of teachers and raise the quality of their teaching than the creation of many such forums. Everything I learned about teaching I learned from my students, from my own experiences as a learner, and from talking, without fear of censure, to other teachers who were as puzzled and frustrated as I was. It is ironic that hardly anyone in the still-small home-schooling movement feels as isolated as do many of the teachers and others working in our giant system of public education. Whatever educators may think of the content of the home-schooling publications, they do offer a rough model of a kind of network of communication and mutual support that, once established, could prove very useful to the public system. One can easily imagine a school district newsletter in which administrators, teachers, students, parents, and the general public share their ideas about the schools.

One reason why many superintendents have been unwilling to allow families to teach their own children is that they fear—and often say candidly—that the schools will lose financial aid. But neither in the school legislation of any of the 50 states nor in existing case law is there any requirement that "attendance" must mean only the bodily presence of a student in a school building. Both in the intent of the laws as written and in established practice, "attendance" means taking part in an educational activity approved by the school. Local school boards can interpret this idea in any way that is acceptable to their constituencies. For instance, because of overcrowding or for other reasons, many districts established off-campus study programs, such as the Parkway Project in Philadelphia, which is now more than 10 years old. No one ever suggested that the schools would lose state aid for all students taking part in such programs. By the same token, school districts are free to register home-taught students in their schools—listing them as participants in a special program and collecting the proper amount of state aid.

But bitter experience has made school superintendents cautious. Some years ago, one of them told me that the average tenure for superintendents was a little more than four years. Thus it is unlikely that many superintendents would choose to run the apparent risks of including home-taught students in average daily attendance figures. Partly for this reason, I have drafted a model home-schooling law, which we hope we can persuade legislatures in every state to enact in one form or another. A vital part of this model legislation is a clause specifically authorizing school districts to enroll home-schooled students in the way I described above and to collect whatever state and other aid their numbers entitle the districts to receive. There is no telling how long it may take for such statutes to become law. But, once enacted, they should remove one of the major obstacles to full cooperation between schools and home-schooling families. Meanwhile, since this model legislation removes the main reasons why educators might fear or object to home schooling, it is certainly deserving of their support. Gaining this support will be an important part of the work of home schoolers.

Another important clause in the model legislation will establish by law the right of home-schooling families to use the facilities of the schools, part time and voluntarily. I believe this arrangement can also work to the benefit of the schools. First, these part-time students, coming to school by choice for their own purposes, can be a valuable asset to the schools. Their presence in the schools will say to the other students that some things taking place there are so interesting or so useful that people actually choose to do them. They will bring to the schools considerable energy, enthusiasm, intelligence, self-motivation, independence, and a wide range of interests. I know from my own experience as a classroom teacher that as few as one or two such students can profoundly improve the morale and atmosphere of an entire class. These part-time, voluntary students will give schools and teachers feedback about the attractiveness and the effectiveness of their offerings of a kind rarely available from regular students, who are often too concerned about staying out of trouble to say much of what they truly think.

There is also the real possibility that, as the number of these part-time, voluntary students increases, some of them may be interested in the possibility of working as aides to teachers of younger children. They could relieve teachers of routine tasks, such as reading to the class, which, though dull for teachers, would not seem dull to young volunteers. Most home-schooled children, unlike their peers who attend school, seem to like younger children and to be kind to them. In home-schooling families I rarely see the kind of bitter sibling rivalry so common elsewhere. Moreover, many children would find it exciting to be in a school, not as students, but as adults. Children both need and love to be useful and valued in the adult world, and working as teacher aides, for as little as a few hours a week, would give them one such opportunity.

Space is too short to discuss some of the other ways in which the home-schooling movement might be helpful to schools, teachers, and schools of education. Readers who would like to explore these possibilities in greater depth can do so by getting in touch with me. Meanwhile, I will close by saying that, since the schools have as much to gain by supporting home schoolers as they have to lose by opposing them, I hope they will hasten to set their feet on the path of cooperation.

Can We Save the Schools?
Yes, But There Isn't Much Time.

John Egerton

John Egerton, free-lance writer in Nashville, Tennessee, has written extensively about various aspects of American education for The Progressive, Saturday Review, *and many other publications.*

Anyone who doubts that public education in the United States is in deep trouble has not been paying attention. Beyond the grim prospects of Reaganomics, beyond all the thorny problems of school finance, an imposing mountain of difficulties has been rising year by year. The woes of the schools have to do with quality and effectiveness, with student achievement and teacher competence, with administrative and governing-board leadership, with basic skills and comprehensive curricula, with standards and values, with the increase in private and parochial school enrollments and the decline in the birth rate, with the weakening of authority and the worsening of violence and disorder, with the pervasive strains of race and class and sex bias, with the acute needs of the poor, the handicapped, the non-English speaking. More money might shrink problems, but it cannot completely solve them, or restore public confidence in the schools, or develop a national consensus on the means and ends of education.

No such consensus exists now. The rising chorus against Federal aid to education is being joined by voices opposing state aid or even local aid—and the proponents of more money for schools from any level of government are losing on every front. Pressure groups demanding specific moral or religious or patriotic content in curricula are countered by opponents who have their own notions of what constitutes "value-free" or "value-fair" material. Sociologist James Coleman's latest education study—a report which holds that private schools are superior to public schools—sets off a furious argument among "experts" over the relative quality of schools (and the validity of Coleman's data).

Anti-busing advocates want neighborhood schools. Textbook crusaders want the power to dictate content. Opponents of standardized testing want abolition of all such tests. New schemes to organize, conduct, and finance education are regularly advanced by all manner of critics and strategists arrayed across the ideological spectrum. Their proposals range from blatantly self-serving to blindly simplistic: tuition tax credits for private school patrons; government vouchers to finance "free-market" schools; segregation by subject matter or test scores or sex or race or socio-economic class; home teaching; instruction through computer terminals and television; the abolition of compulsory education; the "deschooling" of society.

With so much turmoil and frustration abroad in and around the schools, the temptation is almost overpowering to long for bygone

From The Progressive *(March 1982) pp 26–29.* Reprinted with permission from The Progressive, 409 East Main Street, Madison, WI 53703. Copyright © *1982, The Progressive, Inc.*

times when things supposedly were better. But were they? Those who think so argue that schools are now seized with violence and fear, immobilized by bureaucracy, fragmented by special interests, bankrupted by waste and inefficiency, split by philosophical and ideological differences, preoccupied with race and class divisions, filled with incompetence. And yet a persuasive counterargument exists: *There has never been a time when a larger number or percentage of American young people completed the requirements of schooling, left with a greater and more diverse store of knowledge, and went on to advanced training in such a multitude of endeavors.*

Whether for better or worse, the nation's schools have always been more nearly a reflection of the larger society than an expression of its ideals—and now they reflect the soul and substance of a nation gagging on its own divisive juices. Schools are essentially political institutions—they are, after all, the chief instrument for reproducing society—and it is unrealistic to expect them to be otherwise. They will not be agents for social change unless the larger society, through its political forces, is committed to social change. But they will be battlegrounds for competing factions whose interests range from a particular vision of the society of the future to a general determination to preserve and perpetuate educational institutions as they are.

Regardless of our greatly differentiated perceptions and expectations of schools, we are faced with questions we cannot easily answer: How will we pay for education's mission of reproducing society? Can a distinction be maintained between public and private schools? Is such a distinction vital to our democracy or merely an exercise in semantics? Do schools transmit values and indoctrinate the young? Should they? How? Whose values and what doctrines should they impart? Can schools become guarantors of equal opportunity? Can they nourish pluralism and diversity as well as

equality? Should formal schooling for the young be focused only on the basic skills? Could other functions of schools, from the arts and sciences to sports, be better provided by other institutions? Is the advance of technology in schools a promise or a threat to the education of the nation's children?

There is not much evidence that we fully understand the questions, let alone the answers. As taxpayers and parents, we seem instead to be endlessly preoccupied with arguments over taxes and appropriations and budgets, over pupil-teacher ratios and racial percentages and test scores, over credit hours and credentials, over a maze of abstract numbers that obscures our vision and our purpose. Schools have always been a focus of debate and controversy in this country; what is unclear just now is whether the present crisis in education is simply a replay from the past or a new warning sign of impending collapse.

I have always assumed, without really knowing, that faith in public education was rooted in our history; that the rise of schools for "the masses" in the nineteenth century was a belated but genuine attempt to fulfill the egalitarian ideal of the Declaration of Independence.

But in recent years a number of revisionist historians and educational critics have gone beyond the missionary zeal from which so much educational history has sprung, and in the works of this new wave of writers can be found some starkly different perspectives.

It is perhaps oversimplifying, and misleading as well, to paint in one brush-stroke the broad surface of views held by such writers as Bernard Bailyn, Lawrence Cremin, Paul Goodman, Charles Silberman, John Holt, Jonathan Kozol, Michael Katz, Herbert Kohl, Ivan Illich, Peter Schrag, Colin Greer, Joel Spring, Samuel Bowles, and Herbert Gintis. Certainly they are not of one mind about how we got into the mess we're in or how we might best get out of it. But there is in their investigations and insights a wealth of informed opinion that sheds light on both the past and the present. For example:

- The start of public education in this country was not a self-conscious attempt by the State to guarantee equality in the larger society; it was rather an attempt to reinforce tradition and authority and to keep control of a rapidly growing and diversifying population.

- The English principle of politics—that power (and thus education) should be preserved as an exclusive privilege of the rich and well-born—dominated the first 200 years of white settlement in this country, and not even the Revolution altered that fact. It was not until democracy was born on the frontier and swept back East that education, like the franchise, came to be considered a right of the many rather than a privilege of the few—and even so, "the many" were understood to include only white males.

- Waves of immigrants from Europe in the decades preceding the Civil War led liberals and conservatives alike to see schools as a device to encourage assimilation and perpetuate control. Far from giving the native and immigrant masses equal educational opportunity with the upper classes, public schools gave them a general indoctrination in the political, religious, and economic rules of the game—and a little taste of the three Rs for good measure.

- The educational reform movements generally associated with Horace Mann in the antebellum decades and John Dewey in the early part of this century were not intended to raise the opportunities and the status of the poor, or even to broaden the middle class. Their more fundamental objectives were to Americanize foreigners, to train workers for an urban/industrial society, to develop cooperative and compliant atti-

tudes as a means of maintaining social order, and to legitimate inequality by excluding or segregating blacks and others deemed inferior.

I find these views compelling, if not totally convincing. All of us who are old enough to remember the shameful years of legalized segregation must know that however much the public schools promised full freedom and equality for whites, they held no such realistic promise for blacks. We should have known, if we did not, that the economic and social divisions among whites were hardly lessened by the schools; they were, in fact, reinforced.

But even when I suspend belief in the questionable claims of the old missionary historians of education, I am still left with concerns that neither the revisionists nor the contemporary critics of schools have addressed. Two things in particular disturb me.

The first is this: *Public education, for all its flaws and shortcomings, is the nearest thing we have to a publicly owned and operated institution devoted to the general welfare.* (If our mines or our manufacturing plants were so owned and operated, we would properly call them socialist.) From Mann to Dewey to school officials of the present day, there has been and is at least the *rhetoric* of equal opportunity; surely the *reality* of it is closer to our grasp there than in alternative institutions yet to be formed—not to mention private alternatives that already exist.

Until recent years, the strongest attacks on public education came from authoritarian and undemocratic forces opposed to schooling for all at the expense of the state. It would be tragically ironic if the new critics and reformers of the Left gave reactionary opponents on the Right the ammunition that they need to blow public education away once and for all.

Yet opportunities for such destructive mischief already exist. A prime example can be found in current pursuit of tuition tax credits and educational vouchers. Tax credits would bolster private and parochial schools at the expense of the public systems—and that would include the alternative schools of many middle-class liberals as well as those of churches and segregationist groups. Vouchers, or government-issued checks to parents for free-market purchase of educational services for their children, would have essentially the same effect.

In compelling children to attend school, and in compelling the public schools to welcome and teach all who come to them, the State has assured universal exposure to education. The supply-and-demand forces of a so-called free economy do not apply to that process. But with vouchers or tax credits, there could be not more required attendance or required admission. The only compulsion affecting students, parents, and schools would be governed essentially by money—the need for it and the lack of it. Vouchers would create a seller's market, with school administrator-entrepreneurs taking only those students who bring the most money and the least needs and problems with them. Parents, on the other hand, would be limited to what they and their children could "qualify" for—financially, academically, socially. The voucher money from the government would never be enough to buy an equitable and effective school experience for the poor, the handicapped, the underprepared, the unmotivated, the "problem kids"; they would end up in the most marginal schools, while the affluent supplemented their dole from the public treasury with private funds to widen the gap.

The second thing that bothers me about attacks on public education from the Left is that the alternatives advocated by the critics are, to put it mildly, disappointing. Some of them are simply poor imitations of conventional schools; others have attractive features that offer no realistic promise of broad application; still others are riddled with ideological contradictions or based upon pure fantasy.

Ivan Illich led off the contemporary search

for alternatives with his proposal in 1970 for deschooling of society, by which he meant that "the State shall make no law with respect to the establishment of education." School, he said, "is the advertising agency which makes you believe that you need the society as it is." Others have followed with all sorts of alternative proposals to the present structure. The latest comes from John Holt, whose new book, *Teach Your Own,* advocates abandoning schools, which he calls, "babysitting services," and teachers whom he describes as "no more professional than bus drivers," and leaving your kids at home alone with their books.

Such anarchism flavored the proposals of frustrated critics of education in the past, long before Illich and Holt. There was, for example, the Modern School in Shelton, New Jersey, more than a half-century ago, and there have been others similarly devoted to radical re-creation of educational institutions. But now as then, while the alternatives may be interesting or even valuable, they cannot begin to meet the needs of millions of children. It is only the middle and upper classes who can afford to experiment with exotic new forms of schooling, whether their goal is the realization of equality or the enhancement of economic and social advantage.

The poor have less money, more needs and—most important—more children. As the costs of education rise, as the effectiveness of schools diminishes, as more and more unskilled jobs disappear from the nation's economy, and as the affluent, whatever their ideological bent, wander farther in search of educational alternatives for their children, the middle and upper classes are becoming as unmotivated to pay for public schools they'll never use as many of the wealthy are to pay for legal services for the indigent or public transportation or national health insurance or even Social Security.

We are dangerously near a time when public schools could become, like public housing or public jails, places where the poor are confined against their will. If we allow that to happen, it will not be the poor alone who lose; it will be all of us.

Saying the schools have failed and are hopeless is like saying racial integration has failed and can never be achieved. We have, in fact, never agreed upon the goals of education (or integration) or given them a fair trial. It is the society, the system, that has failed, not its ideals—and to give up now is to strengthen the hands of those who want the ideals to succumb.

To the extent that fighting for reform in public education requires or implies defense of it in its present condition, such a posture is at best uncomfortable and at worst indefensible. There is so much wrong with schools as they are, so

much to be critical of, and not enough to inspire spirited defense. Schools that leave thousands of young people illiterate deserve condemnation; so do schools and teachers and administrators and boards of education that value order above freedom, control above creativity, and self-preservation above all.

But realism draws me back to the central question: Where is there an alternative to the present structure of the public education that offers any promise at all of genuine equality and opportunity for almost fifty million school-age children in the United States? I can see none. We will realize a society equal to its ideals—and a school system worthy of it—or we will, quite literally, die trying.

Can We Save the Schools?
No, and They're Not Worth Saving.

John Holt _____

I have to decline your kind invitation to submit a companion article to John Egerton's. I am finishing a book against a tight deadline. With the other work I have to do here, that keeps me busy seven days a week. Sometime in the near future, I expect to begin a book about what kinds of changes in structure, function, philosophy, and methods might lift the "public" schools out of

their downward spiral and into the beginnings of an upward one. But I can't get into that now.

Nonetheless, I want to respond briefly in letter form to some of the points Egerton raises. In the first place, I can think of no meaningful sense in which the "public" schools are public. They are about as public as the Pentagon. In Chicago, the schools are controlled by a small

From The Progressive *(March 1982) pp. 26–29. Reprinted with permission from The Progressive, 409 East Main Street, Madison, WI 53703. Copyright © 1982, The Progressive, Inc.*

board of businessmen. In many cities, including my own, the day-to-day operations of the schools are controlled by judges who are completely outside the political process. In no communities do the citizens and voters exercise any effective control over choice of teachers, curricula (which are more and more determined at the state level), methods, or materials. Indeed, in thousands of communities effective local schools have been closed over the furious protests of the citizens.

The "public" schools are, in fact, a government monopoly, rather like our nuclear monopolies, and about equally sensitive and responsive to public input.

The public schools were never formed for a "public" purpose, and John Egerton half admits that. They were formed primarily to serve the interests of the rich and powerful—specifically, to make sure that the children of the great mass of Americans would turn into obedient and politically passive workers.

The "public" schools—which I call government schools—never did help the poor. My authority for this is Fred Hechinger of *The New York Times,* who wrote in one of his columns that for seventy years and more it has been primarily the children of the poor whom the schools have failed, dropped out, pushed out. No one can dispute this; the record is plain. The government schools have long been bad for most children, but they have always been worst for poor children. They have not increased but decreased the chances of upward mobility in this country. All large schools track or ability-group their students, and every study of these groups has shown that they correlate almost perfectly with social class—the poorer the kids, the lower the group.

In my new book, *Teach Your Own,* I assert that with very few exceptions, the social life of schools and classrooms is mean-spirited, competitive, snobbish, status-oriented, cruel, and violent. I have said exactly the same thing face-to-face to more than 5,000 educators. Not one has ever contradicted me, even after I point out that no one has ever contradicted me. What they say, without exception, is, "That's what the real world is like." I have been told over the years more times than I could count that the schools had to do this or that to get the children ready for "reality." Not one person who has ever said that to me has spoken of this reality, this "real world," as if it were a good place or could be made good, or even better. (I suspect this was not true fifty years ago, when many teachers thought part of their mission was to prepare children to make a better world.)

Indeed, this loss of any sense of humane or noble mission is one of the chief reasons why the schools are worse than they used to be and why their authority and discipline are breaking down so badly. They think, naively and wrongly, that authority and discipline can be made to rest entirely on force, fear, punishment, and the threat of punishment. Any half-smart Army sergeant knows better—and we learned in Vietnam that even an Army cannot maintain its discipline when it loses its sense of mission.

In the late 1960s Charles Silberman and a large team of researchers spent four years examining the government schools all over the United States. It was almost certainly the broadest and most intensive survey of our schools ever made. In his book, *Crisis in the Classroom,* Silberman had this to say about the schools—and please note that this was at the height of the supposed "permissive" revolution:

"Adults . . . fail to appreciate what grim, joyless places most American schools are, how oppressive and petty are the rules by which they are governed, how intellectually sterile and barren the atmosphere, what an appalling lack of civility obtains on the part of teachers and principals, what contempt they unconsciously display for children as children."

I don't know why he says "unconsciously"; many of them do it explicitly and repeatedly. Beyond that, Silberman says nothing at all about the extraordinary amount of physical violence to which children, above all poor children, are subjected in schools.

What we have in these government schools — and many of the private schools are just as bad — is not a preparation for freedom and democracy but a preparation for slavery and fascism. I can understand why the political Right should approve of this, but that the political Left, the "liberals" and "radicals," would do so surpasses belief. If you had talked as much as I have to Middle American audiences, you would know that there is nothing in the world they distrust, fear, and even hate as much as the idea of freedom, the idea that people — above all children — should have some real choices in their lives, should have the right to say No to Authority. In fact, I suspect that the only thing many Americans hate more than freedom is children themselves, perhaps because they are such a living embodiment of it.

Samuel Johnson said, "Patriotism is the last refuge of a scoundrel." We could equally say that it is the last refuge of the incompetent. Having failed dismally to do what they are supposed to do, the schools respond by wrapping themselves in the flag. What astonishes me is that people of the Left let them get away with this. When Charlie Wilson said, "What's good for General Motors is good for the country," liberals were smart enough to give him the horselaugh. But when the $100 billion per year government school monopoly, crammed to bursting with featherbedding administrators, says the same thing, liberals nod in agreement.

Amazing! And frightening!

George Dennison wrote in his wonderful book, *The Lives of Children,* still must reading for anyone concerned about education and especially about the education of poor kids, that even if we had an ideal democracy (which we are far from having) it would not take much more than a generation of government schooling to destroy it. I believe it is fair to say this has already happened. Only a tiny minority of Americans really understand what political and constitutional liberties mean and why they are worth defending. Should we expect otherwise? If we put children, for a large part of their waking lives, into miniature fascist states, why should we expect that at the end of twelve years they will come out understanding or believing in human liberty?

I cannot understand why liberals should object to the idea that poor people, or people of moderate income, should have some of the kinds of choices in education that rich people have always had. The logic is astonishing. Rich people should be able, as they are, to send their children to school wherever they want, but poor people should not have the right, *because it might hurt the government schools.*

Well, enough. I doubt that any of this will seem very convincing to you. But Egerton's piece thrust these thoughts into my mind, and I had to get them down before I could go on to something else.

But What Are the Alternatives?

John Egerton _____

I admire the clarity and quality of John Holt's criticism, and agree completely with most of it. But I am disappointed that my piece only provoked him to repeat the criticisms he has been offering now for a number of years, rather than to address the hard questions I have tried to raise. He says that "sometime in the near future" he intends to "begin a book about what kinds of changes in structure, function, philosophy, and methods might lift the 'public' schools out of their downward spiral and into the beginnings of an upward one." I only wish he would turn his mind to those crucial issues now, instead of giving us yet another analysis of what is wrong.

I can only assume from Holt's comments that he considers public schools and the people who run them beyond redemption, since there is no hint in his letter of anything at all that might be tried to make them more effective or more equitable or more productive. So what do we do next? That is the fundamental issue, as far as I am concerned.

Holt seems to suggest that some sort of tuition tax credit or voucher system would serve us well. "I cannot understand," he writes, "why liberals should object to the idea that poor people, or people of moderate income, should have some of the kinds of choices in education that rich people have always had." I have stated my objections to such schemes; I won't go further here, except to note what an irony is embedded in the notion that so-called free and competitive private enterprise—the folks who brought us Exxon, Ma Bell, Texaco—might bring salvation to a publicly owned and operated school system that has failed us.

The shortcomings of this people's school system must surely be familiar to all of us by now, thanks to the well-aimed critical lights of Holt and others. But the solutions will not be found in transferring the system from the reach of the people to the grasp of the capitalist moneychangers. It is past time for John Holt and all the rest of us to figure out what we're going to do when the school bell rings Monday morning. It would be wonderful to invent a new and better approach to education, if only we had the time.

DISCUSSION QUESTIONS AND ACTIVITIES

1. Why would parents who teach their children at home want to use school classes and facilities part-time? Are they inconsistent in view of their objection to organized schooling?

From The Progressive *(March 1982) pp. 26–29. Reprinted with permission from The Progressive, 409 East Main Street, Madison, WI 53703. Copyright © 1982, The Progressive, Inc.*

2. Holt says that he cannot recall a single well-prepared case for home instruction where the parents lost. Is he equating "well-prepared" with "successful" so that his statement is true by definition? If not, then what does he mean? Can a legally well-prepared case for incompetent or negligent parents be successful?

3. Holt wants school officials to desist from prosecuting parents who opt for home instruction. Does the state, however, have an interest in seeing that children receive an adequate education?

4. Schools, Holt says, are burdened by a set of assumptions about children, learning, and the teaching-learning relationship. State these assumptions; then determine whether these are actually the operative assumptions.

5. Holt indicates some needed research that could more likely be conducted in home instruction. Is this research important, and can it best be carried out in homes rather than schools?

6. Is the main objection to home instruction by school superintendents the fear that schools will lose some financial aid? Would there be no doubts about the adequacy of home instruction?

7. Has Holt offered a convincing case for home instruction?

8. Read Holt's book, *Teach Your Own,* and make a class report of your findings.

9. What evidence does Egerton present to show that a consensus does not presently exist in American education?

10. State the chief criticisms of public education cited by Egerton and the counterarguments he provides. With which view do you side? Why?

11. What does he mean when he says that schools are essentially political institutions, the chief instrument for reproducing society?

12. Egerton criticizes tuition tax credits. Read the two selections in Part II on this innovation and develop your own position about it.

13. Examine and evaluate Egerton's criticisms of Holt's ideas and proposals.

14. Investigate what legal provisions are available in your state for home instruction, and interview parents who educate their children at home.

15. Write an essay on the topic: How to Improve Public Education. Cite pertinent research studies.

SUGGESTED READINGS

Books by John Holt

Escape from Childhood: The Needs and Rights of Children. New York: Dutton, 1974.

Freedom and Beyond. New York: Dutton, 1972; Dell, 1973, paperback.

How Children Fail. New York: Pitman, 1965; Dell, 1975.

How Children Learn. New York: Pitman, 1969; Dell, 1969, paperback.

Instead of Education: Ways to Help People Do Things Better. New York: Dutton, 1976.

Never Too Late. New York: Delacorte, 1978.

Teach Your Own. New York: Delacorte, 1981; Dell, 1982.

The Underachieving School. New York: Pitman, 1969; Dell, 1970, paperback.

What Do I Do Monday? New York: Dutton, 1970; Dell, 1974, paperback.

Cassette Tapes by John Holt

"Freedom and Beyond" (33 minutes). North Hollywood, California: Center for Cassette Studies.

"The Idea of Schools" (48 minutes). Los Angeles: Pacific Tape Library.

"Non-Authoritarian Teaching" (43 minutes). North Hollywood, California: Center for Cassette Studies.

Works about Holt

Broudy, Harry S. *The Real World of the Public Schools.* New York: Harcourt Brace Jovanovich, 1972.

Bumstead, R. A. "Educating Your Child at Home: The Perchemlides Case." *Phi Delta Kappan* 61 (October 1979): 97–100.

Hook, Sidney. "John Dewey and His Betrayers." *Change* (November 1971): 22–6.

Hutchins, Robert M. "The Schools Must Stay." *The Center Magazine* (January/February 1973): 12–23.

Johnson, H. C., Jr. "Some Reflections on Educational Reform." *The Educational Forum* 38 (November 1973): 85–92.

Lucas, Christopher J. "The Invisible Dissenters." *Educational Studies* 2 (Spring/Summer 1971): 1–4.

Pearl, Arthur. *The Atrocity of Education.* St. Louis: New Critics Press, 1972.

Rich, John Martin. "Paternalistic Schools and Children's Rights." *The Journal of Educational Thought* 17 (April 1983): 50–56.

Schrag, Peter. "Education's Romantic Critics." *Saturday Review* (February 18, 1967): 80–2.

Shapiro, B. J. and Shapiro, P. O. "Testing in the Schools: A Response." *Elementary School Journal* 70 (January 1970): 202–05.

Shaw, V. S. "John Holt as I Knew Him." *Grade Teacher* 87 (September 1969): 77.

3
Stimulating Learning and Curiosity

Marva Collins left the public schools in 1975 to open her Westside Preparatory School. She has been hailed as a "miracle worker" who transformed unteachable children.

Her classroom is designed to foster cooperation, collective responsibility, autonomy, and strong adult leadership. Competition is deemphasized. Children are not tested on a regular basis and letter grades are not given; instead pupils are taught to work together cooperatively. Objectives and content are selected by the teacher but pupils can select the books and themes from the content that they prefer to study. Pupils are permitted to use their own native language patterns. She reminds pupils of specific learning tasks and their own personal goals. They are encouraged to show self-direction and think for themselves. Mrs. Collins uses positive reinforcement and adequate time on the task. She has argued that better teachers, not more funds, are needed to improve the school system.

An unemployed teacher uncovered records recently that show that Mrs. Collins has received thousands of dollars from the federal Comprehensive Employment and Training Act. According to Renee Ferguson, a Black TV reporter with station WBBM, the CBS Chicago affiliate, numerous parents have taken their children out of her school because they believed they were not getting their money's worth (tuition is nearly $2000 a year). The most serious charge is that her students do not perform as well on achievement tests as she claims.

"I Take the Kids No One Else Wants!"

Marva Collins: _____

Marva Deloise Nettles Collins (b. 1936) is a Black educator and administrator residing in Chicago. She was reared in Alabama and was awarded a B. A. degree from Clark College. In 1975 she opened Westside Preparatory School, the school for which she received national recognition. Mrs. Collins is the recipient of several honorary degrees and numerous awards, including teacher of the year. She has been the subject of a biography and of a feature film. In 1981, she was offered and declined the position of U.S. Secretary of Education.

She turned down a chance to be secretary of education. She rejected federal funds for her private school because "she wants no strings attached." And, because she believes all kids can learn, even "tough" ones, she teaches children labeled untrainable to memorize poems and to read classical literature. The top-rated television show "60 Minutes" brought her school nationwide attention two years ago, and in December actress Cicely Tyson portrayed her on a CBS "Hallmark Hall of Fame" special, "The Marva Collins Story."

Marva Nettles Collins, 41-year-old elementary teacher and founder of the Westside Preparatory School in Chicago, is described by many as invincible, dynamic, a super teacher, and a miracle worker, while others question her tactics, believing them to be simplistic and ineffectual. She describes herself as no different from many other good, dedicated teachers who she feels just haven't been heard yet. And, in this interview with education writer and former IN-STRUCTOR senior editor Sally Reed, she talks about her students, her techniques, and why she will not quit teaching.

Sally Reed: Mrs. Collins, just six years ago you left the public school system in Chicago and with $5,000 from your pension fund and books from a garbage bin, started this private school in your own home. What prompted you to do that?

Marva Collins: I thought children could learn more than they were learning. But there was no climate of support in the schools for teachers or children. Teachers were against each other. Maybe this was because of poor administrators, or maybe in every profession no one wants to feel that someone is better at doing something than he or she is.

But I would get excited about ideas, reading programs, children's work, and say to other teachers, "Would you look at this?" They would reply, "I don't need to know about that," "I've done that," or "Who does she think she is?"

Now, at Westside Prep we work as a family (four other teachers and 200 children ages 4 to 13). We are totally supportive of one another. This affects everyone's attitude about learning.

You have gained fame for your "no frills"

approach to teaching children diagnosed as learning disabled to read. What exactly do you have them read?

I stick to the classics. Four-year-olds begin with *Aesop's Fables.* The others start with basic books: *Alice in Wonderland, Little Women, Little men,* the C. S. Lewis *Chronicles . . .* and we move to *Uncle Tom's Cabin* or *The Painted Bird,* for example. Children who once never held a book read Dostoyevsky, Flaubert, Tolstoy, Thoreau. . . . There are great lessons to be learned from these people. And so every child reads one book every two weeks, learns one poem per week, and writes one composition every day. We memorize and we drill.

What is your method for getting children to read?

My whole philosophy is to get children to relax and realize they can make mistakes. Many children are nervous about reading, which means they had traumatic experiences somewhere before. But I have as much time to work with them as it takes for them to learn. They know that.

Also, I am consistent. People take too much for granted with children. You cannot hop from subject to subject; children do not learn that way.

My students get the same routine every day. At 7:30 A.M., before school starts, I work with those children having difficulties. We have math from 9 A.M. to 10 A.M. Every morning two reading groups meet: one reads and discusses literature and the other works on comprehension skills. We have a 20-minute lunch break and then "Operation Read" for 30 minutes, during which everyone reads a book, including guests and teachers. We also work on vocabulary, social studies, and science every day.

Students in your class quote Emerson, for example, or Plato, and make connections to prove their points. . . .

If you cannot make connections then what is life about? Who wants to learn only for knowledge's sake? My readings have kept me going.

Are the students in your school any different from those in other schools?

I take children no one else wants—those who have been written off or placed in learning disability classes. But give me one month with them and you'll notice a difference. Within three months, students read two levels above where they started. Four-year-olds read by Christmas their first year. Sixth graders score 7.2 to 11.7 on standarized tests. Last year one girl who scored 2.2 in September scored 7.3 by the middle of the year.

Why? Because that's what we expect. Again, teacher attitude is very important. I believe children should be given a lot of my time. I tell them: "You are here to stay. I love you, but there is no more calling Mommy. No one is going to put you out of school. You are going to learn. You are going to behave."

I repeat this over and over again. I will not argue with a child because I am not his peer.

Would you describe some of your children and how you've handled them?

One child, who used to make my hair curl, was very defensive. Whenever I was about to praise him he would say, "I didn't do it." I told him, "Why don't you listen? I was about to tell you how great your paper is. You don't have to fight me. I am on your side. We are going to work it out here. I have as long as it takes. If I have to take you home with me, I will."

Have you ever done that?

No, I've never had to. I stare children down. I give them the eye and they shape up. But I try to make every child feel special.

Another child had a scalp infection and was completely bald. The children at his former school used to throw his hairpiece around the room. Can you imagine any teacher callous enough to let that happen?

Before he came to my school I told the other children what had happened to him. When he first came to the class we all went to hug him. But he was so afraid that his hairpiece would fall off he pulled away. He was withdrawn and would not play with other children. But we kept loving him. Today, I am happy to see how well adjusted that child is.

Another child had a split personality. When her mother brought her to the schools, she said in front of the girl, "She lies, she does this, she does that. . . ."

But I constantly told that child, "I love you, but I do not think it really happened that way. You just tell me the truth." Gradually she seemed like a new child.

Do you have a definition of a good teacher?

Someone who remembers that he or she does not know everything and that each day, each year is a different process because there are different children.

A good teacher knows the needs of all children: Some children need special skills and special worksheets. With some children you need to be stern. With others you dare not raise your voice.

A good teacher makes the poor student good and the good student superior.

How do you respond to those people who charge that the way you work with children, the way you draw them out, is dependent on your strong personality and cannot be duplicated by others?

That is true—in part. But I started this school and hired other teachers to prove that it is not just Marva Collins. The school works be-

cause we work. The books work because we read them.

I am no miracle worker. People think I am this cosmic force, but they do not see the other side. I cry like other people. I get tired, worn out, frustrated, and depressed. I have the same problems as other teachers.

What keeps you going?

Nourishment from my family, my faith, from a little five-year-old child who says something brilliant, and from seeing progress not just in the children who are clean with their hair neatly combed, but in those who are neglected and dirty, too.

Do you get support from parents?

From a faithful few. It is no different from other schools. But I am tired of people saying, "The parents aren't doing their job." Teachers can't use that as an excuse. If parents are not doing their job then someone has to.

Earlier this year the press was filled with stories about your refusal to take a cabinet post in the Reagan administration. Why did you say no?

It's such a silly question. I cannot understand the way America thinks. It is like having a baby and you drop the baby to go take care of someone else's. What was I supposed to do? Throw down this school completely to run to Washington?

What do you want to do in the future?

I want my own high school, day-care center, and parent setup because parents in this area really need the education children get. I have not finished what I want to do here. Beyond that I cannot say.

Critics Take Marva Collins to Task

Marva Collins, the Chicago "super teacher" who has been critical of public schools and federal involvement in education, has herself come under critical scrutiny in recent months.

Collins, the founder of the private Westside Preparatory School in Chicago, for several years has been acclaimed for her apparent ability to teach "unteachable" children and to turn them into devotees of the likes of Dante, Emerson, Shakespeare and Dostoevsky. She attracted national attention when she was featured on television's "60 Minutes" and was the subject of a "docudrama" starring Cicely Tyson.

But members of the media who have characterized Marva Collins as something of a miracle worker in education are now raising questions about her credibility. Marva Collins' image began to crumble early this year when Len Walter, an anchor reporter for Chicago's WBBN news radio, reported that Collins and two aides had received CETA funds through the Alternative School Network (ASN) despite her insistence on "60 Minutes" and elsewhere that she had never taken federal money.

According to Jack Wuest, head of ASN, Westside Prep had received a total of $69,000 in CETA money. Collins later said that she did not realize that she had been receiving CETA funds through ASN, although Wuest disputes this, arguing it was impossible for Collins not to know the source of her funding.

Walter, whose radio reports were based initially on an in-depth investigative story on Collins by George Schmidt in *Substance,* a publication of a group of Chicago public school substitute teachers, also interviewed a former Westside Prep teacher who claimed that half the students in Collins' class failed the California Achievement Test. Patricia Jergens, who coordinated testing in the school, said that she discovered the poor scores before sending the test to California for machine scoring and that when she told Collins about it, Collins decided not to send the tests out for machine scoring.

A bizarre aspect of the story involves one of the AFT's own publications, the *American Educator.* Walter learned that Collins had written an article for the Sept. 16, 1981, issue of the Chicago *Sun-Times* that bore striking similarities to one by Neil Postman that had originally appeared in the January 1981 issue of *Phi Delta Kappan* and had been reprinted in the Fall 1981 issue of *American Educator,* which was published a few weeks before the *Sun-Times* article.

Postman's article, entitled "Childhood's End" (a phrase that was also used by Collins in her story), charged that the television age is robbing the nation's young people of the characteristics that separate them from adulthood. Both Postman and Collins talked about children losing "innocence and specialness," and both referred to the media creation of the "adult child."

Postman wrote, "Junk food, once suited only to the undiscriminating palates and iron stomachs of the young, is now common fare for adults. Junk literature, junk music, junk conversation are shared equally by children and adults. . . ."

Collins wrote, "Today, children are given junk foods that once were considered palatable

From "Critics Take Marva Collins to Task," American Teacher *66 (April 1982): 4. Reprinted by permission.*

only to those with cast-iron stomachs. Children are allowed to watch junk television, read junk literature in school and listen to junk records."

Both articles included references to youngsters wearing three-piece suits and older men wearing jeans to birthday parties and a reference to a television commercial that sells hand lotion.

When Walter asked Postman to comment, Postman issued a statement indicating that he was "surprised" by the similarities between the two. "While reading her article, I anticipated some attribution, but as none was forthcoming, I will put it down to a remarkable coincidence," said Postman.

A subsequent investigation by Renee Fergeson of Chicago's WBBM TV station put further pressure on Collins. Westside Prep students had reportedly been refused permission to leave their school bus because their parents had not paid $150 monthly tuition, Fergeson reported. She also reported that a test Collins had given to students during a summer course at the Cabrini Green housing project and copyrighted by Collins was an exact duplicate of a test copyrighted by C. H. Schutter (now dead), the principal at the public school where Collins once taught.

Collins said she did not know about the school bus incident and indicated it would not happen again; of the test, her lawyer says that Schutter owned the "registered" copyright and that Collins owned the "common" copyright. Collins also denied any knowledge of a resume that was reportedly circulated among parents listing her as having a degree from Northwestern University; she has a degree in secretarial science from Clark College.

Collins defended herself during a two-part "Donahue" show in which she claimed she had become the victim of a "witch hunt."

AFT president Albert Shanker, commenting on these developments in his weekly column in *The New York Times,* said that much of the blame lay with the "media hype" surrounding the Marva Collins story.

"The terrible thing is not that the media mistakenly gave undeserved recognition to Marva Collins but rather that they did it in such a way as to portray the public schools and their teachers as inept, lazy, unmotivated, bureaucratic, unionized bad guys," Shanker said.

DISCUSSION QUESTIONS AND ACTIVITIES

1. Why did Marva Collins leave the public schools and open her own school? Are the undesirable conditions she found characteristic as well of schools elsewhere? Typical of schools in your community?

2. Describe her curriculum. What reasons does she give for her choice of content? Is knowledge for its own sake one of her reasons?

3. At what age, do you think, children can begin to profit by studying the classics?

4. Are her teaching methods and ways of relating to children likely to prove effective in raising achievement levels and promoting a desirable attitude toward learning.

5. If parents are not doing their job, according to Collins, what then should be expected of teachers?

6. How have various media stories enhanced and damaged her public image? After reading "Critics Take Marva Collins to Task," reevaluate her achievements as a teacher and reformer.

SUGGESTED READINGS

Works by Marva Collins

"I Take Kids No One Else Wants!" *Instructor* 91 (January 1982): 18, 20 (Interview).

Marva Collins' Way. Los Angeles: J. P. Tarcher, 1982.

"Making Lemonade." *Politics Today* 5 (May 10, 1978).

Works About Marva Collins

Alder, J. "The Marva Collins Story." *Newsweek* 99 (March 8, 1982): 64–5.

"Critics Take Marva Collins to Task." *American Teacher* 66 (April 1982): 5.

Hollins, E. R. "Marva Collins Story Revisited: Implications for Regular Classroom Instruction." *Journal of Teacher Education* 33 (January/February 1982): 37–40.

Krance, M. "Those Who Can Teach, Do." *Washington Monthly* 11 (February 1980): 33–5.

Martin, P. "Marva Collins—A Teacher Who Cares." *Good Housekeeping* 187 (September 1978): 60.

Middleton, T. H. "Back to the Blackboard." *Saturday Review* 6 (April 14, 1979): 10.

Reynolds, B. A. "Something Good is Happening Here." *Essence* 12 (October 1981): 106–8.

Smikle, K. "Trashing Marva Collins." *Black Enterprise* 12 (June 1982): 46.

"Westside Story." *Time* 110 (December 26, 1977): 39.

4
Education for Pride and Achievement

Jesse Jackson organized PUSH (People United to Save Humanity) in 1971 to continue the work of Martin Luther King, Jr. He subsequently developed PUSH for Excellence, or EXCEL, as a plan for improving inner-city schools. EXCEL, which has attracted funds from the Ford Foundation, the Department of Education, and metropolitan school systems, has captured nationwide attention.

EXCEL programs strive for total community involvement by bringing the resources of the community together for a common cause, enlisting the aid of parents and other community residents. It emphasizes character education and self-discipline, motivating students and cultivating respect for authority. And the program utilizes a practice-and-study plan that parents and students can apply.

The program's underlying assumptions are that Blacks are behind and need to excel; and although they have legitimate grievances, they must help themselves to rise. This can best be done, Jackson believes, by a program that offers a strong ethical foundation.

The American Institutes for Research (AIR), commissioned by the Department of Education during the Carter Administration to evaluate PUSH-Excel, stated that Jackson had failed to translate his charisma into a workable educational program. "PUSH-Excel is still predominantly a movement inspired by the presentations of the Rev. Jesse Jackson," the report said.

The selection by Eubanks and Levin offers a sympathetic critique and indicates the greatest pitfalls facing the program.

In Pursuit of Equity, Ethics, and Excellence: The Challenge to Close the Gap

Jesse L. Jackson _____

Jesse Louis Jackson (b. 1941) is widely recognized as a charismatic orator and one of the most influential Black leaders since the late Martin Luther King, Jr. He received his bachelor's degree in sociology from the Agricultural and Technological College of North Carolina and did post-graduate studies at the Chicago Theological Seminary. He became an ordained Baptist minister in 1968. Rev. Jackson was a co-founder of Operation Breadbasket, a joint project of the Southern Christian Leadership Conference. He was the national director (1966–71) of the Coordinating Council of Community Organizations, and was founder and executive director of Operation PUSH (People United to Save Humanity). Rev. Jackson has addressed both national and international issues, and recently he spearheaded a drive in many American cities to expand Black ownership, enterprises, and jobs in the business community. He has received more than 25 honorary doctorates and many other awards. A 1980 survey of Black Americans by Data Black National Opinion Poll ranked Rev. Jackson as the nation's leading Black figure; and a poll in Ebony magazine in the same year, which asked readers to vote for the living Black man and woman who had done the most to advance the cause of Black Americans, selected Jackson and Rose Parks, who sparked the 1957 Montgomery, Alabama, bus boycott. Rev. Jackson was one of the Democratic candidates for President in 1984.

The greatest of this generation will be determined by how well we deal with the needs of this day in light of where we need to go as a people. The failure of this generation would be to answer questions that nobody is asking.

Historically, we have been locked out, and our challenge has been to move in.

1954 — *We moved in* to the right of equal educational opportunity (*Brown* v. *Board of Education*).

1964 — *We moved in* to the right of public accommodations (Civil Rights Act).

1965 — *We moved in* to the right to participate politically (Voting Rights Act).

1968 — *We moved in* to the right to buy a house in any neighborhood (Open Housing Act).

The new challenge is to move *up*. Upward mobility is the issue. Our struggle has shifted from the horizontal to the vertical. It was diffi-

From "In Pursuit of Equity, Ethics, and Excellence: The Challenge to Close the Gap," Phi Delta Kappan, (November 1978). Used by permission of the author.

cult marching across the plains, but it will be even more difficult climbing the mountain, often without the help of a rope.

Too many young people in this generation have lost their appreciation for the historic shoulders upon which they stand. The Merediths, the Hunters, and the Holmeses excelled because they served the need of their generation by busting down the barriers to opportunity. They refused to allow death threats, demagogues, dogs, or fire hoses to stand in their way. It was a good fight to create opportunity. But the challenge of this generation is to match opportunity with effort. If this generation is to be great, it must keep these doors of opportunity open, walk through them, and conquer the tasks beyond opportunity.

We must EXCEL because we are behind. There is one white attorney for every 680 whites, one black attorney for every 4,000 blacks; one white physician for every 649 whites, one black physician for every 5,000 blacks; one white dentist for every 1,900 whites, one black dentist for every 8,400 blacks. Less than 1% of all engineers are black. Blacks make up less than 1% of all practicing chemists.

We must EXCEL because resistance to our upward mobility has increased. *Bakke* and Bakkeism have convinced white America, erroneously, that blacks are making progress at white expense. The mass media have conveyed to white America that blacks have gained too much too fast and have come too far in their quest for equality.

We must EXCEL because the sickness of racism, in too many instances, forces us to be superior in order to be considered average.

We must EXCEL because competition is keener. The exportation of jobs to the cheap labor base of the Third World; the increased competition in the world market from Japan, Western Europe, and the Middle East; and cybernation and automation have forced us to compete for jobs requiring greater knowledge.

We must EXCEL because of the joy and fulfillment that comes in the victory of conquering a task and doing it well against odds.

Our goal is educational and economic equity and parity. The goal is to close the gap between black and white, rich and poor, male and female. We are behind in the race, and the only way to catch up is to run faster.

What does EXCEL advise in this race to close the gap? EXCEL is neither conservative nor liberal but focuses on what is basic. And what is basic is that effort must exceed opportunity for change to occur. What is basic is that there is nothing wrong with our genes, but there is something wrong with our agenda. We must change our agenda if we are going to close the gap and catch up.

EXCEL seeks massive involvement and massive effort. Both tears and sweat are wet and salty, but they render a different result. Tears will get you sympathy, but sweat will get you change.

Let me share with you the broad, but basic, concepts and ideas in the EXCEL program.

EQUITY

Racism has forced the black liberation movement to spend most of its time and effort fighting for opportunity. Thus, in 1954, the *Brown* decision allowed us to use the leverage of the law to compete as equals. EXCEL is not a departure from that historic struggle; rather, it is an extension of and a quest for the fulfillment of the historic goal of educational equity and parity. EXCEL supports the foundation laid in the *Brown* decision but argues that we must go beyond the desegregation of our schoolchildren to the desegregation of power.

What do we mean by that? We mean that power has not been desegregated; the same people who were in charge of segregation are in charge of desegregation. Thus black children, black parents, and black educators have no protection. They have no ability to redress their grievances? What protection is needed? Nancy L. Arnez of Howard University suggests this list: 1) loss of teaching and administrative jobs by blacks through dismissals, demotions, or displacement; 2) loss of millions of dollars in projected earned income; 3) loss of racial models, heroes, and authority figures for black children; 4) loss of cherished school symbols, emblems, and names of schools by black children when their schools were closed and they were shifted to white schools; 5) subjection to segregated classes and buses, and exclusion from extracurricular activities; 6) suspension and expulsion of disproportionate numbers of black students; 7) exposure of black children to hostile attitudes and behavior of white teachers and parents; 8) victimization by forced one-way busing policies and the uprooting of black children for placement in hostile school environments; 9) victimization by misclassification in special education classes and tracking systems; 10) victimization by unfair discipline practices and arbitrary school rules and regulations; and 11) victimization by ignorance of black children's learning styles and cultural, social, educational, and psychological needs.

The country's agenda relative to desegregation today is 1) to enforce the present law; 2) desegregate the power; and 3) complete the task of changing people's hearts and minds, not just their behavior and actions.

In addition, we are increasingly confronted with a new phenomenon in our large cities. White flight has left our cities nonwhite and poor. The issue now is not so much segregated schools but segregated school systems. Therefore, we must fulfill the letter and the spirit of the *Brown* decision through metropolitanwide desegregation.

Another impediment threatening to deny us equal educational opportunity is the lack of adequate and equitable funding for our schools. The tax rebellion symbolized by the Jarvis-Gann

Initiative in California; the refusal of the voters to support school bond issues in Cleveland and Toledo, Ohio, and elsewhere; and the Packwood-Moynihan tax credit proposal in Congress threaten to create a three-tiered educational system—a suburban school system based on class, a private school system based on race, and a public inner-city school system based on rejection and alienation.

At present the nation is in the process of a massive prison-building campaign. But building more jails and incarcerating more people is an uneconomic, as well as unethical, proposition. It is unethical because it doesn't attempt to change the individual into a productive citizen. It is uneconomic to the extent that if a young man or woman goes to any state university in this country for four years it will cost $20,000. If he or she goes to the state penitentiary for four years it will cost $50,000.

Yes, education and employment cost less than ignorance and incarceration.

A third impediment is the use of tests to disenfranchise us. Competency tests, too often, are used in a punitive rather than a redemptive way. We support tests and testing, but tests must be used to detect and diagnose, not to delete and eliminate.

Finally, economic equity and parity must parallel educational equity and parity. We cannot educate in an economic vacuum. We can no longer tolerate a white high school dropout getting jobs denied to black and brown high school graduates. An unemployment rate for blacks that is twice that of whites has a negative influence on educational goals. It discourages whites from getting an education because they feel they can get jobs without it. It discourages blacks from getting an education because they feel that even with an education they will not get the jobs.

ETHICS

Ethnic discrimination and an ethical collapse are impediments to excellence. If we are to lift ourselves out of this morass, we must shift our sights from the superficial to the sacrificial.

If we are to close the gap and catch up, we must do so by disciplining our appetites, engaging in ethical conduct, and developing our minds.

A steady diet of violence, vandalism, drugs, irresponsible sexual conduct, and alcohol and TV addiction has bred a passive, alienated, and superficial generation.

Morally weak people not only do not grow in personhood, they contribute to the politics of decadence. A drunken army cannot fight a war for information and close that gap. Minds full of dope instead of hope will not fight for the right to vote. We need a sober, sane, disciplined army to catch up. The challenge of this generation of adults is to regain the confidence of this generation's youth. Only by reestablishing its moral authority can the task be done, for if we reestablish moral authority—that is, our believability, our trustworthiness, our caring—we can then teach discipline, and our children will learn self-discipline.

Truth, like electricity, needs a conduit, a conductor through which to travel. The teacher is the conductor. If the teacher has a healthy respect for the child, the teacher can be a good conductor. But if that teacher has exposed wires and is rotten on race or ethics or character or caring, he will either blow a fuse or set off sparks that burn up a child's life.

Without sounding anti-intellectual, we must be clear that the issues of life flow from the heart, not the head. You cannot teach children against your spiritual will, using only your intellectual skill. You cannot feed children with a long-handled spoon.

The need for a moral and ethical foundation is the reason EXCEL argues for a written code of conduct for students. It is the reason EXCEL argues for character education versus mere IQ education.

EXCEL believes in IQ.

EXCEL believes in developing one's brain.

We are not trying to argue that we ought to substitute consecration for developing our minds. But we must know that on a scale of 10, intellect does not deserve eight points. There are other factors in life. Integrity and drive and commitment and concern above and beyond oneself count also.

PUSH FOR EXCELLENCE

Effort must exceed opportunity for change to occur. Opportunity must be matched by a superior effort, an urge to EXCEL, a will to learn. We are not so dumb that we cannot learn if we study; but we are not so smart that we will learn if we don't study.

The question that has been asked of me most often is. Why are you putting all of this pressure on the victim instead of the victimizer? Why are you letting the "system" off the hook? I'm not arguing that the victimizer is not guilty. I challenge the victimizer everywhere I go. But I know that if the victimizer is responsible for the victim's being down, the victim must be responsible for getting up. It is in the victim's self-interest to get up and go! It is precisely because the slave is in chains that he must run faster.

In this relationship between slave and slavemaster, I have never known of a retired slavemaster.

Our quest for excellence must be balanced between educating the head and the hand. We must know that 80% of our children graduating from high school are going to the world of work and only 20% to college—and less than that 20% graduate. We must balance our emphasis on a liberal education with vocational and career education. We must concentrate on these five basic steps: exposure to knowledge, repetition, internalization, development of convictions about subject matter, and application of knowledge.

We must move from educational existence to educational excellence. We must contrast the politics of the five Bs — blacks, browns, budgets, busing, and balance — with the five As — attention, attendance, atmosphere, attitude, and achievement. When the doors of opportunity swing open, we must make sure that we are not too drunk or too high or too indifferent to walk through.

We must have involvement from the 10 levels affecting education: the board, the superintendent, the staff administrators, the principals, the teachers, the parents, the pupils, the religious institutions, the mass media, and the broader community.

Students must sign pledges that they will study a minimum of two hours every evening with the radio, television, and record player off with no telephone interruptions or social visits. Parents must pledge to monitor their child's study hours, pick up their child's report card each graduating period, and go to the school to see that child's test scores.

At the beginning of the year, the principal must give a "State of the School" address. It should clearly define educational goals, establish rules, set up expectations, and lay out a plan for achieving the goals by the end of the academic year.

Upon graduation, students must be given a diploma in one hand, symbolizing knowledge and wisdom, and a voter registration card in the other hand, symbolizing power and responsibility.

In religious language, we argue that for one to do less than his or her best is a sin. In secular language, we argue that the purpose of life is to develop one's potential to his or her highest capacity.

We must know that if we sow short-term pleasure, we will reap long-term pain. But if we sow short-term pain, we will reap long-term pleasure.

We must teach our children that if they can conceive it and believe it, they can achieve it. They must know that it is not their aptitude but their attitude that will determine their altitude.

Fight for equity.
Fight for ethics.
Fight for excellence.

We must not only close the quantitative gap but the qualitative gap as well. We must . . .

— close the gap with doctors, but doctors who are more concerned with public health than personal wealth;

— close the gap with lawyers, but lawyers who are more concerned with justice than a judgeship;

— close the gap with preachers, but preachers who will prophesy, not merely profiteer;

— catch up in journalism, but we need journalists who will ascribe, describe, and prescribe, not merely scribble;

— catch up in politics, but we need politicians who seek to be of service, not merely seek an office;

— close the gap and catch up in teachers, but we need teachers who will teach for life and not merely for a living.

Believe in yourself. Believe in your ability to close the gap.

Believe in our children. Believe in your ability to teach them and their ability to learn.

Believe in our parents. Believe that if they are consciously sought and planned for, they will participate.

Believe that life is not accidental, that it has a purpose, if you will but seek the way. Hold on. PUSH for Excellence. EXCEL! EXCEL! EXCEL!

I am somebody . . .

The PUSH Program for Excellence in Big-City Schools

Eugene E. Eubanks and Daniel U. Levine _____

Daniel U. Levine (b. 1935) received his degrees from the University of Chicago. He was a teacher in the Chicago public schools and later a Fulbright-Hays research scholar in Athens, Greece. Presently director of the Center for Study of Metropolitan Problems in Education at the University of Missouri—Kansas City, he is co-author of Education in Metropolitan Areas.

Eugene E. Eubanks is assistant dean of education, University of Missouri—Kansas City.

ISSUES IN CARRYING OUT
THE PROGRAM

An educational social program as ambitious and encompassing as the one PUSH is now undertaking inevitably raises a number of important issues connected with definition and implementation. Delineating all these issues and analyzing them at length would require several articles, but some of the most important should be acknowledged, if only in a preliminary and summary fashion.

In our opinion, the most important issues involving the nature and potential of the PUSH Program for Excellence in Education include the following.

1. *Can the program succeed if it is so highly dependent on the leadership of its charismatic leader?* Jesse Jackson is not PUSH, and PUSH is much more than Jesse Jackson. Nevertheless, there is little doubt that much of its initial growth can be attributed to Jackson's dynamic and charismatic leadership. Most of the proposals being put forward by PUSH have been advocated before by parents, teachers, and others who have tried to generate motivation for academic learning among socioeconomically disadvantaged youth, though not in a form as clear and comprehensive. Nevertheless, as Jackson himself has admitted, "I'm saying something that mom and dad say all the time, but it sounds different coming from Jackson." This, of course, is one reason why PUSH efforts in specific school districts include assemblies and meetings at which Jackson speaks with students and parents on their home turf.

The PUSH leadership is well aware of the dangers of having their efforts too dependent on one person, particularly since Jackson has been hospitalized several times in the past few years

From Eugene E. Eubanks and Daniel U. Levine, "The PUSH Program for Excellence in Big-City Schools," Phi Delta Kappan *58 (January 1977): 385-386, 388. Used by permission.*

due to pneumonia brought on by exhaustion and overwork. They are attempting to institutionalize their program and are struggling to obtain resources to employ personnel to work on a day-by-day basis. So far these efforts are being rewarded in growing support, but whether they will succeed at a grassroots level when Jackson is not present to provide inspiration and leadership is still an open question.

2. Can participants in the PUSH program succeed in keeping their roles discrete and effective? Related to the issue of dependence on inspirational leadership is an important question concerning the degree to which actors in the PUSH scenario can each make their special contribution in a cooperative effort to improve social and physical conditions in the inner city. As mentioned earlier, one of Jackson's main tasks is to articulate what others are not in a position to say persuasively or even to say at all. For example, Jackson was able to persuade more than 30 unemployed residents of one inner-city Chicago neighborhood to volunteer security and supervision around an elementary school which had become dangerous to attend. Since these people were unemployed, he argued, why should they not make a contribution to their community and the welfare of its young people? His suggestion, coming from educators, probably would have been mostly ineffectual; and political leaders probably would have been very hesitant to offer it at all.

By the same token, PUSH leaders recognize that they are dependent on educators of technical expertise in improving instruction once classroom conditions have become more conducive to teaching and learning. At some point in the change process, community pressure will have to be brought to bear on faculties lacking the leadership, skill, or motivation to take advantage of this opportunity. At that time major clashes may well occur with teacher or administrator unions and other professional associations.

Jackson and his organization apparently are not trying to force such confrontations; indeed, they tend to view confrontations as a relic of the 1960s, now obsolete. They insist that the most important deficiency in big-city compensatory education has been lack of cooperation as equal partners on the part of all interested parties. Academic reform will come about, Jackson told us, "in proportion to the emergence of active participation of the missing elements," i.e., parents, students, community leaders. Nevertheless, it is only realistic to expect that at some point PUSH will face a crisis that may tear apart the coalition it is trying to put together.

3. Will the PUSH program be perceived as "blaming the victim"? In the past, a number of programs in education and other areas which have attempted to help improve conditions in inner-city neighborhoods have failed largely or partly because they were perceived by their potential clients as "blaming the victim" for his own troubles. Any program designed to help powerless people help themselves may fail for this reason, because in general people will not participate vigorously in an effort which they think maligns and stigmatizes them.

Jackson and other PUSH leaders are well aware of this problem. They are, after all, on the firing lines encountering it first-hand. About all that Jackson or anyone else can do about it is to make his position unmistakably clear at all times, frequently reiterating the truth that self-help neither logically nor practically need be equivalent to blaming the victim. With his outstanding oratory and his great gift for synthesizing many important themes and communicating them to the people he is trying to reach, Jackson so far seems to be succeeding in making this distinction. The situation was aptly summarized by William Raspberry in a *Washington Post* article (March, 1976):

The phrase "blaming the victim" . . . conveys an important truth about the way America has reacted to discrimination against certain of its citizens.

It can describe, for instance, the process of denying job and promotion opportunities to minorities and then contending that the reason for their economic plight is that they have poor work records and too little ambition.

It might also refer to relegating black children to segregated, central-city schools with all the cultural, psychological, and educational deprivation that implies, and then blaming them for their lack of scholastic achievement.

So isn't the Rev. Jesse Jackson "blaming the victim" when he talks about parental neglect, insufficient motivation, and lack of self-discipline as among the reasons black children in inner-city schools are not performing up to par?

It's a question the Chicago-based director of Operation PUSH gave some thought to during a recent, rambling interview.

There is no denying that black people have been, and continue to be, victims of racism, he concedes. And racism must be resisted on every front.

"But to dwell on it in a negative kind of way is to reinforce in the victims a sense of their own victimization and lead them not to action but only to feeling sorry for themselves," he said.

"I'm not saying we should blame the victim. But I am saying we have to stop victimizing ourselves."

4. *Will "practicing" academic subjects yield anything like the same gains which practice may accomplish in sports and physical exercise?* The PUSH program emphasizes such practice. Undoubtedly improvement in academic performance among socioeconomically disadvantaged students depends on their spending more time, both inside and outside of class, on mastering academic subject matter. Recent research tends to verify this commonsense notion. Unfortunately, however, it is very uncertain whether more practice and study by *themselves* would accomplish much. We need improved instructional approaches, for one thing, to diagnose and overcome the learning difficulties of disadvantaged students. Methods of instruction must be modified so that students are not simply practicing the same mistakes over and over

again—as appears to have happened in many after-school or other "add-on" Title I programs

Jackson and other PUSH leaders recognize that practice in academics is only a part of the solution to achievement problems in big-city schools. They have seized upon the practice-and-study idea because it is easy for parents, students, and others to understand, and because it represents something concrete that inner-city residents perhaps can begin to work on immediately. Nevertheless, there are dangers in oversimplifying the learning problem in big-city schools to this degree. It is comparable to the trap some teachers have fallen into when they argue, "They can't learn because they are hungry." Some parents have fallen into it when they say, "If kids aren't learning it must be because teachers aren't teaching."

Practice may even prove dysfunctional if it turns out that the wrong habits are being repeated or if students perceive little improvement after practice and become still more alienated. Moreover, overemphasis on the approach makes PUSH highly dependent on the expertness of teachers now in the schools, teachers who presumably will provide appropriate guidance in telling pupils what and how to study.

5. *Is religion too much commingled with the public schools in PUSH's approach to educational reform?* If only on civil liberty grounds, there are serious questions concerning the central role which PUSH advocates for religion and the churches in seeking to reestablish the "moral authority" its leaders believe is prerequisite to substantial academic improvement in big-city schools. PUSH leaders can point out that their program does not require membership in a church or attendance at church services, but the program is built explicitly on commitment to religious principles, and it sometimes is expressed—as at school assemblies in terms closely reflecting Christian fundamentalism. This may make the PUSH effort at school reform not only vulnerable to legal suits but also repugnant to many potential supporters.

The issue we raise here is really much larger. We live in a scientifically oriented society in which religion plays a lesser part in shaping attitudes and behaviors than it did in previous eras. In this sense our society has become much more "rational" and complex than it was generations ago; indeed, it is partly the complexity of contemporary society which has made big cities almost unmanageable so long as we utilize established political and social institutions and policies. As conditions have deteriorated in big cities, and particularly in the inner city, we have produced a plethora of "scientific" analyses and reports delineating "systems" approaches. We need more science and technology, these reports implicitly tell us, to solve the problems which some would attribute to science and technology in the first place.

Precisely at this point comes Jesse Jackson, arguing that commitment and love are more basic than science and rationalism in solving educational and other problems. It is not that PUSH leaders reject technology and professional expertise; they firmly assert that it must be supplied by the technicians and the professionals. They do insist, however, that community, moral authority, and motivation based on emotional commitment are prior in importance and sequence to solutions based on science and rationality. Who is to say they are wrong?

6. *Can the PUSH program succeed in the face of urban conditions which strongly militate against the success of any organized effort to help the poor and the powerless?* Perhaps this question is too obvious to be worth asking, but the preceding analysis does suggest that it may be worth addressing briefly, in order to place PUSH in an appropriate historical and social context.

PUSH is attempting to bring about what amounts to a revolution in the way inner-city populations and institutions interact and function, explicitly recognizing that anything short of such a revolution probably will fail in the same manner as many earlier programs. As much as anyone, PUSH leaders are aware that the obstacles they face are nearly insuperable, that they are placing a lot of faith possibly weak reeds (e.g., active cooperation on the part of entrenched bureaucracies), and that they may be expanding their program too fast and spreading themselves too thin. They argue with much justification that big-city problems in education, social welfare, employment, etc., are national rather than local in origin and scope; only a comprehensive national effort which reaches directly to the grassroots level of the family and the peer group will have much chance to succeed in local neighborhoods.

One may well quarrel with their diagnosis and program, but hardly with their fortitude and dedication in undertaking so enormous an effort. In assessing their chances, we can do no better than offer the following quote from a *Washington Post* article by William Raspberry:

That sense of entrapment in love may have been a good deal easier to achieve in tiny Greenville, N.C. (population about 12,000 when Mr. Jackson was born there in 1941) than in the teeming cities where uprootedness and unconnectedness combine to produce the very anomie Mr. Jackson is trying to attack.

To a significant degree, what he is proposing is the establishment of small towns in the city, a series of caring communities in which every adult is parent to every child.

Jesse Jackson is, in short, proposing a miracle. And yet, with a little luck and a lot of focused commitment, it could take hold. Not that thugs would suddenly become young gentlemen and hall rovers instant scholars.

But it just may be possible to reestablish in the classrooms a situation where serious scholarship, mutual respect, and discipline are the norm, and where peer pressure serves to reinforce that norm.

It certainly is worth trying.

DISCUSSION QUESTIONS AND ACTIVITIES

1. Does Jackson give cogent reasons why blacks need to excel?
2. Evaluate the list of eleven grievances he claims blacks have today.
3. It is true that "a steady diet of violence, vandalism, drugs, irresponsible sexual conduct, and alcohol and TV addiction has bred a passive, alienated, and superficial generation"?
4. Jackson believes that although intellect should not be neglected, other things, such as character education, are more important. Explain the basis for your agreement or disagreement.
5. Appraise both the logic and feasibility of Jackson's educational plans.
6. Investigate a system that has used EXCEL (PUSH) and report on your findings.
7. Eubanks and Levine believe that at some point PUSH "will face a crisis that may tear apart the coalition it is trying to put together." How did they arrive at this conclusion?
8. Can PUSH avoid the charge that it is "blaming the victim"?
9. Has Jackson oversimplified practice-and-study as a solution to the problems of big-city schools?
10. Does Jackson create problems for his program by infusing it with religious principles?
11. Compare PUSH with other prominent programs for blacks and other minorities used during the past fifteen years.
12. Read and evaluate the articles by B. A. Sizemore and Joyce E. Williams (see bibliography). Both offer a more radical critique than do Eubanks and Levine because they question whether better schooling is the best way for blacks to advance.

SUGGESTED READINGS

Works by Jesse L. Jackson

"Completing the Agenda of Dr. King: Operation PUSH." *Ebony 29* (June 1974): 116.

"Dialogue on Separation." *Ebony* 25 (August 1970): 62.

"Don't Get Mad: Get Smart!" *Journal of National Association of Women Deans Admissions and Counseling* 37 (Fall 1973): 18-26.

"Energy Fraud." *The Progressive* 38 (April 1974): 52.

"Give the People A Vision." *New York Times Magazine* (April 18, 1976): 13. Same abridged in *Reader's Digest* 109 (November 1976): 227.

"Peace in Our Schools." *Saturday Evening Post* 252 (December 1980): 12.

"PUSH for Excellence Can Be One of the Cures." *Ebony* 34 (August 1979): 104-6.

"Reconstruction City." *Ebony* 12 (October 1968): 65-6.

"Unfinished Business of America." *Look* 35 (July 3, 1971): 59-60.

Works about Jesse L. Jackson

Arnold, G., ed. "You Can Pray if You Want To." *Christianity Today* 21 (August 12, 1977): 12-16.

"Black Pocketbook Power." *Time* 91 (March 1, 1968): 17.

"Blacks Wrap Up Slice of Action at Food Chains." *Business Week* (April 26, 1969): 162.

Brooks, Andree. "Watching 'Push for Excellence' Work in the Classroom." *Teacher* 97 (September 1979): 68.

Clayton, M. S., ed. "Jesse Jackson Speaks Out." *Today's Education* 66 (January 1977): 42–6. Interview.

Coggin, T. "Being Somebody Alienates Almost Everybody." *Christianity Today* 23 (September 7, 1979): 66.

Cole, Robert W. "Black Moses: Jesse Jackson's Push for Excellence." *Phi Delta Kappan* 58 (January 1977): 378-382.

A Conversation with the Reverend Jesse Jackson: The Quest for Educational and Economic Parity. Washington: American Enterprise Institute for Public Policy, 1978. 27 p.

Coverson, L. "A Push for Heublein." *Black Enterprise* 12 (June 1982): 50.

Deming, A., and others. "Jackson! Arafat!" *Newsweek* 94 (October 8, 1979): 50.

Dunbar, E. "Rev. Jesse Jackson: A New Kind of Black Cat." *Look* 35 (October 5, 1971): 16-20.

Eaton, W. E. "Jesse Jackson and the Urban School Reform Movement." *Urban Education* 11 (January 1977): 397-402.

"EXCEL: Bringing a Well-Timed Message of Hope and Inspiration." *Phi Delta Kappan* 60 (November 1978): 154-5.

"EXCEL: Mobilization for Excellence." *Phi Delta Kappan* 60 (November 1978): 189S-228S.

Fleming, R. "After Jackson, What?" *Encore* 8 (December 3, 1979): 12-13.

Friedman, R. "Spiritual Electricity of Jesse Jackson." *Esquire* 92 (December 1979): 80-1.

"Further Travels with Jesse." *Time* 114 (October 15, 1979): 63.

"Get Going, and Don't Come Back." *Time* 93 (February 14, 1969): 48.

Gunnings, T. S. and Gunnings, B. B. "In Defense of EXCEL." *Phi Delta Kappan* 60 (January 1979): 370-2.

Heiser, J. D. "There's an Epidemic of Failure in the Public Schools: Jesse Jackson's Fighting It." *Instructor* 86 (August 1976): 200

Interview. *Compact* 12 (Summer/Fall): 14–16.

Interview. *Ebony* 36 (June 1981): 154-6.

"Is He a Troubleshooting Man of God, or a Troublemaking Demagogue?" *People* 12 (December 24, 1979): 85.

"Jackson's Expo." *Newsweek* 78 (October 4, 1971): 24.

"Jesse Jackson: One Leader Among Many." *Time* 95 (April 6, 1970): 14-16.

"Jackson Pushes On." *Time* 99 (January 3, 1972): 30.

"Jesse Jackson Quits SCLC After Being Suspended." *Christian Century* 88 (December 22, 1971): 1488.

"Jesse Jackson's Revolutionary Message." *Center Magazine* (January 1978): 72-3.

Landsmann, L., ed. "Jesse Jackson's Declaration of Excellence." *Instructor* 88 (September 1978): 28-9. Interview.

"Leading With His Jaw." *The Progressive* 43 (March 1979): 12.

"Learning to Excel in School." *Time* 112 (July 10, 1979), 45-6.

Levine, R. "Jesse Jackson: Heir to Dr. King?" *Harper's* 238 (March 1969): 58-64.

Llorens, D. "Apostle of Economics." *Ebony* 22 (August 1967): 78.

Milne, E. "Made in Japan." *Black Enterprise* 11 (November 1980): 24.

Morganthau, T. and S. Monroe. "Jesse Jackson's Troubles." *Newsweek* 98 (July 20, 1981): 29.

Morrow, L. "Gospel According to Jesse." *Horizon* 21 (May 1978): 60-3.

Nauer, B. "Hats Off to Jesse Jackson." *National Review* 28 (June 25, 1976): 674-7.

"Noble Son." *Time* 114 (August 6, 1979): 114.

Page, C. "I Am Somebody! . . . But Who?" *Washington Monthly* 11 (February 1980): 26-36.

Peck, A. "Stones Lyric Protest: Rev. Jackson's Publicity Stunt." *Rolling Stone* (November 16, 1978): 39.

Pekkanen, J. "Black Hope, White Hope." *Life* 67 (November 21, 1969): 67-72.

"PUSH for Excellence." *Ebony* 32 (February 1977): 104-6.

Reynolds, Barbara A. *Jesse Jackson: The Man, The Movement, The Myth.* Chicago: Nelson-Hall, 1975.

Reynolds, Barbara. "Reverend PUSH." *The New Republic* 181 (October 27, 1979): 14–16.

Saar, J. and P. Youngblood. "Jesse Jackson Takes on Pretoria." *Newsweek* 94 (August 13, 1979): 36.

Salpeter, E. "Jesse Jackson's Pilgrimage." *New Leader* 62 (October 22, 1979): 3-5.

Sheils, M. and S. Monroe. "Preaching Pride." *Newsweek* 89 (January 27, 1977): 64.

Sheppard, N. "Jesse Jackson: The Last Charismatic Leader?" *Black Enterprise* 11 (March 1981): 34.

Sizemore, B. A. "PUSH Politics and the Education of America's Youth." *Phi Delta Kappan* 60 (January 1979): 369–70.

"Split in SCLC." *Newsweek* 78 (October 4, 1971): 24.

Tarver, B. J. "Poll Names Jesse Jackson Top Black Leader." 9 (October 1980):22.

Encore "Teachers Must Have a Sense of Sacrifice." *Teacher* 97 (September 1979): 65–8. Interview.

"35th Anniversary Service Awards." *Ebony* 36 (November 1980): 142–3.

Wall, J. M. "Moralists, Politicists and the Middle East." *Christian Century* 96 (October 7, 1979): 995–6.

Williams, Joyce E. "On the Relevance of Education for Black Liberation." *Journal of Negro Education* (Summer 1978): 266–82.

Witt, L. "Jesse Jackson Is Lighting Fires Again." *People* 11 (April 9, 1979), 40–2.

5
Nondirective Learning

Resting at the heart of educational reform are the concepts we hold of teaching and learning, as well as our convictions about the learner. The teaching process has been studied recently in considerable depth by a number of investigators. We now have not only the findings on learning and motivation but also a body of new knowledge on the teaching process and recommendations for its improvement. Knowledge is available about the teacher's verbal behavior and logical reasoning and his nonverbal and affective behavior as well.

Traditional models of teaching have long been under attack, and numerous educators have proposed alternative models for the teaching-learning process. Although Rogers would be an educator of this type, he has gone much further than his colleagues by seriously calling into question the efficacy of teaching itself. He believes that much that goes under the name of "teaching" does not help the student to live meaningfully in a continually changing world. He finds that teaching itself is a relatively overvalued activity and proposes instead that we think in terms of the "facilitation of learning." Rogers presents what he means by this concept in terms of the teacher's relations with students, and ends his essay by citing research evidence to support his position.

While it would be natural to expect some persons to object to a position that marks a considerable departure from established thought—and many have objected to Roger's views on these grounds—few, however, have penetrated the underlying conceptual structure of Rogers's position and offered a significant critique of it. R. S. Peters has penetrated this structure, attempts to show where it is weak and strong, and offers some of his own ideas as a substitute.

The Interpersonal Relationship in the Facilitation of Learning

Carl R. Rogers _____

Carl R. Rogers (b. 1902) is both an educator and a psychologist, known for his non-directive approach to counseling. He received his formal education at the University of Wisconsin and Columbia University and has taught and served in counseling centers at many universities, both public and private. He has been the recipient of numerous awards for his contributions to psychology and counseling. Among his many writings are such well-known books as Counseling and Psychotherapy, Client-Centered Therapy, On Becoming a Person, Freedom to Learn, *and he is co-author of* Psychotherapy and Personality Change. *He is presently a staff member at the Center for Studies of the Person, La Jolla, California.*

I wish to begin this paper with a statement which may seem surprising to some and perhaps offensive to others. It is simply this: Teaching, in my estimation, is a vastly overrated function.

Having made such a statement, I scurry to the dictionary to see if I really mean what I say. Teaching means "to instruct." Personally I am not much interested in instructing another. "To impart knowledge or skill." My reaction is, why not be more efficient, using a book or programmed learning? "To make to know." Here my hackles rise. I have no wish to *make* anyone know something. "To show, guide, direct." As I see it, too many people have been shown, guided, directed. So I come to the conclusion that I *do* mean what I said. Teaching is, for me, a relatively unimportant and vastly over-valued activity.

But there is more in my attitude than this. I have a negative reaction to teaching. Why? I think it is because it raises all the wrong questions. As soon as we focus on teaching, the question arises, what shall we teach? What, from our superior vantage point, does the other person need to know? This raises the ridiculous question of coverage. What shall the course cover? (Here I am acutely aware of the fact that "to cover" means both "to take in" and "to conceal from view," and I believe that most courses admirably achieve both these aims.) This notion of coverage is based on the assumption that what is taught is what is learned; what is presented is what is assimilated. I know of no assumption so obviously untrue. One does not need research to provide evidence that this is false. One needs only talk with a few students.

From Carl R. Rogers, "The Interpersonal Relationship in the Facilitation of Learning," Humanizing Education: The Persons in the Process, *Robert R. Leeper, ed. (Washington, D.C.: Association for Supervision and Curriculum Development, 1967), pp. 1–12. Reprinted with permission of the Association for Supervision and Curriculum Development and Carl R. Rogers. Copyright © 1967 by the Association for Supervision and Curriculum Development. All rights reserved.*

But I ask myself, "Am I so prejudiced against teaching that I find no situation in which it is worthwhile?" I immediately think of my experience in Australia only a few months ago. I became much interested in the Australian aborigine. Here is a group which for more than 20,000 years has managed to live and exist in a desolate environment in which a modern man would perish within a few days. The secret of his survival has been teaching. He has passed on to the young every shred of knowledge about how to find water, about how to track game, about how to kill the kangaroo, about how to find his way through the trackless desert. Such knowledge is conveyed to the young as being *the* way to behave, and any innovation is frowned upon. It is clear that teaching has provided him the way to survive in a hostile and relatively unchanging environment.

Now I am closer to the nub of the question which excites me. Teaching and the imparting of knowledge make sense in an unchanging environment. This is why it has been an unquestioned function for centuries. But if there is one truth about modern man, it is that he lives in an environment which is *continually changing*. The one thing I can be sure of is that the physics which is taught to the present day student will be outdated in a decade. The teaching in psychology will certainly be out of date in 20 years. The so-called "facts of history" depend very largely upon the current mood and temper of the culture. Chemistry, biology, genetics, sociology, are in such flux that a firm statement made today will almost certainly be modified by the time the student gets around to using the knowledge.

We are, in my view, faced with an entirely new situation in education where the goal of education, if we are to survive, is the *facilitation of change and learning*. The only man who is educated is the man who has learned how to learn; the man who has learned how to adapt and change; the man who has realized that no knowledge is secure, that only the process of

seeking knowledge gives a basis for security. Changingness, a reliance on *process* rather than upon static knowledge, is the only thing that makes any sense as a goal for education in the modern world.

So now with some relief I turn to an activity, a purpose, which really warms me—the *facilitation of learning*. When I have been able to transform a group—and here I mean all the members of a group, myself included—into a community of *learners,* then the excitement has been almost beyond belief. To free curiosity; to permit individuals to go charging off in new directions dictated by their own interests; to unleash curiosity; to open everything to questioning and exploration; to recognize that everything is in process of change—here is an experience I can never forget. I cannot always achieve it in groups with which I am associated but when it is partially or largely achieved then it becomes a never-to-be-forgotten group experience. Out of such a context arise true students, real learners, creative scientists and scholars and practitioners, the kind of individuals who can live in a delicate but ever-changing balance between what is presently known and the flowing, moving, altering, problems and facts of the future.

Here then is a goal to which I can give myself wholeheartedly. I see the facilitation of learning as the aim of education, the way in which we might develop the learning man, the way in which we can learn to live as individuals in process. I see the facilitation of learning as the function which may hold constructive, tentative, changing, process answers to some of the deepest perplexities which beset man today.

But do we know how to achieve this new goal in education, or is it a will-of-the-wisp which sometimes occurs, sometimes fails to occur, and thus offers little real hope? My answer is that we possess a very considerable knowledge of the conditions which encourage self-initiated, significant, experiential, "gut-level" learning by the whole person. We do not frequently see these conditions put into effect because they mean a real revolution in our approach to education and revolutions are not for the timid. But we do find examples of this revolution in action.

We know — and I will briefly describe some of the evidence — that the initiation of such learning rests not upon the teaching skills of the leader, not upon his scholarly knowledge of the field, not upon his curricular planning, not upon his use of audio-visual aids, not upon the programmed learning he utilizes, not upon his lectures and presentations, not upon an abundance of books, though each of these might at one time or another be utilized as an important resource. No, the facilitation of significant learning rests upon certain attitudinal qualities which exist in the personal *relationship* between the facilitator and the learner.

We came upon such findings first in the field of psychotherapy, but increasingly there is evidence which shows that these findings apply in the classroom as well. We find it easier to think that the intensive relationship between therapist and client might possess these qualities, but we are also finding that they may exist in the countless interpersonal interactions (as many as 1,000 per day, as Jackson [1966] has shown) between the teacher and his pupils.

What are these qualities, these attitudes, which facilitate learning? Let me describe them very briefly, drawing illustrations from the teaching field.

REALNESS IN THE FACILITATOR OF LEARNING

Perhaps the most basic of these essential attitudes is realness or genuineness. When the facilitator is a real person, being what he is, entering into a relationship with the learner without presenting a front or a facade, he is much more likely to be effective. This means that the feelings which he is experiencing are available to him, available to his awareness, that he is able to live these feelings, be them, and able to communicate them if appropriate. It means that he comes into a direct personal encounter with the learner, meeting him on a person-to-person basis. It means that he is *being* himself, not denying himself.

Seen from this point of view it is suggested that the teacher can be a real person in his relationship with his students. He can be enthusiastic, he can be bored, he can be interested in students, he can be angry, he can be sensitive and sympathetic. Because he accepts these feelings as his own he has no need to impose them on his students. He can like or dislike a student product without implying that it is objectively good or bad or that the student is good or bad. He is simply expressing a feeling for the product, a feeling which exists within himself. Thus, he is a person to his students, not a faceless embodiment of a curricular requirement nor a sterile tube through which knowledge is passed from one generation to the next.

It is obvious that this attitudinal set, found to be effective in psychotherapy, is sharply in contrast with the tendency of most teachers to show themselves to their pupils simply as roles. It is quite customary for teachers rather consciously to put on the mask, the role, the facade, of being a teacher, and to wear this facade all day removing it only when they have left the school at night.

But not all teachers are like this. Take Sylvia Ashton-Warner, who took resistant, supposedly slow-learning primary school Maori children in New Zealand, and let them develop their own reading vocabulary. Each child could request one word — whatever word he wished — each day, and she would print it on a card and give it to him. "Kiss," "ghost," "bomb," "tiger," "fight," "love," "daddy" — these are samples. Soon they were building sentences, which they could also keep. "He'll get a licking." "Pussy's frightened." The children simply never forgot these self-initiated learnings. Yet it is not my purpose to tell you of her methods. I want instead to give you a glimpse of her attitude, of the passionate realness which must have been as evident to her tiny pupils as to her readers. An editor asked her some questions and she responded: " 'A few cool facts' you asked me for. . . . I don't know that there's a cool fact in me, or anything else cool for that matter, on this particular subject. I've got only hot long facts on the matter of Creative Teaching, scorching both the page and me" (Ashton-Warner, 163, p. 26).

Here is no sterile facade. Here is a vital *person,* with convictions, with feelings. It is her transparent realness which was, I am sure, one of the elements that made her an exciting facilitator of learning. She does not fit into some neat educational formula. She *is,* and students grow by being in contact with someone who really *is.*

Take another very different person, Barbara Shiel, also doing exciting work facilitating learning in sixth graders.[1] She gave them a great deal of responsible freedom, and I will mention some of the reactions of her students later. But here is an example of the way she shared herself with her pupils — not just sharing feelings of sweetness and light, but anger and frustration. She had made art materials freely available, and students often used these in creative ways, but the room frequently looked like a picture of chaos. Here is her report of her feelings and what she did with them.

> I find it (still) maddening to live with the mess — with a capital M! No one seems to care except me. Finally, one day I told the children . . . that I am a neat, orderly person by nature and that the mess was driving me to distraction. Did they have a solution? It was suggested they could have volunteers to clean up. . . . I said it didn't seem fair to

me to have the same people clean up all the time for others — but it *would* solve it for me. "Well, some people *like* to clean," they replied. So that's the way it is (Shiel, 1966).

I hope this example puts some lively meaning into the phrases I used earlier, that the facilitor "is able to live these feelings, be them, and able to communicate them if appropriate." I have chosen an example of negative feelings, because I think it is more difficult for most of us to visualize what this would mean. In this instance, Miss Shiel is taking the risk of being transparent in her angry frustrations about the mess. And what happens? The same thing which, in my experience, nearly always happens. These young people accept and respect her feelings, take them into account, and work out a novel solution which none of us, I believe, would have suggested in advance. Miss Shiel wisely comments, "I used to get upset and feel guilty when I became angry — I finally realized the children could accept *my* feelings, too. And it is important for them to know when they've 'pushed me.' I have limits too" (Shiel, 1966).

Just to show that positive feelings, when they are real, are equally effective, let me quote briefly a college student's reaction, in a different course. ". . . Your sense of humor in the class was cheering; we all felt relaxed because you showed us your human self, not a mechanical teacher image. I feel as I have more understanding and faith in my teachers now. . . . I feel closer to the students too." Another says, " . . . You conducted the class on a personal level and therefore in my mind I was able to formulate a picture of you as a person and not as merely a walking textbook." Or another student in the same course,

> . . . It wasn't as if there was a teacher in the class, but rather someone whom we could trust and identify as a "sharer." You were so perceptive and sensitive to our thoughts, and this made it all the more "authentic" for me. It was an "authentic" *experience,* not just a class (Bull, 1966).

---

[1]For a more extended account of Miss Shiel's initial attempts, see Rogers, 1966a. Her later experience is described in Shiel, 1966.

I trust I am making it clear that to be real is not always easy, nor is it achieved all at once, but it is basic to the person who wants to become that revolutionary individual, a facilitator of learning.

PRIZING, ACCEPTANCE, TRUST

There is another attitude which stands out in those who are successful in facilitating learning. I have observed this attitude. I have experienced it. Yet, it is hard to know what term to put to it so I shall use several. I think of it as prizing the learner, prizing his feelings, his opinions, his person. It is a caring for the learner, but a non-possessive caring. It is an acceptance of this other individual as a separate person, having worth in his own right. It is a basic trust — a belief that this other person is somehow fundamentally trustworthy.

Whether we call it prizing, acceptance, trust, or by some other term, it shows up in a variety of observable ways. The facilitator who has a considerable degree of this attitude can be fully acceptant of the fear and hesitation of the student as he approaches a new problem as well as acceptant of the pupil's satisfaction in achievement. Such a teacher can accept the student's occasional apathy, his erratic desires to explore byroads of knowledge, as well as his disciplined efforts to achieve major goals. He can accept personal feelings which both disturb and promote learning — rivalry with a sibling, hatred of authority, concern about personal adequacy. What we are describing is a prizing of the learner as an imperfect human being with many feelings, many potentialities. The facilitator's prizing or acceptance of the learner is an operational expression of his essential confidence and trust in the capacity of the human organism.

I would like to give some examples of this attitude from the classroom situation. Here any teacher statements would be properly suspect, since many of us would like to feel we hold such attitudes, and might have a biased perception of our qualities. But let me indicate how this attitude of prizing, of accepting, of trusting, appears to the student who is fortunate enough to experience it.

Here is a statement from a college student in a class with Morey Appell.

> Your way of being with us is a revelation to me. In your class I feel important, mature, and capable of doing things on my own. I want to think for myself and this need cannot be accomplished through textbooks and lectures alone, but through living. I think you see me as a person with real feelings and needs, an individual. What I say and do are significant expressions from me, and you recognize this (Appell, 1959).

One of Miss Shiel's sixth graders expresses much more briefly her misspelled appreciation of this attitude, "you are a wounderful teacher period!!!"

College students in a class with Dr. Patricia Bull described not only these prizing, trusting attitudes, but the effect these have had on their other interactions.

> . . . I feel that I can say things to you that I can't say to other professors. . . . Never before have I been so aware of the other students or their personalities. I have never had so much interaction in a college classroom with my classmates. The climate of the classroom has had a very profound effect on me . . . the free atmosphere for discussion affected me . . . the general atmosphere of a particular session affected me. There have been many times when I have carried the discussion out of the class with me and thought about it for a long time.
>
> . . . I still feel close to you, as though there were some tacit understanding between us, almost a conspiracy. This adds to the in-class participation on my part because I feel that at least one person in the group will react, even when I am not sure of the others. It does not matter really whether your reaction is positive or negative, it just *is*. Thank you.
>
> . . . I appreciate the respect and concern you

have for others, including myself. . . . As a result of my experience in class, plus the influence of my readings, I sincerely believe that the student-centered teaching method does provide an ideal framework for learning; not just for the accumulation of facts, but more important, for learning about ourselves in relation to others. . . . When I think back to my shallow awareness in September compared to the depth of my insights now, I know that this course has offered me a learning experience of great value which I couldn't have acquired in any other way.

. . . Very few teachers would attempt this method because they would feel that they would lose the students' respect. On the contrary. You gained our respect, through your ability to speak to us on our level, instead of ten miles above us. With the complete lack of communication we see in this school, it was a wonderful experience to see people listening to each other and really communicating on an adult, intelligent level. More classes should afford us this experience (Bull, 1966).

As you might expect, college students are often suspicious that these seeming attitudes are phony. One of Dr. Bull's students writes:

. . . Rather than observe my classmates for the first few weeks, I concentrated my observations on you, Dr. Bull. I tried to figure out your motivations and purposes. I was convinced that you were a hypocrite. . . . I did change my opinion, however. You are not a hypocrite, by any means. . . . I do wish the course could continue. "Let each become all he is capable of being." . . . Perhaps my most disturbing question, which relates to this course is: When will we stop hiding things from ourselves and our contemporaries? (Bull, 1966).

I am sure these examples are more than enough to show that the facilitator who cares, who prizes, who trusts the learner, creates a climate for learning so different from the ordinary classroom that any resemblance is, as they say, "purely coincidental."

EMPATHIC UNDERSTANDING

A further element which establishes a climate for self-initiated, experiential learning is empathic understanding. When the teacher has the ability to understand the student's reactions from the inside, has a sensitive awareness of the way the process of education and learning seems *to the student,* then again the likelihood of significant learning is increased.

This kind of understanding is sharply different from the usual evaluative understanding, which follows the pattern of, "I understand what is wrong with you." When there is a sensitive empathy, however, the reaction in the learner follows something of this pattern, "At least someone understands how it feels and seems to be *me* without wanting to analyze me or judge me. Now I can blossom and grow and learn."

This attitude of standing in the other's shoes, of viewing the world through the student's eyes, is almost unheard of in the classroom. One could listen to thousands of ordinary classroom interactions without coming across one instance of clearly communicated, sensitively accurate, empathic understanding. But it has a tremendously releasing effect when it occurs.

Let me take an illustration from Virginia Axline, dealing with a second grade boy. Jay, age 7, has been aggressive, a trouble maker, slow of speech and learning. Because of his "cussing" he was taken to the principal, who paddled him, unknown to Miss Axline. During a free work period, he fashioned a man of clay, very carefully, down to a hat and a handkerchief in his pocket. "Who is that?" asked Miss Axline. "Dunno," replied Jay. "Maybe it is the principal. He has a handkerchief in his pocket like that." Jay glared at the clay figure. "Yes," he said. Then he began to tear the head off and looked up and smiled. Miss Axline said, "You sometimes feel like twisting his head off, don't you? You get so mad at him." Jay tore off one arm, another, then beat the figure to a pulp with his fists. Another boy, with the perception of the young, explained, "Jay is mad at Mr. X because he licked him this noon." "Then you must feel lots better now," Miss Axline commented. Jay grinned and began to rebuild Mr. X. (Adapted from Axline, 1944).

The other examples I have cited also indicate how deeply appreciative students feel when they are simply *understood*—not evaluated, not judged, simply understood from their *own* point of view, not the teacher's. If any teacher set herself the task of endeavoring to make one nonevaluative, acceptant, empathic response per day to a pupil's demonstrated or verbalized feeling, I believe he would discover the potency of this currently almost nonexistent kind of understanding.

Let me wind up this portion of my remarks by saying that when a facilitator creates, even to a modest degree, a classroom climate characterized by such realness, prizing, and empathy, he discovers that he has inaugurated an educational revolution. Learning of a different quality, proceeding at a different pace, with a greater degree of pervasiveness, occurs. Feelings—positive and negative, confused—become a part of the classroom experience. Learning becomes life, and a very vital life at that. The student is on his way, sometimes excitedly, sometimes reluctantly, to becoming a learning, changing being.

THE EVIDENCE

Already I can hear the mutterings of some of my so-called "hardheaded" colleagues. "A very pretty picture—very touching. But these are all self reports." (As if there were any other type of expression! But that's another issue.) They ask, "Where is the evidence? How do you

know?" I would like to turn to this evidence. It is not overwhelming, but it is consistent. It is not perfect, but it is suggestive.

First of all, in the field of psychotherapy, Barrett-Lennard (1962) developed an instrument whereby he could measure these attitudinal qualities: genuineness or congruence, prizing or positive regard, empathy or understanding. This instrument was given to both client and therapist, so that we have the perception of the relationship both by the therapist and by the client whom he is trying to help. To state some of the findings very briefly it may be said that those clients who eventually showed more therapeutic change as measured by various instruments, perceived *more* of these qualities in their relationship with the therapist than did those who eventually showed less change. It is also significant that this difference in perceived relationships was evident as early as the fifth interview, and predicted later change or lack of change in therapy. Furthermore, it was found that the *client's* perception of the relationship, his experience of it, was a better predictor of ultimate outcome than was the perception of the relationship by the therapist. Barrett-Lennard's original study has been amplified and generally confirmed by other studies.

So we may say, cautiously, and with qualifications which would be too cumbersome for the present paper, that if, in therapy, the client perceives his therapist as real and genuine, as one who likes, prizes, and empathically understands him, self-learning and therapeutic change are facilitated.

Now another thread of evidence, this time related more closely to education. Emmerling (1961) found that when high school teachers were asked to identify the problems they regarded as most urgent, they could be divided into two groups. Those who regarded their most serious problems, for example, as "Helping children think for themselves and be independent";

"Getting students to participate"; "Learning new ways of helping students develop their maximum potential"; "Helping students express individual needs and interests"; fell into what he called the "open" or "positively oriented" group. When Barrett-Lennard's Relationship Inventory was administered to the students of these teachers, it was found that they were perceived as significantly more real, more acceptant, more empathic than the other group of teachers whom I shall now describe.

The second category of teachers were those who tended to see their most urgent problems in negative terms, and in terms of student deficiencies and inabilities. For them the urgent problems were such as these: "Trying to teach children who don't even have the ability to follow directions"; "Teaching children who lack a desire to learn"; "Students who are not able to do the work required for their grade"; "Getting the children to listen." It probably will be no surprise that when the students of these teachers filled out the Relationship Inventory they saw their teachers are exhibiting relatively little of genuineness, of acceptance and trust, or of empathic understanding.

Hence we may say that the teacher whose orientation is toward releasing the student's potential exhibits a high degree of these attitudinal qualities which facilitate learning. The teacher whose orientation is toward the shortcomings of his students exhibits much less of these qualities.

A small pilot study by Bills (1961, 1966) extends the significance of these findings. A group of eight teachers was selected, four of them rated as adequate and effective by their superiors, and also showing this more positive orientation to their problems. The other four were rated as inadequate teachers and also had a more negative orientation to their problems, as described above. The students of these teachers were then asked to fill out the Barrett-Lennard Relationship Inventory, giving their perception of their teacher's relationship to them. This made the students very happy. Those who saw their relationship with the teacher as good were happy to describe this relationship. Those who had an unfavorable relationship were pleased to have, for the first time, an opportunity to specify the ways in which the relationship was unsatisfactory.

The more effective teachers were rated higher in every attitude measured by the Inventory: they were seen as more real, as having a higher level of regard for their students, were less conditional or judgmental in their attitudes, showed more empathic understanding. Without going into the details of the study it may be illuminating to mention that the total scores summing these attitudes vary sharply. For example, the relationships of a group of clients with their therapists, as perceived by the clients, received an average score of 108. The four most adequate high school teachers are seen by their students, received a score of 60. The four less adequate teachers received a score of 34. The lowest rated teacher received an average score of 2 from her students on the Relationship Inventory.

This small study certainly suggests that the teacher regarded as effective displays in her attitudes those qualities I have described as facilitative of learning, while the inadequate teacher shows little of these qualities.

Approaching the problem from a different angle, Schmuck (1963) has shown that in classrooms where pupils perceive their teachers as understanding them, there is likely to be a more diffuse liking structure among the pupils. This means that where the teacher is empathic, there are not a few students strongly liked and a few strongly disliked, but liking and affection are more evenly diffused throughout the group. In a later study he has shown that among students who are highly involved in their classroom peer group, "significant relationships exist between actual liking status on the one hand and utilization of abilities, attitude toward self, and attitude toward school on the other hand"

[Schmuck, 1966, p. 357–58]. This seems to lend confirmation to the other evidence by indicating that in an understanding classroom climate every student tends to feel liked by all the others, to have a more positive attitude toward himself and toward school. If he is highly involved with his peer group (and this appears probable in such a classroom climate), he also tends to utilize his abilities more fully in his school achievement.

But you may still ask, does the student actually *learn* more where these attitudes are present? Here an interesting study of third graders by Aspy (1965) helps to round out the suggestive evidence. He worked in six third-grade classes. The teachers tape-recorded two full weeks of their interaction with their students in the periods devoted to the teaching of reading. These recordings were done two months apart so as to obtain an adequate sampling of the teacher's interactions with her pupils. Four-minute segments of these recordings were randomly selected for rating. Three raters, working independently and "blind," rated each segment for the degree of congruence or genuineness shown by the teacher, the degree of her prizing or unconditional positive regard, and the degree of her empathic understanding.

The Reading Achievement Tests (Stanford Achievement) were used as the criterion. Again, omitting some of the details of a carefully and rigorously controlled study, it may be said that the children in the three classes with the highest degree of the attitudes described above showed a significantly greater gain in reading achievement than those students in the three classes with a lesser degree of these qualities.

So we may say, with a certain degree of assurance, that the attitudes I have endeavored to describe are not only effective in facilitating a deeper learning and understanding of self in a relationship such as psychotherapy, but that these attitudes characterize teachers who are regarded as effective teachers, and that the students of these teachers learn more, even of a conventional curriculum, than do students of teachers who are lacking in those attitudes.

REFERENCES

M. L. Appell. "Selected Student Reactions to Student-centered Courses." Mimeographed manuscript, 1959.

S. Ashton-Warner. *Teacher.* New York: Simon and Schuster, 1963.

D. N. Aspy. "A Study of Three Facilitative Conditions and Their Relationship to the Achievement of Third Grade Students." Unpublished Ed.D. dissertation, University of Kentucky, 1965.

Virginia M. Axline. "Morale on the School Front." *Journal of Educational Research* 38: 521–33; 1944.

G. T. Barrett-Lennard. "Dimensions of Therapist Response as Causal Factors in Therapeutic Change." *Psychological Monographs,* 76, 1962. (Whole No. 562)

R. E. Bills. Personal correspondence, 1961, 1966.

Patricia Bull. Student reactions, Fall 1965. State University College, Cortland, New York. Mimeographed manuscripts, 1966.

F. C. Emmerling. "A Study of the Relationships Between Personality Characteristics of Classroom Teachers and Pupil Perceptions." Unpublished Ph.D. dissertation, Auburn University, Auburn, Alabama, 1961.

P. W. Jackson. "The Student's World." University of Chicago. Mimeographed, 1966.

C. R. Rogers. "To Facilitate Learning." In Malcolm Provus, editor, NEA Handbook for Teachers, *Innovations for Time to Teach.* Washington, D.C.: Department of Classroom Teachers, NEA, 1966a.

R. Schmuck. "Some Aspects of Classroom Social Climate." *Psychology Schools* 3:59-65; 1966.

R. Schmuck. "Some Relationships of Peer Liking Patterns in the Class-Pupil Attitudes and Achievement." *The Social Review* 71:337–59; 1963.

Barbara P. Shiel. "Evaluation: A Self-directed Curriculum, 1965." Mimeographed, 1966.

On Freedom to Learn

R. S. Peters

R. S. Peters, (b. 1919) one of today's leading educational philosophers, is a professor and department chairman and a former dean of the Faculty of Education at University of London's Institute of Education. A member of the National Academy of Education in the United States, he has served as visiting professor at Harvard University and a visiting fellow at Australian National University. Peters studied at Clifton College, Bristol University, Queens College, Oxford University, and Birbeck College, University of London. He has written in the areas of psychology, political thought, philosophy, and philosophy of education. Among his books, are The Concept of Motivation. Brett's History of Psychology, *rev. ed.,* Hobbes, Social Principles and the Democratic State *(co-author),* Perspective on Plowden, Reason, Morality, and Religion, Authority, Responsibility and Education, Ethics and Education, The Concept of Education *(editor),* The Logic of Education *(co-author), and* Educational and the Development of Reason *(co-editor).*

It is, to a certain extent, inevitable that a person's thinking about education will be an extrapolation from a situation with which he is most familiar. Perry (1965) has developed this point with regard to what he calls the "traditional" and the "child-centred" models of education. It is not surprising, therefore, that Carl Rogers' views about education should reflect, in the main, his experiences as a therapist. What is surprising, however, is that an author who strongly advocates openness to the experiences of others should put together a collection of papers that are meant to be of general relevance to educational problems in such a seeming state of ignorance and innocence about educational theory and practice. Freedom is fine; and so is self-directed exploration. But there are other values, both in life and in education—truth, for instance, humility, and breadth of understanding.

Carl Rogers' book about education exem-

From R. S. Peters, "On Freedom to Learn," Interchange, *vol. 1, no. 4 (1970), pp. 111–14. Reprinted by permission.*

plifies both the strengths and weaknesses of his own emphasis. He builds on what he learns and values and much of what he says is perceptive, if rather repetitive; but his passionate assurance is not clouded by any hint of what he does not know and he even seems unaware of the light that others have already shed on some of the positions that he has made his own. Surely, one reflects, as one reads about self-directed learning, work contracts, and the problem-solving approach, Carl Rogers must have heard of the Dalton plan. Surely he has battled his way through Dewey and Kilpatrick as have most American educators; surely he is not so uneducated as to have missed out on Cremin's *The Transformation of the School.* But then, as one reads on, one begins to understand the free-floating character of the book, its lack of any proper historical, social, or philosophical dimensions. It is not really an attempt to think systematically about the actual problems of teaching and learning in a concrete historical context. It is Carl Rogers "doing his thing" in the context of education. Much of the book was actually given as distinct papers and addresses on specific occasions. These various addresses are strung together with other chapters in which Rogers restates his now familiar themes about the organism, interpersonal relationships, self-enhancement, etc., and tries to demonstrate their general relevance for education. This exposition is prefaced by three case studies in which a six grade teacher, a college professor of psychology, and himself try experiments in facilitating learning.

So much by way of general comment on *Freedom to Learn* as a serious sortie into educational theory. But what is to be made of Rogers' specific themes, when due allowance has been made for the limitations of their launching pad? Most of them are to be found in Chapters 4 to 7, after Rogers has presented his case studies in Part I. He gets off to a very shaky start in contrasting teaching, which he thinks unimportant, with the

facilitation of learning, which is the proper concern of the educator. He is led to make this rather stark contrast because the dictionary tells him that teaching means "to instruct" and "to impart knowledge and skill"—some, e.g., Oakeshott (1967), actually wish to *contrast* "instruct" with "impart"—and because he thinks that it is concerned only with the passing on of a static body of knowledge and skill. The Australian aborigines managed all right with teaching because of their unchanging environment; it is, however, useless for modern man because his environment is constantly changing. The goal of education for us must therefore be the facilitation of change and learning.

Every aspect of this thesis is dubious. If Rogers had thought more about the concept of "teaching," or if he had taken the trouble to examine what modern philosophers of education had written about it, instead of just looking it up in the dictionary, he would have grasped that "teaching" is a much more polymorphous concept than this. Was not Socrates teaching the slave in *The Meno,* even though he was not telling him anything? He would have grasped, too, that it is not only knowledge that can be imparted but also modes of thought and experience by means of which knowledge has been acquired and by means of which it can be criticized and revised. Also what is the point, on his own showing, of equipping people to seek knowledge, if no value is to be accorded to its acquisition? It may be salutary, at a time of change, to stress the importance of learning how to learn. But this goal is not inconsistent with acquiring information. My guess, too, is that, in spite of change, modern man needs to acquire much more of it to survive than ever was required by the Australian aborigine.

Having got teaching out of the way, Rogers is then able to give voice to his excitement about a real community of learners, which is worth quoting because, apart from its style, it could have come straight out of Dewey. "To free curiosity; to permit individuals to go charging off in new directions dictated by their own interests; to unleash the sense of inquiry; to open everything to questioning and exploration; to recognize that everything is in process of change—here is an experience I can never forget" (p. 105). How then, is this process of real "self-initiated, significant, experiential, 'gut-level' learning" to be facilitated? And, at this point, Rogers makes his distinctive contribution. It is through "certain attitudinal qualities which exist in the personal relationship between the facilitator and the learner" (p. 106). Findings in the field of psychotherapy apply in the classroom as well. Rogers then outlines the qualities that a facilitator of learning should exhibit to learners, qualities that parallel those of a client-centered therapist to his patients—genuineness, being a real person with his pupils, prizing the learner and caring for him, empathic understanding, and trust. Rogers claims that "individuals who hold such attitudes, and are bold enough to act on them, do not simply modify classroom methods—they revolutionize them. They perform almost none of the functions of teachers. It is no longer accurate to call them teachers. They are catalyzers, facilitators, giving freedom and life and the opportunity to learn, to students" (p. 126).

This is surely an extremely important point to make about teaching. If we avert our eyes from the naive contrast between "teaching" and "the facilitation of learning" there remains a strong case for saying that personal relationships between teacher and pupil, of the type advocated by Rogers, do seem to facilitate learning. This needs to be said loudly at a time when educational institutions are becoming larger and more impersonal and when students are increasingly being treated as subject-fodder and as operatives to be slotted into the occupational structure. Teachers can function as human beings as well as teachers; and if they do so, learning is probably facilitated.

Rogers, however, does not seem altogether

clear about what makes a relationship a personal one as distinct from a role relationship. What seems to me distinctive of a personal relationship is that a response is made to another individual just as a human being—not as an occupant of a role, not as a sharer in a common quest, including that of learning, not even as another moral being who is regarded with respect as the subject of rights (Peters, 1966). Yet Rogers constantly speaks of such relationships as if he views them, in an educational situation, mainly as facilitators of learning. But if they are entered into by the teacher *because he sees them* as facilitating learning they surely cease to be proper personal relationships; for the aspect under which the other is viewed, as a learner, now makes them a species of role relationship. Their spontaneity can thus be spoilt and endless possibilities for *mauvaise foi* are opened up. There is thus inherent in the teacher-pupil relationship a paradox akin to the paradox of hedonism. Learning is facilitated by the teacher entering into personal relationships with his pupils; but such relationships must not be viewed by the teacher as facilitating learning. Indeed a pupil would surely resent being at the receiver end of a "personal relationship" with a "facilitator" that is viewed as aiding his learning, much more than being subject to a straightforward attempt to instruct him. Rogers seems unaware of these difficulties because he does not appreciate that being a facilitator of learning is just as much a role relationship as instructing and that what makes an action a performance of a role is the aspect under which it is viewed by the agent. In other words, Rogers' ideal teacher must, to a certain extent, be capable of forgetting, in his dealing with pupils, that he is a facilitator of learning. He must, from time to time, just respond to his pupils as fellow human beings. This response is something that is valuable in its own right.

Rogers' preoccupations with personal relationships between teacher and pupil are very salutary because progressives, who stress freedom and self-initiated learning, sometimes stress too much "do it yourself" methods. Rogers, of course, advocates these, but he is more than mindful of the bond between teacher and taught that is one of the most potent influences in the development of knowledge, sensitivity, and skill. He does not, however, bring the teacher's role fully out into the open because he is squeamish about direction, and superficial about knowledge. He believes in the growth and self-actualization of the individual. He finds that his clients and pupils move towards genuineness, acceptance of self, openness to others, and self-direction. In other words the self that is realized is not any old self, but one that exemplifies moral values as old as Socrates. Rogers seems to see this as some sort of spontaneous unfolding of dormant potentialities. But he surely must appreciate that there are dormant potentialities for all sorts of other selves and that the emergence of this type of self is very intimately connected with the study influence of persons such as Rogers. Rogers is, of course, an inverterate moralist who passes on his values more by exemplifying them than by trying to instruct others in them — except, of course, when he writes books. This kind of influence is a form of "direction" — perhaps a much more effective form that explicit instruction. I myself share Rogers' moral convictions. But I do think that their ethical status should be made explicit and that some sort of justification of them should be attempted. I also think that persons who believe in them should stop being so squeamish about the manifest "directiveness" involved in passing them on to others — especially if they are teachers.

Rogers' squeamishness about the role of the teacher is connected with his tendency to regard teaching as just instruction in a body of knowledge or code of behaviour. He does not appreciate that a more important aspect of teaching is the initiation of others into modes of thinking and experience that lie behind such bodies of knowledge and codes of behaviour. In teaching science, for instance, one does not just pass on facts and laws; nor does one seek simply to encourage the nebulous sort of adaptability, or learning how to learn, that Rogers advocates. One attempts to get others on the inside of a public form of thinking in which assumptions are challenged and techniques mastered for deciding who is right. Specific types of concepts and truth criteria have to be understood. Above all the passion of truth must be conveyed that gives point to the search for evidence, the abhorrence of irrelevance, incoherence, and arbitrariness, and the love of clarity and precision. Similarly moral education is not just a matter of imposing rules such as those prohibiting stealing and the breaking of promises; it is also a matter of sensitizing persons to principles such as respect for others, truthfulness, fairness, freedom, and the consideration of interests, which are presuppositions of moral experience. Rogers' valuations are intimately connected with this form of experience. It is one that has taken the human race thousands of years to develop and that is constantly threatened by powerful and more primitive tendencies within human nature. It is institutionalized in democratic institutions at their best, and will be perpetuated only if it also is fostered in the consciousness of countless individuals.

Rogers does no service to the tradition that he has inherited by suggesting that his values are private possessions that develop miraculously within the individual soul. And he does a positive disservice by minimizing the role of the teacher as one of the main transmitters of these public forms of life. Rogers contrasts the teacher, who imposes his values, with the facilitator of learning, who sets people free to discover their own. Both pictures are inadequate; for both ignore the public forms of experience underlying, e.g., scientific, moral, and aesthetic achievements and discoveries. The teacher, ideally speaking, is a person whose experience and

...as given him some mastery of of these modes of experience. Rogers manifestly has achieved this in the ...cular mode of interpersonal understanding. His function, in the same way as that of any other teacher, is to initiate others into this form of experience so they can manage on their own. But, as with "creative" artists or scientists, they cannot do so without being introduced in a whole variety of ways, with which good teachers are familiar, into the mode of experience in question. It is against this general background of the role of the teacher that Rogers' important insights, about personal relationships are to be seen in proper perspective.

In Part III Rogers outlines some assumptions about learning and its facilitation and discusses graduate education in the light of them. Generalizations are put forward about the importance of relevance to the learner's purposes, about learning through doing and participation, and about the relationship of threats to the self to learning. Much of this discussion is very apposite; but there is nothing very novel in it. What is missing, however, is any sense of the great differences between the sorts of things that have to be learnt—skills, attitudes, principles, facts, etc., within different modes of experi-

ence. Some generalizations such as those of Rogers can be made about general conditions of learning. But equally crucial for education are the specific features of different types of learning that derive from differences in what is being learnt—these differences affect very much the "facilitator."

Part IV includes a personal confession of what is most significant to Rogers in "being in relationship," some thoughts about the "valuing process," a chapter on Freedom and Commitment in which he outlines his views on free will in contrast to those of Skinner, and an account of the goal of the "fully functioning person." There is no mention of any of the recent work done on moral development and Rogers' handling of the issues in ethics that he raises is so superficial, limited, and confined to his own frame of reference that it would be difficult to know quite where to begin in discussing them. The book ends with a model for revolution in which Rogers recommends T groups, etc., for educational administrators, teachers, and faculty members. This is mildly reminiscent of Plato's suggestion that society can be saved only if philosophers become kings or kings become philosophers. But Plato did know something about politics and institutional change.

REFERENCES

Oakeshott, M. "Learning and teaching." In R. S. Peters (Ed.), *The concept of education.* London: Routledge & Kegan Paul, 1967.

Perry, L. R. "What is an educational situation?" In R. D. Archambault (Ed.), *Philosophical analysis and education.* London: Routledge & Kegan Paul, 1965.

Peters, R. S. "Teaching and personal relationships." In E. L. French (Ed.), *Melbourne studies in education.* Melbourne: Melbourne University Press, 1966.

DISCUSSION QUESTIONS AND ACTIVITIES

1. How does Rogers define teaching? Do you accept his definition? Construct your own definition.

2. What specific reasons does he give for his assertion that teaching is "a vastly overrated function"? Are his reasons valid in terms of

what you know about teaching? Give specific reasons for your answer.

3. By assuming that teaching is only applicable in a certain type of culture, does Rogers thereby lead you to believe that his definition of teaching is overly restrictive?

4. What, according to Rogers, is the goal of education? Evaluate his proposed goal. Develop your own goal.

5. What does it mean to be "a facilitator of learning"? How is being a facilitator different from being a teacher?

6. Evaluate the evidence that Rogers presents as corroborating his position. Do you think his evidence is adequate?

7. Peters charges that Rogers's book does not attempt to think about teaching and learning in a concrete historical context. In other words, the works of his predecessors are ignored. Is it Rogers's responsibility to show earlier educators contributions to his ideas?

8. Peters attacks Rogers's concept of teaching. Explain and evaluate Peters's critique of the concept.

9. Peters argues that Rogers's relationship as a facilitator of learning is a role relationship as distinct from a personal relationship. Evaluate the validity of this charge.

10. What problems, if any, are involved in the concept of spontaneous unfoldment of dormant potentialities?

11. Peters says that Rogers is a moralist but is squeamish about taking a directive role in such matters with students. Peters thinks that Rogers should be less squeamish about doing so. Add ideas of your own if you do not accept the ideas of either author.

12. Peters finds that the teacher who imposes values and the person who is a facilitator of learning are both inadequate because they ignore the public forms of experience underlying codes of behavior and bodies of knowledge. What are the strengths and weaknesses of Peters' counterargument?

13. Peters briefly states his own position. Does it have any weaknesses? If so, what are they? Is it clearly superior to what Rogers has proposed? If so, in what ways?

14. Make observations of one of your teachers for at least one hour. Was your teacher's behavior more in accordance with the ideas of Rogers or Peters?

SUGGESTED READINGS

Works by Carl Rogers

Becoming Partners. New York: Delacorte, 1972.

Carl Rogers on Encounter Groups. New York: Harper & Row, 1970.

Carl Rogers on Personal Power. New York: Delacorte, 1977; Dell, 1978.

Client-Centered Therapy. Boston: Houghton Mifflin, 1951.

The Clinical Treatment of the Problem Child. Boston: Houghton Mifflin, 1939.

Counseling and Psychotherapy. New York: Houghton Mifflin, 1942.

Counseling with Returned Servicemen. New York: McGraw-Hill, 1946.

Freedom to Learn. Columbus, Ohio: Charles Merrill, 1969.

Man and the Science of Man (co-editor). Columbus, Ohio: Charles Merrill, 1968.

Measuring Personality Adjustment in Children Nine to Thirteen Years of Age. New York: Teachers College, Columbia University, 1931.

On Becoming a Person. Boston: Houghton Mifflin, 1961.

Person to Person (with Barry Stevens). Walnut Creek, California: Real People Press, 1967.

Psychotherapy and Personality Change. Chicago: University of Chicago Press, 1954.

"Some Issues Concerning the Control of Human Behavior: A Symposium." *Science* 124 (November 30, 1956): 1057. (with B. F. Skinner)

The Therapeutic Relation and Its Impact (editor). Westport, Connecticut: Greenwood, 1976.

A Way of Being. Boston: Houghton Mifflin, 1980.

Cassette Tapes by Carl R. Rogers

"A Dialogue on Education and the Control of Human Behavior." with B. F. Skinner. 6 cassettes. Jeffrey Norton Publishers, 1976. (INP Tape Library)

Works about Carl R. Rogers

Banta, T. J. "Educating Children for Adulthood." *Young Children* 21 (May 1966): 279.

Barton, Anthony. *Three Worlds of Therapy.* Palo Alto, California: National Press Books, 1974.

Bavelas, Janet Beavin. *Personality: Current Theory and Research,* ch. 9. Monterey, California: Brooks/Cole, 1978.

Bryne, J. T. "Rogers' Counseling Theory and the Nature of Man." *The Catholic Educational Review* 58 (February 1960): 114–18.

"Carl Rogers Joins Ranks of Radical Critics of the Public Schools." *Phi Delta Kappan* 51 (January 1970): 294.

"Carl Rogers, 1902–." *Education* 95 (Winter 1974): 98–101.

Evans, Richard Isadore. *Carl Rogers: The Man and His Ideas.* New York: Dutton, 1975.

Hairston, M. "Carl Rogers' Alternative to Traditional Rhetoric." *College Composition and Communication* 27 (December 1976): 373–7.

Hannoun, Hubert. *L'Attitude Non-directive de Carl Rogers.* Paris: Editions ESF, 1972.

Kemp, C. G. "Another Note on Counseling and the Nature of Man." *Journal of Counseling Psychology* 8 (Summer 1961): 186–88.

Kirschenbaum, Howard. *On Becoming Carl Rogers.* New York: Delacorte Press, 1979.

Lerner, Marcelo. *Introduccion a la Psicoterapia de Rogers.* Buenos Aires: Ediciones Nueva Vision, 1974.

Milhollan, Frank. *From Skinner to Rogers: Contrasting Approaches to Education.* Lincoln, Nebraska: Professional Educators Publications, 1972.

Mintz, A. L. "Encounter Groups and Other Panaceas." *Commentary* 56 (July 1973): 42–9.

Nye, Robert D. *Three Psychologies: Perspectives from Freud, Skinner, and Rogers,* 2nd ed. Monterey, California: Brooks/Cole, 1981.

Pearson, P. H. "Rational Analysis of Rogers' Concept of Openness to Experience." *Journal of Personality* 40 (Summer 1972), 349–65.

Roussel, Fernand. *Le Moniteur d'Orientation Rogerienne.* Montreal: Presses de l'Universite de Montreal, 1972.

Shultz, J. L. "Empathy: Revisited and Updated." *Vocational Guidance Quarterly* 24 (December 1975): 24.

Skinner, B. F. (with Rogers). "Some Issues Concerning the Control of Human Behavior." *Science* 124 (1956): 1057–66.

Smith, M. B. "The Phenomenological Approach in Personality Theory: Some Critical Remarks." *Journal of Abnormal and Social Psychology* 45 (1950): 516–522.

Walerstein, Frida. *Vision Critica de la Psicoterapia de Carl Rogers.* Mexico, Universidad Nacional Autónoma de México. Facultad de Filosofia y Letras 1963.

Wylie, R. C. *The Self-Study Concept: A Review of Methodological Considerations and Measuring Instruments,* rev. ed., vol. I, ch. 2. Lincoln: University of Nebraska Press, 1974.

6
BEYOND FREEDOM
AND DIGNITY

B. F. Skinner's behaviorism avoids deductive theories and relies on an inductive approach in his experimentation. His investigations start with empirical data and proceed tentatively to limited range generalizations. Skinner rejects any method of inquiry that does not depend upon sensory observation. He limits his system to description rather than the customary goal of explanation. His system attempts to avoid reductionism by defining concepts in terms of observables rather than reducing them to physiological states.

The simple unit of behavior is the reflex, which consists of "any observed correlation of stimulus and response." There are two types of behavior: respondent and operant. Behavior is called "respondent" when it is correlated to "specific eliciting stimuli"; behavior is "operant" when no stimuli are present. "Stimulus" means any modification of the environment, and a "response" is a correlated part of the behavior.

Conditioning in the form of respondent behavior is used by Skinner in his experiments with pigeons. Reinforcement (reward) is dependent upon the response. Whenever the pigeon exhibits the desired response as a result of stimuli, the response is reinforced by providing food. On the other hand, with operant conditioning the response comes first and then it becomes reinforced. It is through operant conditioning that the efficiency of behavior is improved. This form of conditioning builds a repertoire by which we handle such processes as walking, playing games, using tools, and other activities.

The selection by Skinner shows why he believes Emile or the free and happy student as an educational aim is fraught with grave dangers. He can well understand why primitive and coercive school systems led educational reformers to espouse this aim; however, he believes his own system of controls would be far superior and should be adopted.

Peters accuses Skinner of holding musty nineteenth century views and attacking straw men. Skinner exhibits a form of utilitarianism that pushes the instrumental approach to life to its limits and poses the danger, according to Peters, of some people using their freedom to deny others their dignity.

The Free and Happy Student

B. F. Skinner

B. F. Skinner (b. 1904) is an internationally known behaviorist recognized for his system of operant conditioning, contributions to programmed learning, and his utopian system of controls based on positive reinforcement. He received an A.B. degree from Hamilton College and M.A. and Ph.D. from Harvard. Professor Skinner was a Research Fellow and Junior Fellow at Harvard before becoming an Instructor of Psychology at the University of Minnesota; in 1942–43 he conducted war research sponsored by General Mills; later he became Professor and Chairman of Psychology at Indiana University; he then returned to Harvard in 1948 and became Edgar Pierce Professor, 1958–74, and Professor Emeritus in 1974. He is the recipient of 24 honorary degrees from American and foreign universities and has been given many awards for distinguished scientific contributions.

His name is Emile. He was born in the middle of the eighteenth century in the first flush of the modern concern for personal freedom. His father was Jean-Jacques Rousseau, but he has had many foster parents, among them Pestalozzi, Froebel, and Montessori, down to A. S. Neill and Ivan Illich. He is an ideal student. Full of goodwill toward his teachers and his peers, he needs no discipline. He studies because he is naturally curious. He learns things because they interest him.

Unfortunately, he is imaginary. He was quite explicitly so with Rousseau, who put his own children in an orphanage and preferred to say how he would teach his fictional hero; but the modern version of the free and happy student to be found in books by Paul Goodman, John Holt, Jonathan Kozol, or Charles Silberman is also imaginary. Occasionally a real example seems to turn up. There are teachers who would be successful in dealing with people anywhere as statesmen, therapists, businessmen, or friends—and there are students who scarcely need to be taught, and together they sometimes seem to bring Emile to life. And unfortunately they do so just often enough to sustain the old dream. But Emile is a will-o'-the-wisp, who has led many teachers into a conception of their role which could prove disastrous.

The student who has been taught *as if he were Emile* is, however, almost too painfully real. It has taken a long time for him to make his appearance. Children were first made free and happy in kindergarten, where there seemed to be no danger in freedom, and for a long time they were found nowhere else, because the rigid discipline of the grade schools blocked progress. But eventually they broke through—moving from kindergarten into grade school, taking over grade after grade, moving into secondary school

From B. F. Skinner, "The Free and Happy Student," New York University Education Quarterly *IV (Winter 1973); 2-6. Reprinted by permission.*

and on into college and, very recently, into graduate school. Step by step they have insisted upon their rights, justifying their demands with the slogans that philosophers of education have supplied. If sitting in rows restricts personal freedom, unscrew the seats. If order can be maintained only through coercion, let chaos reign. If one cannot be really free while worrying about examinations and grades, down with examinations and grades! The whole Establishment is now awash with free and happy students.

DROPPING OUT OF SCHOOL, DROPPING OUT OF LIFE

If they are what Rousseau's Emile would really have been like, we must confess to some disappointment. The Emile we know doesn't work very hard. "Curiosity" is evidently a moderate sort of thing. Hard work is frowned upon because it implies a "work ethic," which has something to do with discipline.

The Emile we know doesn't learn very much. His "interests" are evidently of limited scope. Subjects that do not appeal to him he calls irrelevant. (We should not be surprised at this, since Rousseau's Emile, like the boys in Summerhill, never got past the stage of knowledgeable craftsman.) He may defend himself by questioning the value of knowledge. Knowledge is always in flux, so why bother to acquire any particular stage of it? It will be enough to remain curious and interested. In any case the life of feeling and emotion is to be preferred to the life of intellect; let us be governed by the heart rather than the head.

The Emile we know doesn't think very clearly. He has had little or no chance to learn to think logically or scientifically and is easily taken in by the mystical and the superstitious. Reason is irrelevant to feeling and emotion.

And, alas, the Emile we know doesn't seem particularly happy. He doesn't like his education any more than his predecessors liked theirs. Indeed, he seems to like it less. He is much more inclined to play truant (big cities have given up enforcing truancy laws), and he drops out as soon as he legally can, or a little sooner. If he goes to college, he probably takes a year off at some time in his four-year program. And after that his dissatisfaction takes the form of anti-intellectualism and a refusal to support education.

Are there offsetting advantages? Is the free and happy student less aggressive, kinder, more loving? Certainly not toward the schools and teachers that have set him free, as increasing vandalism and personal attacks on teachers seem to show. Nor is he particularly well disposed toward his peers. He seems perfectly at home in a world of unprecedented domestic violence.

Is he perhaps more creative? Traditional practices were said to suppress individuality; what kind of individuality has now emerged? Free and happy students are certainly different from the students of a generation ago, but they are not very different from each other. Their own culture is a severely regimented one, and their creative works—in art, music, and literature—are confined to primitive and elemental materials. They have very little to be creative with, for they have never taken the trouble to explore the fields in which they are now to be front-runners.

Is the free and happy student at least more effective as a citizen? Is he a better person? The evidence is not very reassuring. Having dropped out of school, he is likely to drop out of life too. It would be unfair to let the hippie culture represent young people today, but it does serve to clarify an extreme. The members of that culture do not accept responsibility for their own lives; they sponge on the contributions of those who have not yet been made free and happy—who have gone to medical school and become doctors, or who have become the farmers who raise the food or the workers who produce the goods they consume.

These are no doubt overstatements. Things are not that bad, nor is education to be blamed for all the trouble. Nevertheless, there is a trend in a well-defined direction, and it is particularly clear in education. Our failure to create a truly free and happy student is symptomatic of a more general problem.

THE ILLUSION OF FREEDOM

What we may call the struggle for freedom in the Western world can be analyzed as a struggle to escape from or avoid punitive or coercive treatment. It is characteristic of the human species to act in such a way as to reduce or terminate irritating, painful, or dangerous stimuli, and the struggle for freedom has been directed toward those who would control others with stimuli of that sort. Education has had a long and shameful part in the history of that struggle. The Egyptians, Greeks, and Romans all whipped their students. Medieval sculpture showed the carpenter with his hammer and the schoolmaster with the tool of his trade too, and it was the cane or rod. We are not yet in the clear. Corporal punishment is still used in many schools, and there are calls for its return where it has been abandoned.

A system in which students study primarily to avoid the consequences of not studying is neither humane nor very productive. Its by-products include truancy, vandalism, and apathy. Any effort to eliminate punishment in education is certainly commendable. We ourselves act to escape from aversive control, and our students should escape from it too. They should study because they want to, because they like to, because they are interested in what they are doing. The mistake—a classical mistake in the literature of freedom—is to suppose that they will do

so as soon as we stop punishing them. Students are not literally free when they have been freed from their teachers. They then simply come under the control of other conditions, and we must look at those conditions and their effects if we are to improve teaching.

Those who have attacked the "servility" of students, as Montessori called it, have often put their faith in the possibility that young people will learn what they need to know from the "world of things," which includes the world of people who are not teachers. Montessori saw possibly useful behavior being suppressed by schoolroom discipline. Could it not be salvaged? And could the environment of the schoolroom not be changed so that other useful behavior would occur? Could the teacher not simply guide the student's natural development? Or could he not accelerate it by teasing out behavior which would occur naturally but not so quickly if he did not help? In other words, could we not bring the real world into the classroom, as John Dewey put it, or destroy the classroom and turn the student over to the real world, as Ivan Illich has recommended? All these possibilities can be presented in an attractive light, but they neglect two vital points:

1. No one learns very much from the real world without help. The only evidence we have of what can be learned from a nonsocial world has been supplied by those wild boys said to have been raised without contact with other members of their own species. Much more can be learned without formal instruction in a social world, but not without a good deal of teaching, even so. Formal education has made a tremendous difference in the extent of the skills and knowledge which can be acquired by a person in a single lifetime.

2. A much more important principle is that the real world teaches only what is relevant to the present; it makes no explicit preparation for the future. Those who would minimize teaching have contended that no preparation is needed, that the

student will follow a natural line of development and move into the future in the normal course of events. We should be content, as Carl Rogers has put it, to trust

> . . . the insatiable curiosity which drives the adolescent boy to absorb everything he can see or hear or read about gasoline engines in order to improve the efficiency and speed of his "hot rod." I am talking about the student who says, "I am discovering, drawing in from the outside, and making that which is drawn in a real part of me." I am talking about my learning in which the experience of the learner progresses along the line: "No, no, that's not what I want"; "Wait! This is closer to what I'm interested in, what I need." "Ah, here it is! Now I'm grasping and comprehending what I need and what I want to know!"[1]

Rogers is recommending a total commitment to the present moment, or at best to an immediate future.

FORMAL EDUCATION AS PREPARATION FOR THE FUTURE

But it has always been the task of formal education to set up behavior which would prove useful or enjoyable *later* in the student's life. Punitive methods had at least the merit of providing current reasons for learning things that would be rewarding in the future. We object to the punitive reasons, but we should not forget their function in making the future important.

It is not enough to give the student advice—to explain that he will have a future, and that to enjoy himself and be more successful in it, he must acquire certain skills and knowledge now. Mere advice is ineffective because it is not supported by current rewards. The positive consequences that generate a useful behavioral repertoire need not be any more explicitly relevant to the future than were the punitive conse-

quences of the past. The student needs current reasons, positive or negative, but only the educational policy maker who supplies them need take the future into account. It follows that many instructional arrangements seem "contrived," but there is nothing wrong with that. It is the teacher's function to contrive conditions under which students learn. Their relevance to a future usefulness need not be obvious.

It is a difficult assignment. The conditions the teacher arranges must be powerful enough to compete with those under which the student tends to behave in distracting ways. In what has come to be called "contingency management in the classroom," tokens are sometimes used as rewards or reinforcers. They become reinforcing when they are exchanged for reinforcers that are already effective. There is no "natural" relation between what is learned and what is received. The token is simply a reinforcer that can be made clearly contingent upon behavior. To straighten out a wholly disrupted classroom, something as obvious as a token economy may be needed, but less conspicuous contingencies—as in a credit-point system, perhaps, or possibly in the long run merely expressions of approval on the part of teacher or peer—may take over.

The teacher can often make the change from punishment to positive reinforcement in a surprisingly simple way—by responding to the student's success rather than his failures. Teachers have too often supposed that their role is to point out what students are doing wrong, but pointing to what they are doing *right* will often make an enormous difference in the atmosphere of a classroom and in the efficiency of instruction. Programmed materials are helpful in bringing about these changes, because they increase the frequency with which the student enjoys the satisfaction of being right, and they supply a valuable intrinsic reward in providing a clear indication of progress. A good program makes a step in the direction of competence almost as conspicuous as a token.

---

[1]Carl R. Rogers, *Freedom to Learn* (Columbus, O.: Merrill, 1969).

Programmed instruction is perhaps most successful in attacking punitive methods by allowing the student to move at his own pace. The slow student is released from the punishment which inevitably follows when he is forced to move on to material for which he is not ready, and the fast student escapes the boredom of being forced to go too slow. These principles have recently been extended to college education, with dramatic results, in the Keller system of personalized instruction.[2]

THE RESPONSIBILITY OF SETTING EDUCATIONAL POLICY

There is little doubt that a student can be given nonpunitive reasons for acquiring behavior that will become useful or otherwise reinforcing at some later date. He can be prepared for the future. But what *is* that future? Who is to say what the student should learn? Those who have sponsored the free and happy student have argued that it is the student himself who should say. His current interests should be the source of an effective educational policy. Certainly they will reflect his idiosyncrasies, and that is good, but how much can he know about the world in which he will eventually play a part? The things he is "naturally" curious about are of current and often temporary interest. How many things must he possess besides his "hot rod" to provide the insatiable curiosity relevant to , say, a course in physics?

It must be admitted that the teacher is not always in a better position. Again and again education has gone out of date as teachers have continued to teach subjects which were no longer relevant at any time in the student's life. Teachers often teach simply what they know. (Much of what is taught in private schools is de-

termined by what the available teachers can teach.) Teachers tend to teach what they can teach easily. Their current interests, like those of students, may not be a reliable guide.

Nevertheless, in recognizing the mistakes that have been made in the past in specifying what students are to learn, we do not absolve ourselves from the responsibility of setting educational policy. We should say, we should be *willing* to say, what we believe students will need to know, taking the individual student into account wherever possible, but otherwise making our best prediction with respect to students in general. Value judgments of this sort are not as hard to make as is often argued. Suppose we undertake to prepare the student to produce his share of the goods he will consume and the services he will use, to get on well with his fellows, and to enjoy his life. In doing so are we imposing *our* values on someone else? No, we are merely choosing a set of specifications which, so far as we can tell, will at some time in the future prove valuable to the student and his culture. Who is any more likely to be right?

The natural, logical outcome of the struggle for personal freedom in education is that the teacher should improve his control of the student rather than abandon it. The free school is no school at all. Its philosophy signalizes the abdication of the teacher. The teacher who understands his assignment and is familiar with the behavioral processes needed to fulfill it can have students who not only feel free and happy while they are being taught but who will continue to feel free and happy when their formal education comes to an end. They will do so because they will be successful in their work (having acquired useful productive repertoires), because they will get on well with their fellows (having learned to understand themselves and others), because they will enjoy what they do (having acquired the necessary knowledge and skills), and because they will from time to time make an occasional creative contribution toward an even

[2]*P.S.I. Newsletter,* October, 1972 (published by Department of Psychology, Georgetown University, J. G. Sherman, ed.).

more effective and enjoyable way of life. Possibly the most important consequence is that the teacher will then feel free and happy too.

We must choose today between Cassandran and Utopian prognostications. Are we to work to avoid disaster or to achieve a better world? Again, it is a question of punishment or reward. Must we act because we are frightened, or are there positive reasons for changing our cultural practices? The issue goes far beyond education, but it is one with respect to which education has much to offer. To escape from or avoid disaster, people are likely to turn to the punitive measures of a police state. To work for a better world, they may turn instead to the positive methods of education. When it finds its most effective methods, education will be almost uniquely relevant to the task of setting up and maintaining a better way of life.

Survival, The Soul or Personal Relationships

R. S. Peters

This book [*Beyond Freedom and Dignity*] was proclaimed in *Science News* as 'one of the most important happenings in twentieth-century psychology', which is perhaps a revealing verdict on the history of psychology in this century. For Skinner's attitudes and ideas belong to the nineteenth century. Basically he is a Utilitarian who values happiness and who thinks that it is attainable if the environment can be more systematically controlled. Things can be fixed up all right for human benefit by the employment of a technology of human behaviour. This technology embodies the old inductivist view of science that generalisations are gradually built up out of systematic experimentation. The principles employed are the old principles of the association of ideas dressed up in their modern guise of the conditioning of responses which subserve the survival of the individual and the species.

Survival, of course, now seems a more urgent question than it did to nineteenth-century perfectibilists. In this respect Skinner's attitudes are less confident, less infected by a belief in the inevitability of progress. For he is very much a contemporary American as well, a member of a nation that has lost its nerve and shed some of its old arrogance. There is the Vietnam war, pollution, the blacks, the student drop-out, drugs and the threat of over-population. These are beginning to look like predicaments, not like problems that can be solved or fixed up—at least not until men are more persuaded of the possibilities

From Review of B. F. Skinner's "Beyond Freedom and Dignity," by R. S. Peters. Times Educational Supplement *(March 3, 1972). Used by permission.*

opened up by Skinner's technology of behaviour.

Skinner passionately wants to persuade his contemporaries that salvation lies in submitting to control of the environment for their own good; but he is thwarted by their obstinate attachment to their freedom and dignity as human beings. Hence his book. And here again his adversary comes straight out of the nineteenth century. For he claims that their attachment is due to their belief in 'autonomous man', which he interprets as implying a belief in a little man within a man. The old Behaviourists, like J. B. Watson, were of course scared stiff of the soul. Hence their onslaught on the immaterial stuff of consciousness of which it was alleged to be composed. Skinner, somewhat quaintly, ascribes similar beliefs to those who nowadays believe in the autonomy of the individual. He sets up straw men to attack who are musty with the smell of Victorian haylofts. I do not think that he wilfully or wickedly misrepresents his adversaries; he is not that sort of man. Basically he is a simple fellow who is too unsophisticated in these matters to understand what they say nowadays.

Skinner admits that the 'literature of freedom' has done much to eliminate aversive practices. But it has placed too much emphasis on changing states of mind instead of the circumstances on which they depend. And, more importantly, escape is sought from all controllers—even from those who control the environment for people's good. Such squeamishness spells race suicide and is based on the superstition of the little man within who is subject to no constraints. These pre-scientific hang-ups are now a luxury that men must do without if they are to survive, though historically they have done some good. Belief in freedom, for instance, has led to opposition to punishment, which is an ineffective form of control; for it induces people not to behave in certain ways but

does not shape their behaviour in a positive direction. The individual has to find his own path—and gets credit for it to boot because of the mysterious workings of conscience, another stronghold of autonomous man.

But the alternatives to punishment proposed by freedom-lovers are also ineffective because they are tied to the superstition of autonomy. Permissiveness, for instance, exonerates the teacher or parent from responsibility for control and simply leaves the child to be controlled by other features of the environment. Socratic midwifery gives the teacher more power and the individual credit. So both are satisfied, but at the cost of more precise knowledge about factors in the environment which are the real determinants of learning. Guidance relies on horticultural metaphors. There is control all right; but it is cloaked by the pretence that the shaping is brought about by inner growth. Dependence on things, as advocated by Rousseau and Dewey, is more effective and saves a lot of time and energy. People, too, can be used as things for shaping others. But the teacher must be careful to arrange such things. Finally there is the more high-minded policy of changing people's minds by urging or persuading them. This is ineffective; for it is really only the changing of behaviour that counts. Mind manipulators overlook past contingencies that are in fact operative and attribute efficacy to the man within.

Skinner sees that hard-headed shaping of behaviour presupposes some view of value; for when is a man in good shape? His answer is Bentham's translated into behaviouristic jargon. Pleasure is positive reinforcement and this becomes both the standard of right and wrong and the throne to which the chain of causes and effects is fastened. Good things are positive reinforcers; so behavioural science is the science of values. Men are guided by their concern for happiness—i.e. by personal reinforcers, that have survival value. They reinforce their fellows who act 'for the good of others'—i.e. who do things that reinforce others. Practices develop that have long-term reinforcing effects. Morals are therefore basically a matter of good husbandry, of fixing things up for human benefit. People tell the truth because they are reinforced for so doing. The scientist does not cook his results because others will check them. This is how men in fact behave and, presumably, how they should—though Skinner, like Bentham, is not altogether clear about the difference.

In the evolution of culture the most important criterion of 'progress' is thus the emergence of enhanced sensitivity to the consequences of behaviour, and increasing ability to predict them. Culture must now be more consciously designed so that long-term goods are promoted. The ingenuity that has produced cars and space-crafts must be turned to fixing up the ghettos, pollution and the use of leisure. Man must accept the view of himself that behavioural science has revealed. It is indeed more appropriate, when contemplating him, to exclaim 'How like a dog' rather than 'How like a god'. God is not dead; for he was never alive. But man will exterminate himself if he does not pay attention to providing the reinforcement contingencies which will shape his survival and turn his back on all the superstitions associated with his own autonomy.

Obviously those who believe in freedom will not take kindly to this paternalistic paean. Neither will their hackles subside when Skinner assures them that controllers are themselves controlled—the master by the slave, the parent by the child, and that a system can be worked out in which controllers have to submit to their own controls. But between their snarls of fitting indignation they can reflect that Skinner's hard-headed *naïveté* performs a useful service. I do not mean just that his uninhibited approach leads him to draw attention to matters that the tender-minded are apt to gloss over—e.g. the

amount of manipulation involved in progressive methods, the inescapability of some form of social control, the ham-handed character of much reform inspired by a hatred of control and injustice. I mean rather that he pushes an instrumental approach to life to its limits and thus reveals a vision of life that is the logical outcome of presuppositions that many seem to share with him.

The Utilitarians, in the main, were not prepared to be completely consistent. They worried about the implication that justice and truth-telling had to be defended instrumentally by reference to their alleged consequences in terms of human happiness. J. S. Mill stood fast on liberty and was half-hearted in his attempt to provide a Utilitarian underpinning for it. He saw its connection with the pursuit of truth, whose connection with the pursuit of happiness he did not explore. Skinner, however, is quite uninhibited. He was nurtured in a cultural *milieu* which enabled William James to proclaim that truth is that which enables the individual to glide happily from one experience to another, and John Dewey to assert that truth is that which works. Happiness becomes the criterion both of what is right and of what is true. Man, the fixer, is the measure of all things. The good life is a smooth flow of positive reinforcement.

But Skinner has pushed this ancient arrogance even further. For, because of his quaint sensitivities about the soul, descriptions as well as justifications are couched in instrumental terms. He thinks states of mind causally inoperative; so he tends to describe them in terms of their overtly observable antecedents and consequences. The result is that, on occasions, one does not literally know what he is talking about. This comes out very clearly in his treatment of human dignity. Understandably he can give no account of this value; for it is connected with the view that we have of a man as having a point of view, as a person who is not to be used or manipulated for his own or anyone else's good. Skinner is reduced to just jibbering about it and to scattering reinforcements around like bird-seed. For it not only starkly confronts his whole instrumental outlook; it also activates his horror of consciousness.

Skinner's set of descriptions are really an attempt to discourse with kings of science whilst retaining the common touch of ordinary speech which is founded on quite different presuppositions. He even fudges things with the use of that blessed term 'the environment'. For what effects people generally are not just the physical properties of things or people but how they view them. 'Responses', too, save at the level of very simple movements, cannot be distinguished without reference to the individual's view of his situation. When he waves his arm, for instance, is he signaling, expressing irritation, or performing a ritual? The basic trouble with Behaviourists is that they have never had an adequate concept of 'behaviour'. Presumably, too, in writing his book Skinner is trying to change people's beliefs about themselves. But he thinks attempts to change people's minds an ineffective way of trying to influence them. How, then, can he justify what he is doing in writing his book, or even give an account of it in terms of his own theory?

Those who believe in 'the autonomous man' do not necessarily subscribe to a belief in the soul. They agree with Skinner that behaviour has 'causes' but they wish to distinguish those that involve the individual's understanding and decisions from those that do not. They also, like Piaget, probably want to distinguish between levels of behaviour—between the level when people (especially children) are induced to act for the sake of reward or approval from the level when they can also act because of genuine reasons connected with the situation itself. Some people, for instance, go to concerts because they genuinely enjoy listening to music, though others may go because of wanting to keep up with their neighbours. Because, in their past, they too may have gone for such extrinsic rea-

sons, it does not follow that they are still just under the influence of that type of 'reinforcement'. Skinner, of course, would probably call all this 'reinforcement'; but that is because, in the face of the refutation of his theory, he has extended the meaning of 'reinforcement' so that it includes every possible form of motivation. So like many other psychological concepts (e.g. 'drive') it ends up by explaining nothing.

In morals, too, it may be the case that, at a certain stage of development, people learn to tell the truth or to keep their promises by being positively reinforced. But they also have to understand what it is to tell the truth and what a promise is. Eventually they may come to see that they should tell the truth because, unless this were the general rule, what is true could not be discovered and communicated. And truth matters—whatever its consequences for survival. For it is one of the values that define a tolerable form of survival. The autonomous man is the person who attempts to be 'authentic' or genuine in his attitudes and beliefs, who tries to free himself from sole dependence on the extrinsic reinforcers so beloved by Skinner. So he values truth and subjects what he is told to constant criticism. He abhors a society, like Skinner's Utopia, in which people believe what it pays them to believe and gladly submit to Pavlovian paternalism.

The value, therefore, of Skinner's naïve fanaticism is to have pushed instrumentalism to its logical limits. He has really no interest in how things are or in people's perspectives on the world. He is concerned only about how things and people will be and in their past as a guide to future manipulations. For him, as for the Puritans whom he despises, salvation lies always ahead, even though it is now downgraded to survival. At the end of his book he says that 'no theory changes what it is about; man remains what he has always been.' But this ignores one of the most important truths about man which is that he alone of creatures lives in the light of theories about himself and behaves differently because of them. The danger is that men may come to believe what Skinner says. They may use their freedom to deny others their dignity.

DISCUSSION QUESTIONS AND ACTIVITIES

1. What are the characteristics of Emile or "the free and happy student," according to Skinner? Why has his so-called education been a failure? Is Skinner's diagnosis accurate?

2. What are Skinner's objections to primitive and coercive treatment in school?

3. But once students have been freed from punishment, says Skinner, they still are not literally free. Why?

4. Why cannot each person learn on his or her own through experience and dispense with formal education?

5. What does Skinner mean by positive reinforcement? Give classroom examples. Evaluate its strengths and weaknesses.

6. What choices can students exercise in Skinner's system of positive reinforcement, and what freedom do they have?

7. Peters accuses Skinner of holding nineteenth century views. What are these views, and why should it be wrong to hold them?

8. Is Peters correct that Skinner's position is a form of utilitarianism?

9. Why is Skinner unable to deal effectively with the concept of "human dignity"?

10. Explain what Peters means by his claim that behaviorists lack an adequate concept of "behavior" and, as a consequence, Skinner cannot give an account, in terms of his own theory, of what he is doing by writing a book.

11. Why is Skinner's treatment of "reinforcement" inadequate for explaining behavior?

12. Observe classrooms where positive reinforcement and programmed materials are used. Interview teachers as to the effectiveness of Skinnerian methods and materials.

13. Organize a classroom debate comparing the relative merits of Carl Rogers' and Skinner's educational ideas and proposals.

14. Read Skinner's *The Technology of Teaching* and make a book report to the class.

SUGGESTED READINGS

Works by B. F. Skinner

About Behaviorism. New York: Knopf, 1974.

The Analysis of Behavior. New York: McGraw-Hill, 1961 (with James G. Holland).

The Behavior of Organisms. New York: Appleton-Century-Crofts, 1938.

Beyond Freedom and Dignity. New York: Knopf, 1971.

Contingencies of Reinforcement. New York: Appleton-Century-Crofts, 1969.

Cumulative Record. New York: Appleton-Century-Crofts, 1972.

Particulars of My Life. New York: Knopf, 1979.

Reflections on Behaviorism and Society. Englewood Cliffs, New Jersey: Prentice-Hall, 1978.

Schedules of Reinforcement. New York: Appleton-Century-Crofts, 1957.

Science and Human Behavior. New York: Macmillan, 1953.

The Shaping of a Behaviorist. New York: Knopf, 1979.

"Some Issues Concerning the Control of Human Behavior: A Symposium." *Science* 124 (November 30, 1956): 1057 (with Carl R. Rogers).

The Technology of Teaching. New York: Appleton-Century-Crofts, 1968.

Verbal Behavior. Englewood Cliffs, New Jersey: Prentice-Hall, 1957.

Walden Two. New York: Macmillan, 1948.

Cassettes

"A Dialogue on Education and the Control of Human Behavior," 6 cassettes. New York: Jeffrey Norton Publishers, 1976. (with B. F. Skinner).

"Interview with B. F. Skinner." 1 cassette, mono 2-track. Los Altos, California: Sound Ed Rpts, 1969.

Works about B. F. Skinner

Carpenter, Finley. *The Skinner Primer.* New York: Free Press, 1974.

Dews, P. B., ed. *Festschrift for B. F. Skinner.* New York: Appleton-Century-Crofts, 1970.

Evans, Richard Isadore. *B. F. Skinner: The Man and His Ideas.* New York: Dutton, 1968.

Freedman, Anne E. *The Planned Society: An Analysis of Skinner's Proposals.* Kalamazoo, Michigan: Behaviordelia, 1972.

Geiser, Robert L. *Behavior Mod and the Managed Society.* Boston: Beacon Press, 1976.

Karen, Robert L. *An Introduction to Behavior Theory and Its Applications.* New York: Harper & Row, 1974.

Machan, Tibor R. *The Pseudo-Science of B. F. Skinner.* New Rochelle, New York: Arlington House Publishers, 1974.

Milhollan, Frank. *From Skinner to Rogers: Contrasting Approaches to Education.* Lincoln, Nebraska: Professional Educators Publications, 1972.

Nye, Robert D. *Three Psychologies: Perspectives from Freud, Skinner, and Rogers,* 2nd ed. Monterey, California: Brooks/Cole, 1981.

_____. *What is B. F. Skinner Really Saying?* Englewood Cliffs, New Jersey: Prentice-Hall, 1979.

Puligandla, R. *Fact and Fiction in B. F. Skinner's Science and Utopia.* St. Louis: W. H. Green, 1974.

Wheeler, John Harvey, ed. *Beyond the Primitive Society.* San Francisco: W. H. Freeman, 1973.

Articles about B. F. Skinner

Bordin, E. S. "Two Views of Human Nature." *New York University Education Quarterly* 12 (Winter 1981): 29–32.

Burton, G. M. "Skinner, Piaget, Maslow, and the Teachers of Mathematics: Strange Companions?" *Arithmetic Teacher* 24 (March 1977): 246–50.

Elias, J. L. "B. F. Skinner and Religious Education." *Religious Education* 69 (September 1974): 558–67.

Gates, L. "Piaget's Model is Superior in Fostering Learning." *Reading Improvement* 15 (Summer 1978): 127–9. Discussion: 17 (Spring 1980): 14–17; 17 (Summer 1980): 97–9.

Harris, D. "Discipline of the Structure, Meaning and Acquisition of Learning, with Special References to Noam Chomsky and B. F. Skinner. *Cambridge Journal of Education* 7, no. 2 (1977): 114–23.

Kitchener, R. F. "Critique of Skinnerian Ethical Principles. *Counseling and Values* 23 (April 1979): 138–47.

Kneller, G. F. and S. L. Hackbarth. "Analysis of Programmed Instruction." *The Educational Forum* 41 (January 1977): 180–7.

Krantz, D. L. "Relation of Reflection and Action: The Intellectual and Clinical Impact of B. F. Skinner and R. D. Laing." *American Journal of Orthopsychiatry* 48 (April 1978): 214–27.

Mowrer, V. M. "Present State of Behaviorism." *Education* 97 (Fall 1976): 4–23. Reply: T. T. Jackson 98 (Fall 1977): 56.

Price, G. "Is Science a Servant or Master?" *Times Higher Education Supplement* 485 (February 19, 1982): 10.

Roper, V. "Influence of Learning Theory on the Behavior of the Teacher in the Classroom." *Educational Theory* 24 (Spring 1974): 155–60.

Royzyck, E. G. "Functional Analysis of Behavior." *Educational Theory* 25 (Summer 1975): 278–302.

Silva, D. "From Skinner to Instruction." *Educational Technology* 19 (May 1979): 51–2.

Teller, G. D. "Is Behaviorism a Form of Humanism?" *Educational Leadership* 34 (May 1977): 637–8.

7
The Pedagogy of Liberation

Viewing education in an international perspective, we find that most of the world's people are destitute — ill-clothed, ill-fed, and ill-housed, and vast numbers have scarcely received the rudiments of an education. These people frequently are unable to rise out of the condition, not only because apathy and torpor crush their spirit but also because those in power exploit them. Paulo Freire worked with the peasants of Brazil and fostered literacy by using materials that taught them the nature of oppression and how it could best be overcome so that a new society could be created. His philosophy is a remarkable admixture of Marx and Marcuse, Mao and Che Guevara, Fromm and Christian love, all welded into an instrument for the transformation of the human condition.

John L. Elias provides a critique of Freire's revolutionary philosophy. He mentions Freire's role in the Popular Culture Movement in Brazil, the connection between his revolutionary ideals and religious beliefs, and shows why it might be difficult to apply his pedagogy. Elias also believes that Freire's theory and strategy of revolution is rather naive and that he has exaggerated education's role in revolutionary activity.

Pedagogy of the Oppressed

Paulo Freire _____

Paulo Freire (b. 1921) devoted seventeen years in devising and refining a program for basic literacy before he was imprisoned for several months after the military seized control of the Brazilian government in 1964. Leaving Brazil, he tested his program in Chile for the next five years. After a year at Harvard University, he became consultant to the World Council of Churches in Geneva. As the political atmosphere in Brazil recently changed, Freire returned in 1981 to his native land and the university in which he originally taught. After a bitter struggle, involving hearings and demonstrations, that involved the State University of Campinas and the governor of the state of Sao Paulo, in which the university is located, agreement was reached to allow students and faculty to elect new directors for the institute and a new rector. In a record turnout, Professor Freire was elected rector over five other candidates. His writings and activities have been influential in literacy programs, adult and continuing education, and the philosophy of education.

The pedagogy of the oppressed, as a humanist and libertarian pedagogy, has two distinct stages. In the first, the oppressed unveil the world of oppression and through the praxis commit themselves to its transformation. In the second stage, in which the reality of oppression has already been transformed, this pedagogy ceases to belong to the oppressed and becomes a pedagogy of all men in the process of permanent liberation. In both stages, it is always through action in depth that the culture of domination is culturally confronted.[1] In the first stage this confrontation occurs through the change in the way the oppressed perceive the world of oppression; in the second stage, through the expulsion of the myths created and developed in the older order, which like specters haunt the new structure emerging from the revolutionary transformation.

The pedagogy of the first stage must deal with the problem of the oppressed consciousness and the oppressor consciousness, the problem of men who suffer oppression. It must take into account their behavior, their view of the world, and their ethics. A particular problem is the duality of the oppressed: they are contradictory, divided beings, shaped by and existing in a concrete situation of oppression and violence.

Any situation in which "A" objectively exploits "B" or hinders his pursuit of self-affir-

___

[1]This appears to be the fundamental aspect of Mao's Cultural Revolution.

mation as a responsible person is one of oppression. Such a situation in itself cónstitutes violence, even when sweetened by false generosity, because it interferes with man's ontological and historical vocation to be more fully human. With the establishment of a relationship of oppression, violence has *already* begun. Never in history has violence been initiated by the oppressed. How could they be the initiators, if they themselves are the result of violence? How could they be the sponsors of something whose objective inauguration called forth their existence as oppressed? There would be no oppressed had there been no prior situation of violence to establish their subjugation.

Violence is initiated by those who oppress, who exploit, who fail to recognize others as persons—not by those who are oppressed, exploited, and unrecognized. It is not the unloved who initiate disaffection, but those who cannot love because they love only themselves. It is not the helpless, subject to terror, who initiate terror, but the violent, who with their power create the concrete situation which begets the "rejects of life." It is not the tyrannized who initiate despotism, but the tyrants. It is not the despised who initiate hatred, but those who despise. It is not those whose humanity is denied them who negate man, but those who denied that humanity (thus negating their own as well). Force is used not by those who have become weak under the preponderance of the strong but by the strong who have emasculated them.

For the oppressors, however, it is always the oppressed (whom they obviously never call "the oppressed" but—depending on whether they are fellow countrymen or not—"those people" or "the blind and envious masses" or "savages" or "natives" or "subversives") who are disaffected, who are "violent," "barbaric," "wicked," or "ferocious" when they react to the violence of the oppressors.

Yet it is—paradoxical though it may seem—precisely in the response of the oppressed to the violence of their oppressors that a gesture of love may be found. Consciously or unconsciously, the act of rebellion by the oppressed (an act which is always, or nearly always, as violent as the initial violence of the oppressors) can initiate love. Whereas the violence of the oppressors prevents the oppressed from being fully human, the response of the latter to this violence is grounded in the desire to pursue the right to be human. As the oppressors dehumanize others and violate their rights, they themselves also become dehumanized. As the oppressed, fighting to be human, take away the oppressors' power to dominate and suppress, they restore to the oppressors the humanity they had lost in the exercise of oppression.

It is only the oppressed who, by freeing themselves, can free their oppressors. The latter, as an oppressive class, can free neither others nor themselves. It is therefore essential that the oppressed wage the struggle to resolve the contradiction in which they are caught; and the contradiction will be resolved by the appearance of the new man: neither oppressor nor oppressed, but man in the process of liberation. If the goal of the oppressed is to become fully human, they will not achieve their goal by merely reversing the terms of the contradiction, by simply changing poles.

This may seem simplistic; it is not. Resolution of the oppressor-oppressed contradiction indeed implies the disappearance of the oppressors as a dominant class. However, the restraints imposed by the former oppressed on their oppressors, so that the latter cannot reassume their former position, do not constitute *oppression*. An act is oppressive only when it prevents men from becoming more fully human. Accordingly, these necessary restraints do not *in themselves* signify that yesterday's oppressed have become today's oppressors. Acts which prevent the restoration of the oppressive regime cannot be compared with those which create and maintain it, cannot be compared with those by which a few men deny the majority their right to be human. . . .

Critical and liberating dialogue, which presupposes action, must be carried on with the oppressed at whatever the stage of their struggle for liberation.[2] The content of that dialogue can and should vary in accordance with historical conditions and the level at which the oppressed perceive reality. But to substitute monologue, slogans, and communiques for dialogue is to attempt to liberate the oppressed with the instruments of domestication. Attempting to liberate the oppressed without their reflective participation in the act of liberation is to treat them as objects which must be saved from a burning building; it is to lead them into the populist pitfall and transform them into masses which can be manipulated. . . .

Through dialogue, the teacher-of-the-students and the students-of-the-teacher cease to exist and a new term emerges: teacher-student with students-teachers. The teacher is no longer merely the-one-who-teaches, but one who is himself taught in dialogue with the students, who in turn while being taught also teach. They become jointly responsible for a process in which all grow. In this process, arguments based on "authority" are no longer valid; in order to function, authority must be *on the side of* freedom, not *against* it. Here, no one teaches another, nor is anyone self-taught. Men teach each other, mediated by the world, by the cognizable objects which in banking education are "owned" by the teacher.

The banking concept (with its tendency to dichotomize everything) distinguishes two stages in the action of the educator. During the first, he cognizes a cognizable object while he prepares his lessons in his study or his laboratory; during the second, he expounds to his students about that object. The students are not called upon to know, but to memorize the contents narrated by the teacher. Nor do the students practice any act of cognition, since the object towards which that act should be directed is the property of the teacher rather than a medium evoking the critical reflection of both teacher and students. Hence in the name of the "preservation of culture and knowledge" we have a system which achieves neither true knowledge nor true culture.

The problem-posing method does not dichotomize the activity of the teacher-student: he is not "cognitive" at one point and "narrative" at another. He is always "cognitive," whether preparing a project or engaging in dialogue with the students. He does not regard cognizable objects as his private property, but as the object of reflection by himself and the students. In this way, the problem-posing educator constantly reforms his reflections in the reflection of the students. The students—no longer docile listeners—are now critical co-investigators in dialogue with the teacher. The teacher presents the material to the students for their consideration, and re-considers his earlier considerations as the students express their own. The role of the problem-posing educator is to create, together with the students, the conditions under which knowledge at the level of the *doxa* is superseded by true knowledge, at the level of the *logos*.

Whereas banking education anesthetizes and inhibits creative power, problem-posing education involves a constant unveiling of reality. The former attempts to maintain the *submersion* of the consciousness; the latter strives for the *emergence* of consciousness and *critical intervention* in reality.

Students, as they are increasingly posed with problems relating to themselves in the world and with the world, will feel increasingly challenged and obliged to respond to that challenge. Because they apprehend the challenge as interrelated to other problems within a total context, not as a theoretical question, the result-

---

[2]Not in the open, of course; this would only provoke the fury of the oppressor and lead to still greater repression.

ing comprehension tends to be increasingly critical and thus constantly less alienated. Their response to the challenge evokes new challenges, followed by new understandings; and gradually the students come to regard themselves as commited.

Education as the practice of freedom — as opposed to education as the practice of domination — denies that man is abstract, isolated, independent, and unattached to the world; it also denies that the world exists as a reality apart from men. Authentic reflection considers neither abstract man nor the world without men, but men in their relations with the world. In these relations consciousness and world are simultaneous: consciousness neither precedes the world nor follows it. . . .

Problem-posing education affirms men as beings in the process of *becoming*—as unfinished, uncompleted beings in and with a likewise unfinished reality. Indeed, in contrast to other animals who are unfinished, but not historical, men know themselves to be unfinished; they are aware of their incompletion. In this incompletion and this awareness lie the very roots of education as an exclusively human manifestation. The unfinished character of men and the transformational character of reality necessitate that education be an ongoing activity.

Education is thus constantly remade in the praxis. In order to *be,* it must *become.* Its "duration" (in the Bergsonian meaning of the word) is found in the interplay of the opposites *permanence* and *change.* The banking method emphasizes permanence and becomes reactionary; problem-posing education — which accepts neither a "well-behaved" present nor a predetermined future — roots itself in the dynamic present and becomes revolutionary.

Problem-posing education is revolutionary futurity. Hence it is prophetic (and, as such, hopeful). Hence, it corresponds to the historical nature of man. Hence, it affirms men as beings who transcend themselves, who move forward and look ahead, for whom immobility represents a fatal threat, for whom looking at the past must only be a means of understanding more clearly what and who they are so that they can more wisely build the future. Hence, it identifies with the movement which engages men as beings aware of their incompletion — an historical movement which has its point of departure, its subjects and its objective.

The point of departure of the movement lies in men themselves. But since men do not exist apart from the world, apart from reality, the movement must begin with the men-world relationship. Accordingly, the point of departure must always be with men in the "here and now," which constitutes the situation within which they are submerged, from which they emerge, and in which they intervene. Only by starting from this situation — which determines their perception of it — can they begin to move. To do this authentically they must perceive their state not as fated and unalterable, but merely as limiting — and therefore challenging.

Whereas the banking method directly or indirectly reinforces men's fatalistic perception of their situation, the problem-posing method presents this very situation to them as a problem. As the situation becomes the object of their cognition, the naive or magical perception which produced their fatalism gives way to perception which is able to perceive itself even as it perceives reality, and can thus be critically objective about that reality.

A deepened consciousness of their situation leads men to apprehend that situation as an historical reality susceptible to transformation. Resignation gives way to the drive for transformation and inquiry, over which men feel themselves to be in control. If men, as historical beings necessarily engaged with other men in a movement of inquiry, did not control that movement, it would be (and is) a violation of men's humanity. Any situation in which some men prevent others from engaging in the process of inquiry is one of violence. The means used are not important; to alienate men from their own decision-making is to change them into objects.

This movement of inquiry must be directed towards humanization—man's historical vocation. The pursuit of full humanity, however, cannot be carried out in isolation or individualism, but only in fellowship and solidarity; therefore it cannot unfold in the antagonistic relations between oppressor and oppressed. No one can be authentically human while he prevents others from being so. . . .

Every thematic investigation which deepens historical awareness is thus really educational, while all authentic education investigates thinking. The more educators and the people investigate the people's thinking, and are thus jointly educated, the more they continue to investigate.

Education and thematic investigation, in the problem-posing concept of education, are simply different moments of the same process.

In contrast with the antidialogical and noncommunicative "deposits" of the banking method of education, the program content of the problem-posing method—dialogical par excellence—is constituted and organized by the students' view of the world, where their own generative themes are found. The content thus constantly expands and renews itself. The task of the dialogical teacher in an inter-disciplinary team working on the thematic universe revealed by their investigation is to "re-present" that universe to the people from whom he first received it—and "re-present" it not as a lecture, but as a problem.

A Critique of Paulo Freire's Revolutionary Theory

John L. Elias _____

John Lloyd Elias (b. 1906) has been a teacher and administrator in the Northwest and has been an officer in a number of community junior college associations. He recently retired after serving as professor of higher education at Seattle University. His interests lie in the areas of adult education and the development of master's programs.

Paulo Freire has the reputation of being an educator who proposes education as a necessary means for achieving revolution. His book, *Ped-*

agogy of the Oppressed, is virtually a handbook outlining the type of education that is necessary for bringing about drastic political and social

From John L. Elias, "A Critique of Paulo Freire's Revolutionary Theory," Cutting Edge, *6 (Spring 1975): 12–21.*

changes in society.[1] What is not as clearly recognized about Freire is that he himself has never actually participated in the type of revolutionary activity which he propounds. This fact is made clear in the preface to his book:

> It is possible that some may question my right to discuss revolutionary action, a subject of which I have no concrete experience. However, the fact that I have not personally participated in revolutionary action does not negate the possibility of my reflecting on this theme.[2]

Freire contends that in his experience as an educator, he has "accumulated a comparative wealth of material which challenged [him] to run the risk of making the affirmations contained in his work."[3]

Francisco Weffort, in his introduction to Freire's *Educacao como Pratica da Liberdade,* explains well the sense in which Freire's work in Brazil might have been considered revolutionary.[4] The goals of Freire were literacy for the Brazilian masses and an increase in popular political participation. Freire was engaged in attempts to democratize Brazilian culture as a member of the Federal Ministry of Education. His work was viewed as revolutionary by certain rightist groups. Weffort described how Freire's work might be considered revolutionary:

> . . . If education for freedom [Freire's literacy campaign] carried the seed of revolt, it would not be correct to say that this is one of the educator's objectives. If it occurs, it is only and exclusively because conscientization discerns a reality in which violence and conflict are the most frequent data.[5]

Weffort criticizes the Popular Culture Movement, of which Freire was a part, for its failure to be more political. He contends that the "forces interested in a popular mobilization failed to perceive and exploit the implications that conscientization had for action."[6] He admits that the popular movements had political relevance. Their ability, however, to be truly effective politically resulted from the fact that these movements were "committed directly or indirectly to the government and thus to the existing institutions which were themselves the objects of popular pressure."[7] The movement failed due to overinvestment in education at the expense of concrete political goals and strategies. Weffort suggests that reformers like Freire were prevented from bringing about necessary changes for the masses because of the state support they received. They were in this way compromised by conflicting loyalties.

A reading of *Education for Critical Consciousness,* a work written immediately after Freire's exile from Brazil and begun while he was in jail, shows no evidence of a revolutionary thrust.[8] He desired while working in Brazil to bring about changes gradually through education.[9] The purpose of this education was to make the people aware of themselves as reflective human persons who created both history and culture. His literacy campaign was promoted by the Goulart government for at least one political purpose: the enfranchisement of the masses who would then support the government in the upcoming elections.

Freire explicitly turned his attention to education as a necessary means for bringing about a revolution in *Pedagogy of the Oppressed.* It has

1. Paulo Freire, *Pedagogy of the Oppressed.* New York: Herder and Herder, 1970.
2. Ibid., p. 24.
3. Ibid.
4. Francisco Weffort, "Education and Politics," introduction to Paulo Freire's *Educacao como Practica da Liberdade.* Cambridge, Mass.: Center for Social Change and Development, 1969.
5. *Ibid.,* p. 11.

6. *Ibid.*
7. *Ibid.,* p. 9.
8. Paulo Freire, *Education for Critical Consciousness* (New York: Seabury Press, 1973). This work contains a translation of Freire's two earlier works: *Educacao como Practica da Liberdade* (1967) and *Extension y Comunicacion* (1969).
9. *Ibid.,* p. 9.

been stated that this book is not based on Freire's experiences in revolutionary movements. This is brought out here because it explains some of the disillusionment with Freire that one encounters in reading him or in attending a training session at which he appears. People expect an active revolutionary, but what they meet is "another religious, middle-class reformer."[10] John Egerton sums up the criticism of Freire at a conference in South Carolina:

> Freire is no more radical than most of us. There is no originality in what he says—it's the same old rap. He has lectured us, criticized our narrow focus on small problems, but his alternative—the global perspective—is stale rhetoric. He is a political and ideological theoretician, not an educator. There is nothing concrete and specific in what he says.[11]

Freire, the revolutionary educator, advised public school teachers to work within the system to do the little that they can do there and also to do the great many things they can do outside this system. At a conference which the author attended at Fordham University in January 1972, similar criticisms of Freire were voiced.

RELIGIOUS JUSTIFICATION OF REVOLUTION

Freire has advocated political revolutions for countries in the Third World. In doing this, he has been sensitive to the question of whether or not political revolution, especially violent revolution, is justified according to Christian principles. The religious inspiration of revolutions has been discussed by a number of scholars.[12] This question has long been debated, especially in the Catholic Leftist circles of Latin America. It is an issue that has brought radical Catholics into conflict with Church hierarchies in Latin American countries. Houtart and Rousseau divided Latin American Christians into four main categories with regard to their attitudes toward revolution in society.[13] One group sees no need for changes in the existing social and political systems. A second group sees the need for some change, but does not think that the church as an institution should be involved in directly working for these changes. A third group sees change as necessary and believes that the church should directly participate in this process. Houtart and Rousseau contend that this is the attitude of many laymen engaged in politics and that it appears to be the attitude of the Catholic Bishops Conference held at Medellin in 1968. Finally, there is a fourth category of Latin American Christians who believe that only violent revolution can effectively change the situation. These Christians commit themselves to the revolutionary process and collaborate with various Marxist movements. In recent years, as Houtart and Rousseau point out, a number of clergymen and theologians have joined the ranks of this latter group.

By 1970 Freire had definitely put himself into league with this latter group of Christians. In speaking of the myths which the oppressor society has imposed upon the oppressed, he points to two particular myths that bear on this issue: "the myth of the heroism of the oppressor classes as defenders of 'Western Christian civilization' [and] . . . the myth that rebellion is a sin against God."[14] The implication here, which is supported by his more recent writings, is that Freire sees rebellion and revolution as acts that can be in accordance with Christian and religious principles. Freire describes revolutionary

10. John Egerton, "Searching for Freire," *Saturday Review of Education,* 1973.

11. *Ibid.,* p. 35.

12. Hannah Arendt, *On Revolution.* New York: Viking, 1963, pp. 18–22; Crane Brinton, *The Anatomy of Revolution.* New York: Random House, 1965, pp. 170–172.

13. Francis Houtart and Anton Rousseau, *The Church and Revolution.* New York: Orbis Press, 1971.

14. Freire, *Pedagogy,* pp. 135–136.

violence in terms which have at least religious connotations surrounding them:

> I am more and more convinced that true revolutionaries must perceive the revolution, because of its creative and liberating nature, as an act of love. For me, the revolution which is not possible without a theory of revolution—and therefore science—is not irreconcilable with love. . . .[15]

Recent writings show Freire even more explicit in his justification of Christian participation in revolutionary action. In the "Letter to a Theology Student," he asserted that:

> We, as Christians, have an enormous task to perform, presuming that we are capable of setting aside our idealistic myths and in that way, sharing in the revolutionary transformation of society, instead of stubbornly denying the important contribution of Karl Marx.[16]

He affirms in the Letter that the Word of God demands a willingness to work for the liberation of man through a process that entails the challenging of the powerful of the earth.

Freire's most explicit treatment of the religious justification for revolutionary action is found in his article, "The Educational Role of the Churches in Latin America."[17] The Church, he contended, cannot remain neutral toward political activity. It must work for the radical transformation of social structures. He criticized conservatives in the churches for "castrating the church's prophetic dimension and fearing the radical transformation of the unjust world."[18] He had praise for the developing political theology of liberation which says something about the revolutionary transformation of the world. Within this prophetic theology, there is room for the view which recognizes "revolution as the road to liberation for the oppressed classes, and the military coup as a revolutionary option."[19] He admits that there may be differences over tactics among Christians dedicated to revolutionary action, but he commends the firm commitment of these Christians to revolutionary action.

Two other religious metaphors are used by Freire in urging Christians to become involved in revolutionary activity. He refers a number of times to the revolution of the oppressed as a Passover or an Easter. These events entailed struggles of life and death. Redemption or liberation from oppression was achieved through active resistance and violent death. Christians are those who involve themselves in a New Passover, a New Easter. The revolutionaries' "setting out is really a sort of Passover in which they will have to die as an oppressed class, in order to be reborn as a class that liberates itself."[20] He speaks of the prophetic church which does not allow itself to be made a refuge for the oppressed masses, but which rather invites them to a new Exodus.

Another encouragement that Freire utilizes in urging Latin American Christians into revolutionary activity lies in the example of the Christ. The image of Christ is of one who is radical, not satisfied with the status quo, anxious to move on, willing to die in order to bring about a continuous rebirth. Freire puts these words in the mouth of those who would counsel conservative activity on the part of Christians: "They say to Christ, 'Master, why push on, if everything here is so beautiful?'"[21]

An interesting development can be ascertained in the writings of Freire. He has become an advocate of revolutionary action for oppressed peoples in the Third World. The difference between *Educacao como Pratica da Liberdade* and

15. *Ibid.*, p. 77.
16. Paulo Freire, "A Letter to a Theology Student." *Catholic Mind*, 1972, 70 (1265), p. 7.
17. Paulo Freire, "The Educational Role of the Churches in Latin America." Washington, D.C.; *LADOC*, 3(14), 1972.
18. *Ibid.*, p. 3.
19. *Ibid.*, p. 12.
20. *Ibid.*, p. 4.
21. *Ibid.*, p. 12.

Pedagogy of the Oppressed makes this clear. This change, however, has been accompanied by a change for a less explicit religious justification of revolution to more explicit religious justification for the necessity of Christian participation in revolutionary activity. The failure to become involved in this type of action in certain countries in Latin America is a failure "to live up to the Gospel."[22]

Freire's open advocacy of revolution on religious principles finds much support in Latin American theologians with whom Freire is no doubt familiar. He has expressed a desire to meet with Latin American theologians who propose a political theology of liberation. Freire's position on the religious justification for revolution is similar to that of one of Latin America's leading Christian theologians, Gustavo Gutierrez. Gutierrez has attempted to give religious justification for more revolutionary political postures of Christian groups in Latin America. He appeals to the message of the Gospel:

> What ultimately brings Christians to participate in liberating oppressed peoples is the conviction that the gospel message is radically incompatible with an unjust society. They see clearly that they cannot be authentic Christians unless they act.[23]

Gutierrez discusses revolution in the context of the biblical symbols of creation, salvation, and the prophetic promises for a kingdom of peace. The case for active church involvement in revolution is put strongly in these terms:

> In Latin America, the church must realize that it exists in a continent undergoing revolution, where violence is present in different ways. The world in which the Christian Community is called on to live . . . is one in social revolution. Its mission must be achieved keeping that in account. The church has

no alternative. Only a total break with the unjust order to which it is bound in a thousand conscious or unconscious ways, and a forthright commitment to a new society, will make men in Latin America believe the message of love it bears.[24]

Freire, on a number of occasions in his writings, makes references to the example of Camilo Torres, the Colombian priest-sociologist who became involved in politics and was ultimately killed as a guerrilla. Freire admired the commitment of Torres to the people—as a priest, as a Christian, and as a revolutionary. Torres is referred to as the guerrilla priest, a loving man. He made a serious attempt to articulate a theory of liberation consonant with orthodox Christian values. Torres stated that the Catholics in Colombia had a moral responsibility to participate in the revolution. A dissertation is currently in progress which attempts to connect the thought of Torres, Freire, and other theologians of liberation.[25]

THEORY AND STRATEGY OF REVOLUTION

It has already been mentioned that Freire has had no direct involvement with revolutionary activity. He indicates that he has received some insights into this activity from his educational experiences in Brazil and Chile. Freire develops his theory of revolution in a most eclectic manner. He draws on the writings of Mao Tse Tung, Marcuse, Fanon, Debray, Che Guevara, Marx, Lenin, Castro, and others.

Freire's theory and strategy of revolution appear to be rather naive, to use a favorite word of his in *Pedagogy of the Oppressed*. He discusses revolution without discussing any particular social and historical contexts. He appears

22. *Ibid.,* p. 5.
23. Gustavo Guttierez, "A Latin American Perception of a Theology of Revolution," in Louis Colonnese (ed.), *Conscientization for Liberation.* Washington, D.C.: United States Catholic Conference, 1971, p. 72.

24. *Ibid.,* pp. 76–77.
25. CF. Stanley Grabowski (ed.), *Paulo Freire: A Revolutionary Dilemma for the Adult Educator.* Syracuse University: Publication in Continuing Education and Eric Clearinghouse on Adult Education, 1972, p. 132.

to be generalizing upon his reflections upon the Brazilian situations in which he was involved. He is like the crusader who, after the brave and good fight, stands ready to generalize his theories and strategies to the situation of all oppressed peoples. *Pedagogy of the Oppressed* appears to have been written by Freire to tell Freire what he and his fellow reformists should have done to bring about real change in Brazil in early 1960's. But the simplistic analysis of Brazilian society into oppressed and oppressors does not even do justice to that historical situation. Its application as a universal theory of social analysis is even more unacceptable.

A fundamental flaw in Freire's theory of revolution is his inadequate treatment of "oppression." For Freire, "any situation in which A objectively exploits B or hinders his pursuit of self affirmation as a responsible person is one of oppression."[26] He further tells us that an act is oppressive when "it interferes with man's ontological and historical vocation to be more fully human."[27] For Freire, the goal of liberation from oppression is the humanization of man. Oppression is always an act of violence. It is to treat a person as if he were a thing.

For Freire, the problem of oppression is reduced to the problem of dehumanization. But he appears to carry within him some intuitive concept of what it means to be human. Without Freire spelling out his criteria for a self affirmation or humanization of the person, his description of oppression becomes not only abstract but also dangerous. Unless one sets down objective criteria for exploitation, the determination of what is oppressive becomes the judgment of each individual and group. Freire would certainly not want to affirm this. He is convinced that, through his pedagogy, the oppressed with their leaders will come to intuit reality the way that it is. Freire's doctrine of objective exploitation comes dangerously close to the concept of the objective enemy which Arendt has criticized:

> The chief difference between the despotic and the totalitarian secret police lies in the difference between the "suspect" and the "objective enemy." The latter is defined by the policy of the government and not by his own desire to overthrow it.[28]

Freire sees only one relationship in the Third World, the relationship of oppression or subjection. Boston indicates a number of other relationships which exist in the Third World.[29] Freire even thinks of relationships in more advanced technological countries in terms of oppressor-oppressed relationships. The oppressors in these societies are those who use technology to manipulate people and produce a mass society. Freire does not condemn technology in itself but rather its harmful effects. The treatment that Freire gives to technology is not extensive. But when he does treat man and technology, the same type of relationship is seen — dependence, subjection, oppression.[30]

The tendency of Freire to see only one type of relationship among men will make it difficult to apply his pedagogy. The cultural, the social, the political, the religious are all cast by him into a single relationship of oppressor-oppressed. It is easy for Freire to do this in *Pedagogy of the Oppressed,* because he fails to root his revolutionary theory in any particular historical or cultural context. In attempting to forge a universal theory of revolutionary pedagogy, he oversimplified to a dangerous degree the concept of oppression and the pedagogical program. He appears to be unaware in *Pedagogy of the Op-*

26. Freire, *Pedagogy,* p. 40.
27. *Ibid.,* pp. 40–41.

28. Hannah Arendt, *The Origins of Totalitarianism.* New York: Meridian Books, 1958, p. 423.
29. Bruce Boston, "Paulo Freire: Notes of a Loving Critic," in Stanley Grabowski (ed.) *Paulo Freire: A Revolutionary Dilemma for the Adult Educator,* p. 88.
30. Paulo Freire, *Cultural Action for Freedom.* Boston: *Harvard Educational Review* and the Center for the Study of Development and Social Change, 1970, pp. 48–50.

pressed that revolutions differ according to varying social and economic situations. Freire's failure to link his revolutionary theory to a particular historical situation and context makes his theory rather abstract. His failure to consider varying social contexts in developing his theory of revolution separates him from such theorists of revolution as Johnson and Arendt who consider these contexts to be essential in defining revolution.[31] It also renders his theory of pedagogy almost impossible to apply, as many groups have found after beginning to work with his ideas.

Freire considers that his main contribution to a theory of revolution is his emphasis on the "dialogical nature" of revolutionary action. By the dialogical nature of revolutionary action, Freire expresses his belief that leaders should be in constant dialogue with the people at all points in the revolution. In fact, he points to his experience in "dialogical" and problem-solving education as giving him the necessary experience to write a book on revolutionary action in which he has never personally participated. *Pedagogy of the Oppressed* was written to defend the eminently pedagogical character of the revolution.

> Critical and liberating dialogue, which presupposes action, must be carried on with the oppressed at whatever the stage of their struggle for liberation. The content of that dialogue can and should vary in accordance with historical conditions and the level at which they can perceive reality.[32]

Freire's commitment to the dialogical character of the revolution is a rather limited one. After he indicates the number of cases where dialogue among equals is to be suspended, there is little left to his theory about the dialogic nature of the revolution. Freire has great difficulty in making his hero, Guevara, an advocate of dialogical revolutionary action. He quotes the revolutionary leader's words:

> Mistrust: at the beginning, do not trust your own shadow, never trust friendly peasants, informers, guides, or contact men. Do not trust anything or anybody until a zone is completely liberated.[33]

Guevara advocated communion with the people after liberation had been achieved. This, however, does not, as Freire would wish it to, make Guevara an advocate of dialogue with the people at every stage of the revolution. Freire commends the realism of the guerrilla leader and still attempts to make him an advocate of dialogue. But this appears an impossibility. By commending Guevara's mistrust of the ambiguity within oppressed human beings and his refusal to dialogue with them, Freire has denied the very essence of his theory of revolutionary action as fundamentally dialogical.

Freire compromises his dialogical theory of revolution in a number of other instances. He denies the necessity or the duty of the revolutionaries to dialogue with their former oppressors. He agrees with Guevara's admonition to punish deserters from the revolutionary group. This must be done in order to preserve the cohesion and the discipline of the group. Freire agrees with the guerrilla leader in his non-toleration of those who are not ready to accept the conclusion that revolution is essential. He speaks of the revolution as loving and creating life: "And in order to create life, it [the revolution] may be obliged to prevent some men from circumscribing life."[34]

Freire, as are many writers on revolutionary theory, is also rather vague in his description of the process and strategy of revolution. Revolutionary leadership will usually be made up of "men who in one way or another have belonged

31. Chalmers Johnson, *Revolutionary Change.* Boston: Little, Brown and Co., 1968; Arendt, *On Revolution,* pp. 18–22.
32. Freire, *Pedagogy,* p. 52.
33. *Ibid.,* p. 169.
34. *Ibid.,* p. 171.

to the social strata of the dominators."[35] Inauthentic leaders will be made manifest through the practice of the dialectic. These leaders are to organize themselves with the people. Freire admits that he has no details on how the revolution is to take place:

> Instead of following predetermined plans, leaders, and people, mutually identified, together create the guidelines of their action. In this synthesis, leaders and people are somehow reborn in new knowledge and new action.[36]

In *Pedagogy of the Oppressed,* Freire valiantly attempts to make his theory of the dialogical character of the revolution hold up against the stated views of revolutionaries. The effort must be pronounced a failure. The forging of a revolution seems to preclude dialogue among equals to arrive at truth by permitting the free expression of ideas.[37] Freire, the educator inexperienced in actual revolutionary activity, has exaggerated the role that the free educational

process is to play in forging a revolution. This stems from a more fundamental problem, his inadequate treatment of education through dialogue.

Briefly, it is Freire's position that somehow through dialogue people will come to see objective reality. In this process, they will denounce what is truly oppressive and at the same time announce or proclaim a new non-oppressive reality. By announcing this new reality, they are already engaged in the process of working for its concrete realization. While developing his educational theory, Freire is convinced that total freedom for denouncing and announcing objective reality must be insured to the people involved in such dialogues. Freire's philosophical position that an objective reality exists, which all will come to recognize through dialogue, fails to do justice to the complex problem of the nature of reality and of human knowledge of it. This leaves little room for relative and pluralistic world views.

DISCUSSION QUESTIONS AND ACTIVITIES

1. Once the oppressed perceive their condition and apprehend the world of oppression, what action would you expect them to take toward their oppressors?
2. Applying Freire's conception of oppression, what groups have you known that you consider oppressed?
3. Why should teacher and student roles not be so fixed that a person invariably is either a teacher or a student?
4. Why is the problem-posing method superior to the banking concept? What distinctive features, if any, do you find in the method?

5. What conception of man does Freire hold? Does it differ from your conception? Clarify any differences and explain why you still believe your conception to be better.
6. How does Freire utilize the student's view of the world in his problem-posing method?
7. Why was the Popular Culture Movement in Brazil, in which Freire was active, not very effective politically?
8. What is the connection between Freire's revolutionary ideals and religious beliefs?
9. Does the fact that Freire sees only one type of relationship among men (oppressor-oppressed) make it difficult to apply his pedagogy?
10. Elias considers Freire's theory and strategy of revolution to be "rather naive." Explain why.

---

35. Freire, *Pedagogy,* p. 162.
36. *Ibid.,* p. 183.
37. Regis Debray, *Revolution in the Revolution.* New York: Grove, 1967, pp. 56, 111.

11. Has Freire in a number of instances compromised his dialogical theory of revolution?

12. Why does Elias believe that Freire has exaggerated the role of education in precipitating revolutionary activity?

SUGGESTED READINGS

Works by Paulo Freire (in English)

Cultural Action For Freedom. Cambridge, Massachusetts: Harvard Educational Review, Monograph Series, No. 1, 1970.

Education for Critical Consciousness. New York: Seabury Press, 1973.

Latin Americans Look into their Social and Religious Problems. Washington, D. C.: Division for Latin America, n.d.

Pedagogy in Process: The Letters to Guinea Bissau. New York: Seabury, 1978.

Pedagogy of the Oppressed. New York: Seabury, 1971.

"People Speak Their Word: Learning to Read and Write in Sao Tome and Principe." *Harvard Educational Review* 51 (February 1981): 27–30.

Works about Paulo Freire

"About Freire." *Interracial Books Child Bulletin* 12, no. 2 (1981): 12–13.

Alschuler, Alfred S. *School Discipline: A Socially Literate Solution*. New York: McGraw-Hill, 1980.

"Application and Practicability of the Ideas of Paulo Freire to Countries, Developing or Developed, That Are Removed from the Region of Latin America: Symposium." *Convergence* 6, no. 1 (1973): 45–92.

Brighman, T. M. "Liberation in Social Work Education: Applications from Paulo Freire." *Journal of Education for Social Work* 13 (Fall 1977): 5–11.

Brown, C. "Literacy in Thirty Hours: Paulo Freire's Process." *Urban Review* 7 (July 1974): 245–56.

Collins, Denis E. *Paulo Freire: His Life, Works, and Thought*. New York: Paulist Press, 1977.

Conti, G. J. "Rebels with a Cause: Myles Horton and Paulo Freire." *Community College Review* 5 (Summer 1977): 36–43.

Crawford-Lange, Linda M. "Redirecting Second Language Curricula: Paulo Freire's Contribution." *Foreign Language Annals* 14 (September/October 1981): 257–68.

Edgerton, John. "Searching for Freire." *Saturday Review of Education* (March 10, 1973): 32, 34–5.

Elias, John L. *Conscientization and Deschooling: Freire's and Illich's Proposals for Shaping Society*. Philadelphia: Westminster Press, 1976.

Elias, John L. "Paulo Freire: Religious Educator." *Religious Education* 71 (January 1976): 40–56.

Evert, D. M. "Proverbs, Parables and Metaphors: Applying Freire's Concept of Codification to Africa." *Convergence* 14, no. 1 (1981): 32–43.

Fiore, Kyle and Nan Elsasser. " 'Strangers No more': A Liberatory Literacy Curriculum." *College English* 44 (February 1982): 115–28.

Fister, J. B. "What We Can Learn from Paulo Freire for Church Education." *Spectrum* 49 (Fall 1973): 11–14.

Gleeson, D. "Theory and Practice in the Sociology of Paulo Freire." *University Quarterly* 29 (Summer 1974): 362–71.

Grabowski, Stanley, ed. *Paulo Freire: A Revolutionary Dilemma for the Adult Educator*. Syracuse, New York: Syracuse University, Publications in Continuing Education and ERIC Clearinghouse on Adult Education, 1972.

Griffiths, Daniel E. "Can Critics Change the Schools?" *New York University Education Quarterly* 4 (1972): 1–6.

Hodder, Geoffrey S. "Human Praxis: A New Basic Assumption for Art Educators of the Future." *Canadian Journal of Education* 5, no. 2 (1980): 5–14.

Hokenson, T. "Process Pedagogy for Christian Education." *Religious Education* 68 (September 1973): 600–07.

Kekkonen, H. "Experiment in Outreach and the Pedagogy of Freire." *Convergence* 10, no. 1 (1977): 53–7.

Knight, P. "Freire's Philosophy Aims to Turn Readers

into Listeners." *Times Education Supplement* 3133 (June 13, 1975): 12.

Lernoux, P. "Brazilian University Embroiled in Conflict as Controversial Educator is Chosen Rector." *Chronicle of Higher Education* (December 16, 1981): 19–20.

Lloyd, A. S. "Freire, Conscientização and Adult Education. *Adult Education* 23 (Fall 1972): 3–20.

McFadden, J. "Bi-Cultural Approach to ESL for Adults." *California Journal of Educational Research* 25 (November 1974): 289–93.

Mackie, Robert, ed. *Literacy and Revolution: The Pedagogy of Paulo Freire.* London: Pluto Press, 1980.

Maring, G. H. "Freire, Gray, and Robinson on Reading." *Journal of Reading* 21 (February 1978): 421–5.

Monette, M. L. "Paulo Freire and Other Unheard Voices." *Religious Education* 74 (September/October 1979): 543–54.

Montieth, M. K. "Paulo Freire's Literacy Method." *Journal of Reading* 20 (April 1977): 628–9.

O'Donnell, J. G. "Education as Awakening." *Religious Education* 76 (September/October 1981): 517–24.

Palmer, Margaret Rose and Ron Newsome. "Paulo Freire's Consciousness Raising: Politics, Education, and Revolution in Brazil." *Educational Studies* 13 (Summer 1982): 183–89.

"Paulo Freire." *Convergence* 3, no. 3 (1970): 62–8.

Plunkett, H. Dudley. "Modernization Reappraised: The Kentucky Mountains Revisited and Confrontational Politics Reassessed." *Comparative Education Review* 22 (February 1978): 134–42.

Sherman, A. L. "Two Views of Emotion in the Writings of Paulo Freire." *Educational Theory* 30 (Winter 1980): 35–8.

Shields, James J., Jr. "The New Critics in Education." *Intellect* 102 (October 1973): 16–20.

Stanley, M. "Literacy: The Crisis of a Conventional Wisdom." *School Review* 80 (May 1972): 373–408.

Further Thoughts on Reformers

Jesse L. Jackson's ideas can best be understood as an outgrowth of the civil rights movement in the United States. The Supreme Court declared in the historic *Brown v. Board of Education of Topeka* (1954) desegregation decision that "separate but equal," as articulated in *Plessy v. Ferguson* (1896), is inherently unequal and violates the equal protection of the law. The Brown decision provided the legal grounds for abolishing *de jure* segregation in schooling and upheld civil rights. The civil rights movement involved many organizations but it was led primarily by Martin Luther King, Jr., from the late 1950s to 1960s and was promoted by the executive leadership of President Lyndon Johnson. These efforts resulted in passage of the Civil Rights Act of 1964 and 1968, which prohibited discrimination in places of public accommodation covered by interstate commerce, and barred discrimination in employment and in housing and real estate transactions.

Rev. Jackson has continued the civil rights activities of Martin Luther King, Jr., by seeking greater economic opportunities for Blacks and by promoting their intellectual, economic, and moral advancement through education. His emphasis is on establishing sound habits and skills, good moral character, and self-help rather than expecting the victimizer to aid the victim. Recalling the reform rationales in the Introduction to Part I, Jackson would appeal primarily to equity; he also appeals to quality in his quest for "excellence."

Marva Collins' approach is somewhat eclectic, as both *essentialism* and *progressivism* are manifested. *Essentialism* is found in the curriculum where emphasis is placed on acquiring basic skills, mastering subjects, and gaining an acquaintance with some great works of the past. *Progressivism* is exhibited in her emphasis on cooperation rather than competition, informal evaluation rather than regular tests and better grades, and pupil self-direction. Though she may appeal to more than one rationale to support her reform proposals, she principally appeals to quality by showing that disadvantaged children can make significant achievement gains (outcomes) and can also begin to enjoy learning more (process). Thus her quality rationale emphasizes improved outcomes first and the process second.

Mortimer Adler is a perennialist. *Perennialism* derives its aims for education from human nature, holding that human nature is everywhere the same, both today and in the past: humans are, above all, rational animals. Since it stems from human nature, the function of man is the same in every age and in every society. Rationality is man's highest attribute and therefore this attribute should be developed to its fullest extent. It can best be developed through educational institutions, whereas other attributes—morality and spirituality—can best be developed in different institutions (e.g., family and church). *Perennialism* holds that truth is absolute, and it is the task of education to impart these truths. These truths can be largely found in the great books of the past. Since the truth is everywhere the same and everyone is a rational being, all students study the same curriculum as is the case with the Paideia Proposal. The reader is more likely to accept the Proposal once the underlying philosophical grounds are accepted. Adler's reform rationale appeals to restoration by prescribing past ideals and standards and reinstating a required curriculum.

John Holt's position is a brand of *libertarianism*. This philosophy holds that all people have the right to make their own choices, so long as they do not interfere with the choices of others. Thus all individuals have rights to their own life and property and a duty to refrain from violating the same rights of others. Rights are violated through the use of force, and government is the principal culprit. Therefore, the role of government should be limited to the protection of life, liberty, and property.

Libertarians generally exhibit suspicion and distrust toward the government's role in education. Many libertarians are acutely dissatisfied with public education and object to the coercive power of government and believe it has usurped parents' rights. They offer legislation and plans for reducing what they consider to be the government's interference in private education and for granting parents primary authority in their child's education. This education might be conducted exclusively in the home or in public, private, or parochial schools; the main point is: parents (or guardians) would choose the education best for their children. Holt's reform rationale primarily appeals to decision-making because he seeks to establish that parents should have ultimate and final authority over their children's education.

Carl Rogers' approach is based on *humanistic psychology*, with special emphasis on nondirective techniques. Humanistic psychology differs from behaviorism and psychoanalysis by taking an organismic and holistic approach to the study of human beings. Such studies are designed to view each individual as a whole person who formulates goals and purposes for which he or she strives to attain. It focuses on the *experiencing person*, each person's experiences, as the unit of study. This focus leads to a research interest in the study of problems that are humanly meaningful and significant rather than those that fit neatly into prior canons of objectivity and limited, but precise, laboratory procedure.

Humanistic psychology, in contrast to the views of Freud, Hobbes, Calvin, and others, believes that observations should be developed from humans at their best. It should be drawn from those individuals who are creative, inventive, original, humane, those who more closely approach the utilization of their full potentials. The goal of psychotherapy, then, would no longer be the elimination of illness and the promotion of adjustment; rather, its aim is to encourage growth and creativity.

Rogers' reform rationale appeals to rights insofar as he seeks to promote student freedom by a release from restrictive and inhibiting classroom environments so that the student can engage in experiential learning and relate to others with attitudes of trust and caring.

In contrast, if a science of behavior is possible as Skinner contends, then more powerful explanations and greater predictability of behavior will be possible, and learning failures and miseducative experiences will largely be a thing of the past. The so-called free and creative student of Rousseauian origin, Skinner avers, is surely not the answer, and this life-style cannot prepare students for the future. By educational systems repudiating punitive methods and substituting positive reinforcement, students will be better prepared for the future. Thus one is left with the question whether Skinner's controlled environment is more educationally valuable than Rogers' open, nondirective relationships. Skinner's reform rationale appeals to quality: educational institutions would utilize his model to bring about both an improved process based on positive reinforcement and better outcomes based on desired behaviors.

Most of the reformers are not socialists. Socialism, though it has many variants, emphasizes what is social as contrasted to the individual, gives priority to social egalitarianism, and advocates that social ownership and control of the basic wealth of the community should replace private ownership. Freire's writings, however, show distinct elements of Marxism and Marxist socialism insofar as he accepts the inevitability of class struggle stemming from unequal distribution of goods and the inability of the masses to gain access to and control the means of production. People, the Marxist says, are forced into two classes: the exploiters and the exploited, and this division assures eventual social conflict. Freire is not merely reciting a party line; he has developed his own distinctive philosophy, which has pronounced Marxist elements. His reform rationale appeals to a combination of equity, rights, and decision-making.

The reformers can be understood in other ways. How do they define education? In what respects do they differ in their conception of education? What educational aims are most important? What reasons are given for adopting a set of aims? Notice that some reformers stress liberating the learner in some way or another. What are they liberating the learner from, and what will he or she be able to do as a result of such liberation? The coerciveness of institutions and their tendency to alienate, dehumanize, and make one feel powerless is a prevailing theme among some reformers. What sort of institutions, if any, will nurture the type of person they believe education should develop?

Another common tendency for reformers is to offer an optimistic view of human nature by stating or, more often, implying that individuals are basically good and when provided a nurturing environment with supportive persons that they will become liberated themselves. These same reformers dismiss those who argue that humans are innately aggressive and destructive or inherently sinful. But how would reformers explain why institutions are oppressive when they are governed by individuals born with these same positive traits? Perhaps Freire's essay provides an answer.

Certain methods of teaching are thought to be superior in promoting education. Freire advocates problem-posing; Adler endorses three types of teaching; and Rogers is suspicious of teaching but in favor of facilitating learning. What is the desired authority relationship in teacher-pupil relations according to the reformers studied? It may also prove helpful to look at different teaching approaches advocated to see if they are consonant with the reformer's goals and view of human nature.

A Parting Scenario

A number of guests, including yourself, are invited to a mountain lodge for a weekend retreat. To your surprise, the guests include all the reformers in Part I. They suddenly begin passionately debating the aims of education. What would they likely say? Who would you side with — and why?

PART II
Innovations and Alternatives

Recent years have been marked by widespread dissatisfaction with public education and numerous attempts to find more successful approaches to educating the young. Not surprisingly, educators have sought to offer innovations and alternatives. Innovation is the introduction of any new idea, method, or device to improve some aspect of the educational process. The idea could lead to a new way of handling gifted or handicapped learners. The innovation may be the project method or the initiation of team teaching, and the device could range from educational television to microcomputers. In contrast, educational alternatives are systems and plans, both inside and outside public education that are different from the typical public school model.

Alternatives first appeared outside of public education as different types of schools (such as free schools), as new organizational plans for redistributing educational resources (vouchers), or plans for home instruction. Alternatives were developed in public education during the 1970s and ranged from schools for performing arts to the back-to-basics alternative.

Although there can be no innovation or alternative without change, most changes are not innovations or alternatives. Change is when something or someone becomes different and may be accidental. An innovation, since it is brought about by human agency to serve a particular purpose, rules out changes in nature and human changes that are unintentional. It is true that some innovations, just as scientific discoveries, are serendipitous. In such cases, however, it is still necessary to make the connection between the discovery and an educational goal and then visualize the innovation within an educational context. Thus, by the time the discoverer finishes, the process has become highly deliberate.

But how novel does something have to be before it is counted as an innovation? Usually it will require some distinctive feature in at least one of the following aspects: rationale, organization, curriculum, or instruction. For instance, the rationale for accountability differs perceptibly from traditional rationales for school organization and evaluation; the organizational procedures of mainstreaming represents a sharp departure from earlier practices in handling handicapped children; and bilingual education differs significantly in curricula and instruction from traditional practices. Although innovations that are highly original are likely to leave a lasting impression, such innovations are also likely to meet with greater resistance from those that require less change. The following survey of key innovations and alternatives of the recent past will clarify these points.

THE CONTINUITY OF INNOVATIONS
AND ALTERNATIVES

Early Innovations in Instruction, Curriculum, and Organization

The Dalton Plan. This is a study plan based on instructional contracts for students. It was named after Dalton, Massachusetts, the district in which it was first introduced in 1920 by Helen Parkhurst. The plan actually attracted more followers overseas — in Europe, China, and Japan — than in the United States.

The plan called for a series of classrooms that were allocated to certain subjects. The classrooms were designated as laboratories and pupils as experimenters. In the English laboratory, pupils had access to significant literary works, and in the geography laboratory the teacher helped pupils use models, maps, charts, and globes. Thus there was a laboratory for each subject taught in school.

The pupil was given a mimeographed guide sheet that listed all the work to be done for the month. The pupil then signed a contract to complete the assignments on the sheet by specified dates. There was no class teaching and pupils could move from one room to another as they choose in fulfilling their contract. It was initially thought that ideally each pupil would receive his or her own assignment sheet, but the burden proved too great for most teachers. One assignment sheet was usually compiled for everyone. Slower learners and indolent pupils required more supervision and direction. Some Dalton followers set aside afternoons for games, gymnastics, and social activities. Enrichment of English was through debates, public speaking, and histrionics; history was supplemented by discussion of current politics, the customs and manners of earlier eras, and other topics.

Despite greater freedom and individual attention than in traditional classrooms, the Dalton Plan came under criticism for insufficient socialization practices and lack of social education. This criticism, however, was more applicable to the original Dalton Plan and not to those that sprang up in various parts of the world where some attempt was made to balance individual learning with social education. Another criticism was that it did not actually individualize instruction because the assignments were not geared to the needs of each student. Nor did it break from the traditional subject curriculum, which some progressives deplored. The plan was suited for a subject curriculum and could be used with any standard subject, except perhaps with foreign languages.

The Winnetka Plan. This Plan was initiated in 1919 by Carleton Washbourne (1889–1968) in Winnetka, Illinois, as a means of individualizing instructions at the elementary level. The curriculum was divided into two parts: the *common essentials,* the 3 R's, sciences, and social studies, and *cultural and creative experiences,* which were taught in a group setting.

The common essentials were individualized at the beginning of the term by evaluating the child in each subject and then establishing assignments that were adjusted to the child's needs. Class recitation was discarded. Instead, pupils would read for the teacher one at a time while the others studied. Once a portion of their work was completed, they could ask the teacher for a test and then move on to the next assignment whenever the test was successfully passed. In the Winnetka Plan, children neither skipped grades nor failed. Thus studies were divided by the teachers into tasks and goals, and each child was given simple directions for proceeding independently.

Half the morning and half the afternoon sessions were dedicated to individual work with the common essentials, while the remaining half of the morning and afternoon was devoted to such cultural and creative experiences as plays, open forums, school journals, self-government meetings, workshops, excursions, shopwork, music, and art.

The Winnetka Plan was more genuinely individualized than the Dalton Plan; and it enabled students to proceed at their own pace, while the Dalton Plan insisted that a pupil could not proceed in any subject until the entire monthly assignment was completed. Studies of the Winnetka Plan under Washburne's direction showed favorable results in terms of student performance or standardized tests, except in spelling where they lagged behind. Washburne used the Winnetka Plan for two decades. However, when adopted elsewhere, it was usually modified considerably to bring it more into line with traditional practices.

Some questions were also raised over what constituted "the common essentials" and whether these subjects were the ones that could best be individualized. Additionally, questions arose over how the two major areas of the program could be connected.

The Activity or Experience Curriculum. This curriculum emerged in elementary schools during the progressive movement in the 1930s. It was based on the assumption that children learn best by experiencing things, rather than by the presentation of subject matter to them. Units of study, furthermore, were constructed from a knowledge of their needs and interests. It was also based on the conviction that learning is an active affair, and involvement in activities will overcome the child's passivity and lack of motivation found in traditional schools. The program usually called for some pupil-teacher planning in which teachers ask children about their needs. Teachers and pupils worked together by using a problem-solving approach in planning, focusing on children's interests for organizational purposes.

This program was aimed at overcoming the interest and motivation problem in the subject curriculum, perhaps meeting some additional needs, and keeping students actively involved. One serious mistake, however, was the assumption that because learning is an active affair, then activity itself will lead to effective learning. One may learn by doing, but not all doing results in learning: Activity may be a necessary condition for some forms of learning but not a necessary and sufficient condition. Moreover, an activity curriculum tends to confuse overt activity with doing. Thinking, however, involves an active role by the learner but may not be observable. Another weakness is that since the child's range of experience is extremely limited, it is incumbent upon the school to broaden interests rather than stick to present ones. Finally, to use needs as a basis for curriculum planning may be untenable. To say that a need exists and that it should be fulfilled is to recognize that it exists to fulfill some objective. Whether or not an objective is desirable is determined by a set of values or the school's philosophy—not an appeal to needs.

The Project Method. William Heard Kilpatrick (1871–1965) believed that the activities found in agriculture and extension work could be applied to other aspects of life through projects. His notion of a project, however, was much broader than the conventional one: "The presence of a dominating purpose." Thus building a boat, making a dress, or staging a play were considered projects as well as any other activity with a dominating purpose. It was important, in Kilpatrick's view, that any given project would lead on to other worthwhile projects, and it was better for each student to choose the project and plan it with teacher guidance, when needed. The project method, Kilpatrick believed, is valuable not just to sustain student interest but because life itself is composed of a series of projects, and therefore, this way of learning will be a suitable preparation for life.

Kilpatrick's definition of the project method, however, was too broad since it tended to equate any goal-directed behavior with a project, even though much of this behavior involved no project in the conventional sense of the term. Futhermore, the project method lacked structure, sequence, and organization; it was difficult to build a curriculum on the basis of projects. Moreover, classroom management was a problem because too many divergent activities were taking place simultaneously. Moving, from one project into another was not always easy and children became bored and restless. Many projects may also only tap lower-level cognitive abilities. The bulk of organized knowledge, as well as skill development, was in danger of being lost with projects as the basis of curriculum. Today the curriculum is not built on projects alone; however, the "pure" project method can still be found in industrial arts, vocational agriculture, and the sciences.

The Platoon System. Many American school districts adopted the platoon system early in this century. The first system was organized by William Wirt (1874–1938) in Bluffton, Indiana, in 1900, where Wirt served as school superintendent. The platoon system divided the school population into two groups. While one group (Platoon A) received instruction in the 3Rs for two hours daily, the second group (Platoon B) studied subjects in specially equipped facilities (shop, gym, art room) for the same length of time. Both groups exchanged places at a predetermined time. This was de-signed to achieve a balance between academic work and social-creative activities. Even the elementary grades followed this compartmentalized plan. This system in-creased pupil capacity by 40 percent without hiring additional teachers.

In 1907, Wirt became superintendent in Gary, Indiana, and established the Gary Plan. In addition to the Platoon System, Wirt adopted Dewey's idea of education as an embryonic community life in which the different community occupations were reflected in art, history, and science. Not only would the school provide greatly ex-panded educational opportunities in art and music rooms, swimming pools, gardens, and the like, but the school would become the community's center for intellectual and artistic life. The schools were open all day, twelve months each year, to persons of all ages, for the ultimate objective of bringing about community improvement.

A team of evaluators commended the Gary Plan for its boldness, organizational innovations, the application of democratic principles to school conduct and disci-pline, and the enrichment of community life through the schools. But it was also criti-cized for not always working well in practice: Some activities wasted time, others were enjoyable but not educative. School records were often inaccurate; instructions in the subjects was not well organized in many cases, sufficient in content, or pre-sented other than conventionally. Despite these criticisms, over 200 cities had adopted the Gary Plan by 1929.

Early Alternative Schools

Francis W. Parker School. An educational reformer who was credited by Dewey as the "father of progressive education," Francis W. Parker (1837–1902) became school superintendent in Quincy, Massachusetts, in 1873, and set about reforming the schools. Parker was a child-centered progressive: He sought to move the child to the center of the educative process and to make the curriculum convey greater meaning to the child. Parker's deification of the child suggests that this philosophy is closer to Rousseau's than Dewey's.

Parker abolished the formalities of the traditional classroom that insisted the child remain perfectly still and quiet and substituted instead observation, laboratory work, and the use of ideas in practice (as in the teaching of arithmetic). Inductive methods were employed in arithmetic; geography was taught by field trips as well as formal study. The emphasis was on observing, describing, and gaining a grasp of things before being introduced to more conventional studies. The program, which was dubbed the "Quincy System," achieved considerable recognition before Parker moved to the Cook County Normal School in Illinois. Here he continued his opposi-tion, first expressed at Quincy, to traditional teaching and stressed instead activity, creative self-expression, the scientific study of education, and prepared special teach-ers for these subjects. In 1901, the Francis W. Parker School was founded in Chicago, staffed by many teachers prepared by Parker; it continued for more than thirty years.

Parker was a founding father of progressive education in the United States and set an example for others to follow. Criticisms of his approach are essentially those made earlier about progressivism of the child-centered variety.

The Dewey Laboratory School. This experimental elementary school began in Chicago in 1896, reached its peak of 140 pupils in 1902, and closed in 1904 after a disagreement with the University of Chicago over the administration of the school. Whereas the Parker School began with practice and later moved to theory, Dewey sought to test theory in the Laboratory School. The school was an experiment in "cooperative living" whereby both individual interests and social life could be satisfied. Dewey sought to reconcile a host of dualisms in the larger culture: interest and effort, individualism and collectivism, work and play, labor and leisure, school and society, the child and the curriculum. The school was experimental and children were allowed to explore, create, and make mistakes in testing ideas.

The organizational focus for the Laboratory School was social occupations. Studying occupations it was thought would not only promote the social purposes of the school but would greatly enliven the school's activities and make the learning of routine skills more interesting. It would also promote a balance between intellectual and practical activities. Since, for Dewey, education was not a preparation for life but was life itself, children were to learn directly about life by the school producing in miniature the conditions of social life. And since many of the children would later become manual workers, they needed an understanding of industrial processes. School subjects in the conventional sense were dispensed with, and even the 3Rs grew out of the child's activities. The social occupations represented human concerns about food, clothing, shelter, household furnishings, the production, consumption, and exchange of goods. Four- and five-year-olds learned about preparing lunch before going home at mid-day; by the age of seven, the emphasis had changed from occupations in the home and neighborhood to an historical approach that traced the emergence of occupations beginning with earliest culture; finally, by the age of thirteen, the emphasis shifted to current events.

The Dewey Laboratory School was a bold experiment and represented the most salient ideas on the leading edge of the Progressive movement. It was criticized because it was difficult to achieve a balanced focus on both the individual (the child) and society. The individualistic or freedom side may have been given greater attention. Systematic follow-up studies were not conducted of the school's graduates and therefore no record is available of the school's impact on their lives. Yet from the records of the school and the extant examples of student work, it appears to have been a soundly managed school with quality teachers.

The Montessori School. Maria Montessori (1870–1952), the first woman in Italy to receive an M.D. degree, worked with mentally defective children and then turned to normal children. Montessori believed that the child needs to escape from the domination of parents and teachers. Children in modern society are victims of adult suppression that compels them to adopt coping measures foreign to their real nature. Teachers must change their attitudes toward children and to organize an environment in which children can lead lives of their own.

In Montessori schools children are placed in a stimulating environment where there are things for them to do and things to study. This environment should be free of rivalry, rewards, and punishments; learning instead is to be through interesting activities. Teachers become directors who see that activities proceed according to a master plan; in fact, Montessori believed that one teacher could handle as many as forty-five children if necessary, but a class of thirty is more desirable. Special materials are used by children in a carefully organized environment. Through regular, graded use of didactic material, children gain skills of manipulation and judgment, and the special senses are separately trained by use of apparatus: Cubes of various sizes are used to build a tower so that children can learn about volume; several kinds of wooden insets exhibit breadth, depth, and volume; sticks of graduated length; cylinders of different sizes are to be placed in the correct blocks. Children learn to develop neuromuscular mechanisms for writing by pouring rice and picking up beans; they learn their letters through a combination of senses: visual, tactile, and auditory. And they learn to associate the sound of the word (sounded phonetically) with an object. In geography, children are given a sandpaper globe, tangible objects, and pictures of people from different cultures. Geography activities lead to the study of history, while learning one's language leads to the study of both subjects. Science, mathematics, and foreign languages are outgrowths of learning one's native language.

The Montessori system spread to many parts of the world prior to World War I, lapsed during the War but had a brief recovery in the 1920s, and was revived again in the United States in the 1950s. Despite their achievements, Montessori schools have been criticized for using equipment too complex and intricate for children, for failure to stimulate the imagination because no imaginary tales are used, for using overly planned and structured learning, and for not promoting social learning sufficiently.

Waldorf Education. Rudolf Steiner (1861–1925), the founder of Waldorf education in 1913, believed in theosophy, a religious movement that originated in India that teaches about god and the world on the basis of mystical insight. Steiner later called his philosophy *anthroposophy*. It was his objective to provide a program of education from a spiritual point of view that recognized the child's physical, emotional, and intellectual development as manifested in three successive stages of growth in seven-year cycles. The first stage is characterized by imitation and expression in active movement. It is inappropriate, Steiner believed, to teach the 3Rs at this stage. The second stage, from seven to fourteen, features the development of feelings and imagination and is the period when basic skills are acquired. The third stage is where the pupil's thinking ability is emphasized through formal study.

During the first two stages, no specialization is permitted and pupils are grouped according to age and intelligence. The greatest need of the child, according to Steiner, is security; therefore, one teacher remains with a group of children throughout the first stage; similarly, another teacher remains throughout the second stage; and only in the final stage, when subject matter specialists are needed, is this pattern altered. No examinations are used because Steiner considered them of no educational value. In addition to traditional subjects, Waldorf education places emphasis on mythology, art, and eurhymthmics (a music-based method of physical training). The Waldorf program strives to develop intellectual and manipulative skills, cultivate social conscience, promote self-expression, and encourage spiritual development. Waldorf schools have a non-denominational Christian outlook. By the 1980s, more than eighty of these schools were established in Europe and the United States.

Waldorf education offers a broad view of education, is holistic, and recognizes different stages (and suitable materials) of pupil development. It may not be appropriate for public education, not only because teachers are unprepared to handle this type of program but because it might raise questions about religious teaching in public schools. Steiner's stages of development do not reflect the latest research findings, and the practice of one teacher remaining with a group of pupils for many years is problematic on pedagogical grounds.

RECENT INNOVATIONS IN INSTRUCTION AND CURRICULUM

Instructional Innovations

Behavioral Objectives. Behavioral objectives arose during the late 1960s to move away from high-sounding educational goals on which performance could not be measured. Instead behavioral objectives (or "instructional objectives," as they were later called) provide precise, observable, measurable statements of goals. Behavioral objectives state exactly what students can be expected to do after completing designated learning activities. (For example, after four weeks in an introductory typing course, students should be able to type at least twenty words per minute on a ten-minute typing test with no more than four errors.) Those planning a course are able to select materials designed to accomplish the objectives. Thus the teacher is able to plan more effectively as well as assess course effectiveness with greater precision. It also means teachers are more accountable for instructional activities, and the student is better informed about what is expected of him or her.

Behavioral objectives, however, have been criticized on a number of grounds. Since objectives for courses are set in advance, they make it difficult for teachers to change plans in the face of special learning needs. This leaves out much learning of an affective, aesthetic, and moral nature that cannot be stated as an objective. While convergent thinking may in many cases be stated behaviorally, it is far less likely that divergent thinking can be stated or measured precisely (though it could be evaluated). Thus many of the more important objectives cannot be stated behaviorally. Emphasis on behavioral objectives may lead to neglect of principles, broad concepts, and understandings that give meaning to behavior. Even if behavioral objectives are sound, they are not feasible because of the enormous amount of time required for teachers to compose innumerable objectives.

Programmed Instruction and Computer-Assisted Instruction. The first teaching machine was developed in the 1920s by Sidney L. Pressey and was revived in the 1950s by

B. F. Skinner in the form of programmed materials. These materials use a carefully planned sequence of learning tasks by breaking the material down into its smallest meaningful units. Students are expected to show mastery of each exercise before proceeding to the next one. Once the exercise is completed, the students know if he or she has mastered the knowledge because the correct answer is given. If the student's answer is incorrect, he or she restudies the material (in a linear program) or is assigned a new exercise, as in alternate or branching programs developed by Norman Crowder.

Programmed instruction has some advantages over traditional teaching. Students have greater recall of material through programmed instruction, master knowledge and skills more rapidly than in traditional instruction, and enjoy the benefits of individualized learning through the use of branching. (Branching is when a learner temporarily ceases work with the main sequence of frames to study a subsidiary or remedial program.)

The disadvantages of programmed instruction are that these materials have not been used to teach higher-order skills and knowledge, students tend to become bored once the novelty has worn off. It is expensive (fifty or seventy-five hours of programming are needed for each student hour of instruction), does not satisfy students whose learning objectives differ from the material; and is atomistic and mechanistic.

Computer-assisted instruction (CAI) operates on similar principles of learning as programmed instruction. Students work individually with a programmed computer by typewriter, touch-manipulation board, or electronic pointer. The computer responds via typewriter, television, slides, recordings, or print. CAI can be used to individualize instruction, supplement classroom demonstrations, promote independent study, and diagnose student learning difficulties.

The advantages of CAI are that students learn faster than by using other methods; it may reduce student drop-outs; it allows students to study at their own pace; students generally react favorably toward it; it is effective for students who do not perform well in traditional instruction; and it aids students to complete courses satisfactorily.

The disadvantages of CAI are that it is expensive, and difficult to exchange programs because of many different computer languages; it is impersonal and lacking human interaction; student excitement over CAI is not easily sustained; teachers generally resist it; and it operates on an atomistic rather than a holistic model of learning.

Mastery Learning. This form of learning is based on the assumption that the mastery of a topic or a human behavior is theoretically possible for anyone given the optimum quality of instruction appropriate to each individual and given the time needed for mastery. Mastery learning began with the work of Henry C. Morrison in the 1920s and continued in the 1960s with further studies by J. B. Carroll and Benjamin S. Bloom.

Carroll's model uses five variables: aptitude, perseverance, ability to understand instruction, quality of instruction, and opportunity for learning. Taken together, these variables predict the degree of student learning for a particular learning task, and they also play an important role in Bloom's strategy for mastery learning. A mastery strategy involves deciding what will constitute mastery for a particular course, determining appropriate procedures, and deciding how mastery will be evaluated. Bloom supplements regular instruction with frequent evaluation to determine student progress and uses alternative methods and materials. Objectives are stated behaviorally; a preassessment of students is used before instruction to determine interest and ability; instruction is adapted to the learner; difficulties are frequently diagnosed; prescriptions for improvement are made; and postassessments are undertaken. A variety of instructional procedures are selected; some are discarded, and new ones added; based on feedback from ongoing instruction. Those students who fail to achieve mastery need to be assessed to determine the problems they are having and given more time to gain mastery.

Mastery learning has the advantages of being workable for virtually any level of schooling for any subject; potentially 90 percent of students can master a course; students can have a role in developing objectives; it can enhance a student's self-concept with a sense of accomplishment; and it promotes cooperation rather than competition for grades.

The disadvantages of mastery learning are that it is more appropriate for learning technical skills; it is unfair if most of the students receive the same grades because grades then become meaningless; teachers are unprepared for mastery learning because of the scarcity of reliable tests to assess the five variables; it is overly teacher-centered by ignoring credit for student effort not reflected on tests; and it overemphasizes outcomes to the detriment of learning processes.

Discovery Learning. This learning is inductive. The student is expected to formulate a rule, devise a formula, and recognize a generalization as a result of first-hand experience with cases or instances of some phenomena. Discovery learning was first advocated by Jerome S. Bruner who held that the most uniquely personal learning is that which the individual discovers for himself. The student, for instance, can discover the generalization that lies behind a particular mathematical operation. Discovery is a process of going beyond the data to develop new insights. This process not only encourages mastery of fundamental ideas about a subject but promotes intellectual excitement about discovery and confidence in one's ability to perceive previously unrecognized relationships. Thus it helps the student acquire information in ways that make it more readily applicable; the student becomes less motivated by external rewards or fear of failure; the act of discovery provides a mode of inquiry in future learning, and the knowledge is more likely to be retained because it is organized in terms of learner interest.

Discovery learning has an outward similarity to Dewey's problem-solving or scientific method insofar as both promote independent, reflective thinking. Dewey's problem-solving, however, is more structured, utilizing a step-by-step sequence; whereas discovery learning is not highly structured and more fully recognizes insight and intuition in the discovery of new knowledge.

One of the basic weaknesses in this area is that researchers have not specified what is to be discovered by the student. In some situations the student is left with almost no cues to discover a simple principle, but without cues it is unlikely that the student can arrive at the principle. If intensive cues, however, are needed by the student, very little discovery will take place. In contrast to an expository approach (where the teacher provides background information and the correct answer), discovery learning is far more time consuming. It is probably truc, though, that discovery methods are preferable to expository teaching if large amounts of time are not consumed by greater learning activity and involvement. Discovery, however, is only one way this involvement can be brought about. Expository teaching could be used to impart basic knowledge, and then students would become more actively involved by applying the knowledge to new situations.

Television Instruction. This form of instruction uses live or prerecorded television lectures or demonstrations in courses. It is used to enlarge slides, documents, pictures; to provide off-campus instruction; to share first-hand field experiences; to provide short demonstrations for videotapes; to observe one's own behavior, as in teaching, in order to improve performance; and to offer professionally prepared educational programs. Television instruction, besides these uses, has certain advantages: It provides instruction to those unable to attend classes (in conjunction with a study guide or syllabus); the broadcasts can be aired repeatedly at convenient times; students generally prefer television instruction to regular lectures; and it enables viewers to see specimens, documents, and pictures more clearly.

Instructional television has some disadvantages: Except in the early grades, students prefer small group discussion; it is essentially a one-way medium that provides no interaction or opportunity to raise questions (unless special provisions are made); it is inferior to other media for music broadcasts; it requires a large audience to be cost effective; and some teachers are averse to using it. When instructional television offers students an opportunity to raise questions and interact, it is at least as effective as other media and methods.

Curriculum Innovations

Structure of the Disciplines Approach. This approach originated with scholars in the 1950s and 60s as a response to their findings of obsolete content and instructional practices in the subject curriculum. While retaining subjects as a framework for organization, the scholars revised and updated content, introduced discovery learning, and deemphasized rote learning in favor of teaching students how to grasp the structure of a discipline. This meant that fundamental axioms, concepts, and other building-blocks of a discipline became the focus of learning so that students could comprehend the underlying structure, attempt to generate fruitful hypotheses, and perceive how scholars generate new knowledge. The concept of readiness was reassessed, and it was found that students could grasp concepts earlier if the concepts were formulated in terms of the student's cognitive development and how students learn best at different ages and levels of maturity. This led to earlier grade placement of subjects and concepts (in mathematics, for instance, set theory was introduced earlier).

The structure of the disciplines approach has certain advantages over the traditional subject curriculum: revision and updating and curriculum content are undertaken more frequently; the emphasis is upon understanding a discipline's structure rather than learning facts for their own sake; stress is placed on critical thinking and intuitive judgment (in discovery learning); concepts are mastered earlier; and, as a consequence of these features, there is a greater likelihood of effective transfer of training.

Despite the promise of this approach and genuine progress in curriculum revision during the 1960s, some shortcomings should be noted. Students face problems in their daily lives that are not restricted to disciplines—problems of relations between the sexes, marriage and the family, race relations, war and peace, ecology, shortages of economic resources, and numerous others that are better approached through interdisciplinary perspectives. Second, a subject or discipline approach to curriculum as opposed to an interdisciplinary one, discourages examination of the curriculum as a whole in order to develop concepts progressively and provide proper continuity and articulation from one grade to the next. Third, this approach emphasizes cognitive learning and neglects social, emotional, and moral development. Stress on cognitive learning slants the approach to the more academically talented and is, in fact, used with highly motivated children in superior schools. A fourth difficulty is that children do not think like researchers in the disciplines, yet the program establishes models of this type of thinking and inquiry. Finally, this curriculum innovation gives little attention to goals and their justification, other than assuming that a mastery of disciplines is the most desirable end—an assumption that is not self-evident and needs to be demonstrated.

Compensatory Education. These are programs that seek to overcome the educational disadvantages of children that arise from personal history, social background, or economic conditions. Research has indicated that retardation may be long-lasting or permanent unless intervention occurs at an early age; consequently, early childhood education programs such as Head Start have been developed. Compensatory education leaves to special education responsibility for physical handicaps, brain damage, and genetic limitations. Among the many approaches used in compensatory education are health programs, reading readiness and remediation programs, emphasis on developing a positive self-concept, expanded guidance services, and curriculum enrichment.

Compensatory education programs were funded under Title I of the Elementary and Secondary Education Act (ESEA) passed by Congress in 1965. This immediately provided $1 billion in Title I funds to supplement and improve the education of poor and minority-group children. By 1965, funds totaled $2 billion per year, or approximately $200 more for each disadvantaged child.

Despite ample funding and federal support, most of these programs were ineffective in raising the cognitive level of disadvantaged children. Numerous reasons account for these early failures: inadequately prepared teachers, a piecemeal approach, consultant fees paid for work improperly done, unethical methods of awarding grants, vague objectives, increased quantity of services without improved quality of program content, and poor evaluation procedures. Results since 1975 have been more favorable as some of these earlier deficiencies have been corrected, better monitoring procedures have been implemented, greater funding has been provided from state and local levels, and program evaluation has improved. Thus programs such as Head Start and Follow-Through have begun to succeed as student achievement in low-income schools in several metropolitan areas is shown to match or exceed the national average. Some studies of early childhood education programs have revealed that they have a lasting effect in raising achievement and IQ scores. The cost, however, of compensatory education is high—$3,000 annually per student—and it is questionable whether funds of this magnitude will be available during a recession or that the public will be willing to provide this level of support.

Organizational Innovations

Middle School. During the 1960s the middle school was developed not only as a new form of organization but a new approach for educating pupils in the sixth, seventh, and eighth grades (in some instances the fifth and ninth grades were also included). Proponents of the middle school believe that the junior high school has not been entirely effective and propose that a separate building and special programs be used to educate pupils in these grades. The middle school is designed to serve as a bridge between childhood and adolescence, a transitional period where existing programs are not suitable for this age group. Thus the middle school seeks to establish its own identity and mission. The program stresses such features as individualized study, team teaching, the integration of extracurricular activities into the formal curriculum, the use of a nongraded plan, and the development of interdisciplinary programs.

One of the dangers is that the middle school will be little different than the conventional junior high school. In some cases middle schools have been used to accommodate excessive enrollments by transferring students to less overcrowded middle schools. Besides the problem of providing a distinctive program and recruiting teachers with the requisite abilities and interests, school buildings geared to these special programs are not always available. Considering it took junior high schools nearly fifty years to acquire buildings adequate for their programs, the likelihood of obtaining buildings does not appear promising. Additionally, the middle school movement has met considerable resistance from proponents of the junior high school; these proponents believe the criticisms of the junior high school are at best superficial. Middle school advocates, however, point to the junior high school as largely an administrative reorganization of secondary education that belatedly developed a curricular rationale, whereas the middle school is a curriculum response to the special needs of this age group. Moreover, the junior high school movement lacks a sufficiently broad research base to validate its effectiveness, whereas the middle school movement has recently accumulated greater data to support its claims.

Nongraded Schools. These schools are a newer form of curricular and instructional organization and are found principally at the elementary level. Grade levels and all expectations associated with separate grades are eliminated. The goals are to individualize instruction and permit each student to learn at his or her own rate of speed. The problem of promotion and retention is overcome, instruction no longer has to be geared to the average student, and student progress is not delayed because of slower classmates. Different age groups work together and learn from one another. A child, for example, may be advanced in arithmetic but slower to grasp social studies; consequently, this student will be placed with others of similar abilities in each subject and will work with them in large and small groups and spend some time working alone.

Nongraded plans, however, are no panacea for curricular and instructional problems. It is still necessary to have teachers adequately prepared for this form of organization and sufficient and appropriate curricular materials (which, generally, are in short supply). Without these two essential ingredients, it would be better to remain with graded plans. Moreover, in some schools the actual organizational pattern required has not been actually put into operation, though teachers and administrators usually assume the plan is nongraded. Other than different reading levels, many so-called nongraded plans are little different than graded ones. Thus many of these plans are conventional homogeneous groupings of pupils within the same grade; curriculum organization and instruction remain the same.

Despite these criticisms, research studies indicate that nongraded school children's achievement scores are significantly higher than those of graded children. Additionally, fewer children are retained, and nongraded schools are especially beneficial for blacks, underachievers, and boys. Most research on nongraded schools, however, was conducted in the early 1970s, and little research has been available since 1973.

Differentiated Staffing. This is a plan for structuring the teaching faculty so that instruction can be individualized by utilizing teachers in different types of assignments according to their competencies. Differentiated staffing is especially suited to merit plans. Public school teachers generally have little differentiation in assignments and responsibilities. People performing the same type of tasks are paid different rates in regular schools; whereas in differentiated staffing teachers receive merit pay but for different types of responsibilities and tasks.

One model of differentiated staffing divides the staff into paraprofessionals and professionals. The paraprofessionals consist of clerical assistants and proctors, technical assistants and instructional assistants, instructional associates, and research assistants. These people serve as the supporting staff to provide clerical and proctoring services, assist in classroom management, supervise the school building and grounds, prepare transparencies and slide presentations, and carry out numerous other tasks that would allow the teacher to concentrate on instruction.

The professional staff consists of the intern teacher, probationary teacher, staff teacher, master teacher, and teacher specialist. The intern teacher is noncertified and teaches part-time or full-time, depending upon the school system. The probationary teacher is equivalent to today's certified teachers who have yet to be awarded tenure. The staff teacher would be tenured, have a fifth year of preparation but not necessarily a master's degree. The master teacher has demonstrated ability to assume leadership in teaching. This teacher has a master's degree and assumes leadership on curriculum committees, serves as a team teaching leader, assists in training of probationary and intern teachers, and undertakes related responsibilities. Finally, the teacher specialist has a doctorate or post-master's degree work and is responsible for research in the area of specialization, planning programs systemwide, demonstrations in experimental teaching situations, and related duties. The teaching specialist is employed on a twelve-month basis, whereas the master teacher is employed on a ten- or eleven-month basis.

Differentiated staffing, according to proponents, breaks the lockstep of traditional plans, affords far better staff utilization, and is more likely than traditional staffing to provide students with superior teaching and services. It also offers greater incentives and rewards for superior teaching, and it relieves teachers of more routine chores so that they can concentrate on professional activities.

Critics, however, say that there are problems in determining the different levels of responsibilities, assigning duties to these levels, and assessing competence. The plan also seems to be a surreptitious way of initiating merit pay. If this is the case a genuine plan of merit pay, based on performance, would be preferable to one based on roles assumed, degrees held, and the like. Second, differentiated staffing fosters specialization and moves the system away from a child-centered approach to one that is subject-centered. Third, the competent teacher is not necessarily the skillful supervisor or coordinator. Thus the Peter Principle may be operating here. Finally, some teachers resent a meritocratic system and a hierarchical arrangement. Although differentiated staffing enlists greater teacher participation in policy-making, some administrators are reluctant to support such changes. Administrators, if they are to make the plan work, will need to involve teachers in organizing it, demonstrate that competencies can be accurately and impartially assessed, and clearly designate the specific types of responsibilities expected in each position.

Team Teaching. This instructional arrangement breaks from the one-teacher-per-class system by involving two or more teachers who plan instruction and evaluation cooperatively for a group of students usually the size of two to five conventional classes. The class may range in size from 50 to over 180 students, two to six teachers may participate, and the class may be organized at times as one group, several small groups, or for individual instruction. Teams may be selected on the basis of the teacher's specialization or teachers who have special talents that complement one another. Usually a team leader with organizational and curriculum development abilities is selected. Differentiated staffing employs team teaching, but this hierarchical model is not a prerequisite for using team teaching, as some plans use teachers of equal or similar status. The ability of competent team members to work together cooperatively, agree upon objectives, and delegate responsibilities is essential for successful team teaching.

Among the advantages of team teaching are: it allows greater utilization of personnel, space, material, and equipment; it offers students an opportunity to find a teacher with whom they relate effectively; it permits students to work in large groups, small groups, and engage in individual study; and it is more likely to provide a more perceptive diagnosis of learning difficulties and a more objective evaluation of achievement because two or more teachers are involved. Teachers benefit as well. They receive stimulation from observing their colleagues, by being observed, and by sharing ideas. Teachers also prepare more carefully and exert greater effort when under observation, and it is an opportunity for more experienced teachers to help less experienced ones.

Yet despite these advantages, many difficulties have arisen in team teaching. One problem lies in organizing the team. Able team leaders and team members are hard to find; large amounts of time are required for preparation and planning and are not always available; and confusion arises at times over the team leader's role—whether to supervise teachers or instruct students. As for students, they may take advantage of different expectations of teachers and pit them against one another. Students may also find that members of the team have different grading practices.

Open Education. This innovation emerged in Great Britain about twenty-five years ago and was popularized in the United States during the 1970s. It drew upon the findings of Susan Issacs and Jean Piaget. The term "open" may be somewhat misleading because it suggests large undivided spaces and removable partitions; however, open education can be conducted in classrooms that are traditional in a physical sense.

A number of characteristics are shared by open education classrooms. In the open classroom, the teacher may observe patterns of growth outlined by Piaget. The teacher instructs and guides learning in small groups or individually rather than instructing the class as a whole. Flexible scheduling is used, with many activities progressing simultaneously. And the abolition of a required curriculum permits children to make some decisions about their work. It is also characteristic that grading is deemphasized; that children learn at their own pace and in terms of their own learning style, and that the teacher's role is that of a diagnostician, guide, and stimulator. Above all, "the whole child" is recognized—intellectually, emotionally, morally, socially, and physically.

Open education, while it shares similarities with the early progressive movement in the United States, differs insofar as it is used in more public than private schools, is more structured, provides an active role for the teacher, and offers more of a planned environment than child-centered progressive schools. Open education also diverges from free schools (which will be discussed shortly) by usually placing more emphasis on cognitive development, providing greater curriculum structure, a more direct leadership role for teachers, and circumscribing more precisely the range and types of choices given to children.

The chief difference between open-space schools and open education is in the flexible architectural arrangements. Research evidence, however, does not support real differences in learning or teaching outcomes. Changes in architectural design in and of themselves do not make a difference. In open education, affective factors such as self-concept, creativity, independence, attitude toward school, and curiosity do show measurable improvement. Nevertheless, the divergent definitions of open education and the evaluative criteria are too varied to arrive at conclusive evidence that open classrooms are better than traditional ones.

Recent Alternatives

Education Vouchers. Dissatisfaction with public education has led to alternative proposals for the use of resources. The voucher plan would finance elementary and secondary education through certificates given by government to parents of schoolage children. The parents select the school of their choice—public, private, or parochial—and present the certificate as payment for instruction in the chosen school; the school then presents the voucher to the government and receives a check for a stipulated amount based on a formula.

Early voucher plans were essentially unregulated and posed threats of violating the separation of church and state and increasing segregated schooling. In contrast, Christopher Jencks and others have developed a highly regulated voucher plan that seeks to overcome the serious shortcomings of the earlier proposals.

The Jencks' plan would create an Education Voucher Agency (EVA) at the community level for receiving government funds for financing schools. It would be locally controlled and would resemble a board of education except that it would not operate any schools of its own; responsibility for operating schools would be retained by public and private school boards. The EVA would determine the eligibility of public and nonpublic schools to participate in the plan.

The purposes of the voucher plan are to provide more education options, break the "monopoly" of the public schools, and enable poor parents to have the same choice as wealthy parents as to where they can send their children to school. The vouchers would offer each applicant roughly an equal chance of admission into any school by taking each student who applied to a particular school, except when the number of applicants exceeded the number of places, in which case a lottery would be used to fill half of its places. Each school would have to show that it had at least accepted as high a proportion of ethnic-group students as had applied. Vouchers from children of lower-income families would have higher redemption value because their education would likely be more costly. Additionally, EVA would pay the transportation costs of all children in order that low-income families would not be inordinately burdened. EVA would also disseminate information about all schools in the area enabling parents to make intelligent choices.

The Office of Economic Opportunity made grants to several communities to study the feasibility of the voucher plan, but only the community of Alum Rock, California, with the aid of a federal grant, decided to try it. Alum Rock's plan, however, differed from Jencks' by using only public schools and providing alternative programs within them, and using the board of education in lieu of EVA. After four years of operation, it was found that teachers, students, and parents liked the plan but standardized test scores were either equivalent to national norms or, in some instances, were below them. In any case, the Alum Rock program does not actually test the original plan; it explores a new option instead.

Excluding Alum Rock, a number of serious deficiencies can be found in voucher plans. A basic tenet of voucher proponents is that public schools constitute a monopoly, and consequently, the use of vouchers would open many new options to parents. Voucher advocates frequently use the free-marketplace analogy that vouchers would do for education what free enterprise has done for the economy and its productivity. Schools, however, are relatively decentralized and do compete with private schools and with each other: in their sports program, for teachers, appropriations, special projects, and the like. The market analogy is misleading insofar as profit-making firms sell their products to anyone who has cash or credit, whereas private schools are selective and not open to everyone. Moreover, for the voucher system to result in the benefits it purports to offer, nonpublic schools would have to be far more innovative and experimental in their programs and organization; as of now only a small number exhibit these characteristics.

Furthermore, once nonpublic schools accept substantial state funds, they are likely to be more thoroughly regulated. It may mean that parochial schools would no longer be able to offer sectarian religious courses, and all nonpublic schools would be subject to desegregation rulings. Voucher plans make no provision for eliminating discrimination in the hiring of teachers. Nonpublic schools may also be required to observe judicial standards of academic freedom.

Public schools, under a voucher plan, would not likely receive additional tax funds but nonpublic schools would be free to increase their endowments, thereby leading to greater inequities. The voucher system could increase public costs by paying nonpublic-school tuitions, staffing and operating the EVA, creating new buildings and facilities for private schools, and underusing those of public schools (because of decreased enrollment, increased transportation costs, and inefficient use of tenured public-school teachers). Thus, in view of the substantial shortcomings of the voucher plan, it may be wiser to offer greater curricular alternatives in public schools.

Performance Contracting. This innovation, which rose and fell in the early 1970s, was one manifestation of the widespread concern that schools should be more accountable to the public at large. Performance contracting is a procedure by which a school system enters into an agreement with a private firm to take over from the school certain instructional tasks in order to achieve a set of designated objectives. The school system can contract with the firm to teach such subjects as reading and mathematics or to assume responsibility for the instructional program of an entire elementary or secondary school. For a stipulated sum of money the firm guarantees certain results within a designated time period. Should the company fall short of its goals, a lesser amount is paid; whereas, when goals are exceeded, some contracts award bonuses. An independent audit team is employed by the local education agency to monitor execution of the contract and certify results to the agency for purposes of payment.

In 1969, a Texarkana, Arkansas, school district entered into a contract with a private firm to take over part of their instructional program. Gary, Indiana, received a four-year grant in 1970 in excess of $2 million to experiment with performance contracting in an effort to overcome "gross underachievement." A number of the other school districts throughout the country have initiated performance contracting. The Office of Economic Opportunity (OEO) in 1970 sponsored eighteen experiments in performance contracting at a cost of $5 to $6 million. The test results at the end of the year for the experimental and control groups show that both groups did equally poorly in terms of overall averages, but these averages, with very few exceptions, are very nearly the same in each grade for the best and worst students in the sample. Thus, the future of performance contracting as a means of insuring accountability — at least in its present form — is seriously in doubt.

Free Schools. As a response to the call for a new type of learning environment, free schools sprang up across the country in the late 1960s. Using city storefronts, old barns, barracks, abandoned churches, and even people's homes, these schools attempted to bring about greater freedom of learning through humanistic principles. Many of the directors of these schools believed that freedom was good, even though "freedom" was not always clearly defined or examined.

While the majority of these schools are organized by middle class white parents and attended by their children, occasionally integrated school settings can be found — in fact, there are a few free schools with little or no tuition located in economically depressed neighborhoods. The free schools utilize both early and neoprogressive methods, borrow ideas on child development from Piaget, and mix in here and there some practices from the English infant schools. Schools range from a Summerhill-type atmosphere to that of a more structured one, but generally children are not pushed to acquire basic skills before they show a readiness to learn.

The precarious financial basis upon which most free schools rest results in an average life span of about eighteen months — scarcely a beginning and surely no time to test out a program. Financial instability, joined with the more independent, idiosyncratic personalities who are drawn to establishing free schools engenders a further basis for their transience. Additionally, free schools have been criticized for being accessible primarily to middle class whites and for giving little emphasis to basic skills and vocational training that ethnic groups might find useful for their survival. With the emergence during the 1970s of alternatives within public schools, there has been less incentive to establish free schools and the movement has rapidly declined.

PLACING INNOVATIONS IN PERSPECTIVE

Educational Theories. Three educational theories that have been influential during the past several decades are behaviorism, progressivism, and essentialism. Proponents of each of these theories have contributed certain perspectives and sponsored or opposed certain innovations.

Behaviorism has been the dominant American psychology since the militant behaviorism first enunciated by John B. Watson in 1913. It spread into education through intelligence testing and then through a larger measurement movement that sought to make education scientific, as in the case of Edward Lee Thorndike who sought to propound laws of learning. Behaviorists study overt behavior and only those human and animal phenomena subject to measurement; thus they reject introspection and mentalistic concepts and rely instead on observing stimulus-response patterns. One of the chief applications of behaviorism in therapeutic situations is the rise of behavior modification.

In education, behaviorists have sponsored teaching machines, programmed learning materials, computer assisted instruction, competency testing, some forms of accountability, homogeneous groupings and tracking. One need not be a behaviorist to support one or more of these innovations; it is just more likely that a behaviorist would do so than someone who espouses a different theory or who is not entirely clear what theory to support. Behaviorists, in seeking scientific precision, are atomistic rather than holistic in approach; they seek to break things down into their smallest meaningful components for either study or educational use. Response patterns can be as simple as finger twitches or knee jerks. Similarly, programmed materials break learning bits to their smallest meaningful units. Since behaviorists also attempt to make accurate measurement of human abilities, they are usually interested in the classification of abilities and placing students in learning situations with peers of similar abilities. Thus they believe that homogeneous groupings will more likely ensure that no one will be held back by slower classmates or have to move more rapidly than they are able to do. Other behavioristic programs include competency education (which is based upon the assumption that human competencies can be identified), student acquisition of designated competencies, and tests designed to measure their attainment.

Essentialism, one of the older theories in the history of education, was prominent in American education during the 1930s and 1950s and then again in the 1970s in the back-to-basics movement. Essentialism emphazies transmitting the cultural heritage to all students, seeing that they are soundly trained in the fundamentals, and ensuring that they study the basic disciplines. In this way students will become educated persons and good citizens. Students, however, cannot always study what strikes their immediate interest, but must study what they need to enable them to assume responsible adult roles. This means that discipline and sound study habits should be stressed in order to master fundamental disciplines. Essentialists believe these disciplines are best grasped in a subject curriculum rather than vitiated in a broad fields curriculum or interdisciplinary programs.

The back-to-basics movement, since it focuses largely on the 3 Rs and firm disciplinary standards, is actually a truncated essentialist program because it fails to give equal weight to the other elements in the cultural heritage. In other words, it is generally consonant with essentialist principles but underdeveloped. Moreover, some back-to-basics programs advocate corporal punishment while some prominent essentialists would not do so. Essentialists would also want schools to be accountable, but the operational principles of accountability follow behavioristic lines more closely.

Progressivism in American education began slowly around the turn of the century; as a formal movement it reached its zenith in the late 1930s only to decline precipitously by the mid-1950s. It rose gain in the late 1960s in different forms and under new rubrics; it was largely submerged, however, by the overriding emphasis on accountability during the 1970s. Early progressives stressed the needs and interests of children and the importance of placing them in a learning environment where they could develop naturally, be free to express themselves, and nurture their creative development. This meant that the progressive teacher would shape learning experiences to students rather than the converse, that the subject curriculum would be modified to take into consideration individual differences, and that the teacher would be a guide, a facilitator of learning, rather than an authority figure.

Essentialists did not appreciate the progressives' departure from exact studies in the disciplines and their alleged abandonment of rigorous standards of scholastic achievement for projects based on immediate interests. Behaviorists found the atomistic approach in conflict with the holistic approach of humanistic education (a form that progressivism took during the 1970s). Rather than precise measurement of abilities and achievement in homogeneous groups, the neo-progressives stressed heterogeneous classrooms and evaluations of a qualitative type. Besides interdisciplinary programs and other departures from the subject curriculum, neoprogressives supported open classrooms, free schools, nongraded schools, alternatives within public schools, and various types of individualized instructional plans.

Ideologies in Education. Among the ideologies in education, meritocracy and egalitarianism have special bearing on innovations. Both of these ideologies have long been prominent in education, but egalitarianism has grown since the civil rights movement and the Elementary and Secondary Education Act of 1965.

The rewards in the meritocratic system go to those who achieve through demonstrated performance, rather than on the basis of race, religion, nationality, seniority, family background, politics, and other artificial distinctions commonly found in most societies. Instead, the abilities, skills, and types of performance are evaluated by merit. And those abilities most prized would be determined by the society's highest values and priorities. A meritocractic system is based on equal access to educational resources and opportunities so that those students with the potentials most valued by a given society would be in a position to best develop them and subsequently be rewarded for their use. Educational institutions are one of the chief mechanisms used by advanced industrial societies to screen and sort out those best qualified to assume careers and tasks that are highly esteemed and that demand greater abilities, responsibility and leadership. Tomorrow's leaders will be sorted out through the process of schooling by its competitive system of grading, promotion, honors, and awards. Those who fail will be notified that they were given a fair chance and must now assume societal roles consonant with demonstrated abilities.

The meritocrat would want to maintain equal access to education to assure that all talented youth have an opportunity to be identified and developed; therefore programs for the gifted and talented would be encouraged and competency education, if not construed too narrowly, would assure that certain measurable outcomes would be achieved. Meritocrats may at times join forces with essentialists in upholding standards, though the meritocrat would be more closely attuned than the essentialist to various sectors of society—government, business, industry, the military—to determine the standards needed.

Egalitarianism as an ideology renounces the policy of equal access because it fails to consider the handicaps and discrimination suffered by racial and ethnic miniorities; thus equal access continues to give children of the white majority an unequal chance to advance. Egalitarians would either favor equal outcomes or substantive equality or both. Equal outcomes would assure that the overall average achievement scores of the different school populations are essentially the same, whereas substantive equality would require a redistribution of wealth in order to abolish poverty (just how this would be handled would depend upon the particular plan). Those egalitarians who have not given up working with public education favor some compensatory education programs, community control of schools, bilingual education, multicultural education, and in some cases vouchers and free schools. These programs and plans, they believe, would best help the less advantaged and help to make society more just and egalitarian. The meritocrat would object to most of these proposals because they allegedly would result in the loss of a nation's talent and a subsequent rise of mediocrity. This would also bring about a leveling process whereby individual initiative and the achievement motive would be discouraged.

Whatever the respective merits of these theories and ideologies, one may want to look more closely at the basis for accepting or rejecting an innovation. It is no longer necessary to choose on an ad hoc basis if one wishes to adopt one of these theories or ideologies.

8
Managing Retrenchment

State aid to Michigan schools was frozen in 1983 by the governor to help solve the state's severe financial crisis. Other states — Illinois, Iowa, Idaho, Virginia, West Virginia, South Carolina, to name a few — have fallen short of state revenues to fulfill the state's budget. In some places, budget cuts were ordered; other states have proposed raising state spending through increases in gasoline and other taxes. School building closures and reductions in teacher salaries are some other measures employed. Proposition 13 in California and Proposition $2^1/2$ in Massachusetts substantially reduced property tax rates, a major source of public school funds.

Nationally, the number of high school seniors peaked in 1979 and will decline through 1994, demographers say. The number of eighteen to twenty-two year olds in the population will drop about 25 percent in those same years. The sharpest decline in births during the post-war baby boom period was among affluent white families. Government aid programs are unlikely to expand to help more lower income students attend college. An increase in the percentage of high school graduates going to college, however, could change the enrollment decline to moderate levels. More women and minority group members are getting a college education and more careers require a college degree. Enrollments are no longer dependent upon the eighteen to twenty-one age group as urban colleges attract more older adults. By 1990, older students will compose half the college population, requiring colleges to offer different educational services. And, if colleges increase the percentage who graduate, it would lessen enrollment drops. Many colleges in declining enrollment areas (Northeast and Midwest) are likely to recruit more vigorously in states where enrollment has not declined (Southwest and West). As for private colleges, more than twice as many private colleges have closed in the past decade as have opened, according to a study by the National Association of Colleges and Universities. Experts predict that as many as 300 of the nation's 1,250 private colleges may close their doors by the end of the decade.

The tenure system is threatened as well. Constrictive state budgets and declining enrollments are prompting many universities to reconsider the tenure process. Under the press of financial exigencies, some colleges and universities have fired tenured faculty. Regents at the University of Colorado and elsewhere have made tenure more difficult to receive and easier to lose. Other universities have eliminated entire departments and programs and have considered varied proposals for modifying the tenure process.

The selection by H. B. Pinkney shows the greater costs of urban schools, the deteriorating sources of financial support, and the paradox of America's wealth and its school financial problems. He offers five proposals for resolving the crisis. Victor J. Rose provides a case study of an Iowa community that engaged community participation in making difficult budget cuts.

An American Dilemma: Financing Public Education

H. B. Pinkney _____

H. B. Pinkney is bureau chief for Program Support Services, State Department of Education, Tallahassee, Florida.

Ever since the passage of Proposition 13 in California, Americans are discussing ways to reform and reduce taxes.

With inflation running rampant and many public school districts already in a financial "straightjacket," tax reform is likely to create still greater financial hardships for schools.

The problems of public school finance deepen as the "flight" of citizens, black and white, continues from urban to suburban areas, leaving those who are poor with the greatest need for all kinds of costly educational services. Garms, Guthrie and Pierce contend that "not only are the higher costs in cities largely unrecognized in school finance formulas, but also there is . . . inadequate compensation for the extra costs associated with educating children of poor and minority parents."[1]

These services require additional expenditures in order to educate those children who are left with so many deficiencies. The cost of educating a pupil is determined by the educational need of that pupil. Those who support and argue in favor of a plan based on the "same for everyone" as being equitable are failing to realize that there are many relevant differences among pupils.

In addition, the high cost of personnel and instructional materials, as well as other operating costs create a real inflation and the need for increased funding of public education. As an excuse, many Americans claim they don't understand the increasing cost of educating today's youth, especially urban. For example:

> There [is] a concentration of disadvantaged and handicapped pupils in the largest cities where the general financial situation [is] undergoing marked deterioration and where the cost of living [is] the highest in the state. Despite this situation, state aid systems [are] still geared to the 1920s when cities were rich and needed little aid, while their environs were poor.[2]

This writer would be the first to recognize and admit that additional funds for education are not positive proof that education for those served will improve. However, research supports the fact that if public education is to sur-

From H. B. Pinkney, "An American Dilemma: Financing Public Education," NASSP Bulletin *64 (November 1980): 68–73. Used by permission.*

---

[1]Walter I. Garms, James W. Guthrie, and Lawrence C. Pierce, *School Finance: The Economics and Politics of Public Education* (Englewood Cliffs, N.J. Prentice-Hall, Inc., 1978), p. 209.

[2]Margaret E. Goertz, Joy H. Moskowitz, and Judy G. Sinkin, *Plain Talk About School Finance,* National Institute of Education, HEW, May 1978, p. 1.

vive in urban or any other areas, adequate funding must be provided. The funding of public education must become a priority in America even if it means outside program monitoring and program changes that will produce effective results for all youngsters. Those citizens who seemingly fail to care about the survival of public education in urban areas fail to realize that the real destiny of all Americans is tied together. The destiny of all school systems (urban, suburban and private) is tied together; we all must share the concerns and blame and put the rhetoric into concrete action.[3]

ARE WE MISSING THE BOAT?

Without adequate funding for the support of public education, especially urban, we are failing miserably to provide meaningful educational programs for literally millions of inner-city and even rural children. And, with the passage of Howard Jarvis' Proposition 13, continued use of the property tax as a basis for financing public education becomes even more obsolete. Throughout legislative halls all over America, the focus is on tax reform and tax cutting.

Until the American people begin to realize the seriousness of the financial problems confronting urban and other school districts, we may be guilty of participating in the destruction of the next several generations of youth. Increasing evidence shows that the "education of the streets" already means more to a large percentage of urban children than what is officially being offered as formal education in the classrooms. The incredibly high rate of absenteeism causes one to wonder about our priorities and who *really* cares: ". . . statistical evidence points to the fact that, in some of our large urban areas, absenteeism (average daily membership) has reached 55 percent.

. . . Regardless of how much rhetoric . . . we utilize, with only 45 percent of the students in school and a large percentage of the others on the streets daily, we are 'missing the boat'."[4]

The continuous struggle for budget survival, in most urban school districts, generally takes a good bit of administrators' time. The "survival game" doesn't allow most urban school administrators time to place a focus upon program planning, program improvement, and problem solving, and those youngsters who are "fenced in" end up without even the basic skills.

The financial problem confronting public education is even more paradoxical when we consider the fact that America is the wealthiest nation in the world. More than one million school-age children recently remained on the streets at the opening of the school year because of a lack of funds.

A TIME TO RE-EXAMINE

Traditionally, public education has depended upon local property taxes for financial support. For years, the formula for funding public education has been inadequate, especially with the deteriorating changes in urban populations over the past three decades. Population shifts have placed a tremendous burden on the schools. As those groups who can most afford increased taxation exit from the cities, property deteriorates and those who are left are unable to or refuse to financially support social organizations such as the public schools. To salvage public education — especially urban — from future destruction, other levels, state and federal, of government must assume a much larger share of the ever increasing cost. "Although the federal government has increased its financial support for education, well over 80 percent of

[3]H. B. Pinkney, "Urban Education: The Rhetoric Goes On," *NASSP Bulletin,* March 1975, p. 48.

[4]*Ibid,* p. 47.

the money for elementary and secondary education still comes from state and local taxes."[5]

With the deteriorating tax base, increased responsibility for support of public education shifts from the local level to state and national levels, especially the former. Based upon the Constitution, public education is a state responsibility. The time has come for state and federal levels of government to re-examine their priorities and at all costs realize the dire need for increased funds for public education.

If state and federal governments fail to increase their financial support for public education for today's children, all levels of government are likely to end up spending many billions to support them when they reach adulthood or drop out of school. The alternative is that we either provide adequate funds for the support of public education and "pay now" as students, or prepare ourselves to "pay later" as adults, with compounded interest through other social agencies for their support.

Those who oppose increased funding of public education by state and federal levels of government under the guise of fear of loss of local control do so at a tremendous expense to millions of poor children who are victims of inadequate and unequal funds for public education. Historically, funds from all levels have been used to support organizations, groups and individuals, yet the myth about rigid state or federal control has not occurred.

Financing public education, especially urban, is a crucial issue and the local property tax can no longer be depended upon to carry a "lion's share" of financial support. This writer strongly recommends the following solutions:

- *Deteriorating Tax Base*—The traditional burden of financial support for public edu-

cation should be shifted from the district's local property taxes to state and federal levels, especially with increased funding by the former. Until this change occurs it will be impossible for urban school districts to improve educational programs for their clientele.

- *Full State Funding*—Vast differences in local property assessment and tax exemptions play havoc with the ratio of assessed valuation per pupil between rich and poor districts. Full state assumption of the cost of public education would solve many of the existing financial inadequacies in education.

  Full state funding would enable states to assume complete funding of public education and enable educational expenditure to be based upon needs rather than upon the wealth of a respective district.

- *Increased Federal Aid*—Increased federal funds must be provided through "categorical aid" to districts based upon the identified needs of the children. In urban or poor school districts where academic achievement is lowest and the need for many different kinds of services exist, the per pupil expenditure should be the highest. The unwarranted fears of federal control should no longer deter increased federal funding. Even if increased federal aid means increased federal control, such would be far less harmful than to permit the demise of public education. Some Americans are already advocating the voucher system as a replacement for public education and many others would support a Proposition 13 for their respective states.

- *Increased Funding vs. Improved Programs*—We can no longer take for granted that increased funding automatically improves educational programs. Quite often in the past, increased funds have not provided evidence of improved educational

---

[5]Leo Averbach, "Crucial Educational Issues," *Innovations and Issues in Education,* edited by Joseph F. Callahan and Leonard H. Clark (New York: Macmillan Publishing Company, 1977), p. 161.

programs. Through increased accountability, the public should demand that increased financial support shall be used for educational programs that will produce positive results for children.

- *Accountability*—Through increased surveillance we should insist that teachers who receive approximately 85 percent of the scarce dollars are held more accountable for the products they produce through some valid form of student growth measurement (testing). Through an effective monitoring system, we should insist that *all* classroom teachers are capable of helping children regardless of their cultural backgrounds. Education stands to benefit if greater official use is made of assessment techniques commonly used in industry (cost-effectiveness analysis). Where cost-effective measures are used, explicit and precise goals are agreed upon and means exist for measuring the degree to which they have been accomplished.

THE NEED IS NOW

The destiny of this nation is tied to the future of our youth. For youngsters in Philadelphia, Toledo, Cleveland, or any other city to be denied educational opportunities equal to others because funds are lacking only increases unsolvable future problems for *all* of us. I am unable to believe or accept Howard Jarvis' statement that even after the tax cut education gets too much money [in California] and everywhere else. Yes, the need does exist for a more cost-effective analysis of educational output, but not for *less* funds.

We often boast and brag about our nation's wealth, our highly industrialized society, our world leadership, and even our concern and services to mankind; yet we have failed to give priority to education with adequate funds. In spite of our bragging, evidence is mounting that urban school systems are deteriorating in many instances because there's a lack of funds. Some writers have even said that the financial problems are cancerous. In most cases, the current system of financing public education remains "unjust and unequal" and if we are really concerned about the future, the urgency now exists for us to put our priorities in rank order.

It is unfair for us to force millions of young people to spend a lifetime waiting and to permit school districts to deteriorate, while through rhetorical arguments and debates we try to decide if the need exists for additional funds or whether or not to support and pass another Jarvis-Gann type Proposition 13 for our states. Our human resources are far too valuable for us to use or create any more arguments or excuses other than to adequately finance public education *now*. The dilemma of financing public education in America must be eradicated.

How to Let the Community Help You Make the Tough Decisions on Budget Cuts

Victor J. Ross _____

Victor J. Ross was formerly an assistant superintendent in the Bettendorf (Iowa) Community Schools and is now an administrator in the Aurora Public Schools, Aurora, Colorado.

"The situation has reached the crisis level," the superintendent solemnly intones. "The legislature has reduced education funding for next year below the level originally promised. We are going to have to cut till we bleed, and there simply aren't going to be any sacred cows."

You look at the grim faces of the board members around the table and reach for an antacid tablet to soothe your churning stomach. It's true, all right. State revenues are down and the federal government is not about to raise taxes to bail out the schools. Those days appear over. But you didn't run for the board of education thinking you'd ever have to make decisions of this magnitude. Cut staff by 10 percent? Eliminate athletics? Close two schools?

It doesn't matter whether the money crunch was caused by a local phenomenon, such as Proposition 13 in California, Proposition $2^1/_2$ in Massachusetts, or the extensive loss of state revenue in Iowa. And there's no use crying over the recession or runaway inflation. What *does* matter is that you don't have the money you need to run the kind of high quality education program you and your community both want and expect.

You're going to have to cut programs and people. But where? Who? Which programs and what people? What's *really* important and *really* essential? Would it be better to kill the athletic program for a year to save $150,000 or to cut ten teachers and let class sizes zoom to 35 or 40?

Whether you're a board member or an administrator in this kind of situation, you undoubtedly are capable of coming up with some answers and decisions, but you probably would like to know how effective those decisions will be. *For sure* you'd like to know how well your public is going to receive them.

Impossible?

Not by a long shot. If you have at least four weeks—two months is even better—then you have enough time to involve parents, teachers, students, and community members in the decision-making process. You have enough time to gather your community together for a conference to assess what works well and what is important in your schools—to learn what your public considers the genuine sacred cows.

Such a conference won't make your job any easier when you cut the budget, but it will give you the confidence to make reductions in areas of lowest priority to your constituents. And you'll have some good data to back you up.

The Bettendorf (Iowa) school system (K-12; enrollment: 5,400), like many others in the country, recently faced a drastic budget situation. The governor first called for a series of across-the-board spending cuts for the current year, and then he unloaded the really bad news: The money promised for next year also was going to be reduced. For our school system, that meant the revenue for next year would be $333,500 less than promised; we would have to cut that much to balance our budget. Put very simply, cutting that much money might mean 20 fewer teachers in our 300-teacher school system.

"Isn't there some way we can find out what's really important, what really makes this the good school system we know it is?" asked our board president. "We've got to know where to start."

But where? Every board member had spontaneous suggestions for cuts, but there was no agreement: "Reopen negotiations," one said. "No, cut teachers," said another. "*Never* cut teachers," grimaced a third. "Let's get rid of the buses." "Defer capital outlay." On and on it went, with much heat and little light.

It began to resemble something out of an old *Mission: Impossible* episode; but the more we thought about the board president's question, the more appealing became the idea of the community conference.

After a few planning meetings, that's what the administration decided to try. These are the steps we followed:

Step One. The administration took the idea to the school system's Citizens Education Council, an advisory group made up of parents from every school in the district. We asked them what they thought of the idea and — if they liked it — whether six or seven of them would serve as a steering committee to help us do it. The answer was Yes on both counts.

Step Two. We met with the steering committee, which comprised five parents and three school board members, and decided to hold the conference one month later. We then drafted a letter of invitation and agreed to aim for a goal of 120 conference participants. We also agreed that, ideally, the 120 should be made up of 30 people representing each of four groups: parents, teachers, students, and community members who no longer have children in school.

Our data processing people provided us with random lists of names for the first three groups within three days. For the final group of community members, we went to the city directory. In three weeks' time we confirmed attendance by 138 participants. Letting people know what was at stake — a priority ordering of school programs to help in budget cutting — had a lot to do with the quick, positive response. Our community conference, we made it clear, was not going to be any ice-cream social. (A special note to keep in mind: When looking for any number of people for a conference, send out twice as many invitations as the number of participants you hope will attend. Even with a critical topic for the agenda, the rate of acceptance is normally about 50 percent. And even if it turns out to be 100 percent, you can only be delighted.)

Step Three. On a Thursday evening, commencing at 7 p.m. in the high school cafeteria, we held the Community Conference to Assess Positive Program Factors.

Our superintendent opened the proceedings with a short, direct speech. He thanked the people in attendance and then explained the situation. "This is not an attempt to find reasons for patting ourselves on the back," Superintendent Lee Grebner said. "We face serious budget difficulties, and we need your help; we *want* your help in determining program priorities. We are going to have to cut the budget, and the cuts are going to hurt. We aren't crying wolf. Please concentrate tonight on helping us identify and set priorities for those things that are most essential to the high quality education program in this school district."

Following Grebner's remarks, the 118 participants (there were 20 no-shows, another inevitability to plan for) viewed a ten-minute tape-and-slide show high-lighting all of the schools' programs. That completed, individual groups received one-page lists of program components and explanations about each item. We tried to list everything we wanted the participants to think about, but we emphasized that it could in no way be considered comprehensive; they could add their own items.

The stage was set. We had done our best to give our participants a crash course in education and to acquaint them—albeit briefly—with important education ingredients they might otherwise not have remembered. It was time to get to work. We asked each six-person group to brainstorm and then to write down responses to this question: "What are the education components that contribute to the excellence of our schools?"

This is not the time to register your complaint about the hot lunch program, we reminded them. Accentuate the positive, and don't pass judgment on someone else's idea. Write it all down.

And write they did. The buzzing at the 20 tables and the complete devotion to the task was enough to warm the heart of the sternest algebra teacher. In 30 minutes, each of the groups had two large sheets of butcher paper filled with ideas.

Next, we had each group exchange papers with the neighboring table; then we directed everyone to review the ideas others had placed on the lists, to write comments in the margins if they wished, and to assign a priority value to each idea: a 1 for a poor idea, a 5 for an excellent idea, or any appropriate number in between.

After 20 minutes, we repeated the exchange with a third table, and 15 minutes later we asked every group to take back its original list and assess the reactions and priority values provided by the other groups. Again, the task received complete attention and concentration. It was remarkable.

By 8:30 p.m., only 90 minutes after the meeting had begun, each group took its own work and began the final step. Participants wrote each idea on an index card, rewriting or clarifying it if necessary, and then assigned it a priority value. This was based on the group's opinion and on the priorities assigned by the other two groups. Shortly after 9 p.m., we had nearly 350 cards, and the conference was adjourned.

Step Four. The steering committee went into action the following week, sorting the cards into groups: staff, special programs, supplemental programs, transportation, and other. Once the cards were assembled in categories, the committee members sorted out duplicate ideas and then added up the total priority points. A quick example: If the school system's reading program was cited as important by eight different groups, and each one gave it a numerical priority rating of 5, then its total value was 40. The results are shown in the table [on page 150].

Were the results helpful?

"Absolutely," attests Superintendent Grebner. "They were invaluable to us when we eventually had to develop a recommendation to cut $333,500 from next year's budget. Staff members were assigned the highest value, obviously, and we also knew which programs were most highly regarded."

Reducing or even eliminating the schools' Outdoor Education program, for instance, was originally considered a strong possibility, according to Grebner. "But when we saw the assessment results [which assigned it Number 7 on the priority list], we knew it was imperative to look harder for something else. We hated to cut Arts in Education [Number 42]. We viewed it as

HOW ONE COMMUNITY RATES SCHOOL PROGRAMS

In Bettendorf, Iowa, we asked 118 parents, teachers, students, and community members to rank every school program according to importance and to assign each one a priority value (**PV**). After tallying the number of times each program ws mentioned (**TM**) and after totaling the priority value points assigned, school officials were able to see how components ranked. Here's what the process revealed:

Rank	Education Component	TM	PV
1.	Teachers	20	98
2.	Elementary music	20	91
3.	Elementary physical education	18	80
4.	Elementary art	17	73
5.	Elementary libraries	14	62
6.	Instrumental music	14	59
7.	Outdoor education	14	52
8.	Athletics	13	52
9.	Intramural sports	13	51
10.	Low class size	10	50
11.	Reading, including Title I	8	40
12.	Community involvement	8	39
13.	Individualized learning	8	38
14.	Gifted and talented education	10	36
15.	Drama	8	36
16.	Basic education	7	33
17.	Instructional supplies and books	7	33
18.	Summer school/curriculum planning	8	32
19.	Libraries (all schools)	7	32
20.	Special education	7	31
21.	Career education	8	29
22.	Foreign language	7	29
23.	Pre-elementary program	6	29
24.	Librarians	6	29
25.	School newspapers	6	22
26.	Testing	5	20
27.	Yearbook		5
28.	Administrators		4
29.	Neighborhood schools		4
30.	Maintenance staff		4
31.	Custodians		4
32.	Vocal music		4
33.	Counselors		4
34.	Athletic trip transportation		4
35.	Project READY		4
36.	Driver education		3
37.	Excellent facilities		3
38.	Debate		3
39.	Buses (regular routes)		3
40.	Secretaries		3
41.	Computers (courses and equipment)		3
42.	Arts in education		3
43.	Staff inservice		3
44.	Strong academic program		2
45.	Communications		2
46.	Industrial arts		2
47.	Curriculum-related field trips		2
48.	Class guides		2
49.	Teacher associates		2
50.	Instrumental music-lessons		2
51.	Special education busing		2
52.	Planetarium		2
53.	Swimming pool		2
54.	Teacher recruiting and hiring		1
55.	Clerks		1
56.	Capital improvments		1
57.	Audiovisual equipment		1
58.	Speech therapy program		1
59.	High school cooperative program		1
60.	Length of school day		1
61.	Overtime pay		1

one of our most innovative and highly regarded programs, but it was clear from the assessment conference that our people don't see it that way." When selected administrators met later, they considered whether any federal or state regulations prevented cutting any program that the conference participants placed low on the priority list; fortunately, this wasn't a factor in deciding what to cut. Outdoor Education stayed. Arts in Education didn't.

Board members, teachers, parents, and students all agreed that trimming an already tight budget was difficult, but the positive program assessment took a good deal of the sting out of the process. If you have from four to eight weeks to make critical decisions, then it pays to take the time to assess your program through a community conference.

The payoff: a balanced budget. When Bettendorf's school board met a month after the conference to vote on Superintendent Grebner's recommendations, members faced an audience of more than a hundred people and three television news cameras. But they also had the assess-ment results in front of them, and the board unanimously approved Grebner's recommendations for cuts. There were literally *no* discouraging words from the audience.

DISCUSSION QUESTIONS AND ACTIVITIES

1. Why is a finance plan based on the same for everyone actually inequitable, according to Pinkney?

2. Why are costs higher in city schools?

3. Why are local property taxes inadequate for sufficient public school support?

4. What financial reforms does Pinkney propose? What is the likelihood that these proposals, taken as a package, will achieve the results claimed?

5. Would increased federal aid lead to greater federal control?

6. Pinkney recommends the use of accountability and monitoring student achievement. Review the selections in this book on com-petency education to determine whether this proposal is warranted.

7. Read some of the Suggested Readings below and compare them with Pinkney's proposal.

8. Should the community be involved in decisions about public school budget cuts? If they should participate, to what extent and in what ways?

9. Analyze the effectiveness of community participation in the case study of the Bettendorf (Iowa) Public Schools. What would you have done differently?

10. Attend a local school board meeting when the budget is to be discussed. Observe how the budget is handled and report to class on your findings.

SUGGESTED READINGS

Retrenchment in Public Schools

Adams, E. Kathleen. "The Fiscal Conditions of the States." *Phi Delta Kapan* 63 (May 1982): 598–600.

Bakalis, Michael J. "American Education and the Meaning of Scarcity." *Phi Delta Kappan* 63 (October 1981): 102–5.

Benson, C. S. *The Economics of Public Education,* 3rd ed. Boston: Houghton Mifflin, 1978.

DeLuca, Nicholas. "Don't Camouflage Budget Cuts." *Executive Educator* 4 (April 1982): 30.

Doherty, Victor W. and James J. Fenwick. "Can Budget Reduction be Rational?" *Educational Leadership* 39 (January 1982): 253–57

Garms, W. I., J. W. Guthrie, and L. G. Pierce. *School Finance: The Economics and Politics of Public Education.* Englewood Cliffs, N.J.: Prentice-Hall, 1978.

Kirst, Michael W. "How to Improve Schools Without Spending More Money." *Phi Delta Kappan* 64 (September 1982): 6–8

"One Hundred Ways to Cut Costs in Your School System." *American School Board Journal* 165, No. 10 (1978): 37–45.

Parpart, Edmund R. and Mary Jane Broncato. "Avoiding Devastation When Confronted With Budget Cuts in Education" *Illinois School Research and Development* 18 (Winter 1982): 1–5.

Tyack, David and Elizabeth Hansot. "Hard Times, Hard Choices: The Case for Coherence in Public

School." *Phi Delta Kappan* 63 (April 1982): 511–15.

Tyler, Ralph W. "Dynamic Response in a Time of Decline." *Phi Delta Kappan* 63 (June 1982): 655–58.

Whetten, David A. "Organizational Response to Scarcity: Exploring the Obstacles to Innovative Approaches in Education." *Educational Administrative Quarterly* 17 (Summer 1981): 80–97.

Retrenchment in Higher Education

Bieschke, Suzanne M. *Retrenchment Review.* San Diego: Planning Office, University of California at San Diego, 1978.

Boland, James. "Retrenchment: Panacea or Placebo?" *Action in Teacher Education* 3 (Summer-Fall 1981): 85–89.

Campbell, Stephen D. "Response to Financial Stress." *New Directions for Higher Education* No. 38 (Successful Responses to Financial Difficulty) 10 (June 1982): 7–16.

Doyle, K. L. "Managing Higher Education in a Climate of Contraction: A Conceptual Model." *Journal of Tertiary Administration* 2 (October 1980): 139–49.

Hellweg, Susan A. and David A. Churchman. "The Academic Tenure System: Unplanned Obsolescence in an Era of Retrenchment." *Planning for Higher Education* 10 (Fall 1981): 16–18.

Ishler, Richard D. "Educational Retrenchment: A Model for Institutions of Higher Education." *Action in Teacher Education* 3 (Summer-Fall 1981): 75–80.

Journal of College and University Personnel Association 31, No. 1 (Spring 1980): 7–104. A series of articles from different perspectives on faculty retrenchment.

Journal of College and University Personnel Association 31, No. 3-4 (Fall-Winter, 1980): 136–203. Another series of articles about retrenchment, focusing on doctorate granting institutions, comprehensive universities and colleges, liberal arts colleges, and two-year colleges and universities.

Lepkowski, Wil. "Research Universities Face New Fiscal Realities." *Chemical Engineering News* 59 (November 1981): 23–24, 29–32.

Leslie, Larry L. "The Financial Prospects for Higher Education in the 1980's." *Journal of Higher Education* 51 (January-February 1980): 1–17.

Mayhew, Lewis B. *Surviving the Eighties.* San Francisco: Jossey-Bass, 1979.

Mingle, James R. and Associates. *Challenges of Retrenchment.* San Francisco: Jossey-Bass, 1981.

Nolting, Earl. "Recession in Academe: Development of Policies for Retrenchment." *Personnel and Guidance Journal* 60 (November 1981): 165–68.

Ratcliff, James L. "The Role of Needs Assessment in a Period of Retrenchment." *Community Services Catalyst* 12 (Spring 1982): 21–23.

Schutz, Richard E. "The Conduct of Educational R & D in an Era of Limits." *Educational Researcher* 10 (December 1981): 13–18.

Stevenson, Mike R. and R. Don Waller. "Financial Decision Making in a Period of Retrenchment." *New Directions for Community Colleges* 9 (September 1981): 83–93.

Weathersby, George B. "Scarce Resources Can Be a Golden Opportunity for Higher Education." *Change* 14 (March 1982): 12–13.

9

Competency Education and Minimal Competency Testing

A growing grass roots movement, beginning with parents, employees, and interested citizens, has been pushing for minimal competency testing. These concerns have recently made their impact on legislators so that now six states have passed legislation, a dozen states are close to passage, and ten state boards have changed requirements on their own authority. Of the thirty-six states developing minimal competency tests, less than half plan to use the examinations as a requirement for high school graduation. By the mid-1980s most states will likely have instituted minimal competency standards. It is widely held that incompetent students lacking in basic reading and mathematical skills have been certified as competent by being awarded high school diplomas and, even in some cases, granted college degrees. Norms on standardized achievement test scores, college admission scores, and National Assessment of Educational Progress show declines in student achievement over the past decade. Proponents of minimal competency testing believe that the use of such tests will actually increase achievement by motivating students to learn in order to attain certain goals and rewards.

Competency education holds that not only are there certain competencies needed in the respective professions—law, medicine, engineering, and others—but a basic set of competencies are needed by each high school graduate in order to function successfully in society. Though the experts may differ over the specific competencies to be included, they do agree that every student should at least attain a minimal level before being awarded a diploma. It is also believed that these competencies can be observed and measured through the performances of students in testing situations, even though differences of opinion exist about the content of such tests and to whom and under what circumstances they should be administered. One aspect of competency education is minimal competency testing; another is competency based teacher education, designed to assure that prospective teachers demonstrate designated competencies that a good teacher would be expected to have.

Various objections have been raised against minimal competency testing. Some wonder whether the tests will be fair if imposed on secondary students late in their program with little prior notice. School programs may also have to be changed to prepare students for these competencies which may, in turn, become the curriculum itself—a serious threat to reduction and narrowing of curricula. Danger also lies in the minimum becoming the maximum. Others ask how the minimum is to be determined.

Competency Based Education

H. G. Rickover

Hyman George Rickover (b. 1900) took his B.S. degree at the U.S. Naval Academy and received an M.S. in Electrical Engineering from Columbia University. His naval career began in 1922, and he rose in the ranks, serving in the submarine project with Atomic Energy Commission at Oak Ridge in 1946 and continued in developing the atomic submarine with the Bureau of Ships, 1947–81. He was responsible for the development and construction of the first atomic submarine, U.S.S. Nautilus, and the first nuclear powered electric utility station at Shippingport, Pennsylvania. Admiral Rickover has been decorated by both British and French governments, is the recipient of the Enrico Fermi award for contributions to atomic science, and the Presidential Medal of Freedom. During the late fifties and early sixties Admiral Rickover's tough criticisms of American education were expressed in his Education and Freedom, Swiss Schools and Ours: Why Theirs are Better; *and* American Education — A National Failure. *Philosophically, he is an essentialist.*

Members of the education community suggest that I have no business speaking on education — that I should leave education to the experts. They say, in effect: "If you don't tell us how to run our schools, we won't tell you how to design your nuclear ships." A professor from Columbia University Teachers College once told *The New York Times* I advocated that we "educate the best and shoot the rest." When he was questioned about this, he replied that I had not actually said this, but he thought it was what I believed. The one I like best, though, is what the superintendent of my local school district has called me — a "Neanderthal reactionary."

I believe it is a fundamental responsibility and moral obligation of every citizen to point out problems of public concern when he sees them, and to do what he can to set them right. If you do not feel comfortable with what I have to say, I want to reassure you that my remarks are intended to challenge, not to alienate. I speak as a friend of education, not as an adversary.

During the past quarter of a century as head of the Navy's Nuclear Propulsion Program, I have had a unique opportunity to judge the products of our schools. In searching out young officers to meet the demands of this program, I have interviewed, over the last three decades, more than 12,000 top graduates from 150 colleges and universities. I look for people with the ability to think for themselves; who understand the basic principles of the courses they have taken; and who speak clearly. I find some who are well-qualified. But a growing number do not measure up to their diplomas.

It is not uncommon to interview a recent graduate from a so-called "good" college with a degree in mathematics who cannot solve a tenth grade algebra problem. I find graduates with degrees in electrical engineering who do not know the difference between direct and alternating current.

In case after case, not only in engineering, mathematics, and science, but in history, foreign language, economics, and other fields, I find students who have excellent academic records, but who are unable to discuss even the fundamentals of their disciplines. From what I see, the basic knowledge shown by recent graduates is much less than that shown by those I interviewed 15 years ago. Yet each had received good grades, and therefore, believed he had learned what was expected of him.

I also see the products of our secondary schools—the enlisted men in the naval nuclear program. These are selected from the top high school graduates. Yet, in recent years, I have had to teach remedial courses in the basics of mathematics, physics, and chemistry to prepare them for nuclear power school.

Similar problems obtain elsewhere in the Navy, where there is difficulty finding young men who read well enough to perform their jobs. For example, recently a sailor tried to repair a diesel engine simply by looking at the illustrations, because he could not read the instructions. He caused $250,000 damage. Because many recruits cannot read adequately, the Navy now has to conduct a six-week remedial course to raise the reading skill of high school graduates to the sixth grade level.

This problem is not unique to the Navy. A parallel to the Navy's experience exists in nearly every aspect of life. Employers must now teach basic skills that should have been learned in elementary school. More and more colleges are compelled to conduct remedial courses for high school graduates who are inadequately prepared in reading, writing, and mathematics. A few colleges, like American University in Washington, D.C., have now begun to require all students to pass competency tests in reading, writing, and mathematics, before receiving a degree.

Despite rising grades, test scores on college entrance examinations and various achievement tests have been dropping steadily for over a decade. The National Assessment of Educational Progress reports that the writing ability of teenagers has declined. Diplomas, or even good grades, no longer accurately represent actual academic accomplishment.

Many factors have contributed to this decline in student achievement. We live in a society governed by conspicuous waste. We squander human energies in the pursuit of meaningless diplomas. With our ever-increasing obsession with television, homework and leisure reading have become endangered species. Hard work is no longer a driving force.

Parents are also responsible. Many spend little time with their children or do not show enough interest in their children's school work. They subscribe to the belief, common in our affluent society, that any problem can be solved by spending more money. But the education of youth requires more than money; it requires of parents personal dedication and investment of time.

Schools cannot fully compensate for lack of parental involvement or for all manner of societal problems. But they do bear substantial responsibility for the decline in student achievement. Many schools, spurred by parent and school board demand for "innovation," have made it possible for students to avoid courses that provide a solid grounding in reading, writing, and mathematics. There has been a decline in enrollment for basic academic courses. These have been supplanted by less demanding electives or pleasant extracurricular activities. Moreover, in many schools the number of instructional hours per school year has declined.

Many schools have become preoccupied with instilling "relevance" in education. Substantial sums have been wasted in programs directed more toward providing amusement than developing the ability to sort facts and make intelligent decisions.

These programs are couched in the jargon of systems analysis and other pseudoscience mumbo-jumbo. They place a high priority on freedom of choice in selecting courses, without ensuring that the choices are structured to meet academic needs. At this stage in their development, most children are not competent to decide what is in their own best interest or how much "creative freedom" they should be permitted.

Many schools foster attitudes that do not prepare students for the world's harsh realities. They promote the notion that learning must be easy and entertaining. This idea is cruel to the child and dangerous to society; children then grow up believing they need not struggle to excel. There is simply no way to combine the instant provision of happiness with the business of learning to read, write, and calculate.

Learning can be interesting, rewarding, and exciting, but it requires effort. It is work. No learning takes place, just as no ditch gets dug, without work. Mental sweat is required of the student who would acquire the skills, concepts, and information necessary to master a subject. Preaching the doctrine that learning should be easy implies that society has an obligation to make life easy, and promotes the already far too prevalent attitude against hard work. If our goal is to entertain our children, we can do so far more cheaply than by sending them to school.

There is also the matter of "equal educational opportunity," a noble concept which some educators, by carrying it to illogical extremes, have subverted. Properly, equal educational opportunity means removing the access barriers to education, especially for minorities. It means giving each student a chance to grow to the limits of his ability without regard to race or class.

Unfortunately, some educators distort this concept to mean that all children are entitled to the same academic recognition, whether they have earned it or not. As a result, poor academic performance is often overlooked or rewarded, especially if the student is a member of a minority or is poor.

Many students who have not mastered the subject matter are promoted anyway, so they will not feel inferior to their fellow students, or so that parents or teachers will not be embarrassed. Eventually the student gets so far over his head academically that all learning stops; he then becomes a discipline problem or a dropout.

This twisted philosophy is detrimental to the academically talented child as well as to the slow learner. Many special programs that challenge intellectually gifted children have been dismantled as being unfair to other students. Sometimes these programs are charged with fostering "elitism" or racism—as if intellectual talents are limited to upper middle class whites. Giftedness is color blind and not class conscious. In fact, it is the economically disadvantaged gifted student who is the most common victim of neglect.

Equal opportunity is an important goal I strongly support. However, we should never neglect students' needs in the name of educational equality. Children have unequal mental ability and learn at different speeds. Lowering expectations and instruction to the level of the least capable may allow the mass to move forward together and to claim the same recognition, but it does not do justice or produce well-educated citizens.

Without objective measures of how well schools are preparing students for the demands of our society, our educational system has fallen prey to the exaggerated claims of designers of new curricula and teaching methods. Too late we have learned how ineffective or even harmful some of these changes in subject matter and instruction have been.

Most developed countries have definitive

and known standards of intellectual accomplishment. But in our country, what a child should know at a given stage of his academic career has remained undefined. Most achievement tests do not measure what a student should know. They merely show his relative standing compared to other test-takers. It is little consolation to find out you know more than your contemporaries about swimming if none of you can swim.

Particularly in the basic subjects of reading, writing, and mathematics, there should be objective measures of student performance in relation to clearly defined standards of educational proficiency. Parents should be able to find out how well their children are really doing without having to rely solely on the judgment of individual teachers or school officials. Too often, students and their parents are misled by automatic promotion and grade inflation into believing that students are learning the necessary skills. A glaring example occurred two years ago in Washington, D.C. when a high school valedictorian failed to meet the acceptance requirements of a local college because his entrance examination scores were but half of what was expected.

The public has become increasingly aware of the importance of competency standards and testing as a way to help ensure that their children are graduating with the skills necessary to function effectively in society. A 1976 Gallup Poll showed that two out of three Americans favored a standard nationwide examination as a prerequisite for high school graduation. According to a survey of Washington, D.C. area residents in May 1978, 85 percent believe that high school students should be required to take a standard competency test in basic subjects before being allowed to graduate.

Yet, some educators and educational organizations who purport to speak for the entire educational community have fought the development of academic standards and competency testing programs. They argue that there is already too much emphasis on test scores as a measure of student performance; or that competency standards and tests would be unfair to miniorities and the disadvantaged; or that teachers and students would set their sights on minimum standards and not try to progress beyond them. The National Education Association, running true to form, released a report this month which said that competency testing would humiliate minority children.

These arguments make no sense to me. Obviously, no test is perfect, and a single test score does not tell us everything about a child's intellectual development. But testing—particularly testing against objective standards—is an essential step in gauging student progress and achievement.

Furthermore, minorities and the disadvantaged are the very ones who have most to gain from competency standards and tests. Many leaders of minority groups recognize that to expect less from minority children is a cruel form of discrimination and they now endorse competency standards and tests as a means to help their children get a fair education.

As to the contention that "the minimum would become the maximum," I do not believe good teachers would reorient their courses and reduce content in order to prepare all students to meet merely the minimum competency standards. Instead, schools whose students are not meeting standards for reading, writing, and mathematics would be required to focus the necessary attention on developing these skills.

Despite opposition from some educators and in response to public pressure, more than thirty states have now enacted laws or issued regulations involving competency testing. In addition, several localities have undertaken development of their own competency testing programs, independent of efforts at the state level. There are reports of dramatic improvement in student attitudes and performance from some school districts that have implemented competency testing programs.

On the other hand, some states have simply

issued "motherhood" statements and directed local school boards to establish their own competency standards and tests. This is a difficult task, and the results vary with the locality. Some states and localities simply require competency testing only at the high school level, when it is already too late to do much with the results. Others have made their tests ridiculously easy, so that a politically acceptable percentage of those tested can pass. This is like trying to make a cold room warmer by shifting the scale on the thermometer.

Some opponents of competency testing cite these problems as proof that competency standards and tests will not work. I disagree. We need to improve our competency testing programs, not abolish them.

Last year, I recommended to the House and Senate Education Committees the establishment of voluntary national competency standards and tests in reading, writing, and mathematics. The key features of my proposal are as follows:

- The Federal Government would assemble a panel of nationally prominent persons in representative walks of life to develop standards in the basic skills.

- These standards would define what children should know and be able to do in reading, writing, and mathematics at the second, fourth, sixth, eighth, tenth, and twelfth grade levels.

- This panel would contract with testing firms or universities to devise appropriate tests against these standards.

- Use of these standards and tests would be voluntary, not mandated by the Federal Government.

- Parents would be able to have their children tested against the standards—if necessary, at Government expense.

Unlike much of the so-called "research" traditionally sponsored by the Department of Health, Education and Welfare, these model standards and tests would be a tangible and practical form of Federal assistance. States and localities which have not begun to develop competency tests could save time and money if national standards and tests were available. And those states and localities desiring to improve their existing competency testing programs might also find the national standards and tests helpful.

Yet, the proposal to develop voluntary national standards and tests has encountered strong opposition from segments of the educational community, especially the National Education Association and the U.S. Office of Education, which seems to be NEA's official ambassador to the Executive Branch. The most common arguments against national standards and tests are that federal involvement is wrong because competency testing should be based on local needs; that voluntary national standards and tests would eventually lead to federal control of education; and that federal efforts would interfere with state and local development of standards and tests which is already underway.

These arguments are specious. The concept that schools should educate children to fit into the local environment belongs to an earlier, less complex age, when people were less mobile and the need for literacy was not as great as it is today. With today's highly transient population, every American child, regardless of cultural or geographic background, has the same need for competency in reading, writing, and mathematics. Also, it amazes me how education officials can denounce development of voluntary standards and tests as a threat to state and local control of education, while at the same time demanding and accepting ever-increasing sums from the Federal Government for programs they themselves advocate.

Since the national standards and tests would be voluntary, they would not interfere with either control of curriculum, or development of competency programs by states and localities. Rather, the national standards and tests would benefit those states and localities which, like Virginia, are considering using commercially prepared tests because developing their own tests would be too expensive and time consuming.

I believe that the absence of competency standards is fundamental to many of the problems facing American education today. Lord Kelvin said: "When you can measure what you are speaking about, you know something about it; but when you cannot measure it, your knowledge is of a meager and unsatisfactory kind." To operate our schools without appropriate standards and tests is tantamount to getting vaccinated and not caring to find out if the vaccination "took."

Just as no community can exist without norms and standards of some kind distinguishing acceptable from unacceptable behavior, so too quality education cannot flourish without generally accepted standards of academic performance. I urge you to support the use of competency standards and tests in your school. You should welcome federal development of voluntary model standards and tests in reading, writing, and mathematics to help accommplish this task.

Competency testing of students, while important, is merely an indicator of whether students are learning. It takes a properly balanced curriculum taught by competent and dedicated teachers to provide quality education. In this regard, I have the following recommendations:

First, ensure that the primary goal of schools is the intellectual development of the children.

One of the major problems today is that the world is changing faster than the institutions that have to deal with the world's needs. We are living in a time of revolutionary change and have not adjusted to it either at home or abroad. Everywhere, governments are being asked to de-

liver more services, while resources have been shrinking under the pressure of inflation.

It seems that whenever a need in our society becomes pressing, someone is sure to look to the schools to fulfill the need. For example, it has recently been proposed that, since cardiopulmonary resuscitation could save many of the 650,000 Americans who die from heart attacks each year, this technique should be taught as part of the curriculum and be made a requirement for graduation from high school.

The response—a flood of letters of approval and commendation—was overwhelming. Doctors, nurses, and hospital administrators were most enthusiastic. Some found it "inconceivable that our high school students are not required to learn and be proficient at a skill so basic to the health of our country." Educators were equally enthusiastic. The chorus of approval included police and fire officials, leaders of civic groups, health organizations, state and local legislators, military personnel, and ordinary citizens.

But today, basic education in our schools is already competing with, and being overwhelmed by, career education, consumer education, energy education, drug education, sex education, and many others. Our educational system is being asked to do too many things; as a result, it is doing few of them well. The schools should concentrate on what they can do best—and must do—developing the mind and passing on knowledge to the younger generation through systematic study under expert instruction.

I recommend that, whenever someone proposes to add a new subject to the school curriculum, he should be required to identify which subject will be eliminated to allow for the new addition, or to recommend instead how much the school year must be lengthened to accommodate the new subject.

You must ensure that instructional programs are developing in each child the ability to read, to write clearly, to calculate, to think critically and logically, and to acquire knowledge of the world through history, literature, science, and art.

Second, require teachers to be knowledgeable in the subject matter they teach, and to demonstrate the reading, writing, and mathematical skills necessary to evaluate student performance and serve as appropriate models for them.

Sadly, many teachers today do not have the basic skills the students themselves lack. Too often, unfortunately for our children, teachers are the products of teachers' colleges which emphasize the *theory* of education. They are then supposed to be capable of teaching any subject, regardless of their knowledge of that subject. Some states foster this concept by qualifying teachers based on the number of education courses in teaching techniques rather than on competence and skill in subject matter.

While classroom managment, discipline, and method of presentation are necessary, they are not a substitute for mastery of the subjects being taught. It is essential that teachers themselves be proficient in the reading, writing, and mathematics they are trying to teach our children. Teachers should be required to demonstrate through written examination, their own expertise in these basic skills before being allowed to teach. This is a revolutionary concept. Can you imagine the NEA's reaction?

Third, provide close supervision of teachers by administrators and principals who are competent and experienced teachers themselves.

For any endeavor to be successful, those responsible must involve themselves in the details of day-to-day operations. The supervision and training of subordinates is the single most important duty of the one in charge. Yet school teachers are among the most unsupervised workers in our society. The notion of academic

freedom, combined with tenure protection, often results in each teacher determining on his own what subject matter is taught and how it is presented. And some school administrators are not themselves experienced or competent teachers and are not capable of evaluating teacher performance. Nowhere else is such a situation tolerated.

Fourth, improve in-service training of teachers.

In too many schools, training of teachers consists merely of granting them time off to attend conventions and symposia or requiring that they periodically take additional courses in subjects of interest to them, but often of no value to their teaching function.

Fifth, free teachers insofar as possible from responsibilities extraneous to their teaching.

The effectiveness of good teachers can be enhanced by freeing them from burdensome administrative and extracurricular duties. Far too much of this is of little use and is merely a job-making device. Teachers burdened with large amounts of clerical and administrative work have a strong incentive to structure their courses so as to minimize such work. This results in simplified tests and little demand for written work. It is not surprising that true-false examinations or multiple choice tests have largely replaced written assignments so essential to the development of writing and reasoning.

Sixth, in allocating school expenditures, give academic programs and quality teaching precedence over building improvements, athletic programs, and other extracurricular activities.

Too often, the accoutrements of education are given more attention than the intellectual needs of our children. Time and money are spent on new buildings and equipment or competitive sports programs which may be attractive to parents and students but add little or nothing to a student's mental development. What our children need and desire most is a good education, not beautiful buildings or entertaining extracurricular activities.

From 1960 to 1975, spending on public elementary and secondary education increased 315 percent while enrollments went up only 24 percent. Between 1972 and 1976, classroom teachers increased by only 4.5 percent, while the number of all other school personnel rose by more than 15 percent. Public education is costing us more each year, yet the increased expenditures appear to be aimed toward administrative and other non-instructional areas.

With the public's growing rebellion against high taxes — as evidenced by California's Proposition 13 — there will be pressures to reduce school spending. This can be a blessing in disguise. It can enable you to institute savings by reducing staffing, eliminating programs, and reducing overhead services not essential to good education. With the present taxpayer mood, this can be achieved with little opposition.

As school administrators and principals, you cannot be held accountable for the actions of parents and school boards. But you can and should create an environment in the schools where teaching is the primary objective, where performance is demanded and excellence rewarded for teacher and student. Without such an environment, the most diligent efforts of parents and school boards to raise achievement will be ineffective.

Schools cannot guarantee that their pupils will become well-adjusted citizens. What schools can do is provide an opportunity to learn. But it is the children who must do the learning. This must be made clear to parents, so they understand and accept responsibility for their own role in the education of their children.

A school administrator's job is a difficult one — in many respects more difficult than managerial positions in the business community. Factory managers, for example, can specify the type and quality of their material; school administrators must work with children of varied backgrounds and abilities. Factory managers have complete control over material during production; whereas school children are subject to outside influences over which administrators and teachers have little or no control. Factory managers can fire incompetents, but tenure agreements effectively bar school administrators from doing the same.

Despite the many problems, it is your job to educate children to take part in our modern society. This requires determination more than money. It requires that you place the needs of education ahead of all other considerations; that you demand professional performance from teachers; that you instill throughout your schools an appreciation and respect for excellence.

Parents have entrusted you with the educational development of their children. In carrying out this responsibility, you must act as if these children were your own. In this connection, I believe it would be a good idea for a community, wherever possible, to appoint school board members and administrators from among those whose own children are attending the schools they supervise.

Above all you must feel personally responsible for the quality of your schools. Responsibility is a unique concept: it can only reside and inhere in a single individual. You may disclaim it, but you cannot divest yourself of it. Even if you do not recognize it or admit its presence, you cannot escape it. If responsibility is rightfully yours, no evasion, or ignorance, or passing the blame can shift the burden to someone else.

Can Minimum Competency Testing Be Justified?

Jerrold R. Coombs

Jerrold Coombs is a professor of education at the University of British Columbia. He received his Ph.D. in philosophy of education from the University of Illinois, and has taught previously at Florida State University. His publications include articles on teaching, indoctrination, equality, and values education. He is currently working on problems in philosophy of curriculum.

The many minimum competency testing (MCT) programs that have appeared in the past few years share two essential features. Each involves the use of a test, usually a standardized test, which is purportedly a measure of the minimum competencies or basic skills any person must possess if he is to be successful in life. In some cases the tests are called "functional literacy" tests, implying that they measure competencies deemed necessary for adequate functioning in one's society. Some proponents of MCT go so far as to claim they are testing for competencies that are necessary for "survival" in our society. The second essential feature of MCT programs is that they involve the application of sanctions to those who fail the test. Usually this takes the form of denying promotion to those in junior grades. Both testing for basic skills and denying graduation diplomas to students who fail to meet certain standards of performance are established practices in public education. What is new in MCT programs is the way in which these two elements are combined, and the fact that the power of the state is used to enforce them.

Much has already been written about both the desirable and the undesirable consequences of MCT programs.[1] I do not want to recapitulate those arguments here. Rather, I wish to raise certain fundamental questions about the justification of MCT programs. First I will examine the adequacy of the justifications actually given for MCT programs. This done, I will explore the issue of whether or not MCT programs can be adequately justified. Finally I want to raise certain issues concerning the purpose of education, which, although not completely ignored in MCT debates, have not received the attention they deserve.

ARE THE PRESENT JUSTIFICATIONS ADEQUATE?

What sort of justification is usually given for instituting MCT programs? The reasons which recur most often appear to be the following: 1) It will make the high school diploma

From "Can Minimum Competency Testing Be Justified?" by Jerrold R. Coombs, First published in The High School Journal, *vol. 62, January 1979. © 1979 The University of North Carolina Press. Reprinted by permission of the publisher.*

---

[1]For a good review of the major arguments for and against MCT see *Phi Delta Kappan*, May, 1978.

mean something or be worth something, 2) It will motivate students to work harder to learn the basic competencies, and 3) It will motivate schools and teachers to do a better job of teaching the basic competencies. Let us examine each of these reasons in turn, leaving open for the moment the question of what competencies count as basic.

Many people are concerned that the high school graduation diploma has become meaningless or worthless because of the prevalence of the practice of promoting and eventually graduating persons who have not achieved any significant proficiency in such things as reading, writing and mathematical computation. If a diploma does not signify that at least these skills have been acquired, they argue, then it doesn't mean anything. The concern that a high school diploma should stand for or mean something is quite understandable. Diplomas are, after all, meant to signify *achievements*. If it does not signify some achievement, there is no point to having it. What is not so readily understandable is *why* a high school diploma must signify the achievement of these particular competencies. Why must it even signify the same set of competencies in each case in which it is conferred? Would the high school diploma be meaningless if one student got it for competence in art and sports whereas another got it for competence in reading and mathematics? If the diploma would not be worthless in such a circumstance, then it is not clear that MCT is needed to make the diploma mean something. Just what a high school diploma should mean is a question to which we will return shortly.

Claims that MCT programs will motivate students to work harder to achieve basic competencies and that they will motivate teachers to do a better job of teaching them are as yet unverified. Unverified, too, is the supposition that an increase in motivation will produce a significant increase in achievement of basic competencies. Persons who opt for MCT as a motivating de-

vice betray a very deep distrust of both students and schools. They are saying, in effect, that students and teachers could do a better job if they really tried. What they need in order to make them try harder are greater penalties for failure. This reasoning is rather curious. If these achievements designated as minimum competencies really *are* necessary for survival or even just for success in life, then it should be possible to make students see that this is the case. Doing this should provide the strongest possible motivation for mastery of the minimum competencies, far stronger than that provided by MCT. Such motivation would be particularly strong for persons who tend to be motivated by fear of failure, which is the only sort of person that MCT is likely to affect.

The supposition that MCT will motivate teachers is similarly flawed. It is odd to suppose that a teacher would have stronger motivation for helping students get diplomas than for helping them learn what is demonstrably necessary for survival or for success in life. My experience is that teachers are highly motivated to teach what they regard as basic skills, particularly the skills of reading, writing and mathematical computation. Moreover, their efforts in this direction tend to be successful with the majority of students. What teachers lack is knowledge of sufficiently powerful means to teach these skills to *all* students in the present social context. MCT does nothing to help overcome this problem.

Even if MCT programs were to prove effective in bringing about increased learning of skills which everyone could accept as basic, we might still be unjustified in instituting such programs. To be justified, MCT must not only be an effective means, it must be the best available means. This point will be discussed more fully in the next section of the paper. It is mentioned here because it seems very likely that school boards and state departments of education, with their control of curriculum, funding and administration, have ample power to assure that schools devote maximum effort to developing basic skills. Thus it is far from clear that MCT is the best available means of increasing the acquisition of basic skills.

Up to this point I have argued that the reasons typically given in support of present MCT programs are insufficient to justify them. Now I want to consider what an adequate justification of an MCT program must include, and whether or not such programs can be justified.

WHAT MUST AN ADEQUATE JUSTIFICATION OF AN MCT INCLUDE?

Perhaps we can gain a better perspective on these issues if we begin by considering the justifications for competency testing in other areas. Competency testing has been with us for many years. Doctors, lawyers and accountants, among others, must pass tests to establish their competency before they are licensed to practice their professions. Presumably there are things which anyone must know or be able to do if he is to be competent to practice law, for example. Consequently, it makes sense to require the same minimum competencies of all who would practice law. There are good reasons also for a state's requiring competency testing in such areas. A client can be badly hurt by the incompetence of his doctor, lawyer or accountant. Since the average person lacks the background necessary for assessing the competence of practitioners in these areas, the state is justified in taking action to protect its citizens from incompetent doctors, lawyers, accountants and the like.

What are the essential features of these cases of competency testing which seem to have good justification? First, the testing is applied to persons who aspire to perform a particular service for other people, a service that requires the use of specifiable knowledge and skills. Second, the testing is applied in order to protect other people from suffering harm at the hands of those being testing. It is *not* applied in order to help members of the tested group. Finally, the testing is applied in cases where prospective clients are unable to determine the competence of those being tested.

It should be obvious that competency testing for high school graduation cannot be justified in the same way as competency testing is usually justified. Conferring a high school diploma is not meant to signify that the recipient is qualified to perform a particular service for others which requires the use of specifiable knowledge and skills. Nor is it the case that competency testing for graduation is needed in order to prevent harm to clients of high school graduates. For a high school graduate, the closest approximation to a client is an employer or a university. It is unnecessary to protect employers from high school graduates who are incompetent, for employers have ample means to test prospective employees for whatever competencies they deem necessary or desirable. Nor is it necessary to protect universities. They too are well able to screen prospective students and to weed out those that are incompetent. For whose protection, then, is competency testing of high school graduates needed?

There is one further important difference between competency testing for high school graduation and the justified cases of competency testing we have been examining. They take place in very different sorts of moral contexts. One *chooses* to enter the legal profession because of his interests and aptitudes. If one fails the test required to practice law, he can turn to some other occupation. In our society children are *required* by law to attend school; they are not free to choose in this matter. If one fails the test to graduate from high school, he cannot turn to some alternative field of endeavor, for there is none. He is certified by the state to be incompetent, not merely to do a particular job, but as a person. He is deemed to be functionally illiterate and incapable of a successful life. We should remember too that high school graduation has been made a prerequisite for all sorts of occupations which could easily be performed by persons who have not graduated. In the present social and economic context, to deny a high school diploma to someone is in itself sufficient to decrease his chances of having a successful life. It should be clear that the legally mandated sorting and labelling of human beings implicit in MCT is morally hazardous in a way that competency testing of lawyers, doctors and accountants is not.

What would count as an adequate justification of an MCT program? At the least such a justification must show the following to be the case: 1) That the MCT program would either prevent significant harm to persons, provide some significant benefits to those being tested, or promote the general welfare of members of our society, 2) That the MCT program is the best available means of achieving the desired result and 3) That the good to be promoted, or harm to be prevented would not be outweighed by the harm caused by the MCT program.

Recent critiques of MCT have made abundantly clear the harms that are likely to be caused by MCT programs. They include such things as reinforcing inequality of opportunity presently existing among members of different social classes, increasing the number of school dropouts, decreasing concern for individual differences in interests and talents and depreciating the significance of achievements not considered basic. What, then, are the goods to be promoted or the harms to be prevented by an MCT program that will outweigh the harms it is likely to cause? There are two possible answers: 1) an increase in the acquisition of competencies *necessary* for adequate functioning in life, or 2) an increase in the acquisition of competencies which are *desirable* because they increase the likelihood of adequate functioning or success in life. Acquiring skills necessary to adequate functioning in life is a more significant good

than acquiring skills that are merely desirable. Consequently, if an MCT program promotes this good, we are more likely to judge that the good it promotes outweighs the harm it does.

WHAT COMPETENCIES ARE NECESSARY FOR SUCCESSFUL LIVING?

We will put aside temporarily the question of whether or not MCT programs are likely to produce the results they were designed to produce. Instead, let us consider whether or not the competencies that MCT programs typically attempt to foster are actually necessary for a person to function adequately or for a person to have a successful life. The competencies most often identified as basic are skills in reading, writing, and mathematical computation. These are thought to be necessary if one is to be able to do such things as understand a contract for a loan, fill out a tax return, do comparison shopping, vote intelligently, follow a recipe, and the like. One difficulty in the way of showing that these skills are necessary is the fact that sensible people disagree as to what counts as adequate functioning or a successful life. Conceptions of the successful life include such diverse things as being economically self-sufficient, being happy, developing one's talents, improving the lot of mankind, and finding God. To make his case, an MCT proponent must show that these basic skills are necessary for achieving any sort of life that could defensibly be called successful or adequate.

Given even a very ordinary conception of an adequate or successful life, the basic skills appear not to be necessary to its realization. Consider, for example, the skill of reading. A person who cannot read may be unable to do many things the average person does, but can we show that he is unable to have a successful life? I think not. A talented artist or artisan could likely be self-supporting, happy and well-informed without being able to read. Understanding contracts and filling out tax forms need not be a serious problem for him, for a person of average means can afford to get help with such matters. Had he the inclination, he could even enjoy novels recorded on tape. It is still harder to make the case that proficiency in writing and mathematical computation are essential for success. Many adults whom we would ordinarily judge to be successful do little writing or computation.

Although proficiency in reading, writing and mathematical computation cannot be shown to be necessary for success in life, it seems clear that they are desirable skills for anyone to have. Having these skills increases one's chances of having a successful life, however that life is defined. Reading seems particularly important since it is one of the principal means by which a person gains new knowledge. Suppose, then, that the basic skills are only *desirable* rather than *necessary* for having a successful life. Does increasing the degree to which they are acquired constitute a good that is significant enough to outweigh the harm that is likely to result from MCT programs? I believe that most people, were they in possession of the relevant facts, would require an enormous increase in the degree of basic skills acquisition before they would judge that this good is significant enough to outweigh the potential harm of MCT programs. Personally, I think the potential harms so egregious that no amount of increase in basic skills acquisition could outweigh them. This brings us to the question set aside earlier. What degree of increase in basic skills acquisition are MCT programs likely to achieve? MCT programs have not been underway long enough to yield any substantial results, but it would be very surprising if they were to increase basic skills acquisition enormously.

The final component which an adequate justification of an MCT program must have is a demonstration that the program in question is the best means available for promoting in-creased acquisition of the basic skills. Why do we need to make such a strong case for MCT? Basically it is because MCT involves using the power of the state to regulate the lives of its citizens, and because this action of the state has the potential of causing harm to some of its citizens. In such a case we require assurances that the action taken by the state is the best available means of promoting the good in question. So far as I know, no one has mounted even a plausible argument showing that MCT is the best available means for increasing either the number of students acquiring basic skills or the degree to which individual students acquire them. To make this case one would have to show that no other available means is as effective as MCT or has fewer undesirable consequences. My judgment, which I mentioned earlier, is that there *are* means available that are likely to be as effective as MCT and have fewer undesirable consequences.

I want now to return to the two questions which I earlier deferred: the question of whether or not there are any achievements that are basic to the adequate functioning of persons, and the question of what achievement a high school diploma should signify. These fundamental questions deserve serious consideration by both educators and the general public. One of the virtues of the MCT movement is that it has made manifest the need for such consideration. Unfortunately the debates concerning MCT have not as yet satisfied this need.

WHAT ARE THE REAL BASICS?

I think a plausible case can be made for the view that there are achievements which are basic to persons. To call someone a person is not merely to identify him as a member of a certain biological class; it is also to identify him as a member of a group that has certain moral status. A person is someone who has both rights and responsibilities. To be without either is to be in a significant sense a non-person. The achievements that are basic to adequate functioning as an adult person are those which are necessary to recognizing and exercising one's rights, and those which are necessary to recognizing and fulfilling one's responsibilities. Taken as a whole, the acquisition of such achievements constitutes the acquisition of rationality and autonomy. Not surprisingly, our concept of education, as opposed to our concept of schooling, has built into it the ideal of developing rational, autonomous persons. An educated person is not merely one who is well informed, socialized or trained for a vocation. To be an educated person is to be a person who can think for himself, one who makes his own decisions about what to believe, value and do on the basis of relevant reasons and evidence.[2]

---

[2]For a fuller discussion of the concept of education see Richard Peters, *Ethics and Education*. London: George Allen & Unwin Ltd., 1966.

In sum, the abilities, dispositions and inclinations that are necessary to making rational decisions about what to believe and do are basic to persons and are implicit in the idea of educating persons. If our schools are meant to educate persons, then ideally a high school diploma should signify some significant attainment of these abilities and dispositions. Nonetheless, I would not advocate instituting an MCT program having such attainments as its basis. I know of no way to establish the minimum degree of attainment which all persons must have that is not completely arbitrary. Moreover, it is exceedingly difficult to test for the ability to think rationally, for this is captured more in how one thinks than in what one thinks.[3]

---

[3]For a discussion of what is involved in thinking rationally, at least in the area of making value decisions, see Jerrold Coombs, "Objectives of Value Analysis," in Lawrence Metcalf, ed., *Values Education*. Washington, D.C.: National Council for the Social Studies, 1971.

DISCUSSION QUESTIONS AND ACTIVITIES

1. Despite rising grades, college entrance examination scores have fallen and basic knowledge needed by workers in many occupations has shown increasing deficiencies, according to Rickover. Are his data correct, and if it is, how can this phenomenon best be explained? Are schools and colleges primarily responsible for this decline?

2. Rickover believes that there is less interest in basic academic courses and more interest today in "relevance" and providing freedom of choice. Why does he find this trend dangerous?

3. Why is Rickover against the doctrine that learning should be easy?

4. How can a distortion of the concept "equal educational opportunity" lead to lowering educational quality?

5. Would minority children likely be hurt by competency tests?

6. Review Rickover's proposal for voluntary national standards and tests and give reasons for your agreement or disagreement with his proposal.

7. Rickover claims that our educational system is trying to do too many things and, consequently, it is doing few of them well. What, then, should schools be doing? Has he supported his position adequately?

8. Would Rickover's proposals improve the quality of teaching?

9. Why should a high school diploma signify

the achievement of minimal competencies on a test?

10. Will such testing programs motivate students to achieve the basic competencies and teachers to do a better job of teaching?

11. According to Coombs, do teachers generally lack motivation for teaching basic skills or do they lack something else?

12. For whose protection is competency testing of high school graduates needed? What would be an adequate justification for the use of such tests?

13. Investigate the mandated legislative provisions for minimal competency testing in your state or province and report to class on your findings.

14. Make a case study of a school system which employs minimal competency testing. Explain why the school system adopted this kind of testing, characteristics of the tests used, the extent to which the tests achieve their objectives, and whether the objectives could have been achieved more effectively using some other approach.

15. Invite as a classroom speaker a proponent of minimal competency testing.

SUGGESTED READINGS

Proponents

Abrams, Joan D. "Precise Teaching is More Effective Teaching." *Educational Leadership* 39 (November 1981): 138.

"Accountability, Competency Testing, Back-to-Basics" (Symposium). *NASSP Bulletin* 62 (October 1978): 1–93. Divergent viewpoints.

Bailey, Gerald D. and Robert K. James. "Competency-Based Education: Its Elements and Potential." *School Science and Mathematics* 81 (November 1981): 563–71.

Cohen, Arthur M. and Florence B. Brawer. "The Technology of Instruction." *Community and Junior College Journal* 53 (September 1982): 35–37.

Holmes, Mark. "Competency Based Education—Is It Time? Can It Work?" *School Guidance Worker* 35 (March 1980): 5–11.

Irish, Gladys H. "Maximizing Functional Competencies and Basic Skills: Lessons of a Special Project." *Adult Literacy and Basic Education* 4 (Spring 1980): 17–22.

Jones, Edward Everett. "Incorporating Competency-Based Education Into Minimum Competency Testing Programs." *School Science and Mathematics* 81 (February 1981): 145–52.

Peterson, Gary W. and Roger G. Stakenas. "Performance-Based Education: Method for Preserving Quality, Equal Opportunity, and Economy in Public Education." *Journal of Higher Education* 52 (July-August 1981): 52–68.

Pollock, Marion B. "Speaking of Competencies." *Health Education* 12 (January-February 1981): 9–13.

Popham, W. James and Stuart C. Rankin. "Minimum Competency Tests Spur Instructional Improvement." *Phi Delta Kappan* 62 (May 1981): 637–39.

Reynolds, Sherrod. "A Marriage Proposal: Competency Based Education and Experiential Learning." *Journal of Experiential Learning* 4 (Fall 1981): 34–39.

Rickover, H. G. "Do We Really Need a National Competency Test? The Testimony." *National Elementary Principal* 57 (January 1978): 48–56. Discussion: 57–70.

Rockler, Michael J. "Competence and Creativity—Can We Have Both?" *Curriculum Review* 18 (December 1979): 366–70.

Tyo, John. "Ten Suggestions to Help Implement Competency-Based Education." *NASSP Bulletin* 64 (November 1980): 58–63.

Ulmer, Curtis. "Adult Competency Based Instruction." *Community College Review* 8 (Spring 1981): 51–56.

Critics

Bell, Wendell D. "Caveat on Competency Based Education." *Journal of Industrial Teacher Education* 17 (Spring 1980): 6–21.

Black, Mary J. "Matthew Arnold and Proficiency Tests." *English Journal* 71 (January 1982): 18–20.

Clements, Millard. "Performance Based Education: A Social Alchemy." *The Educational Forum* 46 (Spring 1982): 315–25.

"Down and Out in the Classroom: Surviving Minimal Competency." (Symposium) *National Elementary Principal* 58 (January 1979): 11–59.

Jacob, Kay. "Brave New English Curriculum." *English Journal* 71 (January 1982): 48–51.

Kazanas, H. C. and E. L. Frazier. "A Comparison of Instructional Approaches." *Journal of Studies in Technical Careers* 4 (Fall 1980): 312–20.

Pruitt, K. Wayne 'Speaking Out: The Rush to Competency-Based Education." *The Clearing House* 54 (September 1980): 4.

Ross, Dorene D. "Competency Based Education: Understanding a Political Movement." *The Educational Forum* 46 (Summer 1982): 483–90.

Willems, Arnold J. and Max H. Brown. "Competency-Based Curricula: Another Perspective." *The Educational Forum* 44 (January 1980): 225–30.

10
Microcomputers in Education

Some hail it as a "revolution" while others claim, "It's just another fad." These disputes are over the introduction of the microcomputer in education. Some observers believe that within a few years the ability to program and use microcomputers may be as important as the ability to read, write, type, drive, or use a telephone.

Automated teaching devices began in the 1920s with the first teaching machine, which did not achieve popularity until the 1950s. As the work of these early machines could be handled in simpler, more economical ways, programmed materials supplanted them during the 1950s and 1960s. The emergence of computer-assisted instruction (CAI) in the late 60s was heralded as a breakthrough, only to find it constrained by prohibitive costs — to establish a CAI program in a school system costs in excess of $100,000.

In contrast, the spread of microcomputers stems largely from the cost reductions of microtechnology, with microcomputers available from $200–400 and up to $5,000–6,000. The National Science Foundation projects one million units available in elementary and secondary schools by 1985. Hardware development is outpacing software development and implementation, and the present microcomputers will probably be replaced in several years. In the next ten to twenty years networks will likely emerge that will permit microcomputers to access the resources of larger computers. Proponents claim, however, that present microcomputers can improve educational programs.

Computers have been widely adopted in business and various organizations. Most universities offer courses in computer science, graduate courses are available in computer-based education, and many computer literacy workshops are offered. Many school districts are identifying teachers who can be consultants for inservice sessions in the use of microcomputers. Still, there is no agreement on the precise knowledge needed for computer literacy.

The quality of programs is a problem in the field microcomputer, as in the case of CAI where the development of programs is an extremely time-consuming and expensive task. Thousands of programs written for CAI have limited instructional value. Suitable microcomputer programs for instruction are just beginning to emerge. Some serious problems, however, need to addressed.

The new information technologies (including microcomputers) could lead to a further centralization of authority because they favor decentralization of activities while promoting centralized decision-making. This technology contributes to the trend of large corporations making decisions for remote areas. The new technology also reduces personal contact and shrinks interpersonal communication.

Despite these shortcomings, the new information technology is likely to spread rapidly. Some observers envision future home instruction or neighborhood learning centers capable of providing basic instruction that consumes most of the school day, leading to a shift of accountability and competency education from the schools to the home. The role of teachers would be transformed from transmitters of knowledge to providers of higher-order learning experiences.

Shane explores the microcomputer breakthroughs in relation to larger developments in the information society, and then shows the likely changes that microcomputers may bring about in education. Dean explains in what ways microcomputers still have deficiencies to overcome.

The Silicon Age and Education

Harold G. Shane _____

Harold G. Shane (b. 1914) has a Ph.D. from Ohio State University. He has been a teacher, principal, and superintendent in school systems in Ohio and Illinois. A former dean of the School of Education at Indiana University, he now is University Professor of Education. Professor Shane has been a consultant to USOE and other agencies, a recipient of awards, former president of the Association for Supervision and Curriculum Development, and the author of numerous books, including Education for a New Millenium.

"Change [must] be accepted . . . when it can no longer be resisted."

Victoria Regina (c. 1895)

The microchip is a tiny slice of silicon, an "electronic book" that stores information in a binary code consisting of zeros and ones.[1] Far too small to be seen by the naked eyes,[2] the chip requires a read-out terminal that converts the electronic transistor codes into the language of the viewer. Screens displays the textual material at viewer-controlled speeds.[3]

But this article is not concerned primarily with the technical aspects of silicon chips and other computer hardware. The implications of the computer revolution for education are my primary concern. Indeed, a large portion of the Western world already can be considered a computerized society. Our task is coping with and using constructively the new social environment that is emerging as computers approach an era of virtually exponential growth.

Human communication has gone through four distinct revolutions. The first was occasioned by our species-specific skills of complex speech—a development that created an important role for memory. It also permitted the nongenetic transfer of our human qualities, our mental achievements, from one generation to another.

The art of writing heralded the second revolution; its various forms—cuneiform, hieroglyphics, and the script of scribes—remained of prime importance for thousands of years. The art of writing became the victim of a third revolution, triggered by Johann Gutenberg, who, in the 15th century, presumably became the first European to use movable type in his printing

From Harold G. Shane," The Silicon Age and Education," Phi Delta Kappan *(January 1982) pp. 303–08. Used by permission of author and publisher.*

[1]The zeros and ones are symbolic representations of the presence or absence of electronic current.
[2]As of the early 1980s, the transistor or "chip" cell measured three microns. This is less than half the diameter of the seven-micron human red blood cell.
[3]Space constraints preclude more detailed information regarding computer hardware, but it is readily available in books by Christopher Evans and Robert Moody. See footnotes 5 and 6.

press. Soon thereafter the printed word was available to millions of people who could neither afford nor, in many instances, even read books lettered in medieval script.

The fourth and potentially most profound revolution—one still in the full vigor of its youth—has been wrought by the enormous advances in telecommunications in the span of a single lifetime. Although the telegraph, telephone, and radio played an important role, not until the last decade has our globe begun to become a "wired planet"—an information society created by the microchip.

As John Platt points out in a superbly provocative essay:

> It is important to realize how far we have gone in the new direction. We are living already in what McLuhan has called the Electronic Surround. Half of the jobs in the American economy are now "tertiary" or information-handling jobs, and more and more of them have become computerized or electronic. Banks and businesses are linked together by credit cards and data processing. Government records, science, and the military are all dependent on big computers. Everywhere there are pocket calculators, transistor radios, citizens' band radios, and stereo sets with records and tapes. We have electronic monitors in stores and entryways, and videotapes for learning tennis. Telephone and television are linked by global satellites, while the home begins to have two-way cable electronic games, and video recordings on cassettes and disks.[4]

The revolution in telecommunications—the silicon chip revolution—and the resultant changes in the world of work demand that educators understand the new life patterns and interactions that are coming into being. Not only our work in schools but our very ways of thinking, our global awareness, our concepts of power and political priorities—all must come under scrutiny.

BACKGROUND AND FUTURE PROSPECTS

The microprocessor is both the source *and* support system of the transitions already under way. In the computer, it is analogous to a combined heart and brain in humans. One may wonder why such an astute observer as Alvin Toffler failed to mention the microprocessor in *Future Shock*. The answer is simple. The microprocessor didn't even exist in 1970!

According to Christopher Evans, the idea behind the computer is an old one. Charles Babbage, a British engineer born in 1791, first conceived the idea of a calculating machine but lacked the technology to build an efficient model. He and a gifted mathematician, Ada, the Countess of Lovelace (Lord Byron's daughter), probably deserve credit as the parents of what they called a "Difference Engine," the first primitive autocalculator.

But only within recent memory did the development of a general-purpose computing machine begin. ENIAC, the first digital computer, was built at the University of Pennsylvania in 1946.[5] It cost half a million relatively uninflated dollars to build, weighed 30 tons, and required the floor space of an average-sized house. Its 18,500 special vacuum tubes required 130,000 watts.

The development of a computer on a microchip—accomplished by Intel Corporation of Santa Clara, California, about 10 years ago—was the real breakthrough that presaged the silicon age. Evans describes what has happened as miniaturization techniques were used to etch complete, integrated circuits on a chip: "The units of which computers are made are getting smaller and smaller, shrinking beyond the range of ordinary microscopes into the infinites of the molecular world."[6]

---

[4]John Platt, "Education in the Electronic Society," in John Y. Cole, ed., *Television, the Book, and the Classroom* (Washington, D.C.: Library of Congress, 1978).

[5]Robert Moody, *The First Book of Microcomputers* (Rochelle Park, N.J.: Hayden, 1978). pp. 3, 4.
[6]Christopher Evans, *The Micro Millennium* (New York: Pocket Books, 1979), p. 51.

By 1980 it was possible to etch the equivalent of 60,000 to 70,000 vacuum tubes on a microchip; by the spring of 1981, in a U.S. laboratory, 750,000 tube equivalents were squeezed onto a chip. Million-unit chips small enough to balance on a paperclip are just over the horizon. In fact, they may already have appeared by the time this issue of the *Kappan* is off the press. Already there are computers with a switching potential of nanoseconds—machines capable of billions of switchings in a one-second clock-tick. The incredible speed of the chip is, perhaps, more readily understood when one understands that a nanosecond is one thousand-millionth of a second.

Consider this: If a Rolls Royce had improved as much in cost-efficiency as the microcomputer has in the last decade, it would have a sticker price of just $3. A 1945 all-tube computer capable of doing the work of the present-day table-top computer would have had to be the size of New York City; it would have required more power than the whole of the city's subway system.

The microprocessor is the latest stage in the development of transistors (invented in 1947 by William Shockley) and a basic element in the computer. It is a small semiconductor with impurities that permit electrons to move under the impulse of an infinitesimal amount of energy. Its importance resides in the way it links three components: 1) *matter* (the semiconductor's impurities); 2) *information,* expressed in a universal binary language; and 3) the actuating power of *energy.*

Before contemplating what the microprocessor may portend for education, let us examine some of the results of the marriage of computer technologies and telecommunications. The first commercially feasible microcomputer became available in 1975, just six years ago. Since then:

• As of the summer of 1981, about three million microcomputers had been sold in the U.S. alone, over a million of them as personal computers. The dollar value of the computer industry (including software) was $2.6 billion in 1980. If present trends in the sales of information processing equipment continue in the U.S., sales—including supplies and services—could exceed $62 billion in 1985.[7]

• In 1980 information workers (those who handled information and dispensed communications in their many forms) constituted approximately 50% of U.S. workers, far outstripping other service occupations (29%), industry (17%), and farm workers (4%).

• Within three to five years European televiewing will be saturated by three satellites that will beam a broad spectrum of commercial programs to 250 million Europeans. "Digital sound" equipment developed for use in Europe will permit many viewers (by pressing their choice from among four buttons) to hear programs dubbed in their own language.

• By late 1981 physicians in New York and Tokyo exchanged information on the treatment of glaucoma by means of a "symposium" held via satellite.[8]

• "Smart machines" performing jobs formerly done by humans are proliferating; the field of robotics, made possible and profitable by the microprocessor, is becoming a major element in industry. About 4,000 robots are in use in the U.S., mostly in the auto industry, and more than 11,000 are at work in Japan, as of 1981. Some can be in-

---

[7]Estimate from G.T.T. Molitor, president, Public Policy Forecasting. Cf. the *Futurist* (April 1981) 23–30. *Time* magazine (5 October 1981, p. 69) reports that the cost of an Apple II personal computer (about $1,500) is only the beginning. One can also spend as much as $800 for eight software programs.

[8]*Indianapolis Star,* (4 October 1981); p. 1

structed to see, hear, feel, and even make simple decisions. Robots can now beat most humans at chess, they can perform, and they can "learn." General Motors is installing 10 "programmable universal machines for assembly" that can screw light bulbs into dashboard panels, spray paint, weld, load and unload parts, follow typed directions, and even respond to simple verbal directions. In handling hot casings, robots such as these have cut the number of rejects by 15% and increased production by 10% while reducing the need for human labor by 70% — all for $4.60 per hour.[9]

THE CHIP AND THE CURRICULUM

Following the example of Ned Lud, an angry worker who smashed two textile frames belonging to his Leicestershire employer, the Luddites in early 19th-century England literally attacked the new labor-saving machinery which they saw threatening them with wage cuts and unemployment. French workers also railed against the Industrial Revolution by jamming *sabots,* their wooden shoes, into the spinning equipment that was eliminating many of their jobs (thus the word *saboteur*).

Let me begin my discussion of the chip and its effects on the curriculum by suggesting that the teaching profession avoid an understandable urge to feel threatened by the microcomputer—lest we become educational Luddites. Rather, let us strive to anticipate the influence of the microchip and of telecommunications on 1) subject matter, 2) components of the educational community (pre-primary through postsecondary), and 3) the ultimate goal of educating for a sustainable society. First, however, a quick review of terminology.

Schooling, Education, and Learning. As used hereafter, *schooling* refers to a program of planned and organized instruction designed to build a sense of identity with one's culture and to preserve or to transmit those values prized by the society. *Education* is used here in a broad sense to include the divers experiences and continuing out-of-school learning of adults and youths. *Learning* refers to the sum of the internalized knowledge, values, and ways of thinking that determine behavior. The microchip is influencing each of the three.

Schooling and the chip. The microprocessor is likely to encourage a number of desirable changes and innovations in the overall scope of the school. Increasing use of the hand calculator, greater use of videotapes and videodiscs, and increased use of suitable TV offerings should begin to permeate the classroom. The significant use of microcomputers will reside in the interactive relationship between learners and increasingly "smart machines" — not in the use of microcomputers as "electronic flash cards."

"Computer literacy" will begin to receive more attention, too, and the idea and the basic purposes of "computer camps"[10] for pre-teen and teenage youngsters will probably be quickly co-opted within school walls. The National Education Association, for example, announced last summer that it was negotiating an agreement with Control Data Corporation to provide a computer literacy program for teachers.

As a part of this trend educators are forced to question the necessity of routine math drill

---

[9]The *Futurist* (vol. 15, nos. 1, 2, and 4, 1981) published a sequence of excellent and provocative articles on microelectronics and robotics.

[10]By mid-1981 the computer camp was enough of a growing phenomenon to command notice in such publications as *Time* and *Le Monde*. In the camps, children learn computer languages such as BASIC and PASCAL, devise electronic games, learn programming skills, etc. (See *Time*, 3 August 1981, p. 70.) A concomitant development in the opening of "computer stores" for children. In Indianapolis, for example, there is a store in which children pay tuition and receive instruction after school hours.

when $10 calculators can instantly compute percentages and square roots. I suspect that tomorrow's schools will deemphasize the *mechanics* of ciphering but place more stress on pupils' acquiring a greater understanding of the *meaning* of numbers, including how to recognize reasonable solutions or answers to math problems fed to the calculator.

The microprocessor will also be used to facilitate work in traditional courses—mathematics, English, social studies—and a sprinkling of novel ideas will surface. By "novel ideas" I mean such strategies as using an IBM model 1620 to help teach singing: At Stanford University a computer has been used to print out notes to be sung by students. The machine compares the learner's pitch to true pitch and then selects proper remedial practice.

One puzzle yet to be solved is the future of computerized foreign language instruction. It is quite possible that within two decades handheld computers with voice input and output will provide translating devices virtually as fluent as and perhaps more grammatical than many native speakers. How will this affect practices and methods in the classroom? What might occur in the realm of bilingual education?

As the computer changes the work place, schools will find themselves pressured to modify vocational education and guidance programs to make them respond more rapidly to change. Lifelong education—including vocational reeducation or "retrofitting" for those replaced by robots—for mature (over 30) and senior (over 55 or 60) learners seems likely to open new, highly used social roles for the school. Retrofitting may become particularly important. Many of the persons who are likely to become unemployed as a result of developments in robotics will not necessarily have the skills needed to fill new jobs that are created by applications of the microcomputer.

I do not, however, see any radical or wrenching changes in schooling during the short-term future (five to 10 years) as a result of the silicon chip. Budget cuts and federal fiscal policies seem likely to impede major investments in computers and in material for at least another five years. (Even so, schools from the elementary level to the university are giving high priority to the equipment. For instance, the Indiana University School of Education, despite financial constraints, is installing 18 microcomputers for student and faculty education and use.) Moreover, computer-assisted instruction, at least in some fields of study, now has few advantages over a well-programmed text (although the availability of high-quality software seems likely to improve during the Eighties). Then too, some teachers will resist change either because they feel insecure in an electronic milieu or because they believe that any "computer takeover" would abort established routines or stifle creative planning and innovative teaching.

Perhaps one of the gravest impediments to the rapid development of suitable software is the lack of agreement among educators at all levels as to which methods of instruction are "best" and what the goals of education should be. Moreover, software producers (as well as educators) still have much to learn about the learning process and about individual differences in learning styles. Lacking such knowledge, we could end up merely cloning inadequacy more rapidly by means of the computer.

The Chip and Education. Education as a lifelong process will be more profoundly changed than schooling during the next 10 to 15 years. Learners of all ages are likely to find their homes becoming "electronic cottages," a term coined by Alvin Toffler in *The Third Wave*. In a knowledge-rich society many homes may become work places through the use of telecommunications, including 3-D holography—a development that could reduce the need for personal transportation as energy reserves wane.

Another important development—one with

implications for both the electronic cottage and off-campus education—occurred in 1976–77 when the first commercial lightwave systems were built. Bell, Corning Glass, and ITT, among others, succeeded in fabricating fiber glass cables—cables that carried lightwave communications made possible by laser beam technology. A 600-mile Boston-New York-Washington system planned by AT&T is expected to carry 80,000 telephone calls simultaneously through these new "glass pipelines." Within a few years fiber optics may link stores, homes, schools, and offices, and make "glass-wired" telecommunications inexpensive and commonplace.[11]

Telephone conferences, including doctoral orals for which the candidates remain overseas while their committees convene in the U.S. and special telephones that are linked to the resources of powerful computers already are feasible and available in a learning society. Fiber optics technology seems sure to faciliate such communications. However, as these changes occur, we must be careful not to confuse information with education. One is an *item,* the other a *process* to which the *item* may contribute.

As the robot revolution in industrialized nations creates the likelihood of a three- or four-day work week, education for the wise use of leisure takes on new importance. A shortened work week also should provide the hours needed to educate, or at least to retread, workers displaced by the robots that already perform some assembly-line tasks with greater skill, efficiency, and patience than humans. This and other opportunities for extending the schools' domain appear likely to characterize tomorrow's practices.

Furthermore, even widely acclaimed TV programs ("Sesame Street," for instance) tend to be stronger in production, in special effects, and in charisma than in sustained educational merit.

Since this is likely to remain true for some time to come, there is sure to be a growing need for professionally prepared teachers, educational psychologists, and media specialists to work on the improvement of the population's general education via the media.

For both educators and the general public, novel technological innovations and new solutions also create new problems,[12] among them:

- the need to produce specialists and at the same time preserve the merits of a general education;

- the question of striking a balance between the amount of reference material that theoretically can be stored and the amount actually needed;

- learning to cope with the prospect that as many as half of the jobs in U.S. industry may be eliminated by 2000 or 2006;

- teaching learners to use information carefully rather than carelessly as it becomes more abundant and more available;

- educating the relatively few who master and direct the use of the new information technologies to use their advantage with prudence, integrity, and in the human interest;

- at least for the immediate future, dealing with "perhaps the most paralyzing aspect of the microelectronics industrial revolution": namely, "the inability of lawmakers and sociologists to cope with what is occurring, because no one knows where to begin";[13] and

- perhaps most important, striking a balance between what is made technically possible by microelectronics and what is educationally desirable in learning situations.

[11]See Daniel L Askin. "The R & D Story," *Passages,* October 1981, pp. 54–66.

[12]For additional examples, see Jan Henrick Nyheim's list in "The Age of Doubt," *Intermedia,* March 1981, pp. 10, 11.

[13]Adam Osborne, *Running Wild: The Next Industrial Revolution* (Berkeley, Calif.: Osborne/McGraw-Hill, 1979). p. ix.

Telecommunications, the Chip, and Learning. In the long-range future (i.e., by 2000 or 2010), we may discover that the most significant socioeducational mutation wrought by the microprocessors in our Electronic Surround is what they do to enhance learning, the outcome of experiences that shape and improve our subsequent behavior. Advances in technology are already forcing us to think previously unthinkable thoughts. At a meeting in Paris last fall, a group of educators, predominantly scholars from the Third World, discussed at length the possible merits of totally by-passing the Gutenberg Revolution, moving immediately beyond the era of books, and introducing the world's illiterate masses to an unprecedented approach to learning: a new "electronic literacy" based on means of communication other than print.

A member of this UNESCO panel, a woman from the Ministry of Education in a Southeast Asian nation, said, "When I go to a village with a radio, I find all the people there gathering around me eager to listen. Can you imagine the drawing power that a large-screen TV set would have — and the way carefully developed programs may be designed to help those who are now blinkered and muzzled by their illiteracy to become more informed and effective humans."

As microcomputers and robots improve in their ability to *see* gestures, *feel* textures, *hear* commands, *accept* directions, and *speak,* extraordinary, almost preternatural, human-and-computer learning relationships may develop. Christopher Evans, an experimental psychologist and computer scientist, has discussed possibilities that are both exciting and vaguely disturbing. "The old teaching machines," he tells us:

> were electromagnetic gadgets, combining the subtle swiftness of electricity with the unhappy slowness of machinery. . . . Teaching computers, on the other hand, are basically all-electronic, with no moving parts—other than electrons—and are easy to mass produce . . . and they have the great advantage of being extremely reliable.

> Their value is not so much in *what* they teach as *how they will go about it.* The flexibility of a modern computer, small or large, is, to all intents and purposes, infinite, and the range of tasks it can perform is limited only by the range of programs which can be written for it.[14] [Emphasis in original]

Evans contends that, by "learning" to recognize a student's voice patterns, computers will eventually be able to converse and to adjust their programmed responses to the learner "in a wide variety of ways, constantly giving the impression that they are 'interested' in teaching by the way in which they structure their communication to meet the needs of the moment."

Seymour Papert, an M.I.T. professor, contends that the "computer presence" actually can contribute to mental processes. To Papert, there is a world of difference between what computers can do to nurture learning and what society and its schools may choose to do with them as they face what may seem a threatening change. "It is hard to think about computers of the future," Papert says:

> without projecting on to them the properties and limitations of those we think we know today. And nowhere is this more true than in imagining how computers can enter the world of education. It is not true to say that [my] image of a child's relationship with a computer . . . goes far beyond what is common in today's schools. My image does not go beyond: It goes in the opposite direction.

> In many schools today, the phrase "computer-aided instruction" means making the computer teach the child. One might say the computer is being used to program the child. In my version, the child programs the computer and, in doing so, both acquires a sense of mastery over a piece of the modern and powerful technology and establishes an intimate contact with some of the deepest ideas

---

[14]Evans, p. 193.

from science, from mathematics, and from the art of intellectual model building.[15]

Contending that "it is possible to design computers so that learning to communicate with them can be a natural process . . . like learning French by living in France,"[16] Papert says that the computer presence will enable us to modify out-of-school learning environments to the point that "schools as we know them today will have no place in the future. But it is an open question whether they will adapt by transforming themselves into something new or wither away and be replaced."[17]

The "new curriculum" characteristic of our electronic age has certain features with which it is difficult for the school curriculum to compete. The TV and silicon age curricula are becoming ever more pervasive, often are more persuasive, combine images and narration, can provide immediate gratification, are relatively noncompetitive, and are irrefutable. This creates a fascinating potential development for educators: namely, that with the aid of computers some—perhaps many—of our young learners, a decade or two hence, may be taught the coping skills that life demands and that reading currently provides, with the help of an audiovisual-microchip support system.

Today it can take years for textbooks to begin to reflect current events. While textbooks will continue to be of value, schools of the eighties are likely to discover that they will need to install more computer terminals and other electronic equipment for using tapes, videodiscs, and the myriad of analogous resources that the Electronic Surround has begun to provide. While the microchip is not likely to cause a decline in the teaching profession, the status of teachers and what they *do* is likely to be different as they work at developing the planet's great-

est resource: the valuable deposits of "gray matter" in the heads of young and old learners alike. With the help of the tools for improving teaching and learning that the chip provides, the skills of professionals should help to guarantee that the world retains the capacity to move toward a decent, civilized future.

AN ULTIMATE GOAL

I have attempted to summarize some of the possible developments regarding schooling, education, and learning that are presaged by the silicon revolution. There is an ultimate goal, however, both short- and long-term, related to schooling, education, and learning. This is the goal of creating what Lester R. Brown has called a "sustainable society."

Today most of us are painfully aware of the great strains that humanity is placing on our planetary resources. Erosion, biological systems under stress, the changing prospects for maintaining food production for more than 4.6 billion people, the probable twilight of our petroleum-based culture, nuclear weaponry, and divers socioeconomic stresses have been problems for 20 years or more.

To this end I believe that the curriculum should, at appropriate age levels, begin to educate for world society through:

- emphasizing the need to create a timetable for stabilizing world population;

- stressing the need to move from a throwaway society to a preserving, conserving society;

- directing attention toward more ways of powering the planet with unexploited energy sources;

- redirecting research and development in a context of global need rather than in the mere quest for ways to produce more material things;

- using school, community, and national *example* rather than *precept* to change values

---

[15]Seymour Papert, *Mindstorms* (New York: Basic Books, 1980), p. 5.

[16]Ibid., p. 6.

[17]Ibid., p. 9.

and shift priorities so that, in a resource-short world, we stop teaching our children and youths to want and expect what isn't there; and

- becoming more mindful of the social fissures between the haves and the have-nots and beginning to patch them.

In effect, we have changed an old pattern of life in which many people often borrowed from their parents. Now, too many humans are borrowing from our children and grandchildren, many as yet unborn, as they seek to prolong their contemporary binge of conspicuous consumption. We need instead to move toward the voluntary simplicity that the future well-being of our posterity requires.[18]

How do these concluding points bear on education and on the marvels of the microchip? They bear on them because of the potential for improved communication, for more rapid problem identification, and for more effective problem solving that could characterize the silicon chip age. As Jean-Jacques Servan-Schreiber sees it:

> Computerized infrastructures for the Third World could make it possible for whole stages of [socioeconomic] development to be by-passed. From abacus to the multiplication table to the logarithmic rule to adding machines to the first computers to transistors took centuries. And from this long series of innovations emerged the microprocessor—a wonderful device [in] which the . . . basic elements of all wealth converge. . . ."[19]

One hopes that the less-industrialized nations, thanks to the silicon revolution, can greatly improve the lives of their citizens through a blend of technological revolution and improved educational options. As a Dutch Nobel laureate, economist Jan T. Tinbergen, sees it, the information society can make possible a uniquely reconceived educational network with the potential for breaking down the festering poverty and continuing turmoil that is endemic in much of the Third World and thus avoid what otherwise could become an accelerating slide toward disaster.

Thus far, schooling and education have done relatively little to prepare us for the emerging information society. Nor has much been done to recognize or to remedy the need of less-developed nations for not merely a new *deal* but for a new economic *order*. Furthermore, teachers, the curriculum, and the media lag far behind in educating for a sustainable society. I am convinced that endeavoring to achieve this goal will prove to be education's greatest task and its more important responsibility as the 20th century winds down and a new millennium begins. And the microchip just might be the ally that puts the odds in our favor as the profession tackles the job.

---

[18]A number of points made above are developed in detail by Lester R. Brown, *Building a Sustainable Society* (New York: W.W. Norton, 1981).

[19]Jean-Jacques Servan-Schreiber. *The World Challenge* (New York: Simon and Schuster, 1980), p. 268.

What's Holding Up
the Show?

Jay W. Dean _____

Jay W. Dean is a graduate student in Agricultural Education at the University of Minnesota at St. Paul.

As computers become better suited — both in design and in cost — to school purposes, the teacher's ability to use them effectively becomes more important. Two limitations on this ability remain: lack of useful programs (*software,* also called *courseware* in education) and lack of a computer language that teachers can use to create or adapt courseware suited to their own classes. Even these limitations, however, seem destined shortly to give way.

Perhaps the most confusing factor teachers have to deal with at present is the plethora of courseware that is becoming available. Computer vendors, textbook publishers, and public agencies face the competition of hundreds of small software houses that have sprung up in response to the need for good educational software.

Often this software is the brain-child of talented and creative programmers but lacks the pedagogical soundness necessary for the classroom setting. In other instances the product is that of teachers who have the pedagogy and the subject matter content in hand but lack the technical skills necessary to use the computer to the best advantage.

Software often fails to take account of knowledge about the learning process — of such factors as the learning sequence, the use of rele-

vant cues, and key item-response patterns. Thus evaluators should be aware of how selected software relates to theories on learning, cognitive development, instructional psychology, and adaptive instruction.

I recently examined a beautifully designed piece of arithmetic software that was meant to teach "the missing addend." Developed by two creative and resourceful programmers, it demonstrated a masterful utilization of the computer's capabilities. The graphics and sound were excellent, and the algorithm was presented in a way that would intrigue the child.

The missing addend is normally introduced in the first grade or the beginning of the second grade. Unfortunately, the program was written at a fifth or sixth grade reading level. Disparities of this type are common, and teachers with grade-level experience can identify them best.

Evaluators must also be familiar with the other side of the coin. They must know what computers are capable of providing if they are to avoid simply using the new technology in the same manner as the old.

Are the lessons in a piece of courseware personalized and written in a way that draws the student into the learning process? Do they make appropriate use of the color, sound, and graphics capabilities of the computer? Does the pack-

From Jay W. Dean, "What's Holding Up the Show?" Today's Education *(April/May 1982) pp. 21-23. Used by permission of author and publisher.*

age include the documentation that is necessary if a student is to use the materials successfully and with the least possible frustration and distraction?

Fortunately, there is now emerging a scattering of software that is creative, involving, and educationally sound. To ferret out and thoroughly evaluate good programs, however, will continue to take an enormous amount of energy and tenacity.

A complicating factor is that microcomputer software which comes on floppy diskettes or cassette tapes lends itself to illegal duplication. To date, a skilled technician or a state-of-the-art duplication program can circumvent most security precautions. As a result, software developers often hesitate to send out programs for evaluation. Gone are the days of free examination copies or 30-day approvals. This means that districts may have to rely on sales presentations or third-party evaluations, both of which can be time-consuming and risky.

Partially in response to this phenomenon, centers for software evaluation have organized around the country. These can often gain access to commercial software that schools have a difficult time obtaining for evaluation. Their thorough and accurate evaluations can save individual school districts a considerable amount of time and money.

The Northwest Regional Education Laboratory is among these agencies. It has established many criteria for evaluation that can also be useful to school districts that have the opportunity to evaluate software.

To be credible, evaluations should be done by teachers with appropriate subject matter knowledge and experience. Such evaluators will have a feeling for the student characteristics that greatly determine whether a unit of instruction will work with a particular set of learners. In the end, the most crucial question they can ask may be whether the computer is the most suitable way to teach a particular instructional objective.

A second difficulty blocks the development of educational use of computers. No existing computer language is really suitable for teachers' use. Currently, *BASIC* is the most common programming language in education. Much of its popularity is due to the fact that it is a compact, easy-to-use language that is suitable for solving computational problems. It has few commands, which means that the beginning programmer can focus more on the algorithm and less on the structure of the language.

These same characteristics make BASIC less than suitable for many educational applications. It becomes clumsy and difficult to use in applications that involve words and language.

Another drawback of BASIC is that it comes in several versions. A BASIC program written for one computer may not run on any other computer, even another model from the same manufacturer. Often all that is needed to make a program run under these circumstances is to change a few listings, but if teachers lack programming skills, even making simple changes is an arduous task.

While teachers have no need to become BASIC programmers, some proficiency in the language is necessary for those who want to cope with computers in the classroom. By sitting in on an introductory programming class, interested teachers should be able to garner the information necessary to make the kinds of simple changes described above. They will also be able to modify programs to make them better teaching tools. This might involve standardizing the processes by which students enter data or increasing the meaningfulness of a program by adding supplemental text.

PILOT is a dialogue-oriented computer language which deals nicely with words and text. The syntax is simple, which means it can be learned quickly and easily. It can generate sound effects and limited color graphics. People with no previous programming experience can begin to use PILOT in a matter of hours. Anyone who fully exploits its facilities can produce worth-while courseware.

Pascal is perhaps the most suitable language for education. It has been designed to lead to more efficient programming, fewer errors, and easier revision. It is in the final stages of being internationally standardized. Programs written in Pascal for one system will run on other computers. It is in the public domain, and the compilers are inexpensive.

Kenneth Bowles at the University of California, San Diego, (UCSD) has increased the computer assisted instruction (CAI) capabilities of Pascal by making it easier to use words, clauses, and sentences in dealing with student input. UCSD Pascal also contains enhanced graphics capabilities.

This inexpensive, logically structured, relatively easy-to-use language system holds great promise for teachers. While UCSD Pascal is not difficult to understand, however, to become proficient in using it takes considerable time and effort.

A well-structured language comes from the Massachusetts Institute of Technology Artificial Intelligence Laboratory. This language, called *LOGO,* has been described as "easy, forgiving, and user-friendly."

The developers of LOGO shaped it in accordance with two basic ideas: that children should be in control of their own learning and that schools can accomplish this by providing computer-based environments in which students can learn in a natural fashion. As part of this environment, LOGO includes a robot turtle that students can program.

Seymour Papert, in his book *Mindstorms: Children, Computers, Powerful Ideas,* describes how students using LOGO can gain some control over the learning process. They can solve the problem of drawing a circle, for example, by pretending that they are the turtle, walking out what they want the turtle to do, and then describing what they have done in "turtle language."

Papert points out that this process allows the students to practice some very powerful ideas. They are applying a heuristic principle, they are using mathematics as a language, and they are learning that mathematics is not just an abstract ritual but something they can use for personal ends. These features, coupled with the fact that LOGO is now available for the microcomputer, are causing a lot of excitement in education.

Still missing is a language that is easy to learn and easy to use, one that resembles natural dialogue, allows for variations of style, and can be mastered in a few hours.

Only when we put such a tool in the hands of classroom teachers can we expect the consistent development of creative, pedagogically sound software. It is the individual classroom instructor who knows best what will work in the classroom and what types of courseware are needed.

DISCUSSION QUESTIONS AND ACTIVITIES

1. What are the four distinct revolutions, according to Shane, that human communication has experienced?
2. What technological breakthroughs made the microcomputer possible?
3. List four changes in school that the micro-computer is likely to bring about. Are all of these changes desirable?
4. What changes outside of schools are likely to result in the next ten to fifteen years from the dissemination of microprocessors?
5. What additional changes can be expected in

the long-range future, by 2000 or 2010?

6. Shane believes that the curriculum should help educate for a world society. Evaluate the directions he outlines for the curriculum.

7. According to Jay W. Dean, software for microcomputers is deficient in a number of ways. State these different deficiencies.

8. What can be done to improve software?

9. What are the problems in developing a computer language suitable for teacher use, and what is being done to overcome these problems?

10. Explore the courses available at your college designed to promote computer literacy.

11. Survey your local school district in terms of their use of microcomputers. Interview persons in charge of these programs; then assess the overall effectiveness locally of this innovation.

12. Compare the more widely used microcomputers used in schools and colleges with those available for home instruction in terms of costs, programs, characteristic uses, and other features.

13. Invite an expert to speak in class and to provide an introductory demonstration of computer uses.

SUGGESTED READINGS

Aiker, Robert M. "The Golden Rule and Ten Commandments of Computer Based Education." *Technological Horizons in Education* 8 (March 1981): 39–42.

Alexander, Wilma Jean. "Microcomputers: Impact on Society and Education." *Business Education Forum* 35 (May 1981): 19–21.

Anderson, David O. "Microcomputers in Education." *Journal of Learning Disabilities* 15 (June-July 1982): 370–72.

Bolton, Harold and David K. Mosow. "Microcomputers in the Classroom: A Foot in the Door." *Educational Computer Magazine* 1 (September-October 1981): 34–36.

"Computers in the Schools: What's Really Happening Around the Country." *Learning* 11 (October 1982): 30–31, 34, 36, 38, 42, 46.

Cornish, Blake M. "The Smart Machines of Tomorrow: Implications for Society." *Journal of Epsilon Pi* 7 (Fall 1981): 8–14.

Cox, Dorothy and Carl F. Berger. "Microcomputers are Motivating." *Science and Children* 19 (September 1981): 28–29.

Cunningham, Sandra. "Off to a Good Start with Microcomputers." *Educational Computer Magazine* 1 (September - October): 38–39.

Cuthbert, L. G. "Microcomputers in Schools?" *Physics Education* 16 (May 1981): 136–41, 151.

Daneliur, Carl and Annette Wright. "Instructional Uses of Microcomputers: The Why, What and How of the B.C. Approach." *Education Canada* 21 (Fall 1981): 4–11.

Frederick, F. J. *Guide to Microcomputers.* Washington, D.C.: Association for Educational Communications and Technology, 1980.

Hamrin, Robert D. "The Information Society: Its Effect on Education." *Education Digest* 47 (December 1981): 46–47.

Jelden, D. L. "The Microcomputer as a Multi-user Interactive Instructional System." AEDS *Journal* 14 (Summer 1981): 108–117.

Lewis, R. "Education, Computers, and Micro-Electronics." *Technological Horizons in Education* 8 (January 1981): 47–49, 54.

Lopez, Antonio M., Jr. "Microcomputers: Tools of the Present and Future." *School Media Quarterly* 9 (Spring 1981): 164–167.

Martin, Kathleen. "The Learning Machines." *Arithmetic Teacher* 29 (November 1981): 41–43.

"Microcomputers in Education." (Symposium) *Educational Technology* 19 (October 1979): 7–67.

"Microcomputers in the Classroom." *Today's Education: Social Studies Edition* 71 (April-May 1982): 14–30. A series of articles.

Milner, S. D. "How to Make the Right Decisions About Microcomputers." *Instructional Innova-*

tor 25 (September 1980): 12–19.

Phi Delta Kappan 63 (January 1982): 303–325. A series of articles about microcomputers.

Senter, Joy. "Computer Technology and Education." *The Educational Forum* 46 (Fall 1981): 55–64.

"Tracking Students with a Computer." *American School and University* 54 (September 1981): 48.

Zakariya, Sally Banks. "The Computer Goes to School." *Principal* 61 (May 1982): 16–20, 52–54.

11
Bilingual Education

Bilingual education has become an important part of American and Canadian education, marked by the testing of a number of approaches during the 1960s and the growth and spread of bilingual education during the 1970s. Historically, the United States has tended to assimilate foreign speaking people from European backgrounds, but American Indians, Puerto Ricans, and Mexican-Americans have been less linguistically assimilated. In Canada, even before the Bilingualism and Biculturalism Commission's report (1968), educators urged the introduction of French (or English in French-speaking schools) in elementary grades at as early an age as possible.

Bilingual children traditionally tended to find that neither language served them well in coping with academic work. Educators, however, have generally underestimated the influence of the home language and culture. Those who survive academically are frequently asked to choose between their heritage and the dominant culture, a choice that may result in isolating themselves from their culture and their family.

Bilingual education seeks to overcome these problems. Bilingual education is designed to provide schooling fully or partly in a second language for the purpose of enabling students to acquire proficiency in the second language while simultaneously maintaining their proficiency in the first language and fully promoting their overall educational development. English is learned not as an end in itself but as one of many tools—the home language is another—for the development of skills, attitudes, and basic concepts.

At one time school officials, in those cases where there were few bilingual children, did nothing about the problem or perceived it as a problem of low IQ. Some early programs focused on vocabulary items without building a syntactic framework for using words. This was followed by an approach in the 1950s and early 1960s of teaching English as a second language by using drill exercises; however, this approach found little role for the mother tongue. As late as 1967 in the United States, the Bilingual Education Act developed curricula and Spanish language instruction but gave little attention to the development of bilingual teachers.

George Blanco distinguishes between equality and equity and seeks to determine whether bilingual education programs are effective and where the focus on bilingual education should be. However, *The Christian Science Monitor* contends that immersion in English is a better educational approach.

Equity, Quality, and Effectiveness in Bilingual Education

George M. Blanco _____

George M. Blanco (b. 1937) has taught at the elementary, high school, and the university levels. His main interests have been in the areas of second language teaching and learning and bilingual education. He held the position of Director of Foreign Languages at the Texas Education Agency and, later, that of Director of the Office of Bilingual Education at The University of Texas at Austin. He has served as a consultant to state and federal agencies, as well as to American schools in various Latin American countries. He currently teaches full time in the area of bilingual education at The University of Texas at Austin.

Federal and state attention to bilingual education in the United States during the past 18 years has been characterized by controversy and debate concerning its effectiveness, its cost to the taxpayer, its philosophy, and its lack of a conceptual framework with the necessary research underpinnings. Bilingual education during this period has also been characterized as compensatory in nature, i.e., designed primarily for lower socioeconomic students of limited English-language proficiency. It has also been implemented as a transitional program whereby the students' first language is eventually replaced altogether by English for instructional purposes.

Essentially, the goal of bilingual education in the United States has been to ensure that non-English speaking (NES) or limited English-speaking (LES) students acquire a good command of the English language and to succeed academically in the subjects that comprise the school curriculum.

This paper addresses the issue of equity of instruction for a segment of the student population referred to by Hawley (1982:207) as "children at risk." In his words:

> . . . children at risk are assumed to have special needs that set them apart, at least to some extent, from other children and, therefore, disadvantaged. . . . What children at risk have in common is a set of circumstances which, while different, are likely to reduce the effectiveness or, in some cases make inappropriate, conventional educational practices. Business as usual for children at risk is risky business.

NES/LES children fall into the category of children at risk by virtue of the linguistic and cultural circumstances which make them different from the monolingual English speaker of the majority culture in the United States. The issue that NES/LES children are linguistically and culturally different has always worked to their

Condensed from "Quality Education and Educational Equity for Students of Limited English Proficiency," in Equity and Educational Excellence. *New York-New Jersey Coalition for Equity; Consortium for Educational Equity; Rutgers State University of New Jersey; NODAC-Institute for Urban and Minority Education; Teachers College, Columbia University; The Metro Center, RADAC-New York University, 1984.*

disadvantage—the fact that they spoke a language other than English was *their* problem, not the school's, and it was *their* duty to conform to the school's all-English model from the outset. This was usually the case, despite the much touted maxim heard by several generations of future teachers: "Begin where the child is."

The U.S. Supreme Court case, *Lau vs. Nichols,* decreed that English-only educational programs did not provide equal educational opportunity to Chinese-speaking students in San Francisco. In the educational arena, the terms "equal" and "equitable" have often been used synonymously. According to Salomone (1982: 11) equality ". . . refers specifically to division, partition, and redistribution . . . it refers to numerical equality and to equal treatment or inputs. Equity, on the other hand, is a broader concept encompassing justice, equality, humanity, morality, and right."

Following this line of thinking, children at risk need not only educational opportunities that are equal, but also opportunities that are equitable. Educational equity for NES/LES students, as it is implemented in the schools, refers to special programs, strategies, and materials which go beyond those regularly in place for monolingual English-speaking students. The mounting of special programs for children at risk, then, is seen as a necessary step toward assuring that equity be present before true equality can exist. Given the fact, however, that programs for children at risk, such as bilingual education, are compensatory in nature, the question of quality, effectiveness, and excellence surfaces.

EDUCATIONAL QUALITY AND EFFECTIVENESS

While there is a considerable body of literature regarding bilingual education outside the United States (Paulston, 1978), research in this country has been supported in a concerted manner by the federal government since 1979 through funding under Part C Research Agenda of ESEA Title VII. Prior to this effort, most of the research conducted fell into the area of program evaluation using a quantitative paradigm. Comparative studies using a quantitative paradigm required large student samples to provide reliable statistics. According to Goodrich (1980), the only language groups that have large enough numbers of students to warrant use of quantitative comparisons are the Spanish, French, and Navajo. Vázquez (1981) feels that this observation is important because cultural and linguistic differences affect such elements as educational practices, student achievement, motivation, etc., thus rendering interlanguage group comparisons less reliable. Research to show bilingual education effectiveness, or lack thereof, has been difficult to conduct. The evaluation of Title VII Spanish/English bilingual education programs conducted by the American Institutes for Research (AIR) (Danoff, 1978) has been criticized for its inadequacies (Gray, 1977 and 1978; O'Malley, 1978). Yet, Troike (1978) states that not all of the negative findings can be dismissed and that program weaknesses should be corrected. Both Saravia Shore (1979) and Vázquez (1981) feel that effectiveness is a relative term concerning several critical questions: What is to be measured? In relation to what? Using what criteria? Selected by whom?

Troike (1978 and 1981) in his reviews of bilingual education program evaluations in the United States concludes that quality programs can be effective in providing equal educational opportunities for NES/LES children. He feels strongly that if a program does not provide equal educational opportunities, there is something wrong with the program. It is interesting to note that in the programs examined by Troike, the students in the bilingual education programs generally performed as well as, and in some cases better than, students in monolingual programs at the district or national levels in a variety of subjects. It is particularly noteworthy that the standardized tests used in these programs were in English. One of the main criticisms about bilingual education has been the notion that children are either not exposed sufficiently to the English language, or that time spent on instruction in the native language takes valuable time away from exposure to English.

There has been considerable research, both at the applied and the theoretical levels, to show that learning through two languages not only helps children learn the required subject matter, but that it also promotes their mastering the English language better than an all-English setting. Saravia Shore and Arvizu (in press) compiled a descriptive summary of a series of research projects which also support the general use of the students' native language for a portion of the instructional program.

We return to the issue of effectiveness, since its definition or definitions are of prime importance to the concept of bilingual education. The major part of the literature on effective instruction deals with monolingual settings. Even in such settings, it is highly improbable that there exist universal conditions of teaching, given the complex nature of the classroom teaching and learning (Tikunoff and Vázquez-Faría, 1982).

Barnes (1981:2) provides an operational definition of the "effective teacher":

> The "effective teacher" is the teacher whose classes regularly score higher on standardized achievement tests than do classes of other teachers of similar students after entering differences among classes are statistically removed.

Barnes (1981:10) goes on to state that ". . . teachers who establish both a task or work-oriented atmosphere in the classroom and a warm, supportive environment for their students are providing those students with a successful learning environment." *The Significant Bilingual Instructional Features Study* (SBIF)

(Tikunoff, et al., 1981) was based on the premise that effective instructional strategies are probably generic and are similar in monolingual and bilingual settings. The SBIF Study did not use traditional achievement test performance as a measure of effectiveness. Actual observation was used, based on an adaptation of the observation system used by Good and Grouws (1979). Two types of student outcomes were used for 232 students in 58 classrooms: Academic Learning Time (ALT), and establishing the students' competent participation in instructional work activity. ALT is the amount of time a student spends in a content area engaged in learning tasks with a high degree of accuracy. These students achieved a success rate of 80 percent, which averages to 84 minutes per student per day of ALT. The second student outcome, participation in instructional work activity, is particularly important for NES/LES students. Participation requires ". . . that a student understand what is going on, what the task requirements are, what the completed product must look like, what the steps are for completing the task what the teacher's expectations are with regard to task completion, etc." (Tinkunoff and Vázquez-Faría, 1982:249–50). It is obvious, then, that if students do not understand the language of instruction, they will not perform satisfactorily and will fall behind academically.

The SBIF Study speculates that the teacher sample used was effective, as judged by their use of active teaching behaviors and by their producing desired student performance in terms of ALT and student participation in instruction. Further, three skills or behaviors distinguish successful teachers in the sample from effective teachers in monolingual settings:

1. Teachers in the sample used *both* L1 and L2 [first language and second language] for instruction. . . . Particularly for NES/LES who have no English or little English is proficiency, this allows access to instruction.

2. Teachers focused some instructional time on English language development, using variations of the bilingual instructional strategies . . . designed to develop English language proficiency while concurrently ensuring that NES/LES will have access to regular instruction in the content areas so that they don't fall behind while learning English.

3. Preliminary analysis of the descriptions of instruction for teachers in the sample reveal frequent use of behavior which appears to be culturally relevant and specific for the ethnolinguistic group of NES/LES in a given classroom. . . .

For children to participate successfully in the instructional process, they must understand what is going on and what is expected of them. Equitable instructional programs, therefore, require that a school go above and beyond the regular school curriculum for children at risk who do not understand or speak the school language. Equally important, however, is the finding that effective teachers exhibit similar behaviors whether the setting being evaluated is monolingual or bilingual.

There are, of course, studies to support an anti-bilingual education stance. The AIR Study (Danoff, 1978) cited earlier, is perhaps, the best known example. Paulston (1978:188) states that "A study can be found to support virtually every possible opinion." The issue, then, is not so much whether bilingual education, ESL, or any other educational treatment "works" for the NES/LES children but whether students can participate actively in the instructional activities of the curriculum. Of the present options available, bilingual education seems to be the only approach that promotes understanding and thus encourages active participation by NES/LES students in the instructional activities, as far as the content areas are concerned.

Critics of dual-language instruction, however, are quick to point out that time learning

subject matter in L1 is time taken away from the learning of English. As was shown by some of the studies reviewed by Troike (1978), participation in a sound bilingual education program does not retard student academic progress nor the learning of English. There is abundant anecdotal information regarding the academic success experienced by foreigners, such as Mexicans, who come to the United States and who often surpass their Spanish-speaking classmates born in this country (Lazos, 1981). The fact that foreign-born students often surpass their U.S.-born classmates in English (and consequently in the content areas) is, perhaps, best explained by the work of Cummins (1979) and the research conducted in Scandinavia by Skutnabb-Kangas and Toukomaa (1976) and Skutnabb-Kangas (1980).

Cummins has come forth with two hypotheses which may help to explain the anomalous situation of foreign-born students achieving a higher level of academic success than U.S.-born NES/LES students. The first is the Threshold Hypothesis which proposes that certain levels of L1 development must be attained by children to avoid cognitive deficits and to obtain cognitive benefits of bilingualism. If children's L1 is interrupted and discontinued before reaching the "threshold," around the age of 10 or 11, their cognitive development will be retarded. Cummins (1979) and Skutnabb-Kangas and Toukomaa (1976) have advanced the hypothesis that the cognitive aspects of L1 and L2 are interdependent and that proficiency in L2 is partially a function of the L1 proficiency level at the time the child was intensively exposed to L2. Since L1 and L2 Cognitive/Academic Language Proficiency are manifestations of the same underlying linguistic proficiency, literacy in L1 will have a direct bearing on literacy in L2. These hypotheses appear to be supported by the work of Skutnabb-Kangas and Toukomaa (1976) who indicate that, in general, the better students preserve their native language, the better are their prerequisites for learning a second language. These researchers report that the ability to do abstract thinking in the mother tongue is a prerequisite for learning mathematical concepts.

From the standpoint of cognitive development for NES/LES students, then, the research strongly supports the idea of ensuring L1 development until they have reached the "threshold" level and have attained the necessary literacy skills. From the point of view of English language development, the research also suggests a strong L1 base, since proficiency in L2 is directly related to proficiency in L1. This relationship has also been supported by some of the research reported by Saravia Shore and Arvizu (in press). An equitable solution to the dilemma would be to ensure a quantitative and qualitative *continuation* of the children's L1 for a longer period of time than is now commonly done. The issue does not revolve solely around the question of whether children can exit from a bilingual program to participate in an all English learning environment. Rather, it deals with the notion of ensuring the most efficient type of instruction for NES/LES students. By exiting students from the bilingual education program before L1 is firmly established, we may be truncating their cognitive/academic skills and their English language development.

LANGUAGE ATTITUDES

Sociolinguists maintain that the importance and prestige of a language are essentially based on the persons who use it, the audience, the purpose, and place where it is used (d'Angelan and Tucker, 1973; Fishman, 1972; Labov, 1966). If students perceive their native language to be unimportant by virtue of its minimal use or its use in a begrudging fashion, the result can only be negative. Tikunoff and Vázquez-Faría (1981:252–53) agree, stating that:

A strong argument for bilingual instruction for NES/LES rests with the assumption that when instruction is provided only in English, a hierachy of language use is constructed. At the top of that hierarchy is English, and those who can use it competently thereafter are perceived to be somehow "better" than those who cannot. If the NES/LES never hears his/her home language used in the classroom for instruction, or hears it only in a negative context for reprimands, attitudes might develop which place English in a positive frame and the child's home language in a negative frame.

Hansen and Johnson (1981), in their extensive review of the literature on language attitudes, found that language learning is related to self-esteem. "This literature clearly demonstrates that some language varieties are generally held to be inferior to others, and that children quickly adopt the dominant evaluations, perhaps to the detriment of their own self-esteem or cultural identity" (Hansen and Johnson, 1981:4). Positive self-esteem is seen as promoting positive attitudes toward learning and participating and succeeding in school work (Tikunoff and Vázquez-Faría, 1981).

The question of language attitudes in general and toward minority languages and minority groups in particular is an extremely complex one. Whatever the source of language attitudes or attitudes toward ethnolinguistic groups may be, it is quite evident that children adopt "dominant evaluations," to reiterate Hansen and Johnson's term. Children very often exhibit negative attitudes toward their native language, even in a bilingual education program. The pressure to abandon the native language in favor of English, exclusively, is significant, and it is pervasive throughout the educational system, the students' homes, and society at large.

The learning of English is one, if not the primary, goal of bilingual education programs in the United States, and it is vital that NES/LES students learn English and learn it well. The work of Cummins (1979) and the Scandinavian research cited earlier (Skutnabb-Kangas and Toukomaa, 1976), have a direct bearing on the ability of bilingual education students to learn English well. If children are tacitly or openly encouraged to abandon their native language in favor of English before reaching the threshold level, bilingual education will not go beyond a compensatory program with all of the negative opinions that accompany such programs. It is my contention that effective teaching in bilingual or monolingual programs is directly related to and, indeed, shaped by forces outside the school itself. The school, as one of the main purveyors of the mainstream culture, necessarily reflects the attitudes and values of that society. This perspective is not new, and it is supported in the literature on language attitudes and on social and educational change.

FACTORS BEYOND THE CLASSROOM

Paulston (1978) contends that questions regarding bilingual education have shifted with more attention focused on factors outside the programs themselves as causal variables. Bilingual education has usually been looked on as the independent variable and the children's behavior as the dependent variable. Paulston (1978:191) goes on to state that:

We can begin to understand these questions only when we see bilingual education as the *result* of certain societal factors, rather than the *cause* of certain behaviors in children. Unless we attempt in some way to account for the sociohistorical, cultural, economic, and political factors which lead to certain forms of bilingual education, we will not be able to understand or to assess the consequences of that education.

The issue of research which focuses on the classroom, as opposed to research which looks at the larger context within which the classroom exists is examined by Akinasso (1981). This researcher states that the sociolinguistic studies of educational inequality have been criticized by such writers as Ogbu (1974) Karabel and Halsey (1977) for emphasizing micro rather than macrocosmic processes. These studies result in explanations that tell *how,* but not *why.* Gumperz (1980) feels that one cannot dismiss the classroom, altogether. Since students spend a significant part of their formative years in school, he says that what happens there can either change or reinforce values and attitudes brought from outside the classroom.

Hansen and Johnson (1981:2) synthesize this whole issue:

Classroom learning is seen as more than a simple acquisition of knowledge and skills such as reading, writing and arithmetic; it is seen as a process of active effort to understand and cope with the demands, opportunities and restrictions of the social environment of the classroom and school— demands, opportunities and restrictions that are themselves changing, and often are symbolically created not only by teachers, administrators and policy makers, but also by the child's community and family, and by new technologies of teaching, learning and living.

It is my opinion that the negative attitudes about minority ethnolinguistic groups and their languages have a direct effect on the nature of the instructional program and on the learning processes of the students themselves. We have evidence that bilingual education can be effective, that it can promote academic quality, that students can learn the required subject matter and that they can learn the English language . . . provided that the right educational and societal circumstances are present.

CONCLUDING REMARKS

The school and societal contexts in which programs for children at risk operate are as important, if not more so, than the actual instructional strategies used by the teacher. Programs, such as those using a dual-language approach, often operate as an appendage, as something to be tolerated, rather than as an integral part of the instructional and curricular program. The result is circular: the programs are appendages because of negative attitudes and the fact that the programs are appendages further reinforces these attitudes. The opinion held about such programs on the part of all teachers, administrators, parents, the community and society at large determines what the teacher can or cannot do. Negative attitudes about programs for children at risk and about their native language and cultural group breed equally negative attitudes, on the part of the students, about the special instructional efforts and about themselves.

Educational quality, achievement, effectiveness, and equity are not mutually exclusive concepts. Quite the contrary, these concepts should be mutually supportive to produce the desired educational results.

REFERENCES

Akinnaso, F. N. "Research on Minority Languages and Educational Achievement: A Synthesis and an Interpretation." 1981. ERIC Document ED 216 517.

Barnes, S. *Synthesis of Selected Research of Teaching Findings.* Austin, TX: The University of Texas at Austin, Research and Development Center for Teacher Education, 1981.

Cummins, J. "Cognitive/Academic Language Proficiency, Linguistic Interdependence, the Optimum Age Question and Some Other Matters." in *Working Papers on Bilingualism,* No. 19. Toronto: Ontario Institute for Studies in Education, 1979.

d'Anglejan, A. and G. R. Tucker. "Sociolinguistic Correlates of Speech Style in Quebec." In R. W. Shuy and R. W. Fasold, eds., *Language Attitudes: Current Trends and Prospects.* Washington, D.C.: Georgetown University Press, 1973.

Danoff, M. N. *Evaluation of the Impact of ESEA Title VII Spanish/English Bilingual Education Programs: Overview of Study and Findings.* Palo Alto, CA: American Institutes for Research, 1978.

Fishman, J. A. *Sociolinguistics: a Brief Introduction.* Rowley, MA: Newbury House Publishers, 1972.

Good, T. L. and D. Grouws. "The Missouri Mathematics Effectiveness Project: An Experimental Study in Fourth Grade Classrooms" *Journal of Educational Psychology,* 1979, 71, 335–362.

Goodrich, R. L. *Planning Factors for Studies of Bilingual Instructional Features. Bilingual Instructional Features Planning Study.* Vol. 3. Washington, D.C.: National Institute of Education, 1980.

Gray, T. C. "Response to AIR Study." (Duplicated.) Arlington, VA: Center for Applied Linguistics, 1977.

————. "Challenge to USOE Final Evaluation of the Impact of ESEA Title VII Spanish/English Bilingual Education Program." (Duplicated.) Arlington, VA: Center for Applied Linguistics, 1978.

Gumperz, J. J. "Conversational Inference and Classroom Learning." In J. L. Green and C. Wallat, eds., *Ethnography and Language in Educational Settings.* Norwood, NJ: Ablex, 1980.

Hansen, D. A. and V. A. Johnson. *The Social Contexts of Learning in Bilingual Classrooms: An Interpretive Review of the Literature on Language Attitudes.* Rosslyn, VA: National Clearinghouse for Bilingual Education, 1981.

Hawley, W. D. Preface, "Effective Educational Strategies for Children at Risk." *Peabody Journal of Education,* 1982, 59 (4), 207–208.

Karabel, J. and A. H. Halsey. "Educational Research: A Review and an Interpretation." In J. Karabel and A. H. Halsey, eds., *Power and Ideology in Education.* New York: Oxford University Press, 1977.

Labov, W. *The Social Stratification of English in New York City.* Arlington, VA: Center for Applied Linguistics, 1966.

Lazos, Héctor. *A Study of the Relationship of Language Proficiency in the Motor Tongue and Acquisition of Second Language Reading Skills in Bilingual Children at Age Twelve.* Unpublished Doctoral Dissertation. The University of Texas at Austin, August 1981.

Ogbu, J. U. *The Next Generation: An Ethnography of Education in a Urban Neighborhood.* New York: Academic Press, 1974.

O'Malley, J. M. "Review of the Evaluation of the Impact of ESEA Title VII Spanish/English Bilingual Program." *Bilingual Resources,* 1978, 1 (2), 6–10.

Paulston, C. B. "Bilingual/Bicultural Education." In L. S. Shulman, ed., *Review of Research in Education,* 6. Itaska, IL: F. E. Peacock Publishers, Inc., 1978.

Salomone, R. M. "Public Policy and the Law: Legal Precedence and Prospects for Equity in Education." 1982, in press.

Saravia-Shore, M. "A Ethnographic Evaluation/Research Model for Bilingual Programs." In R. V. Padilla, ed., *Bilingual Education and Public Policy in the United States.* Ypsilanti, MI: Eastern Michigan University, 1979.

Saravia-Shore, M. and S. Arvizu, eds. *Cross-Cultural and Communication Competencies: Ethnographies of Educational Programs for Language Minority Students.* West Cornwall, CT: Horizon Communications (in press).

Skutnabb-Kangas, T. *Language in the Process of Cultural Assimilation and Structural Incorporation of Linguistic Minorities.* Rosslyn, VA: National Clearinghouse for Bilingual Education, 1980.

Skutnabb-Kangas, T. and P. Toukamaa. *Teaching Migrant Children's Mothertongue and Learning the Language of the Host Country in the Context of the Sociocultural Situation of the Migrant Family.* Helsinki: Finnish National Commission for UNESCO, 1976.

Tikunoff, W. J. and J. A. Vázquez-Faría. "Successful Instruction for Bilingual Schooling." *Peabody Journal of Education,* 1982, 59 (4), 234–271.

Tikunoff, W. J. et al. *Preliminary Analysis of the Data for Part I of the Significant Bilingual Instructional Features Study.* San Francisco: Far West Laboratory for Educational Research and Development, 1981.

Troike, R. C. "Research Evidence for the Effectiveness of Bilingual Education." *NABE Journal,* 1978, 3 (1), 13–24.

Troike, R. C. "Synthesis of Research on Bilingual Education." *Educational Leadership,* March 1981, 498–504.

Vázquez, J. A. "The Social, Political, and Instructional Contexts of the Bilingual Public Education Movement in the U.S.: A Brief Overview." In W. J. Tikunoff, et al., *Preliminary Analysis of the Data for Part I of the Significant Bilingual Instructional Features Study.* San Francisco: Far West Laboratory for Educational Research and Development, 1981.

Bilingualism Is Not the Way

Of all the major educational issues confronting the American people, perhaps none is as contentious as that of bilingual education. Thousands of school-age children receive instruction in public schools primarily in their native language. Given the fact that public schools are now called upon to teach huge numbers of children from minority backgrounds, the bilingual approach is not surprising. In Texas alone, minorities make up close to half of the school-age population. About two-thirds of that group are Hispanic. Many of those children speak only Spanish. In California, minorities comprise two-fifths of the school children. Again, many children can communicate only in their native language.

The motive for bilingualism, of course, is well-intentioned: namely, to ensure that the children have access to an appropriate and comprehensive education in the only language they understand, until such time as they acquire skills in English.

Unfortunately, good intention does not necessarily promote sound public policy.

There is strong evidence that bilingualism is short-changing for the long-range educational and social needs of the children and unduly burdening financially strapped school systems. Worst of all, a sentimental embracing of multiculturalism may be working against the assimilation so necessary to ensure that the United States remains a unified nation.

The better educational approach, it seems to us, is that recommended by the Twentieth Century Fund's task force on federal elementary and secondary education policy. The report stresses the importance of literacy in English as an overriding educational objective. It would achieve this through a preliminary program of total immersion in English language courses followed by a "catch up" period in courses such as mathematics, science, history, etc., which may have been neglected during the immersion process. This is the reverse of current practice.

Immersion in English—and moving away from bilingualism—makes sense. The issue is not one of denying children necessary instruction in their home language and culture. During a transition period teachers must be patient and not equate unfamiliarity with English with stupidity. And each school system should work out a program of immersion based on its particular circumstances—the children involved, which language they speak, their grade level, and so on. But the primary goal should be fluency in English.

To reject such an approach means continuing to subject school systems to impossible demands in finding foreign language instructors (as many as 56,000 would be needed for bilingual programs around the US, according to the Department of Education). Also, even if schools accommodate a use of languages other than English, this merely postpones the reality of the larger society, which does not.

The United States has always been a nation of many peoples, whose languages and cultures are respected. But English is the official and functional language of the United States. Its official records, its laws, its public discourse, its commerce have under almost all circumstances been conducted in English. It is that very commonality provided by the English language that has helped to give unity, shape, and direction to such a diverse society. At a time when young people need to know far more than the mere rudiments of good English just to obtain jobs in an increasingly sophisticated technological society, this would hardly seem to be the moment to create an educational system that downplays, minimizes, or even ignores English.

DISCUSSION QUESTIONS AND ACTIVITIES

1. Who are the "children of risk"?
2. What is the difference between *equality* and *equity*? Is it a valid distinction?
3. Why is research to demonstrate bilingual education effectiveness difficult to conduct?
4. Does time spent on native language take away valuable time from the study of English?
5. The issue, according to Blanco, is not whether bilingual education works but "whether students can participate actively in the instructional activities of the curriculum." What does he mean by this statement? Do you agree?
6. Should the focus in bilingual education be on the classroom? Forces beyond the classroom? Both?
7. Why does *The Christian Science Monitor*'s editorial claim that immersion in English is a better educational approach than bilingual education?
8. Will immersion in English place nonEnglish-speaking students at a distinct disadvantage?
9. Do the needs of the larger society indicate that immersion in English, rather than bilingual education, is necessary?
10. What common values will immersion in English help support?
11. Observe bilingual programs in operation and report to the class on your observations.
12. Invite a bilingual educator to relate his or her teaching experience in the program.
13. Ask students who grew up in bilingual homes about their early school experiences.

SUGGESTED READINGS

Research Studies

Andersson, Theodore and Boyer, Mildred. *Bilingual Schooling in the United States,* 2 vols. Detroit: Blaine Ethridge, 1976.

Barik, H. C. and Sevain, M. "English-French Bilingual Education in the Early Grades: The Elgin Study." *Modern Language Journal* 58 (December 1974): 392–403.

Canada Royal Commission on Bilingualism and Biculturalism. *A Preliminary Report.* Ottawa: Queen's Printer, 1971.

Cohen, A. D. *A Sociolinguistic Approach to Bilingual Education: Experiments in the American Southwest.* Rowley, Mass.: Newbury House Publishers, 1975.

Cummins, J. "Cognitive/Academic Language Proficiency, Linguistic Interdependence, the Optimum Age Question and Some Other Matters." In *Working Papers on Bilingualism,* No. 19. Toronto: Ontario Institute for Studies in Education, 1979.

_____ . "The Cross-Lingual Dimensions of Language Proficiency: Implications for Bilingual

Education and the Optimal Age Issue." *TESOL Quarterly,* 1980, 14(2), 175–187.

Dulay, H. C. and M. K. Burt. *Why Bilingual Education? A Summary of Research Findings.* 2nd ed. San Francisco: Bloomsbury West, 1978.

Fishman, Joshua. *Bilingual Education: An International Sociological Perspective.* Rowley, Mass.: Newbury House Publishers, 1976.

Gaarder, Bruce A. "Teaching the Bilingual Child: Research, Development, and Policy." *Modern Language Journal* 49, No. 3 (March 1965): 165–75.

Hansen, D. A. and V. A. Johnson. *The Social Contexts of Learning in Bilingual Classrooms: An Interpretive Review of the Literature on Language Attitudes.* Rosslyn, Va.: National Clearinghouse for Bilingual Education, 1981.

Paulston, C. B. "Bilingual/Bicultural Education." In L. S. Shulman, ed., *Review of Research in Education,* 6. Itaska, Ill.: Peacock Publishers, Inc., 1978.

Ramirez, Manuel and Castaneda, A. *Cultural Democracy, Bicognitive Development and Education.* New York: Academic Press, 1974.

Saravia-Shore, M. and S. Arvizu, eds. *Cross-Cultural and Communication Competencies: Ethnographies of Educational Programs for Language Minority Students.* West Cornwall, Conn.: Horizon Communications (in press).

Proponents

"Canada and the U.S.: There's So Much We Can Share and Learn from Each Other About Education." *American School Board Journal* 162 (March 1976): 31–5.

Center for Applied Linguistics (CAL). *Bilingual Education: Current Perspectives.* Arlington, Va.: CAL, 1977.

Gray, T. C. "Challenge to USOE Final Evaluation of the Impact of ESEA Title VII Spanish/English Bilingual Education Program." (Duplicated) Arlington, Va.: Center for Applied Linguistics, 1978.

Johnson, L. S. "Bilingual-Bicultural Education: A Two Way Street." *Reading Teaching* 29 (December 1975): 231–9.

O'Malley, J. M. "Review of the Evaluation of the Impact of ESEA Title VII Spanish/English Bilingual Education Program." *Bilingual Resources* 1(2) (1978): 6–10.

Salomone, R. M. "Public Policy and the Law: Legal Precedence and the Prospects for Equity in Education." (in press)

Tikunoff, W. J. and Váquez-Faría, J. A. "Successful Instruction for Bilingual Schooling." *Peabody Journal of Education* Vol 59, (1982): 234–271.

Troike, C. "¡Bilingual-Sí!" *Principal.* No. 3 Vol. 62, (1983): 9, 46–50.

Critics

Carrison, P. "¡Bilingual-No!" *Principal.* No. 3 Vol. 62, (1983): 9, 41–44.

Danhoff, M. N. *Evaluation of the Impact of ESEA Title VII Spanish/English Bilingual Education Program: Overview of Study and Findings.* Palo Alto: American Institutes for Research, 1978.

Duhamel, R. J. "Bilingual Immersion." *Education Canada* 16 (Spring 1975): 28.

Texas Monthly. "Double Talk." *Texas Monthly* (July 1980): 78–83.

12
Multicultural Education

When waves of immigrants were coming to American shores the melting pot ideology held sway over the thinking of educators. This ideology viewed the role of the school as that of assimilating the immigrant into the life of the culture by teaching the dominant values and beliefs. Many youth were assimilated and some rose in the socioeconomic scale but frequently at the cost of turning their backs on their own culture. Ethnic minorities today generally find public schools alien to their values and belief systems. Multicultural education has been proposed as a remedy. Multicultural education may emphasize ethnic literacy so that the different groups, including the white majority, will gain an understanding of cultural differences. Pluralists (proponents of multicultural education) generally believe that when assimilationists talk about promoting the common culture they frequently mean Anglo-American culture rather than a culture that reflects ethnic and cultural diversity. Through multicultural education minority students can not only acquire social and economic skills but skills to promote significant social change. Thus it will teach members of racial and ethnic groups how to bargain from a position of strength in order to gain full participation in society.

But critics note that such programs may exaggerate differences among groups and thereby be as harmful as the older practice of ignoring real differences. Additionally, should a situation arise where each group demands its own autonomy, it could cause fragmentation, cultural separation, and divisiveness. Usually it is assumed that racial bias is centered on the white middle class; however, ethnic minorities have prejudices that might be exacerbated by a narrow conceptualization of their grievances. Ethnic programs, critics add, assume monolithic groups and ignore variations in age, sex, occupations, social class, and the racially mixed backgrounds of many Americans. Though complaints may be sound about teaching a common culture founded on majoritarian values, and greater emphasis upon interdependence rather than competition may be more appropriate for a complex, interdependent society, some basic democratic values—liberty, justice, and equality—need to be taught.

In his essay, James A. Banks traces the early treatment of ethnic and nationality groups, states principles on which multicultural programs can be based, and notes some dangers to be avoided. Harry S. Broudy indicates some further problems facing multicultural education.

Cultural Pluralism and the Schools

James A. Banks

James A. Banks (b. 1941) studied at Chicago City College, Chicago State University, and Michigan State University, has held an NDEA Fellowship for three years and was a Spencer Fellow. He has taught in elementary schools and is presently a professor of education at the University of Washington in Seattle. In addition to serving as a consultant on ethnic studies to various professional organizations, he has written Multiethnic Education, Teaching Strategies for Ethnic Studies, Black Self-Concept, *and other works.*

During the Colonial period, many different ethnic and nationality groups immigrated to North America to practice freely their religious and political beliefs and to improve their economic status. These groups were provincial, ethnocentric, and intolerant of ethnic differences. Each nationality group tried desperately to establish European institutions on American soil and to remake North America in the image of its native land.[1]

Very early in Colonial history the English became the dominant ethnic group, and controlled entry to most social, economic, and political institutions. The English did not allow immigrants from other nations to participate fully in the social system. Thus, the French Huguenots, the Irish, the Scotch-Irish, and the Germans were victims of overt discrimination in Colonial America. The attainment of Anglo characteristics became a requisite for full societal participation. Immigrants who remained distinctly "ethnic" were punished and ridiculed.

THE MELTING POT IDEOLOGY

The public schools, like other social institutions, were dominated by Anglo-Americans. One of their major functions was to rid children of ethnic characteristics and to make them culturally Anglo-Saxon. The schools taught the children of immigrants contempt for their cultures and forced them to experience self-alienation and self-rejection. The melting pot ideology, which was popularized by the English Jewish author, Israel Zangwill, became the philosophical justification for the cultural and ethnic destruction which the schools promoted. All European cultures, it was argued, were to be blended and from them a novel and superior culture would emerge. Most immigrants, how-

[1]Maldwyn Allen Jones. *American Immigration.* Chicago: University of Chicago Press, 1960.

ever, abandoned their cultures and attained Anglo cultural characteristics. One dominant culture emerged rather than a synthesis of diverse cultures. Most of the nonEnglish cultures stuck to the bottom of the mythical melting pot.

In many significant ways, the Anglo-dominated society, and the schools which helped to perpetuate it, succeeded both in acculturating European-Americans and in helping them to attain inclusion into mainstream American life. Once they attained Anglo-American characteristics, most European-Americans were able to participate fully in the social, economic, and political life of American society. We should, however, not underestimate the psychological pain which this process of self-alienation and re-socialization caused European immigrants and their descendants. Today, most American children of European descent find the school culture highly consistent with their culture, although a few, such as Amish and Appalachian youths, do not. However, this is not the case for most minority youths.

THE ALIEN SCHOOL CULTURE

Many ethnic minority youths find the school culture alien, hostile, and self-defeating. Because of institutional racism, poverty, and other complex factors, most ethnic minority communities are characterized by numerous values, institutions, behavior patterns, and linguistic traits which differ in significant ways from the dominant society. The youths who are socialized within these ethnic communities enter the school with cultural characteristics which the school rejects and demeans. These youths are also dehumanized in the school because they are nonWhite. Because of the negative ways in which their cultural and racial traits are viewed by the school, educators fail to help most minority youths to acquire the skills which they need to function effectively within the two cultural

worlds in which they must survive. Consequently, many of them drop out of school, psychologically and physically.

THE SCHOOL'S ROLE IN A PLURALISTIC SOCIETY

What should be the role of the school within a society which has a dominant culture and many other cultures which, according to the democratic ideology that we extol, have a right to thrive? The school in this type of society has a difficult task, especially when those who make most of the major public decisions do not value, and often disdain, the minority cultures. This harsh reality must be seriously considered when we talk about the role of the school in a pluralistic society. Although cultural pluralism exists within American society, most major decisions in government and in industry are made by Anglo-Americans, many of whom are ethnocentric and intolerant of cultural, ethnic, and racial differences.

The school must help Anglo-Americans to break out of their ethnic encapsulations and to learn that there are other viable cultures in the United States, aspects of which can help to redeem and to revivify the dominant culture. The school should also help all students to develop *ethnic literacy,* since most Americans are very ignorant about cultures in the United States other than their own. Americans are socialized within ethnic enclaves where they acquire the belief that their ethnic cultures are the only valid and functional ones. To attain social and economic mobility, minorities are required to function in the dominant culture and are thus forced out of their ethnic encapsulations. However, Anglo-Americans are able to remain within their ethnic enclaves. Most minorities, nevertheless, are very ignorant about other minorities. Most Mexican-Americans know little about the cultures and problems of Afro-Americans. Most Afro-

Americans know as little about the diverse and complex cultures of Mexican-Americans.

THE NEED FOR BROADLY CONCEPTUALIZED ETHNIC STUDIES PROGRAMS

Broadly conceptualized ethnic heritage programs should be devised and implemented in all schools. Such programs should teach about the experiences of all American ethnic groups, including Jewish-Americans, Polish-Americans, and Puerto Rican-Americans. Most ethnic studies programs now in the schools deal only with the history and culture of the ethnic minority group which is present or dominant within the local school population.

Thus, it is rare to find an ethnic heritage program within a predominantly Black school which teaches about the experiences of Asian-Americans, Mexican-Americans, and Puerto Rican-Americans. Such narrowly conceptualized ethnic studies programs are parochial in scope and do not help students to develop the global view of ethnicity in the United States which they need to become effective change agents in contemporary society. We have reached a point in our history in which multiethnic approaches to the teaching of ethnic studies are not only appropriate but essential.[2]

MAXIMIZING CULTURAL OPTIONS

The school within a pluralistic society should maximize the cultural and economic options of students from all income and ethnic groups. Minority students should be helped to attain the skills needed to function effectively both within their ethnic cultures and within the dominant culture. Black children who speak "Black English" should leave the school sensitive to the utility of their native dialect but proficient in standard English. If Black high school graduates are unable to speak and to write standard English, their careers and social options will be severely limited.

By arguing that the school must help minority youths to attain the skills needed to function effectively within the dominant culture, I do not mean to suggest that the school should conduct business as usual, and continue to demean the languages and cultures of minority students. Rather, educators should respect the cultural and linguistic characteristics of minority youths, and change the curriculum so that it will reflect their learning and cultural styles and greatly enhance their achievement.[3] Minority students should not be taught contempt for their cultures. Teachers should use elements of their cultures to help them to attain the skills which they need to live alternative life styles.

Anglo-American students should also be taught that they have cultural options. We severely limit the potentiality of students when we merely teach them aspects of their own cultures. Anglo-American students should realize that using Black English is one effective way to communicate, the Native Americans have values, beliefs, and life styles which may be functional for them, and that there are alternative ways of behaving and of viewing the universe, which are practiced within the United States that they can freely embrace. By helping Anglo-American students to view the world beyond their cultural perspectives, we will enrich them as human beings and enable them to live more productive and fulfilling lives.

---

[2]This point is further developed and illustrated in: James A. Banks. *Teaching Strategies for Ethnic Studies*. Boston: Allyn and Bacon, Inc., 1975.

[3]Alfredo Castañeda. "Persisting Ideological Issues of Assimilation in America: Implications for Assessment Practices in Psychology and Education." In: Edgar G. Epps, editor. *Cultural Pluralism*. Berkeley, California: McCutchan Publishing Corporation, 1974. pp. 56–70.

TEACHING FOR SOCIAL REFORM

It is necessary but not sufficient for the school to help minority children to acquire the skills which they need to attain economic and social mobility. It must also help equip them with the skills, attitudes, and abilities needed to attain *power* so that they can effectively participate in the reformation of the social system. We will perpetuate the status quo if we merely acculturate students so that they will fit into the Anglo-Saxon mold. They must acquire both the skills and the commitment to engage in *radical social change* if we are ever going to create a society in which individuals and groups can freely participate without regard to their ethnicity, sex, and social class. If the school acculturates as well as politicizes students so that they become committed to radical reform, we should realize that it will be contradicting its historic mission of perpetuating the status quo and will be engaging in a subversive task.[4]

CULTURAL PLURALISM: A CAVEAT

While the school should reflect and perpetuate cultural diversity, it has a responsibility to teach a commitment to and respect for the core values, such as justice, equality, and human dignity, which are expressed in our major historical documents. If carried to its logical extreme, the *cultural pluralism* argument can be used to jus-

tify racism, cultural genocide, and other cultural practices which are antithetical to a democratic society. There is also a danger that *cultural pluralism* may become the new myth, replacing the *melting pot*. This concept must be rigorously examined for all of its social and philosophical ramifications. The works of earlier advocates of cultural pluralism, such as Horace M. Kallen, who originated the concept, and of Julius Drachsler, merit serious study.[5]

We should not exaggerate the extent of cultural pluralism in the United States, and should realize that widespread cultural assimilation has taken place in America.[6] To try to perceive cultural differences where none exist may be as detrimental as ignoring those which are real. The school should foster those cultural differences which maximize opportunities for democratic living, but vigorously oppose those which do not. We should realize that racism, sexism, and dehumanization are also aspects of human cultures which can be justified with the cultural pluralism argument. Emerging concepts and unexamined ideas must not be used to divert attention from the humanistic goals that we have too long deferred, or from the major cause of our social ills — *institutional racism*.

---

[4]Mildred Dickeman. "Teaching Cultural Pluralism." In *Teaching Ethnic Studies: Concepts and Strategies.* James A. Banks, ed. Washington, D.C.: National Council for the Social Studies, 1973. p. 18.

[5]Horace M. Kallen. *Cultural and Democracy in the United States.* New York: Boni and Liveright, 1924; Julius Drachsler. *Democracy and Assimilation: The Blending of Immigrant Heritages in America.* New York: The Macmillan Company, 1920. Milton M. Gordon presents a perspective critique and analysis of *cultural pluralism* in: *Assimilation in American Life: The Role of Race, Religion, and National Origins.* New York: Oxford University Press, 1964. pp. 132–59.

[6]Gordon, *op. cit.,* argues that widespread *cultural assimilation* has taken place in American life but that American society is *structurally pluralistic.*

Cultural Pluralism: New Wine in Old Bottles

Harry S. Broudy

Born in Poland in 1905, Harry S. Broudy emigrated to the U.S. in 1912 and became a naturalized citizen in 1936. He studied at Boston and Harvard Universities, taught at North Adams (Mass.) State Teachers College and for many years at the University of Illinois, Champaign, until in 1974 he became Emeritus Professor of Philosophy of Education. During his long career he served as a visiting distinguished lecturer at many colleges and universities, was past president of the Philosophy of Education Society, the Association of Realistic Society, and an editor of The Educational Forum. *His books include* Building a Philosophy of Education, Enlightened Cherishing, *and* The Real World of the Public Schools. *Philosophically, Professor Broudy is a classical realist or perennialist.*

Whenever another bandwagon to reform American public schools is launched, it may be taken as a signal that somebody has dug up some old bottles and is trying to sell new wine under an old label. For bandwagons, besides being bright, shiny, and noisy, need a motto wherewith to capture attention and pull in customers. For this purpose such slogans as career education, competency-based education, accountability, humanized education, basic education, and value education are eminently useful, because they conjure up sentiments and traditions that no self-respecting citizen or school person would wish to deny. But the predicament to which the bandwagon is responding may not be that for which the old bottles and their labels were designed; it may be new and strange wine indeed.

Cultural pluralism is a case in point. It is an old bottle with venerable labels carrying the mind to the Statue of Liberty, the American Dream, the freedom of the new world versus the despotisms, wretchedness, and limitations of the old, naturalization ceremonies and tears in the eyes of the new citizens drawn from a bewildering variety of nations and ethnic enclaves. Cultural pluralism was a concept developed by Horace Kallen in which he attempted to allow for some degree of cultural diversity within the confines of a unified national experience.[1]

One feature stood out in the old version of cultural pluralism American style, namely, that

[1]Horace Kallen. "Democracy vs. the Melting Pot." *The Nation*, February 18 and 25, 1915. A careful discussion of the various attitudes toward immigrant cultures is contained in Chapter III of a forthcoming book by Paul Violas to be published by G. P. Putnam's Sons.

over and beyond hospitality to ethnic, religious, and national differences, there were common aspirations for a decent and prosperous life in a free, democratic society. Perhaps equal opportunity and political equality were more slogans than descriptions of reality, but no amount of revisionist history can negate the fact that, for some immigrants and their children, economic and social mobility became a reality. The streets were not paved with gold, as many an immigrant had been led to believe, but if one were willing to work very hard, sacrifice a lot—much more than the established families—get some schooling, and take some risks, one could "make it."

These immigrant groups, one can be fairly sure, did not like to give up their customs, language, and traditions. These cultural differences were to be respected (not derided or denigrated) and on certain occasions (such as holidays) celebrated with folk song, costume, and ritual; but they were not expected to become autonomous cultures to be set over against the common culture. After all, these immigrants had chosen to come to this country.[2]

This common culture was predominantly white, Protestant, and Anglo-Saxon, but it had been absorbing elements and flavors from many sources that were being incorporated into the language, diets, and the very ethos of this country. Americans are rarely mistaken for English, French, or Germans regardless of their origins or those of their ancestors.

---

[2]In this respect the Blacks and the Indians pose a moral problem quite different from that of ethnic groups that voluntarily come to this country. If it was morally wrong to bring the Blacks against their will to this country and for the Indians to be pushed and swindled out of their land, then the preservation of the indigenous cultures of these groups is more valid than the preservation of the culture of the Slovenes or the Irish or the Italians. However, whether the present generation of Blacks and Indians would be best served by such preservation and whether such preservation would morally atone for the original wrongs is debatable.

A DIFFERENT VINTAGE

The new cultural pluralism is of a different vintage. It was fermented in the early and mid-60s, when the Civil Rights and Great Society legislation was being translated painfully and erratically into economic and educational programs.

In the first place, the ethnic minorities directly involved in the push for cultural pluralism were Blacks, Puerto Ricans, Mexicans, and Indians. Of these, only some of the Mexicans were immigrants in the ordinary sense of that term, and even they were connected with the special problems of migrant labor and a common border as the other immigrant groups were not. These minorities suffered from a low socioeconomic status that was caused or sustained by discrimination in schooling, housing, and jobs. The new cultural pluralism is not invoked to liberate or raise the consciousness of immigrant Irish, Poles, Jews, Italians, French, Chinese, and Japanese. On the contrary, among the most stubborn foes of the economic and educational reforms of the 60s were the earlier ethnics, who had achieved membership in the various layers of the middle class. They perceived themselves as bearing the brunt of the burden of these reforms.

In the second place, the current press for cultural pluralism does not always share the traditional ideal of a common culture with interesting but not fundamentally important variations. In the more extreme and militant forms, it is a demand that minority cultures be regarded as separate and equal. Each cultural group presumably is to participate in the various activities of the nation on its own terms, and it is expected that the public schools will facilitate their doing so.

How much diversity is compatible with the existence of a viable society is itself an interesting question. Social organization necessitates varying degrees of interdependence, whereas cultural diversity that claims complete autonomy for each cultural group can only result in aggregates of groups with a minimum of dependence on each other. Taken seriously and interpreted strictly, it leads to cultural separatism or atomism.

The advocates of cultural pluralism do not agree on how far toward such separatism they wish to go. They are united, however, in demanding that the schools take into account the linguistic and other cultural differences that children of minority groups bring to the classroom, and that the schools refrain from imposing the majority culture both in its language and ethos on these children.

Schools are asked—and even mandated—to create special programs for children with bilingual home backgrounds, that various dialects be given equal status with the standard English dialect; children are to be encouraged to study their ethnic origins and cultures. Much can be said in favor of these demands. Some are justified by the exigencies of instruction and some by the importance of ethnic pride to the self-concept of the pupil. But these claims can—and in some instances have—become claims that only Blacks can teach Blacks and only Puerto Ricans can teach Puerto Rican children. There is even the suggestion that all instruction throughout the grades be conducted bilingually.

Writing of bilingual schooling, Bayard Rustin, noted leader in the Civil Rights movement and President of the A. Philip Randolph Institute, said:

> . . . the concept of bilingual teaching is all too often being advocated as a means of creating a separatist, alternative culture in which the speaking of English does not play a pivotal role. . . .We must recognize that the object of education is to help students cope with an increasingly complex society. Those who minimize this goal are doing inestimable harm to the very children who need quality education more than any other group. Instead of producing students who are fluent in two lan-

guages, the proponents of cultural isolation would produce bilingual illiteracy on a massive scale.[3]

Accepting the need for bilingual instruction as a means to quicker and more efficient entry into the common culture is far less debatable than to use bilingualism as a way of refusing to participate in that culture. Even more debatable is the wisdom of "accepting" a dislike for formal schooling, the work ethic, and the standards of health and morals prevalent in the majority culture. Indeed, if "feeling comfortable with" or "being turned on by" are the final criteria for legitimacy of a cultural pattern, then we must be prepared to "accept" without "getting uptight" the gang, drug, and crime cultures that some groups "feel comfortable with." Whatever may be the ultimate metaphysical defense for such a view, it is simply not the case that the potentials of diverse cultures for coping with a modern technological society are equal, and the public schools ought not to conspire to foster the illusion that they are.

An even more important consequence of the view that all cultures are separate, autonomous, and equal is that some groups will be encouraged not to participate not only in the culture of this country but also in the intellectual and artistic achievements of the human race. To these achievements many races and cultures have contributed, albeit not equally or uniformly. Nevertheless, one theme unifies the diversity of knowledge, art, and religion—the attempt to define and realize the peculiar virtues (excellences) of the human species.

As far as the school is concerned, this theme is expressed in and transmitted through the scientific, humanistic, and artistic subject matters we call the disciplines. The modes of inquiry and the forms of feeling exhibited in these disciplines

---

[3]Bayard Rustin. Quoted in: Albert Shanker. "Where We Stand." Advertisement in *The New York Times,* July 6, 1975.

are not class-bound or culture-bound. To be disciplined by these disciplines is what has customarily been called liberal education and quality education. Cultural pluralism was never intended to bless the evasion of this kind of education.

If the new cultural pluralism is used to justify such an evasion, it will be of doubtful value to those whom it is intended to liberate. We should look with some skepticism at proposals for alternative curricula, the substitution of "relating" for cognitive achievement, and the distortion of scholastic standards to accommodate cultural differences; they may only "con" the children of minority groups out of their right to the real thing.

The old cultural pluralism denoted an ideal of the kind of unity in diversity that a great orchestra or indeed any great work of art exhibits, where the whole is discernible in every part and every part gets its full meaning from the whole. Once the new cultural pluralism absorbs the flavor of this ideal, it can mature safely in the old bottles.

DISCUSSION QUESTIONS AND ACTIVITIES

1. What is the melting pot ideology and why was it used?
2. What does Banks mean by "ethnic literacy" and what would be the purpose of such programs?
3. How does Banks propose that minorities gain the types of skills needed to function effectively in the larger culture?
4. Should schools teach a set of core values? Of what should they consist? How can the problem of bias be avoided?
5. In what respects were the experiences of early immigrants significantly different from today's ethnic and minority groups?
6. How much diversity can a democratic society tolerate and still operate effectively?
7. Is there danger, as Broudy claims, that some groups will not be encouraged to participate in the intellectual and artistic achievements of the human race?
8. Can we freely encourage racial and ethnic groups to study the disciplines and their forms of inquiry because they are not class-bound or culture-bound?
9. Ask those class members of racial and ethnic minorities to comment on their own schooling in light of the essays.
10. Invite to class as a speaker a teacher or administrator of a multiethnic program.
11. Survey what your local community is doing in multicultural education and make recommendations for needed programs.

SUGGESTED READINGS

Banks, James A. *Teaching Strategies for Ethnic Studies.* Boston: Allyn and Bacon, 1975.

Chase, Josephine. *Multicultural Spoken Here: Discovering America's People through Language Arts and Library Skills.* Santa Monica, Ca.: Goodyear Publishing Co., 1979.

Claydon, Leslie, et al. *Curriculum and Culture Schooling in a Pluralist Society.* Winchester,

Mass.: Allen and Unwin, 1978.

Colangelo, Nicholas; Foxley, Cecelia H.; Dustin, Dick, eds. *Multicultural Nonsexist Education: A Human Relations Approach.* Dubuque, Iowa: Kendall/Hunt, 1979.

Cross, Delores, et al. *Teaching in a Multicultural Society.* New York: The Free Press, 1976.

DeLo, James S. *Multicultural Transactions: A Workbook Focusing on Community Between Groups.* Saratoga, Ca.: Century Twenty One, 1981.

Epps, Edgar G., ed. *Cultural Pluralism.* Berkeley, Calif.: McCutchan, 1974.

Glazer, N. *Affirmative Discrimination.* New York: Basic Books, 1975.

Gold, M. J., Grant, C. A., and Riulin, A. N. *In Praise of Diversity: A Resource Book for Multicultural Education.* Washington, D.C.: Teacher Corp, Association of Teacher Education, 1977.

Klassen, Frank H. and Gallnick, Donna M. *Pluralism and the American Teacher: Issues and Case Studies.* Washington, D.C.: Ethnic Heritage Center for Teacher Education of the American Association of Colleges for Teacher Education, 1977.

McLeod, Keith A., ed. *Multiculturalism, Bilingualism, and Canadian Institutions.* Toronto: Guidance Center, Faculty of Education, University of Toronto, 1979.

Pusch, Margaret D., ed. *Multicultural Education: A Cross-Cultural Training Approach.* La Grange Park, Ill.: Intercultural Network, 1979.

Tiedt, Pamela L. *Multicultural Teaching: A Handbook of Activities, Information, and Resources.* Boston: Allyn and Bacon, 1979.

13
Mainstreaming

An increasingly widespread concern over the education of handicapped children and doubts whether their special education is adequate to their needs have led to the development of mainstreaming. Mainstreaming involves moving handicapped children from their segregated status in special classrooms and integrating them into regular classrooms. The handicapped child would be in a regular classroom for all or part of a day and receive the necessary supportive services of both special and general education. Mainstreaming for some students might only entail integrating with other students for nonacademic work such as physical education, but for others it might involve assignment to a regular classroom and provision therein for special education as appropriate. The theory of mainstreaming holds that children have a right, and would benefit from, participation in the least restrictive educational program they can manage.

The United States courts have so far decided that handicapped children have a right to participate in public education regardless of the classification or the severity of the handicap, and that an education should be furnished appropriate to individual learning needs, including treatment and therapy according to the disability.

One problem of labelling children with disabilities is that they may be misclassified, which might mean being almost indefinitely trapped in the wrong program and segregated from peers. Minority groups seem especially likely to be misclassified. At times children have been singled out for some behavior quirk or learning habit, labeled, and placed in a special classroom; this practice has led to emphasizing their differences rather than similarities with students in regular classes.

But even those in favor of mainstreaming recognize a number of difficult problems: regular classroom teachers need special preparation and assistance in working with handicapped children; these children may not be accepted by their classmates and may not receive special help needed from them in performing routine school activities; modification of the physical plant may be necessary; changes in curriculum and class size will be needed; and additional funding exclusively for such programs is essential. Moreover, research seems to suggest that while those in regular classes learn more, those in special classes are better adjusted.

Martin Tonn, drawing upon arguments and research findings, states directly and succinctly why the mildly mentally retarded child should be integrated into regular classrooms. Edwin W. Martin, on the other hand, points out many problems and barriers that may lead to unsuccessful programs, and he warns against exaggerated claims that are unlikely to be successfully fulfilled because of difficulties of implementation.

The Case for Keeping Mentally Retarded Children in Your Regular Classrooms

Martin Tonn _____

Martin H. Tonn (b. 1921) studied at the University of Iowa and held a USOE special education fellowship. He has been a speech therapist in the public schools, a consultant on speech and hearing to government agencies, and has held office in speech and hearing associations. In addition to articles in professional journals, he has written humorous articles and articles on child care for mass circulation magazines. Tonn is director of special education at Moorhead State College, Moorhead, Minnesota.

Before the turn of the century, mentally handicapped children faced one of two rather bleak prospects: an isolated existence at home or institutionalization. In the early 1900s a third choice was opened for these children: special, segregated schooling (mentally handicapped children were placed in self-contained, special classrooms and taught by special education teachers). Only in the last decade or so has another option been offered: integration of handicapped children into the regular classroom program. It's something you should know more about.

The idea of placing mentally handicapped children in the mainstream of the school program gained impetus from a November 1968 magazine article published in *Exceptional Children*. The article's author, I. M. Dunn, spoke out against the exclusive use of self-contained classes for the educable mentally handicapped. Dunn did not call for abolishing all special classes, but he offered evidence to support the use of alternate programs. His article sparked further research and debate that, in turn, have changed some of the traditional recommendations for teaching moderately retarded children.

Support for integrating educable mentally handicapped children into regular classes rests on these seven points:

1. Dunn and others say research shows that, with one exception, mentally handicapped children do better in regular classes than in special classes. The exception: peer acceptance.

2. Labeling and stigmatizing children by sending them to "retarded" classes may prove detrimental to them.

3. Special classes isolate children, preventing meaningful contact that could be helpful both to mentally handicapped and other students.

4. Many special classes do not meet—in a real way—the educational and social needs of children.

5. Special classes have an unrealistically high

From Martin Tonn, "The Case for Keeping Mentally Retarded Children in Your Regular Classrooms,"
American School Board Journal *161 (August 1974)* p. 45. Reprinted with permission.

proportion of minority children and children from low socioeconomic backgrounds. This lack of balance, researchers claim, is the result of a middle-class oriented test bias and of environmental deprivation, rather than of actual intellectual inferiority inherent in the child.

6. Isolating students in special classes is not in keeping with our democratic philosophy of education.

7. Results from standardized IQ tests are not sufficient evidence for placing children in special classes.

More about the final point: Psychologists and educators know that standardized IQ tests are subject to fluctuations caused by factors such as emotional problems, environmental deprivation, sensory defects, and special learning disabilities. At the educable level, children with IQs of 50 to 75 generally are placed in special classes. Studies have shown, however, that some students with moderate mental handicaps perform better (on a battery of various cognitive tests) than do children who have IQs above 75 and who attend regular classes.

Several alternative programs have been devised by school officials who are convinced that a number of mentally handicapped children can profit from experience in the regular classroom. In some districts, handicapped children are placed in ordinary classes when they reach a certain level of achievement in their special classes and when their special class teachers recommend the transfer. A mentally handicapped child who moves into the traditional classroom setting receives help each day from a special education resource teacher. This additional assistance is flexible—increased when the child is experiencing problems and decreased as he progresses with his school work. Resource teachers also can help classroom teachers plan curriculum programs for handicapped children.

A program called Individually Prescribed Instruction continually assesses and monitors the abilities and progress of a mentally handicapped child who attends a regular class. Special instructional materials are produced for the child as he reaches each new or different level of learning. This method allows a handicapped child to work at his own pace.

The Harrison Resource Learning Center in one of Minneapolis' inner-city schools provides prescriptive instruction to those moderately mentally handicapped youngsters who attend regular classes. The amount of time each child spends in the Resource Learning Center is flexible and based on individual needs. With the help of this program, a number of mentally handicapped children have been enrolled full time in regular classes.

No one is suggesting the elimination of all special classes for retarded children, some of whom may suffer from severe handicaps or a combination of emotional and physical problems. These children may be served best in special classes.

But this question *is* being asked: Do all special children necessarily need special classes? Donald MacMillan, writing in *Focus on Exceptional Children* poses the question this way: "To what extent, and under what circumstances, can a wider range of individual differences be accommodated in the regular class than is presently the case?"

School board members and superintendents should be aware of the district-wide implications of this trend to integrate certain handicapped children into the traditional classrooms:

1. More resource teachers and teacher aides will be needed.

2. Smaller classes will be beneficial, if not necessary.

3. Regular classroom teachers who work with mentally handicapped children will need more specialized inservice training.

4. Top school officials should ensure that administrators, teachers, parents, and the general community are aware of the goals and objectives of new programs for handicapped children within their districts.

Some Thoughts on Mainstreaming

Edwin W. Martin _____

Edwin Wilson Martin (b. 1931) took his doctorate at the University of Pittsburg and served a number of years as co-director of the speech and hearing clinic at the University of Alabama before joining the federal government in various capacities. A recipient of several awards and former Director of Education for the Handicapped, United States Office of Education, he is now President, Human Resources Center, Inc., in Albertson, New York.

Several weeks ago, our CLOSER LOOK program, which provides information to parents and others about education for handicapped children, received a letter from a young girl, a seventh or eighth grader, asking if we could help find a special school for a retarded girl in her class. The letter went on to express her grievances that the retarded girl was given too much of the teacher's attention and that she received good grades for work that others would have received poorer grades for. In all, the writer felt this retarded youngster should be put somewhere else, a suitable place.

Her letter, while clearly understandable from a young, maturing person, summarizes in one short page the major historical response of our schools and our culture to the needs of handicapped people. They are different, they trouble us in deep, unexplainable, irrational ways, and we would like them somewhere else, not cruelly treated, of course, but out of sight and mind.

If in advocating mainstreaming, we don't plan today for these societal patterns of response to the handicapped we will be painfully naive, and I fear we will subject many children to a painful and frustrating educational experience in the name of progress.

THE REASONING BEHIND MAINSTREAMING

Let's focus attention for a minute on why so many of us favor increasing the positive interactions between handicapped and non-handicapped learners, which is the essence of mainstreaming.

Our experience with segregated societal institutions has shown them to be among our most cruel and dehumanizing activities. I recently heard former Attorney General Ramsey Clark make this point very well. Think for a moment about the conditions within Indian reservations, about the internment of Japanese-Americans in World War II, about the Willowbrooks, about the jails, about the racially segregated schools. In each instance we have created these institutions, supposedly for the good of those to be incarcerated, or at least to provide them humane treatment, and in each, there has been a classic pattern of neglect, isolation, rejection, and ultimate dehumanization of the persons on whose behalf society was supposedly acting. This has been true (fortunately in some lesser degree) of our approach to handicapped children within public education. Yet we all know of the insufficient budgets, the unqualified teachers, the condemned buildings, the lack of materials, the failure to provide effective identification, and the out of sight/out of mind syndrome.

On this basis alone, *the human concern for human beings,* we must attempt to have handicapped children, in sight, in mind, and in settings where they will receive the fullest measure of our educational resources. If we also believe their actual achievement in educational terms will also prosper—so much the better.

BARRIERS IN OUR WAY

I am concerned today, however, about the pell-mell, and I fear naive, mad dash to main-stream children, based on our hopes of better things for them. I fear we are failing to develop our approach to mainstreaming with a full recognition of the barriers which must be overcome.

First, is the question of the attitudes, fears, anxieties, and possibly overt rejection, which may face handicapped children, not just from their schoolmates but from the adults in the schools. Principals, teachers, and teacher aides, after all, are only human. Their attitudes are created by their experiences and most have had no formal training or experience with the handicapped child. In fact, as any of you who have worked on revision of college curricula know, efforts to include such training for regular educators have been fiercely resisted for the most part.

If the majority of handicapped children—the mildly and moderately retarded, the children with behaviorial disorders, the children with language and learning problems, the children with orthopedic difficulties—are to be spending most or much of their time in regular classrooms, there must be massive efforts to work with their regular teachers, not to just "instruct them" in the pedagogy of special education but to share in their feelings, to understand their fears, to provide them with assistance and materials, and in short, to assure their success.

Can you imagine what the educational experience for handicapped children will be if they and their teachers are left to sink or swim by one sudden impulsive administrative judgment?

SOME OTHER PROBLEMS

While no one wants such a condition to occur, my discussions with people suggest we need to be aware of some of the problems we face.

First, efforts to provide training and experiences for regular classroom teachers are not keeping pace with the efforts to mainstream. We can predict that much of this training will be rationalistic and skill oriented and fail to respond to the feeling and attitude issues. It may also be that the practical involvement which should be part of the training will be relatively laissez-faire and not carefully or intensively supervised. This is all too true of much current training.

Second, there is a range of logistical problems. Children come and go from class at inappropriate times. Special educational resource teachers use different sets of materials from the regular classroom teachers, and the fact that the teachers are parts of separate administrative budgets may mean that they can't get together on materials.

One major ingredient in mainstreaming, frequently cited as essential, is the development of educational prescriptions or programs for each child. Reports reach me that we need to look carefully at this process. In some instances, there is not enough material effort in developing the programs. The special education or school psychology people are drawing up plans for the teachers to follow. My prediction is that this approach will fail, that it will be seen as too externally oriented a device. Further, in some instances the manpower shortages mean that such plans can only be drawn annually or perhaps semiannually. These plans are likely to be quickly obsolete and relegated to the desk drawer, with psychologists' reports and other educational artifacts.

Finally, there is all too frequently a failure to evaluate carefully the child's progress toward specific educational objectives so that we will have to rely, as in the past, on our subjective judgments as to whether or not the child is, in fact, better off in mainstreamed settings. I would like to add, parenthetically, that our observations on the effectiveness of programs must include the emotional and social aspects of the children's lives, for much of our hope for mainstreaming lies in this realm.

CONCLUDING COMMENTS

I have used this discussion to speak to several major issues or concerns, societal attitudes, mainstreaming itself, new demands for teacher education, new demands for effective educational planning and programming and finally the need for a more effective evaluation of our work.

There is a mythical quality to our approach to mainstreaming. It has faddish properties, and my concern is that we do not deceive ourselves because we so earnestly seek to rectify the ills of segregation. We must seek the truth and we must tolerate and welcome the pain that such a careful search will bring to us. It will not be easy in developing mainstreaming, but we cannot sweep the problems under the rug.

Alexander Solzhenitsyn in the last letter he circulated among his friends in the Soviet Union called on them to renounce the lies in that society and its governance. He spoke not only of the lies that the intellectuals and writers were called upon to write to speak under government pressure but also of the lies which others spoke and about which they had chosen to remain silent. He predicted that if that small brave band of dissidents would refuse to lie, the pattern would spread from 100 to 1,000 to many thousands and the weaknesses in their system would be forced to change, quickly.

There are many messages for Americans in Solzhenitsyn's words and especially for us in special education. We cannot keep silent about some of the lies in our present system—the failure to provide services, the poor facilities, the failure to identify learning problems, the failure to move children out of institutions or out of special programs into regular settings.

But we must also avoid those well intentioned lies that ignore the weaknesses in a well intentioned system, because we are afraid that exposure will hurt our cause. We should not allow our belief in the promises of mainstreaming to cause us to be silent if we see faults in its application. With the newly recognized *rights* of children to the education we offer, there must be an equal *responsibility* to see that those rights are truly fulfilled.

DISCUSSION QUESTIONS AND ACTIVITIES

1. What are the seven points that support the integration of educable mentally handicapped children into regular classes?

2. What alternative programs are provided for those mentally handicapped children who are mainstreamed?

3. Can those school systems that use mainstreaming dispense with all special education classes?

4. Gather evidence on school systems where mainstreaming has generally proven successful and those where the results have been unfavorable. What are the ingredients for successful programs?

5. Martin is concerned that in the rush to mainstream children, we overlook the barriers that must be overcome. What are these barriers?

6. What type of preparation do regular classroom teachers need in order to work successfully with handicapped students?

7. Invite to class as visiting speakers, teachers of special education classes and regular classroom teachers who have integrated handicapped children.

SUGGESTED READINGS

Proponents

Blackhurst, A. Edward. "Competencies for Teaching Mainstreaming Students." *Theory Into Practice* 21 (Spring 1982): 39–43.

Borg, Walter R. and Frank R. Ascione. "Classroom Management in Elementary Mainstreaming Classrooms." *Journal of Educational Psychology* 74 (February 1982): 85-95.

Dumas, Wayne. "Mainstreaming and Four Red Herrings." *The Clearing House* 55 (February 1982): 282–83.

Dunn, L. M. "Special Education for the Mentally Retarded—Is Much of It Justifiable?" *Exceptional Children* 34 (1968): 5–22.

Hart, Verna. *Mainstreaming Children with Special Needs.* New York: Longman, 1981.

Hegarty, Seamus. "Meeting Special Educational Needs in the Ordinary School." *Educational Researcher* 24 (June 1982): 174–81.

Kopit, Marvin. "Restructuring Curriculum and Instruction Courses to Accommodate Mainstreaming Studies." *Teacher Education and Special Education* 5 (Winter 1982): 11–18.

Lehr, Joan K. "Teacher Training Programs for Exceptional Classes." *Music Educators Journal* 68 (April 1982): 46–48.

Paul, James L., Anne P. Turnbull, and William M. Cruickshank. *Mainstreaming: A Practical Guide.* Syracuse, N.Y.: Syracuse University Press, 1977.

Salend, Spencer J. and Donne Viglianti. "Preparing Secondary Students for the Mainstream." *Teaching Exceptional Children* 14 (February 1982): 137–40.

Strain, Philip S. and Mary Margaret Kerr. *Mainstreaming of Children in Schools: Research and Programmatic Issues.* New York: Academic Press, 1981.

Critics

Bates, Louise. "Mainstreaming: We Have Come Full Circle." *Childhood Education* 58 (March-April 1982): 238-40.

Gickling, E. E. and J. T. Theobold. "Mainstreaming: Affect and Effect." *Journal of Special Education* 9 (Fall 1975): 317-28.

Kunzweiler, Charles. "Mainstreaming Will Fail Unless There Is a Change in Professional Attitude and Institutional Structure." *Education* 102 (Spring 1982): 284-88.

Longo, Paul. "Mainstreaming: The Promise and the Pitfalls." *Urban Education* 17 (July 1982): 157-79.

Mosley, W. G. and H. H. Spicker. "Mainstreaming for the Educationally Deprived." *Theory into Practice* 14 (April 1975): 73-81.

Ringlaben, Ravic P. and Carol Weller. "Mainstreaming the Special Educator." *Education Unlimited* 3 (Fall 1981): 19-22.

Turney, David. "Mainstream or Quiet Eddy?" *Contemporary Education* 46 (Writer 1975): 146.

14
Educating the Gifted

The gifted and talented are once more the object of attention after a period of relative neglect. When the Soviet Union launched Sputnik in 1957, alarm swept through the land that the United States had fallen behind in the space race and therefore more scientists, engineers, and mathematicians would be urgently needed. The National Defense Education Act of 1958 provided funds to promote the intellectually talented in those fields. But by 1965 with the Elementary and Secondary Education Act, interest in culturally different learners and compensatory education became a dominant concern; this trend was followed by provisions for handicapped children. Until recently many administrators assumed the gifted could make it alone. Now interest has again returned to the gifted and talented, and some important changes are evident since the earlier years.

An important development is that giftedness is no longer restricted to intellectual talent. In 1972, the USOE's Office of Gifted and Talented defined these two terms as referring to children capable of high performance in any one or more of these areas: general intellectual ability, specific academic aptitude, creative and productive thinking, leadership ability, visual and performing arts aptitudes, or psychomotor ability. By this definition, three to five percent of the school age population could be considered gifted. An elementary teacher with a class of 35 would likely have one or two gifted children each year. Or, to use another example, out of a hypothetical roomful of 100 children who represent all children in the fifth grade, 68 of them are likely to be average learners, 13 above average, 13 below average, three retarded, and three gifted.

The two educational approaches to the gifted are acceleration and enrichment. Acceleration may involve early enrollment in kindergarten, skipping grades, advanced placement, and early high school and college entrance. Acceleration, however, removes the child from age mates and may cause social isolation. Enrichment programs, which are now part of many elementary schools, enable the child to spend most of the time in the regular classroom but meet several hours each week with other gifted children.

Federal education programs for the gifted were funded in 1976. Presently 30 states make some statutory provision for educating the gifted.

In the selections that follow Donald Thomas surveys the present status of education for the gifted, including programs, legislation, type of teachers needed, and the role of parents. James J. Gallagher shows that Americans have generally had an uneasy and an ambivalent attitude toward the gifted, caught between the fear of a special elite as opposed to egalitarianism. Can these conflicting attitudes be reconciled? Will greater attention to the gifted neglect the handicapped and disadvantaged?

Gifted and Talented Children: The Neglected Minority

Donald Thomas

Donald Thomas (b. 1926) studied at the University of Dubuque and received a doctorate from the University of Illinois. He has been a high school teacher of English, speech, and remedial reading, and a counselor, principal, and superintendent in several school systems. He is presently superintendent in Salt Lake City School District. Dr. Thomas has been a lecturer at a number of colleges and universities, a consultant to various organizations, and has contributed articles to many professional journals.

Youngsters with unusual talents number in the millions and many need special help in school. Some of our most gifted students have had difficulty in school, while others have passed through without using many of their talents.

Unfortunately, the education of gifted and talented students has not been given the attention it deserves. As a result, some of the brightest students have dropped out of school.

In the past decade our schools have made good progress in the education of handicapped students. Strides have been made in providing special services to the blind, the deaf, the retarded, the emotionally disturbed, the physically handicapped, and the disadvantaged. At the same time, however, little attention has been given to those who are gifted and talented.

GIFTED CHILDREN MISUNDERSTOOD

Some people may find it difficult to see why gifted children require special attention. The reason is that our schools are not equipped to deal with future Beethovens, Jeffersons, Newtons, and Einsteins. Such children often appear different, out-of-the-ordinary, and out-of-step with the rest of the class. They are often misunderstood, considered uncooperative, antisocial, or defiant.

Thomas Edison stopped going to school because his teacher claimed that he could not learn. Gregor Mendel failed an examination four times. Newton was considered a slow student. So were Darwin, Churchill, and Eisenhower. Shelley, Whistler, and Poe were expelled from school because they could not abide by the rules. Einstein found school to be so extremely boring that he learned mathematics from his uncle.

Those who study gifted children believe that a large number of these children simply do not survive the ordinary school programs. What is needed, they say, are learning activities especially suited to the needs of superior children. They need unique materials, highly skilled

From Donald Thomas, "Gifted and Talented Children: The Neglected Majority," NASSP Bulletin 60 (October 1976): 21–24. Used by permission.

teachers, special attention, and sympathetic understanding.

Now that schools have provided special services to the "disadvantaged" and the "handicapped," it is time that we better educate our most able children. The following questions and answers consider the current status of education for gifted and talented students.

Who are the gifted and talented children? Gifted and talented children are those who have high potential or performance in one or more areas. Such students may be extremely bright. Some have leadership talent. Others are outstanding in the performing arts. Many show great decision-making ability. Their talents range from the ability to read far above their grade level to the ability to solve intricate social problems. Such children come from all walks of life, and are the children of parents from a wide spectrum of occupational fields.

How many gifted and talented students are there? Estimates vary widely. The U.S. Office of Education estimates that three to five percent of our children are gifted. This means that between 1.5 and 2.5 million gifted and talented children are in our schools. The School Management Study Group (SMSG) states that there are between three and five million gifted students in the public schools alone. Some educators who are authorities in the education of the gifted claim that the number of talented students is far higher than can be measured by our present tests. Others claim that all children are gifted in some way.

Why should gifted and talented children receive special attention? Being gifted is often as much a handicap in our schools as being retarded. These children need special programs to realize their potential. They need challenging learning activities, understanding teachers, and highly individualized learning opportunities. Without

special assistance such children often conceal their talents, become bored, show hostile behavior, or withdraw from others. Human talent is the greatest resource possessed by any nation. It is the talents of our children that must be discovered and nurtured by our teachers.

What kinds of programs exist for the gifted and talented? Some 30 states have enacted legislation to implement programs for highly talented students. Twenty state departments of education have full-time directors to promote the education of gifted. Several states provide special funding as an incentive to develop educational programs for superior children. Five states that have strong programs for the gifted are Illinois, California, North Carolina, Idaho, and Ohio.

The Illinois Gifted Program was initiated in 1964, and provides supplementary funds to districts that voluntarily establish programs for gifted students. California has had the Mentally Gifted Minors (MGM) program for many years, and it has served thousands of bright children. The Marin County, Calif., "College for Kids" program has sufficiently shown that children can do more than is ever required of them.

Both Illinois and California define a gifted child as one who receives a high score on a test of academic ability. Some states have introduced the so-called "multiple-talent" programs promoted by Calvin Taylor, a psychologist at the University of Utah. Taylor believes that all children have "hidden" talents that must be nurtured and encouraged by teachers.

In explaining what happens to talented students, Taylor gives the example of a Utah mining process. In years past, miners extracted copper from the mountainside and deposited the waste products on the valley floor. Today we are discovering that what was believed to be waste contains metals of a larger value than the ones already extracted. Taylor believes that the talents of many gifted children are buried in underachievement.

What is the federal government doing in this area? The federal government has become very active in the education of gifted and talented. In March 1972, Congress received a major report, *Education of the Gifted and Talented.* Since then it has enacted the Education Amendments of 1974 to provide special funds in this area. In addition, the U.S. Office of Education operates a division of gifted and talented. It supports studies, provides information to Congress, awards grants to states and local school districts, and provides training in the education of the gifted and talented.

The U.S. Office of Education has taken a new interest in stimulating interest in the education of bright children. The office disseminates information, provides technical assistance, and encourages states to provide special help to extremely able children.

What kind of teachers are needed for gifted and talented students? Talented and gifted children need highly sensitive teachers. They should be trained in child development and learning theory. Without special training, some teachers are indifferent (or hostile) to the needs of bright children.

Generally, teachers who succeed with gifted children have special gifts themselves. Such teachers have a wide range of interests, a sense of humor, are student-centered, are enthusiastic about their work, and speak positively about children. They usually participate in renewal activities for themselves and can tolerate the divergent behavior of superior students. They are able to motivate, to encourage, and to nurture the "hidden" talents of their students.

What can parents do to stimulate interest in programs for gifted and talented? Parents can work with local school districts to encourage special programs for talented children. They can work

through the PTA, attend board of education meetings, and talk with state legislators. Parents can also become familiar with programs for the gifted. Information can be obtained from the local library, the superintendent of schools, or the state board of education. Free material can be obtained from the Office of the Gifted and Talented, U.S. Office of Education, Washington, D.C. 20202, or The Council for Exceptional Children, 1920 Association Dr., Reston, Va. 22091.

With the help of parents, local schools can provide special services to gifted children. Parents can develop talent banks, can assist teachers, and can supervise enrichment activities. Parents can also organize to assist the legislature to provide special funds for gifted programs. Schools welcome the help of parents in this area.

What are the benefits of special programs for the gifted and talented? The gifted and talented youngster has the potential to make more than the average contribution to our troubled society. It is, therefore, in the national interest to provide special services for the gifted. Senator Jacob Javits said it well when he spoke to the Council for Exceptional Children: "Without the development of these neglected traits, the brightest individual is greatly handicapped and much of his potential is lost."

Special programs for the gifted and talented children may make it possible for hidden abilities to be discovered and for potential genius to be sympathetically encouraged. Such programs may reduce the loss of talent, the frustration of not being in tune with the rest of the class, and the boredom that occurs among so many bright children.

William James estimated that only 10 percent of human capacity is ever utilized. He believed it to be even less among the gifted. The challenge of our schools, therefore, is great. It is our schools that must implement and establish programs for the education of gifted and talented children.

The vastness of man's potential can be seen in the "Grandma Moses effect." It illustrates that each boy and girl may have abilities that are never uncovered. Our hope, however, is that students will not have to wait until old age to find a new talent. It may be possible, with some special help, to uncover those gifts at an early age in our schools.

Issues in Education for the Gifted

James J. Gallagher _____

James J. Gallagher (b. 1926) is presently Kenan professor of education at the University of North Carolina at Chapel Hill. He studied at the University of Pittsburg and Pennsylvania State University, taught at several universities, and served in the Bureau of Education for the Handicapped, HEW. He is the recipient of several awards and has written Teaching the Gifted Child *and was editor of* Application of Child Development Research to Exceptional Children.

AMERICA'S LOVE-HATE RELATIONSHIP WITH THE GIFTED

The gifted scholars of tender years are often told by their elders that they are the future of the nation and that we are delighted with their academic performance and look eagerly to their forthcoming contributions to the society. These gifted students might well be confused by the conflicting messages they receive because even the most perceptive of them has a difficult time grasping the fundamental point that we adults do not say everything we mean, nor do we mean everything we say, about their talent.

A strong case can be made for the presence in the American society of a love-hate relationship with giftedness and talent. On one hand, we revere the gifted individual who has risen from humble background. We are proud to live in a society where talent can triumph over environment or family status. At the same time, since our origins came from battling an aristocratic elite, we are suspicious of attempts to subvert our commitment to egalitarianism. We do not

From James J. Gallagher, "Issues in Education for the Gifted." In The Gifted and Talented: Their Education and Development *(ed. by A. Harry Passow). 78th Yearbook, Part I of National Society for the Study of Education. Chicago: The Society, 1979. Used by permission.*

wish a new elite class to develop, and as a result we seem to waver in our attitudes. We design our elementary and secondary programs for gifted students in ways that can be defended by careful administrators as giving no special favors, no tipping the scales in favor of the socially powerful or the specially endowed.[1]

Sometimes satire is the best way to illustrate the ambiguous positions in which we find ourselves. Kurt Vonnegut, Jr. has carried one of the common feelings about the gifted in our society to a logical conclusion in a short story entitled *Harrison Bergeron,* set in some future society:

> The year was 2081, and everybody was finally equal. They weren't only equal before God and the law, they were equal in every which way. Nobody was smarter than anybody. No one was better looking than anybody else.[2]

The reason for this enforced equality was that people who were outstanding in various ways were given handicaps. Those that could dance well had to wear sandbags on their feet, those who were strikingly good looking would have to wear a mask so as not to embarrass those who did not have those characteristics. And those with high intellectual ability?

> George, while his intelligence was way above normal, had a little mental handicap radio in his ear. He was required by law to wear it at all times. He was tuned into a government transmitter. Every twenty seconds or so, the transmitter would send

out some noise to keep people like George from taking unfair advantage of their brains.[3]

The essentially destructive approach to "equality" does not really pass until we reach higher education when a miraculous transformation takes place. The United States has created the most complex and extensive higher education and professional school establishment in the world. We do not call the Stanford Medical School or the Harvard Law School a program for gifted students, but we know that they are and no apologies are made that only the "best" students should be allowed to attend. After all, some of us may need a good lawyer from time to time, others may need an excellent surgeon, and others would like to get some good advice from a competent psychiatrist.

As we view the needs of the society, the agenda of unsolved problems such as pollution, population, energy, and a lacking sense of national purpose, we feel the need for the best and the brightest to be well prepared and well motivated, not only to achieve their individual destiny, but also to aid the society as a whole.

At the local, state, and federal levels we vacillate in our public school program between the need to be "fair" and the need to be "effective." At times when the society seems to be threatened, such as in the Sputnik era and recently with the variety of problems surrounding energy shortages, we lean toward the productive use of all talent. In more placid eras such as the early 1950s, the post-World War II decade, when there seemed to be little to worry and threaten us, we sought "equality" as a more appropriate goal. At the very least, we need to make these conflicting values visible so that a more mature societal decision can be made.

---

[1] John Gardner, *Excellence: Can We Be Equal and Excellent Too?* (New York: Harper and Row, 1961).

[2] Kurt Vonnegut, Jr., *Welcome to the Monkey House* (New York: Dell, 1950), p. 7.

[3] Ibid.

DISCUSSION QUESTIONS AND ACTIVITIES

1. How do we determine who are the gifted and talented? Are they likely to be found primarily in certain segments of the population?

2. What are the arguments used to support special programs for the gifted? Are the arguments valid?

3. What special characteristics do teachers of the gifted need?

4. Why do some democratic societies evince an ambivalent attitude toward the gifted?

5. How would you explain the fact that in the U.S. during certain periods the gifted are given special attention and in other periods are neglected? Cite examples. Can you think of any societies in which the gifted are consistently given preferential treatment? Explain why they are accorded this status.

6. Investigate what provisions have been made in your home community for educating the gifted, and determine the adequacy and success of these programs.

7. Invite a teacher or administrator experienced in working with the gifted to your class to speak.

8. In his *Excellence: Can We Be Equal and Excellent Too?* John Gardner sought to find a place in a democratic society for both equality and talent. Read his book to determine whether he was able to do so convincingly.

9. In John Rawls' *A Theory of Justice* (Cambridge, Mass.: Harvard University Press, 1971) he articulates two fundamental principles: (1) each person is to have an equal right to the most extensive total system of equal basic liberties compatible with a similar system of liberty for all; and (2) social and economic inequalities are to be arranged so that they are both (a) to the greatest benefit of the least advantaged, and (b) attached to offices and positions open to all under conditions of fair equality of opportunity. Although the first principle has priority over the second one, would we still assume that the gifted would receive less resources if these two principles were adopted? In other words, would the second principle allocate extra resources to the handicapped, mentally retarded, and culturally disadvantaged? Thus, what would be just and fair in the use of scarce societal resources for educating the gifted?

SUGGESTED READINGS

Alexander, Patricia A. and Mula, Joseph A. *Gifted Education: A Comprehensive Roadmap.* Rockville, Md.: Aspens Systems Corp., 1982.

Anthony, John B. and Anthony, Margaret M. *The Gifted and Talented: A Bibliography and Resource Guide.* Pittsfield, Mass.: Berkshire Community Press, 1981.

Baskin, Barbara H. and Harris, Karen H. *Books for the Gifted Child.* New York: R. R. Bowker, 1980.

Gardner, John. *Excellence: Can We Be Equal and Excellent Too?* New York: Harper & Row, 1961.

Getzels, Jacob W. and Jackson, Philip W. *Creativity and Intelligence.* New York: Wiley, 1962.

Karnes, Frances A. and Collins, Emily C. *Assessment in Gifted Education.* Springfield, Ill.: C. C. Thomas, 1981.

Khatena, Joe. *Educational Psychology of the Gifted.* New York: Wiley, 1982.

Maker, C. June. *Curriculum Development for the Gifted.* Rockville, Md.: Aspen Systems Corp., 1982.

Marland, Sidney P., Jr. *Education for the Gifted and*

Talented, Vols. I and II: Report to the Congress of the United States. Washington, D.C.: U.S. Government Printing Office, 1972.

Passow, A. Harry. *The Gifted and Talented: Their Education and Development*, 78th Yearbook, Part I. Chicago: National Society for the Study of Education, 1979.

Stanley, Julian C.; George, William C.; and Solano, Cecilia H. *The Gifted and the Creative: Fifty Year Perspective*. Baltimore: Johns Hopkins University Press, 1977.

Terman, L. M. and Others. *Genetic Studies of Genius.* Stanford, Ca.: Stanford University Press, 1925.

Terman, Lewis M. *The Gifted Group at Mid-life.* Stanford, Ca.: Stanford University Press, 1967.

Torrance, E. Paul. *Guiding Creative Talent.* Huntington, N.Y.: R. E. Krieger Publishing Co., 1976.

15
Cognitive Moral Development

The concern over moral education is not new. Educational systems in various cultures since antiquity have usually espoused more than cognitive outcomes. These systems sought, in most cases, to develop a certain type of individual, a person, among other things, of sound character. And character, of course, was formulated according to the dominant norms of society or the values of those who controlled the educational system. Leading educators, both past and present, usually expressed their educational philosophy in terms not only of intellectual changes but moral outcomes as well.

Yet ostensibly educational systems may go through different cycles. One reaction in the United States to the Soviet Union's launching of Sputnik during the late 1950s, for instance, was to place greater emphasis upon science, mathematics, and cognitive learning in general. Following a period of attention to culturally different learners in the late 1960s, there has been a recrudescence of interest in moral education—not only in the United States but in Canada and England as well. Thus it is much more than a post-Watergate phenomenon; among the many factors, an emerging world of eroding traditions and temporary, fragmented social relations contribute to a heightened interest in the examination of values.

Values are no stranger to schools. Value decisions are involved in choosing aims and selecting the means for their achievement, in allocating funds in terms of a set of priorities, in determining curriculum content, in attempting to establish desired outcomes for the instructional process, and in developing a professional code of ethics. Whether consciously or not, the teacher influences the student's behavior and his or her attitudes toward learning the teacher's choices and the example he or she sets. Not only the content of the message but the teacher's voice, facial expression, and muscular tension are also important. Today more educators believe that value acquisition should not be left to informal cues and chance but must be deliberately developed in the most effective way.

In the development of moral judgment, theories of moral development describe how children learn a moral code and how thought and action change. These developmental changes have usually been stated in terms of stages of moral growth and judgment. Such theories serve to clarify moral judgments and to apprise educators of what to expect so that a suitable program can be established.

Lawrence Kohlberg's cognitive-developmental approach is indebted to Jean Piaget's pioneering work and was influenced by Dewey's psychological writings. Kohlberg's studies have yielded six developmental stages allotted to three moral levels. These stages are based on ways of thinking about moral matters. Kohlberg believes that a necessary, but not sufficient, condition for morality is the ability to reason logically. His theory, he claims, is both psychological and philosophical, and his findings generate a philosophy of moral education designed to stimulate moral development rather than teach fixed moral rules. Kohlberg believes that a philosophic concept of morality and moral development is required, that moral development passes through invariant qualitative stages, and that moral development is stimulated by promoting thinking and problem solving. Justice, Kohlberg holds, is the key principle in the development of moral judgment.

R. S. Peters' reply acknowledges the importance of Kohlberg's research but he chides him for generally ignoring his critics and thereby failing to make a number of needed changes in his approach.

Moral Development:
A Review of the Theory

Lawrence Kohlberg
Richard H. Hersh _____

An expert in developmental and social psychology, Lawrence Kohlberg (b. 1927) had clinical psychological experience during and after his studies at the University of Chicago. He has been a fellow at the Institute for Advanced Study in Behavioral Science and held faculty positions at Yale University and the University of Chicago, where he was director of the child psychology training program before assuming his present position with the Laboratory of Human Development at Harvard University. Professor Kohlberg is internationally recognized for his significant research in moral development and moral education.

Richard H. Hersh (b. 1942) is professor of education and associate dean of teacher education at the University of Oregon.

. . . Whether we like it or not schooling is a moral enterprise. Values issues abound in the content and process of teaching. The interaction of adults and students within a social organization called a school results in human conflict no less so than does such interaction in social organizations labeled "families." Yet moral education has been viewed as the exclusive province of the family and/or church. Disregarded or misunderstood has been the nature of the school as an important moral education institution. Because schools have not been viewed as legitimate institutions of moral education, society has avoided concepts of morality and ethics in evaluating the effects of these institutions on the social development of children and adolescents. Terms like "socialization" or "acculturation" or "citizenship" have been used to refer to the moral impact on students. Such terms ignore the problem of the standard or principle of value implied by such terms. We must face the issue of choice as to whether the outcome of the growth and education process is the creation of a storm trooper, a Buddhist monk or a civil rights activist. All are equally "socialized" in terms of their social group. To consider "socialization" or the "acquisition of values" as moral education, is to consider the moral principles children are developing (or are not developing). It is also to consider the adequacy of these principles in the light of an examined concept of the good and right (the province of moral philosophy) and in the light of knowledge of the moral processes of human development (which is the province of psychology).

We are concerned with the traditional prohi-

From Lawrence Kohlberg and Richard H. Hersh, "Moral Development: A Review of the Theory," Theory Into Practice *16 (April 1977): 53–59, College of Education, The Ohio State University. Used by permission.*

bition of schools from teaching values or "morality" normally felt to be the province of the home and church. In keeping family, church, and school separate, however, educators have assumed naively that schools have been harbors of value neutrality. The result has been a moral education curriculum which has lurked beneath the surface in schools, hidden as it were from both educators and the public. This "hidden curriculum"[1] with its emphasis on obedience to authority ("stay in your seat, make no noise, get a hallway pass"; and the feeling of "prison" espoused by so many students), implies many underlying moral assumptions and values, which may be quite different from what educators would admit as their conscious system of morality. Schools have been preaching a "bag of virtues" approach—the teaching of a particular set of values which are peculiar to this culture or to a particular subculture, and which are by nature relativistic and not necessarily more adequate than any other set of values. But the teaching of particular virtues has been proven to be ineffective. We wish to go beyond this approach to moral education and instead to conceptualize and facilitate moral development in a cognitive-developmental sense—toward an increased sense of moral autonomy and a more adequate conception of justice.

Moral development, as initially defined by Piaget[2] and then refined and researched by Kohlberg,[3] does not simply represent an increasing knowledge of cultural values usually leading to ethical relativity. Rather, it represents the transformations that occur in a person's *form* or structure of thought. The content of values varies from culture to culture; hence the study of cultural values cannot tell us how a person interacts with his social environment, or how a person goes about solving problems related to his/her social world. This requires the analysis of developing structures of moral judgment, which are found to be universal in a developmental sequence across cultures.[4]

In analyzing the responses of longitudinal and cross-cultural subjects to hypothetical moral dilemmas it has been demonstrated that moral reasoning develops over time through a series of six stages. The concept of stages of cognitive development refers to the structure of one's reasoning and implies the following characteristics:

1. Stages are "structured wholes," or organized systems of thought. This means individuals are consistent in their level of moral judgment.

2. Stages form an invariant sequence. Under all conditions except extreme trauma, movement is always forward, never backward. Individuals never skip stages, and movement is always to the next stage up. This is true of all cultures.

3. Stages are "hierarchical integrations." Thinking at a higher stage includes or comprehends within it lower stage thinking. There is a tendency to function at or prefer the highest stage available.

The stages of moral development are defined by the following characteristics:

DEFINITION OF MORAL STAGES

I. Preconventional Level

At this level, the child is responsive to cultural rules and labels of good and bad, right or

[1] P. Jackson, *Life in the Classrooms,* (New York: Holt, Rinehart & Winston, 1968).

[2] J. Piaget, *The Moral Judgment of the Child* (1932), (New York: Free Press, 1965).

[3] L. Kohlberg. *Stages of Moral Development as a Basis for Moral Education,* in C. Beck and E. Sullivan (eds.), *Moral Education,* (Toronto: University of Toronto Press, 1970).

[4] L. Kohlberg, "Moral Stages and Moralization: The Cognitive Developmental Approach," In T. Lickona (ed.), *Moral development and behavior: Theory, Research, and Social Issues,* (New York: Holt, Rinehart & Winston, 1976).

wrong, but interprets these labels either in terms of the physical or the hedonistic consequences of action (punishment, reward, exchange of favors) or in terms of the physical power of those who enunciate the rules and labels. The level is divided into the following two stages:

Stage 1: The punishment-and-obedience orientation. The physical consequences of action determine its goodness or badness, regardless of the human meaning or value of these consequences. Avoidance of punishment and unquestioning deference to power are valued in their own right, not in terms of respect for an underlying moral order supported by punishment and authority (the latter being Stage 4).

Stage 2: The instrumental-relativist orientation. Right action consists of that which instrumentally satisfies one's own needs and occasionally the needs of others. Human relations are viewed in terms like those of the marketplace. Elements of fairness, of reciprocity, and of equal sharing are present, but they are always interpreted in a physical, pragmatic way. Reciprocity is a matter of "you scratch my back and I'll scratch yours," not of loyalty, gratitude, or justice.

II. Conventional Level

At this level, maintaining the expectations of the individual's family, group, or nation is perceived as valuable in its own right, regardless of immediate and obvious consequences. The attitude is not only one of *conformity* to personal expectations and social order, but of loyalty to it, of actively *maintaining,* supporting, and justifying the order, and of identifying with the persons or group involved in it. At this level there are the following two stages:

Stage 3: The interpersonal concordance or "good boy – nice girl" orientation. Good behavior is that which pleases or helps others and is approved by them. There is much conformity to stereotypical images of what is majority or "natural" behavior. Behavior is frequently judged by intention — "he means well" becomes important for the first time. One earns approval by being "nice."

Stage 4: The "law and order" orientation. There is orientation toward authority, fixed rules, and the maintenance of the social order. Right behavior consists of doing one's duty, showing respect for authority, and maintaining the given social order for its own sake.

III. Postconventional, Autonomous, or Principled Level

At this level, there is a clear effort to define moral values and principles that have validity and application apart from the authority of the groups or persons holding these principles and apart from the individual's own identification with these groups. This level also has two stages:

Stage 5: The social-contract, legalistic orientation, generally with utilitarian overtones. Right action tends to be defined in terms of general individual rights and standards which have been critically examined and agreed upon by the whole society. There is a clear awareness of the relativism of personal values and opinions and a corresponding emphasis upon procedural rules for reaching consensus. Aside from what is constitutionally and democratically agreed upon, the right is a matter of personal "values" and "opinion." The result is an emphasis upon the "legal point of view," but with an emphasis upon the possibility of changing law in terms of rational considerations of social utility (rather than freezing it in terms of Stage 4 "law and order"). Outside the legal realm, free agreement and contract is the binding element of obligation. This is the "official" morality of the American government and constitution.

Stage 6: The universal-ethical-principle orientation. Right is defined by the decision of conscience in accord with self-chosen *ethical principles* appealing to logical comprehensiveness, universality, and consistency. These principles are abstract and ethical (The Golden Rule, the categorical imperative); they are not concrete moral rules like the Ten Commandments. At heart, these are universal principles of *justice,* of the *reciprocity* and *equality* of human *rights,* and of respect for the dignity of human beings as *individual persons.*[5]

Given that people have the psychological capacity to progress to higher (and therefore more adequate) stages of moral reasoning, the aim of education ought to be the personal development of students toward more complex ways of reasoning. This philosophical argument is based on the earlier contributions of John Dewey:

The aim of education is growth or development, both intellectual and moral. Ethical and psychological principles can aid the school in the greatest of all constructions—the building of a free and powerful character. Only knowledge of the order and connection of stages in psychological development can insure this. Education is the work of supplying the conditions which will enable the psychological functions to mature in the freest and fullest manner.[6]

Like Piaget, Dewey's idea of development does not reflect an increase in the *content* of thinking (e.g., cultural values) but instead, a qualitative transformation in the *form* of the child's thought or action. This distinction has been elaborated elsewhere:

What we examine in our work has to do with form rather than content. We are not describing or classifying what people think is right or wrong in situations of moral conflict, for example, whether draft-evading exiles should be given amnesty or thrown in prison if and when they return to this country, or even changes in what individuals think as they grow older. Nor are we assuming that we can specify a certain behavioral response as necessarily "moral" (in the descriptive or category sense, as distinguished from non-moral), for example "cheating," and then discuss moral-development in terms of the frequency with which individuals engage in this behavior as they grow older, perhaps in different kinds of situations ranging from spelling tests to income tax. As distinguished from either of these two avenues of research that might be said to be dealing with moral content, our work focuses on the cognitive structure which underlie such content and give it its claim to the category "moral," where "structure" refers to "the general characteristics of shape, pattern or organization of response rather than to the rate of intensity of response or its pairing with particular stimuli," and "cognitive structure" refers to "rules for processing information or for connecting experienced events." From our point of view it is not any artificially specified set of responses, or degree of intensity of such responses, which characterizes morality as an area of study. Rather, it is the cognitive moral structurings, or the organized systems of assumptions and rules about the nature of moral-conflict situations which give such situations their meaning, that constitute the objects of our developmental study.[7]

Based on this crucial difference between form and content, the aim of moral education should be to stimulate people's thinking ability over time in ways which will enable them to use more adequate and complex reasoning patterns to solve moral problems. The principle central to the development of stages of moral judgment, and hence to proposals for moral education, is that of *justice.* Justice, the primary regard for the value and equality of all human beings and for reciprocity in human relations, is a basic and

[5]L. Kohlberg, "From Is to Ought," in T. Mischel (ed.), *Cognitive Development and Epistemology* (New York: Academic Press, 1971), pp. 164–165.

[6]J. Dewey, "What Psychology Can Do for the Teacher," In R. Archambault (ed.), *John Dewey on Education: Selected Writings* (New York: Random House, 1964), p. 207.

[7]D. Boyd and L. Kohlberg, "The Is-Ought Problem: A Developmental Perspective," *Zygon,* 1973, *8,* 360–361.

universal standard. Using justice as the organizing principle for moral education meets the following criteria: It guarantees freedom of belief; it employs a philosophically justifiable concept of morality, and it is based on the psychological facts of human development. The stages may be seen as representing increasingly adequate conceptions of justice and as reflecting an expanding capacity for empathy, for taking the role of the other. And in the end the two are the same thing because the most just solution is the one which takes into account the positions or rights of all the individuals involved. The expansion of empathy thus, in turn, leads to an expansion of points of view and this expansion defines the three levels of moral judgment into which the six stages subdivide.

At the first or preconventional level the individual sees moral dilemmas in terms of the individual needs of the people involved. Situations of moral conflict are seen as situations in which needs collide and are resolved either in terms of who has the most power in the situation (Stage1) or in terms of simple individual responsibility for one's own welfare (Stage 2) except where bound by simple market-place notions of reciprocity.

These formulations are perfectly consonant with the child's experience. For a young child power is perhaps the most salient characteristic of his social world (Stage 1) and as he learns to see conflicts between conformity to power and individual interests, he shifts to a notion of right as serving individual interests. However, as the child becomes increasingly involved in mutual relationships and sees himself as a sharing and participating member of groups, he sees the individual point of view toward morality as inadequate to deal with the kinds of moral conflicts which confront him. He has then two choices: he can hold on to his preconventional philosophy and simplify experience, or he can expand his philosophy so that it can take into account the expanding complexity of his experience.

The second two stages of moral development are termed "conventional" in that moral conflicts are now seen and resolved in group or social terms rather than in individual terms. Right or justice is seen to reside in interpersonal social relationships (Stage 3) or in the community (Stage 4). At the conventional levels there is an appeal to authority but the authority derives its right to define the good not from greater power as at Stage 1, but from its social sharedness and legitimacy.

However, if society defines the right and the good, what is one to think when one recognizes that different societies choose differently in what they label as good and bad, right and wrong? Eskimos think it is right to leave old people out in the snow to die. When abortions were illegal in this country, they were legal in Sweden. With the increasing exposure of everyone to how others live, there is a greater recognition of the fact that our way is only one among many.

If one cannot simply equate the right with the societal and the legal, then what is one to do? We have found that adolescents may go through a period of ethical relativism during which they question the premises of any moral system. If there are many ways to live, who can presume to say which is best? Perhaps everyone should do as he or she chooses.

The way out of this moral relativism or moral nihilism lies through the perception that underneath the rules of any given society lie moral principles and universal moral rights, and the validity of any moral choice rests on the principles that choice embodies. Such moral principles are universal in their application and constitute a viable standard against which the particular laws or conventions of any society can and should be judged. When obedience to laws violates moral principles or rights, it is right to violate such laws.

At the last two stages, then, choice is based on the principles that supersede convention, just as previously the claims of society or convention were seen as the grounds for adjudicating differences between individuals. This, then, is the sequence of moral development.

What spurs progress from one stage to another and why do some individuals reach the principled stages while others do not? Moral judgment, while primarily a rational operation, is influenced by affective factors such as the ability to empathize and the capacity for guilt. But moral situations are defined cognitively by the judging individual in social interactions. It is this interaction with one's environment which determines development of moral reasoning.

Social interaction requires the assumption of a variety of roles and the entering into a variety of reciprocal relationships. Such relationships demand that one take others' perspectives (role-taking). It is this reworking of one's role-taking experiences into successively more complex and adequate forms of justice which is called moral development. Thus moral development results from the dialogue between the person's cognitive structure and the complexity presented by environment. This interactionist definition of moral development demands an environment which will facilitate dialogue between the self and others. The more one encounters situations of moral conflict that are not adequately resolved by one's present reasoning structure, the more likely one is to develop more complex ways of thinking about and resolving such conflicts.

What can teachers and schools do to stimulate moral development? The teacher must help the student to consider genuine moral conflicts, think about the reasoning he uses in solving such conflicts, see inconsistencies and inadequacies in his way of thinking and find ways of resolving them. Classroom moral discussion are one example of how the cognitive-developmental approach can be applied in the school. Much of the moral development research in schools has focused on moral discussions as the vehicle for stimulating cognitive conflict. But such discussions, if too often used, will become pedantic. The classroom discussion approach should be part of a broader, more enduring involvement of students in the social and moral functioning of the school. Rather than attempting to inculcate a predetermined and unquestioned set of values, teachers should challenge students with the moral issues faced by the school community as problems to be solved, not merely situations in which rules are mechanically applied. One must create a "just community."

At present, the schools themselves are not especially moral institutions. Institutional relationships tend to be based more on authority than on ideas of justice. Adults are often less interested in discovering *how* children are thinking than in telling them *what* to think. The school atmosphere is generally a blend of Stage 1, punishment morality, and Stage 4, "law and order," which fails to impress or stimulate children involved in their own Stage 2 or Stage 3 moral philosophies. Children and adults stop communicating with one another, horizons are narrowed and development is stunted. If schools wish to foster morality, they will have to provide an atmosphere in which interpersonal issues are settled on the basis of principle rather than power. They will have to take moral questions seriously and provide food for thought instead of conventional "right answers."

We do not claim that the theory of cognitive moral development is sufficient to the task of moral education. . . . There are three major areas in which the cognitive developmental approach to moral education is incomplete: 1) the stress placed on form rather than content 2) the focus on concepts of rights and duties rather than issues of the good 3) the emphasis on moral judgment rather than behavior.

We have previously mentioned the distinction between form and content. That we have chosen to delineate the form or structure of moral judgments does not deny the importance of the moral content of school curriculum. That textbooks and other curricula materials have reflected and perhaps reinforced racism, sexism and ethnocentrisms is to be decried. It is imperative that the content of curriculum for moral education be constructed so as to avoid unfair characterizations of others as well as promote opportunities for structural development. The integration of curriculum content is exemplified by articles in this issue by Lickona, Bramble and Garrod, and the Ladenburgs. Additional work in this content dimension is required if educators wish to incorporate the cognitive developmental approach to moral education in the curriculum.

We have stressed in this "theory" the concern for what is right, what is just or fair. To ask "what is right?" or "what ought I do in this situation?" presumes that notions of what is "good" are in conflict. But,

> We are not describing how men formulate different conceptions of the good, the good life, intrinsic value, or purpose. Nor are we discussing how men develop certain kinds of character traits and learn to recognize these traits in judgments of approbation and disapprobation. Instead, we are concentrating on that aspect of morality that is brought to the fore by problematic situations of conflicting claims, whether the conflict is between individuals, groups, societies, or institutions, and whether the source of the conflict lies in incompatible claims based on conceptions of the good, beliefs about human purpose, or character assessments. In short, we intend the term "moral" to be understood in the restricted sense of referring to situations which call for judgments involving denotological concepts such as right and wrong, duty and obligation, having a right, fairness, etc., although such judgments may (or may not) involve either or both of the other two basic concepts or their derivatives.[8]

This is not to say that questions of "good" are less important or need not be asked. Rather it is an acknowledgement that the cognitive developmental approach is limited in scope and requires that attention be paid to such issues in the development of any moral education program.

The relationship between moral judgment and moral behavior is not fully defined. That is, moral judgment is a necessary but not sufficient condition for moral action. Other variables come into play such as emotion, and a general sense of will, purpose or ego strength. Moral judgment is the only distinctive *moral* factor in moral behavior but not the only factor in such behavior. Educators who are looking for answers as to how to "get children to behave" often meaning to rid themselves of discipline problems will not find *the* answer in one theory. We hypothesize that behavior when informed by mature moral judgment is influenced by level of moral development.[9] Further research in this crucial area is needed.

Cognitive developmental moral education is rooted in a substantial empirical and philosophical base. The theory is complex and as suggested above insufficient to the task claimed by "moral education." Within limits, however, the theory has informing power for the practitioner. Resourceful practice is required both to validate and inform the theory.

---

[8]*Ibid.,* p. 360.

[9]The relationship between moral judgment and moral behavior is more fully discussed in: Kohlberg, 1976 "Moral Stages," L. Kohlberg, "Stage and Sequence: The Cognitive Developmental Approach to Socialization," in D. A. Goslin (ed.) *Handbook of Socialization Theory and Research,* vol. I (New York: Russell Sage Foundation, 1964), pp. 383–432.

A Reply to Kohlberg
"Why Doesn't Lawrence Kohlberg Do His Homework?"

Richard S. Peters

Someone said to Bernard Shaw that he was like the Venus de Milo. What there was of him was excellent. The same, I think, needs to be said of Kohlberg. The trouble is, however, that Kohlberg remains quite impervious to criticisms of the limitations of his view of moral education. He has never answered, for instance, a series of very constructive criticisms leveled against him by myself and Bill Alston in the Binghampton conference of 1969.[1] It is not that the stuff he continues to ladle out is not very good. It is, and I have made much use of it myself.[2] It is simply that he remains oblivious of the many other important aspects of moral education, and there is a danger that the unwary will think that he has told the whole story. In a commentary of this length, I can only list the main omissions.

1. He suffers from the rather touching belief that a Kantian type of morality, represented in modern times most notably by Hare and Rawls, is the only one.[3] He fails to grasp that utilitarianism, in which the principle of justice is problematic, is an alternative type of morality and that

people such as Winch have put forward a morality of integrity in which the principle of universalizability is problematic.[4] I think this can be carried forward, actually. A morality of courage as exemplified by train robbers, the old "virtue" of Machiavelli's *Prince,* is a defensible morality. So also is a more romantic type of morality such as that of D. H. Lawrence, in which trust must be placed in "the dark God within." It is either sheer legislation to say that Kohlberg's morality is the true one, or it is the worst form of the naturalistic fallacy which argues from how "morality" is ordinarily used to what morality is.

2. He does not take "good-boy" morality seriously enough either from a practical or from a theoretical point of view. Practically speaking, since few are likely to emerge beyond Kohlberg's States 3 and 4, it is important that our fellow citizens should be well bedded down at one or the other of the stages. The policeman cannot always be present, and if I am lying in the gutter after being robbed it is somewhat otiose to speculate at what stage the mugger is. My regret must surely be that he had not at least got a con-

From Richard S. Peters, *"A Reply to Kohlberg,"* Phi Delta Kappan, *LVI (June 1975): 678.*

[1]See Theodore Mischel, *Cognitive Development and Epistemology* (New York: Academic Press, 1971).
[2]See articles collected in Part 2 of Richard S. Peters, *Psychology and Ethical Development* (London: Allen and Unwin, 1974).
[3]See Richard S. Peters, *Reason and Compassion* (London: Routledge and Kegan Paul, 1973) and Iris Murdock, *The Sovereignty of Good* (London: Routledge and Kegan Paul, 1970).
[4]See Peter Winch, *Ethics and Action* (London: Routledge and Kegan Paul, 1972) and Søren Kierkegaard, *Purity of Heart* (London: Fontana Books, 1961).

ventional morality well instilled in him. Theoretically, too, the good-boy stage is crucial; for at this stage the child learns from the inside, as it were, what it is to follow a rule. Unless he has learned this well (whatever it means!), the notion of following his *own* rules at the autonomous stage is unintelligible. Kohlberg does not appreciate, either, that moral rules have to be learned in the face of counter-inclinations. Otherwise there would, in general, be no point to them. Hence the necessity at these stages for the type of reinforcement advocated by Skinner and others and for the modeling processes so stressed by Bronfenbrenner in his *Two Worlds of Childhood.*[5] In particular, he ignores the masterly chapter on "The Unmaking of the American Child." He seems sublimely unaware, too, of the mass of evidence about other aspects of moral education collected by Hoffman in Mussen's *Carmichael's Manual of Child Psychology.*[6]

3. As Bill Alston stresses in his article[7] and I stress elsewhere, Kohlberg, like Piaget, is particularly weak on the development of the affective side of morality, of moral emotions such as "guilt," "concern for others," "remorse," and so on.

4. Finally, Kohlberg, in his references to ego strength, sees the importance of will in morality, but offers no account of the type of habit training which encourages or discourages its growth.[8]

I and others have written a great deal about these other aspects of morality and moral learning and development; it is a pity that Lawrence Kohlberg does not start doing some homework!

---

[5]Urie Bronfenbrenner, *Two Worlds of Childhood* (London: Allen and Unwin, 1971).

[6]Paul H. Mussen, *Carmichael's Manual of Child Psychology* (New York: Wiley, 1970).

[7]See Alston's remarks in Mischel, op. cit., and Richard S. Peters, "Moral Development: A Plea for Pluralism," in the same volume.

[8]See Richard S. Peters, "Moral Development; A Plea for Pluralism," in Mischel, op. cit., and "Moral Education and the Psychology of Character," in Richard S. Peters, *Psychology and Ethical Development,* op. cit.

DISCUSSION QUESTIONS AND ACTIVITIES

1. How do many schools presently handle value issues? Why does Kohlberg believe his approach to be superior to these practices?

2. What does Kohlberg mean by the stages of moral development?

3. What, for Kohlberg, should be the aim of moral education? How adequate is this aim?

4. Why should justice be used as an organizing principle of moral education?

5. Does Kohlberg suggest a plausible way to avoid ethical relativism? Should it be avoided?

6. Why does Kohlberg conclude that "schools themselves are not especially moral institutions?

7. Is it the case, as Peters claims, that Kohlberg has overlooked alternative types of morality, and if so, is this matter as serious as Peters would have us believe?

8. Does Kohlberg neglect the affective side of morality?

9. Has Kohlberg failed to offer a form of habit training of will in morality?

10. Check what programs of moral education are used in your local community. Visit such

classrooms and, even if Kohlberg's approach is not employed, see what types of moral judgment are made and classify them according to Kohlberg's moral stages.

11. Study some of your friends carefully over a period of time by recording in a notebook their oral moral judgments. After sufficient judgments have been collected, classify each person according to one of Kohlberg's stages. Then determine the extent to which their moral actions are consonant with their moral judgments. (This exercise, be forewarned, may not promote lasting friendships.)

SUGGESTED READINGS

Principal Works by Lawrence Kohlberg

"Continuities and Discontinuities in Childhood and Adult Moral Development" (with R. B. Kramer). *Human Development* 12 (1969): 92–120.

"The Development of Children's Orientations Toward a Moral Order: 1. Sequence in the Development of Moral Thought." *Vita Humana* 6 (1963): 11–33.

"The Development of Moral Character and Moral Ideology." In *Review of Child Development Research,* Vol. 1, ed. M. L. Hoffman and L. W. Hoffman, pp. 383–431. New York: Russell Sage Foundation, 1964.

"Early Education: A Cognitive Development View." *Child Development* 39 (1968): 1031–62.

"Education for Justice: A Modern Statement of the Platonic View." In *Moral Education: Five Lectures,* ed. Nancy F. and Theodore R. Sizer. Cambridge, Mass.: Harvard University Press, 1970, pp. 57–83.

"From Is to Ought: How to Commit the Naturalistic Fallacy and Get Away with It in the Study of Moral Development." In *Cognitive Development and Epistemology,* ed. T. Mischel. New York: Academic Press, 1971.

The Just Community Approach to Corrections: A Manual, Part I (with others). Cambridge, Mass.: Education Research Foundation, 1973.

"Moral Stages and Moralization: The Cognitive Developmental Approach." In *Moral Development and Behavior: Theory, Research, and Social Issues,* ed. T. Likona. New York: Holt, Rinehart & Winston, 1976.

"Moral Development and Moral Education" (with E. Turiel). In *Psychology and Educational Practice,* ed. G. Lesser. Chicago: Scott, Foresman, 1971, pp. 410–65.

The Philosophy of Moral Development: Moral Stages and the Idea of Justice. San Francisco: Harper & Row, 1981.

"Stage and Sequence: The Cognitive Developmental Approach to Socialization." In *Handbook of Socialization Theory and Research,* ed. D. S. Goslin, pp. 347–480. Chicago: Rand McNally, 1969.

"Stages of Moral Development as a Basis for Moral Education." In *Moral Education,* ed. C. Beck and E. Sullivan. Toronto: University of Toronto Press, 1970.

Proponents

George, Paul S. "Discipline, Moral Development, and Levels of Schooling." *The Educational Forum* 45 (November 1980): 57–67.

Gross, Francis L., Jr. "Teaching Cognitive-Moral Development in College (A Generalist Appoach)." *Journal of General Education* 32 (Winter 1981): 287–308.

Herring, Mark. "Social-Moral Development and Individualized Instruction." *The Educational Forum* 46 (Fall 1981): 23–30.

Hersh, Richard H.; Paolitto, Diana Pritchard; and Reimer, Joseph. *Promoting Moral Growth: From Piaget to Kohlberg.* New York: Longman, 1979.

Larsen, John A. "Applying Kohlberg's Theory of Moral Development in Group Care Settings." *Child Welfare* 60 (December 1981): 659–68.

Leming, James S. "Curricular Effectiveness in Moral/Values Education: A Review of Research." *Journal of Moral Education* 10 (May 1981): 147–64.

Mosher, Ralph L. "Parenting for Moral Growth." *Journal of Education* 163 (Summer 1981): 244–61.

Novak, Barbara. "Morality Reasoning among High School Students." *The Clearing House* 55 (October 1981): 73–79.

Olson, John R. "Curbing Vandalism and Theft." *Educational Horizons* 59 (Summer 1981): 195–7.

Rorvik, Harald. "A Comparison of Piaget's and Kohlberg's Theories and Tests for Moral Development." *Scandinavian Journal of Educational Research,* 25, n. 3 (1981): 99–124.

Rosen, Hugh. *The Development of Sociomoral Knowledge: A Cognitive-Structural Approach.* New York: Columbia University Press, 1980.

Critics

Codd, John S. "Some Conceptual Problems in the Cognitive Developmental Approach to Morality." *Journal of Moral Education* 6 (May 1977): 147–57.

Conroy, Anne R. and John K. Burton. "The Trouble with Kohlberg: A Critique." *The Educational Forum* 45 (November 1980): 43–55.

Evans, Charles S. "Reliability of Moral Judgment Interview: Written Version." *Journal of Moral Education* 11 (May 1982): 200–02.

Falikowski, Anthony. "Kohlberg's Moral Development Program: Its Limitations and Ethical Exclusiveness." *Alberta Journal of Educational Research* 28 (March 1982): 77–89.

Frankel, Jack R. "The Kohlberg Bandwagon: Some Reservations." *Social Education* 40 (April 1976): 216–222.

Gibbs, John C. "Kohlberg's Stages of Moral Judgment: A Constructive Critique." *Harvard Educational Review* 47 (February 1977): 43–58.

Peters, R. S. "Moral Development: A Plea for Pluralism." In *Psychology and Ethical Development,* pp. 303–335. London: George Allen & Unwin, 1974.

Rich, John Martin. "Moral Education and the Emotions." *Journal of Moral Education* 9 (January 1980): 81–87.

Schmitt, Rudolf. "The Steps of Moral Development—A Basis for an Educational Concept?" *International Review of Education* 26, no. 2 (1980): 207–16.

Sichel, Betty A. "The Relation Between Moral Judgment and Moral Behavior in Kohlberg's Theory of the Development of Moral Judgments." *Educational Philosophy and Theory* 8 (April 1976): 35–67.

Sullivan, Edmund V. *Kohlberg's Structuralism: A Critical Appraisal.* Toronto, Ont.: Ontario Institute for Studies in Education, 1977.

16
Values Clarification

Values clarification is one way to help students to choose their values freely while maintaining an open mind. It was initiated by Louis Raths and further developed by Sidney Simon, Howard Kirschenbaum, and Merrill Harmin. It is widely used in the United States today in many areas of the curriculum, including drug education, social studies, environmental education, reading, language arts, vocational education, marriage and family life, and other areas.

The program avoids indoctrination and inculcation of a fixed set of values; instead, it is based on a valuing process for examining, clarifying, and accepting or rejecting values. It posits values based on three processes: choosing, prizing, and acting. Choosing should be (a) freely done, (b) from alternatives, (c) after thoughtful consideration of each alternative. Prizing involves (d) cherishing and being happy with the choice and (e) willingness to affirm the choice publicly. Acting consists of (f) doing something with the choice and (g) doing it repeatedly, in some life pattern.

The teacher's role is to help students become aware and appreciative of their value position. The teacher does this by eliciting value statements from students, accepting their ideas nonjudgmentally, and raising questions that will help them think about their values. Many different strategies are used: "values voting" permits students to indicate publicly what they believe and discover what others believe; "rank ordering" enables students to choose among alternatives and explain their choices: "name tag" asks students to look more closely at themselves and tell others about one's values. Other strategies employed are values sheets, discussions, role-playing, and interviews. Many classroom materials are available.

Roberta P. Martin's interview conveys the evolution and present status of values clarification, in what areas and settings it is used, its relation with other movements, and why certain criticisms of it are unwarranted. Alan L. Lockwood identifies and explains what he considers to be five shortcomings of values clarification.

Values Clarification: The State of the Art for the 1980s

An Interview with Sidney Simon and Howard Kirschenbaum

Roberta P. Martin _____

Roberta P. Martin is an assistant professor in the Department of Counselor Education, Mississippi State University. Sidney Simon is a professor at the Center for Humanistic Studies, University of Massachusetts, Boston. Howard Kirschenbaum is Co-Director of Sagamore Institute and Executive Director of the National Coalition for Democracy in Education, Saratoga Springs, New York.

Values clarification is a process that has been used widely in the past two decades by counselors and teachers in almost every facet of the educational world. The following is an interview conducted in August 1980 with Drs. Sidney Simon and Howard Kirschenbaum, two major leaders in the field. The interview attempts to assess the impact of values clarification during the preceding 20 years and to project the future directions of values clarification in the 1980s. The interviews were conducted separately, but since the same basic questions were asked to both Dr. Simon and Dr. Kirschenbaum, they have been combined for clarity and continuity.

Roberta Martin: Sid, you have been a major leader in values clarification since the beginning. What is your assessment of what has happened in the values clarification movement? Did it change, and, if so, how?

Sid Simon: Well, the 70s were the great verdant, vibrant opening expansion of values clarification. The word was first used in 1957, to my recollection, and that was by my teacher, Louis Raths, when I was a graduate student at New York University. He first came up with that phrase, and how exciting those times were, Roberta. The next few years were spent in trying to refine strategies and in beginning to understand the theory better. That finally culminated in our book in 1966, *Values and Teachings* (Raths, Harmin, & Simon, 1966), a book which had phenomenal success. I am not sure many people realize it, but that book sold well over a half million copies and was adopted by hundreds of colleges and teacher education institutions. Well, that took us into the 1970s, and in 1972 we published *Values Clarification: A Handbook of Practical Strategies for Teachers and Students* (Simon, Howe, & Kirschenbaum, 1972), which was clearly the thing that gave the movement its momentum. That book also sold over a half million copies and from what I understand it is one of the books most widely ripped off at libraries and from teachers' desks. I'm not sure exactly if I should be proud of that, but it does happen!

The Values Clarification Handbook led to dozens of workshops all around the country. People came out in droves to learn values clarification. So, the 70s for us was the great sweeping introduction and attracted thousands of people to the values clarification work. Kirschenbaum recently made an estimate, and he said that to his best guess, a million people probably have had a values clarification workshop or seen a presentation on values clarification—that's a lot of people—so values clarification is known.

The year of the 1970s saw the extension of the values clarification strategies approach, and this was best expressed in two other major books. One was *Clarifying Values Through Subject Matter* (Harmin, Kirschenbaum, & Simon, 1973), which raises the notion that we can teach subject matter content with the values clarifying approach. It is a very useful book, and I hope that people who are reading this article are familiar with it. The other was a book of *Readings in Values Clarification* (Simon & Kirschenbaum, 1973), which is expansive articles on theory and application of values clarification. From that point on, the remainder of the 1970s began to see an abundance of books—books on values clarification in teaching foreign languages, books on values clarification teaching English, books on values clarification teaching human sexuality, et cetera. Values clarification began to be the underpinning of a whole range of discipline. It was during this time that more and more counselors became aware of values clarification, and I doubt that there are many counselors in these days who do not use values clarification as one of the tools in their repertoire. So we have seen the word spread, we have seen it go off in new directions, and we see it

now coming . . . at clearly a crossroads in its existence.

Martin: Where do you see values clarification work going in the 80s? What will the changes be?

Simon: Well, I anticipated the spreading to audiences that have not yet been reached. For example, I think we'll see the health professions use values clarification in its practices, in its training, and in its applications. It is clear that nurses' daily tasks are dominated by values issues. Physicians, too, have come to realize that the simple problem of getting a patient to take his or her medications is a values issue. The physician can prescribe it and have hopes that it will cure the diagnosed disease or ailment, but until a patient makes a commitment to take the medication nothing much can transpire. The physicians are finding that it is very difficult to prescribe an exercise program or a diet change. These are also values issues that must be dealt with by that profession. I think we will also see more and more applications of values clarification in industrial centers. Business is coming to realize that, clearly, choices are based on values, and value choices dominate the market and also dominate employee relationships and personnel policy. We will see a use of values clarification in industrial business efforts. We will also see, I hope, an increasing use of values clarification in child rearing and the family setting.

All of these are places where values clarification needs consideration. Just this afternoon we had an exercise in asking people to decide where they spent the last four Saturday nights. We are coming to realize that these kind of choices are things that many of us need to consider more carefully. It is not only teenagers who need to make those choices. We need to take a closer look at our lives. I continue to believe the phrase that Emerson said, "The unexamined life is not worth living." Values clarification strategies and the theory which supports those strategies create enormous possibilities of getting people to live life at a deeper intensity and help them to reach the fullest of their potential.

Martin: Howie, you too have been deeply involved in the development and growth of values clarification. What are your thoughts on the future of values clarification in the next decade?

Howard Kirschenbaum: It occurs to me that to some extent I give a response to that question in the book *Advanced Values Clarification* (Kirschenbaum, 1977), in the chapter under the "Futures of Values Clarification." I talk about what I think are some of the paradoxical trends. In many cases values clarification will become integrated and absorbed into peoples' professional styles, and it will fade from the scene as a separate approach: yet, at the same time more people who have not had prior exposure will be discovering values clarification. I think that graduate students will continue to do a considerable amount of doctoral research on it. I think the techniques will be taught in colleges of education and inservice programs, but not necessarily called values clarification. The techniques of values clarification are part of the education profession and other helping professions now, and they will be passed on. Some people will use values clarification to teach decision-making skills, others to teach value-clarifying skills, others as moral development strategies, others as just strategies to help students work more effectively in groups — but the activities are here to stay.

I think the basic thing that values clarification does — which is to identify an important issue that has value dimensions and to provide an effective way for young people to identify their own beliefs and feelings on this issue and to share these and to interact with others — is something that is a part of quality education and something that is going to continue to take place.

Martin: You have mentioned that values clarification is becoming integrated with other approaches. This brings another question to mind. How will the interfacing or blending of values clarification with other aspects of humanistic education affect values clarification?

Simon: Well, what are the threads of humanistic education? One is an awareness of the whole person which includes the transpersonal, the spiritual, and — or intuitive. Values clarification is in perfect harmony with that. We happen to be more grounded in cognitive exercises, but we have a deep respect for the part that the transpersonal and the spiritual play in our lives. In addition, the benefits of touch and the tactile senses, the kinesthetic, have deep commitment in my own work. It is a natural extension of values clarification. I see values clarification being in perfect harmony with some of the therapies that are clustered under humanistic psychology or related to humanistic education. Glasser's Reality Therapy is so compatible with values clarification and so is Ellis's Rational Emotive Therapy. I think the threads of Gestalt and transactional analysis and reevaluation counseling all can be enhanced by the use of values clarification because the insights that have come from therapy need to be translated into change, and values clarification has always had its focus on change. So it is absolutely compatible with so many branches of humanistic education.

Martin: Are there any other changes that either of you see?

Simon: Well, I'm sure values clarification will have to face and deal with the "return to basics" movement. It's hard to deal or to talk to parents who are anxious about the economy who feel that unless their own children get all of their training in basics that are needed, they will not be suitable for the job market. It is hard to talk with them and show them what in Joel

Goodman's phrase is "a return to the basics and a forward move to fundamentals." One of the basic fundamentals has got to be values clarification—how to make choices, how to know what you really love, how to take action, how to look at alternatives, examining the consequences. All of these processes are essential to what we would call a basic education. But we are going to have to do our homework and we are going to have to talk to parents and administrators in non-threatening ways to convey this message. Maybe we ought to do an article on how to talk to parents or to administrators about values clarification and why we have it.

Kirschenbaum: One of the main things we can say to parents and administrators is that values clarification can be combined with teaching subject matter so that students learn even more of the basics than they would otherwise. I describe research in *Advanced Value Clarification* showing how this assertion was supported in elementary reading, in high school biology, in driver education, and in other areas. The reason is not difficult to understand. Values clarification activities help the students relate the subject matter to their own lives—their feelings, choices, and behavior. This dramatically increases the students' motivation with respect to the subject. It also makes class a lot more interesting, enjoyable, and memorable.

Martin: The 80s obviously set forth some strong challenges for values clarification, challenges which will require homework as you say. There are those who say that values clarification is a fad that is passing. It is my observation in watching school districts really become involved in values clarification over a period of time that changes are taking place slowly, gradually, gently. Is it not possible that the seeds planted during the prolific fast-moving 70s are just now beginning to show growth? There is a time for forging ahead and there is a time for waiting. Does that make sense?

Simon: Yes, it does. I think you have outlined the problems very, very carefully. The numbers of people coming to workshops have fallen off. There still are millions of people that need to know about values clarification, but there will not be the period of time of enthusiasm of the 1970s. And what we are in is what you have clearly outlined—a period of carefully filling in the holes—of people doing methodical, thoughtful work, to see that curricula contain values clarification, to see that work with the parents is done ever more effectively, to build support groups for teachers who do values clarification. We're out of the period of the flashy work and we're into what you call the solid building of the waiting work, and I think that it is very important that it be done and be done well.

Martin: There are those who oppose humanistic education in general and values clarification in particular. How are such groups affecting or going to affect values clarification?

Kirschenbaum: There are attempts to ban values clarification. Every now and then a piece of legislation or a school board decision says that values clarification cannot be used in schools. But that is untenable. That's like saying school teachers cannot identify an important issue for students to talk about and that teachers and students cannot talk to one another about their ideas on a topic. You can't ban that. Among other things, it is protected by the Constitution. Students and teachers have a right to think for themselves and say what they think.

But I think it's yet to be seen what effect certain elements will have in their attacks on humanistic education and education in general. It's becoming increasingly clear that there are well-organized and well-financed oppositions to humanistic education, values clarification, sex education, students' choosing some of the directions of their education, and so on. I think that it starts with the attack on humanistic education and, if that is successful, it goes on to banning sex education of any type in the schools, and then it goes on to eliminating a large number of books in the school library and reading programs, and it goes on to disallowing certain people who are different—whether they are homosexual or have liberal beliefs—from the teaching profession. And who knows where it will go from there.

So, I think as this becomes increasingly clear, as I hope it will, that those who have belief not only in the importance of humanistic education but in the importance of free thought and quality education in the schools will recognize that some very important issues are at stake and will get together to see what needs to be done to enable our schools to remain a very important part of our democratic system. I don't know which way it is going to go. I would like to be optimistic and say that people are going to realize pretty soon what's happening, and that the major organizations in the education profession, like the NEA and the UFT, will be among the leaders in standing up for the rights of professionals to do a good job of educating students for democratic living.

Martin: Two of the specific contentions of those who oppose humanistic education are that values clarification and humanistic education are amoral and atheistic. How do you address these concerns?

Kirschenbaum: I think that most humanistic education approaches are highly moral approaches. Basic to so many of them is the respect for persons, an advocacy to tolerance within the classroom, and emphasis of the importance of people understanding one another and working out their conflicts in a way that respects the rights and beliefs of all individuals. I think many of the humanistic education approaches and the curriculum that have come out of the field have encouraged young people to take a look at the real issues and problems in the

real world outside and get involved in working on them. I think many of the approaches of humanistic education have asked students and taught students to take responsibility for their own behavior and to recognize the consequences of their behavior on other people. So it seems that some of the basic moral values of respect for persons, positive conflict resolution, communication among family, friends, and colleagues, and social responsibility—some of the great moral concerns that both conservatives and liberals share—are very much reflected in humanistic education.

In terms of religion, humanistic education doesn't take a stand on religious issues. It is not meant to. Reading programs in schools are *nontheistic,* which is different than *a* theistic. Most science curriculums are nontheistic. Math is nontheistic. Some of the skills that humanistic education teaches are nontheistic. What that simply means is that humanistic education, like most other aspects of public schools, doesn't attempt to tamper with people's religious beliefs and values. The fact is that many humanistic educators are priests, ministers, rabbis, and lay people who have firm religious beliefs! I would imagine that some humanistic educators are atheists and agnostics as well. I think many of the moral values of humanistic education are consistent with the moral values of most world religions, but it's not a theistic system and was never meant to be.

Simon: Well, values clarification and humanistic education have been attacked by certain fundamentalist groups in this country. And I feel sad about that because I can't think of anything that is being done in the schools that has a deeper base in paralleling what wise, sensitive parents are doing with their children at home. I clearly don't understand what the furor is about. But what we are doing seems utterly consistent with Christian beliefs expressed by almost any person who calls himself or herself a Christian. And still we are working in a secular setting. We try very, very hard to give equal voice, to allow people to express their opinions. But not just anything is called a "value." A value in our framework has a most demanding set of criteria—it must be prized and cherished, chosen after considering consequences, acted upon, et cetera. We insist on a rigorous search for values. What parents don't want their kids to look at the consequences of their choices or act on their beliefs? What I would dream of would be that the fundamentalists would become allies, realizing that millions of children don't get a fundamental background at home at all. And they come to school without any guidance training whatsoever. The genuine concern that is expressed by some fundamentalists are concerns that we have, too. What we need, however, is that they actually read our materials and present their arguments in context with things they have difficulty with. We don't need uninformed reactions that come from propaganda because then no dialogue can ensue.

Kirschenbaum: With regard to values clarification being amoral, I just think the critics are wrong. I think it is as powerful a tool for building good people who live respectable and responsible lives as any set of tools I know. Just

the rigors of the seven criteria which demand critical thinking, which demand the testing of consequences, and which demand closing the gap between your creeds and your deeds make it an extremely moral discipline. What some people are concerned about is that we raise moral issues at all, and that's true. We do sometimes raise questions, as the students raise questions about sexuality, religion, politics, families, money, and the like. Some people would ban these topics from the classroom. Well, that can't be done. If it relates to the subject area being considered—and there are certainly a fair share of moral issues connected to social studies, literature, science, and health, among other subjects—then I think the First Amendment and the traditions of academic freedom say the teacher and student have every right to read about, to write about, and to share their views on these topics.

Martin: Is there anything either of you would like to add?

Simon: Yes. Louis Raths died in 1978. This was 30 years after his conception and his brilliant innovation, and how proud I am to be carrying on the work which that noble man started.

REFERENCES

Harmin, M.; Kirschenbaum, H.; & Simon, S. *Clarifying values through subject matter.* Minneapolis: Winston, 1973.

Kirschenbaum, H. *Advanced values clarification.* La Jolla, Calif.: University Associates, 1977.

Raths, L.; Harmin, M.; & Simon, S. *Values and teaching.* Columbus, Ohio: Charles E. Merrill, 1966.

Simon, S. B., Howe, L.; & Kirschenbaum, H. *Values clarification: A handbook of practical strategies for teachers and students.* New York: Hart, 1972.

Simon, S. B., & Kirschenbaum, H. (Eds.). *Readings in values clarification.* Minneapolis: Winston, 1973.

What's Wrong with Values Clarification

Alan L. Lockwood _____

Alan L. Lockwood is professor of education at the University of Wisconsin and has written widely on moral education.

I deliberately chose this negative title because I assume that Howard Kirschenbaum will try to explain what is right with Values Clarification. He has a much tougher job than I do. There are a number of serious conceptual, ethical, and practical flaws with the Values Clarification approach to values education.[1] Among them are:

1. The failure to distinguish moral from non-moral value issues.
2. The embodiment of an unacceptable moral point of view best characterized as ethical relativism.
3. The reliance on assumptions and methods of approaches to therapy.
4. The use of methods which jeopardize the privacy rights of students and their families.
5. The absence of a persuasive body of research to support claims of effectiveness.

In the remainder of this commentary, I will briefly summarize these five shortcomings of Values Clarification.

The failure to distinguish moral from non-moral value issues. Values Clarification asks students to clarify their values on a wide variety of topics ranging from favorite foods to whether mercy-killing should be legalized. For example, suggested questions for the "Public Interview" strategy cover such topics as one's views on welfare policy, community injustices, career preferences, favorite sports, and current toothpaste preferences.

It appears that, for the advocates of Values Clarification, a value issue is a value issue; that there are no fundamental distinctions between decisions affecting the rights and welfare of other persons and decisions regarding one's personal tastes. Clearly, however, not all value issues are of the same type. A decision to support policies involving the termination of human life is different from a decision involving one's preferences in entertainment. Decisions of the former type are moral value decisions, while the latter are non-moral value decisions.

The moral/non-moral distinction is not always easy to make, but to pretend that it does

From Alan L. Lockwood, "What's Wrong with Values Clarification," Social Education 41 (May 1977): 399–401. Reprinted with permission of the National Council for the Social Studies.

---

[1]The position taken in this commentary is a distillation of more detailed argumentation developed in other papers. A. Lockwood, "A Critical View of Values Clarification," *Teachers College Record*, September, 1975. A. Lockwood, "Values Education and the Right to Privacy," unpublished mimeo, University of Wisconsin-Madison. G. Wehlage, and A. Lockwood, "Moral Relativism and Values Education," in *Moral Education . . . It Comes With the Territory*, Purpel and Ryan (eds.). McCutchan, Berkeley, 1976.

not exist is a serious shortcoming, especially in curricula used by social studies teachers. Social studies teachers have a general responsibility to engage in citizenship education. As part of this responsibility we should help students recognize the importance of social-ethical issues and the need to make considered, defensible decisions when confronted with such issues; we have no compelling interest in how citizens decide on matters of personal taste, Curricula, such as Values Clarification, which blur the distinction between moral and non-moral value issues are a disservice to one of the major goals of citizenship education.

The embodiment of ethical relativism. Simply put, ethical relativism is the view that no value beliefs can be proven better than others; so, therefore, all value beliefs are equally valid. Two features of Values Clarification suggest that it, perhaps unwittingly, holds the relativistic point of view: (a) the advocacy of a non-judgmental classroom environment, and (b) the absence of justificatory requirements in the seven-step valuing progress.

Participants in Values Clarification are urged to be non-judgmental in their treatment of others' point of view. The desired atmosphere is one of acceptance, nurturance, and unconditional positive regard. Disagreement over the rightness or wrongness of persons' views is discouraged; empathy, supportiveness, and trust are encouraged. The stress is on helping students make decisions with which they feel personally comfortable, rather than on helping them make decisions which they believe are morally justified.

In addition to the general absence of ethical argumentation, the recommended seven-step valuing process does not include any suggestions or criteria for such debate. Indeed, the seven criteria fit an almost limitless array of value positions. For example, the views of Adolph Hitler, Charles Manson, Mahatma Gandhi, and Jesus

Christ clearly fulfill the Values Clarification criteria for possession of a value. Surely Values Clarification does not intend to nurture morally indefensible points of view, but, as currently formulated, it does nothing to inhibit them.

Any values education curriculum which rules out debate on the propriety or defensibility of moral value decisions is susceptible to charges of promoting ethical relativism. Relativism may be quite acceptable in the realm of non-moral value decisions, but it is inadequate for making moral value decisions. Moral judgments require sound justifications, not simple expressions of personal taste. If not, how could we fairly and rationally oppose the views and practices of Hitlers, Mansons, Watergaters, and the like?

The reliance on assumptions and methods of therapy. A variety of Values Clarification strategies and assumptions are drawn from therapeutic theory and practice. For example, note the strategies "Rogerian Listening," "Self-Contracts," "Chairs or Dialogue With Self," "Partner Risk or Sharing Trios," "R D As," and others in *Values Clarification* by Simon, Howe, and Kirschenbaum.[2] Similarly, the general orientation presented in *More Values Clarification,* by Simon and Clark,[3] is in the tradition of self-disclosure group therapies.

Currently, most teachers are neither trained in nor authorized to engage in therapy with their classes. (Whether they should be is a separate question.) Inexperienced, amateur therapists in public school classrooms are likely to do more harm than good. I believe most teaches recognize this and would not intentionally choose to play such a role without training and public ac-

---

[2]Sidney B. Simon, Leland W. Howe, and Howard Kirschenbaum, *Values Clarification* (New York: Hart Publishing Co. 1972). Strategies are on pages 295, 319, 221, 177, 358 in the order mentioned above.

[3]Sidney B. Simon and Jay Clark, *More Values Clarification* (San Diego, California: Pennant Press, 1975).

ceptance/authorization for the performance of therapy.

The advocates of Values Clarification occasionally assert that Values Clarification is not therapy. This blanket claim is most misleading given many of their recent recommendations to teachers. Values Clarifications should admit the therapeutic derivation and orientation of many of their suggestions and strategies and present them separately from the more conventional strategies. This would allow teachers and other curriculum decision-makers to better decide what aspects, if any, of Values Clarification they feel competent and justified in employing.

Practices which jeopardize privacy rights. Many Values Clarification strategies are designed to encourage students to disclose information about themselves and their families. This is done through both explicit questioning and the use of projective techniques. Some examples of explicit questions are: Do you have any brothers or sisters? How do you get along? What does your mother do? Does she like it? Reveal who in your family brings you the greatest sadness, and why. How did you first learn to kiss? Did you ever cheat on tests? How many of you are in love right now?

In addition to explicit questions designed to obtain personal information, projective techniques are used. One example is the sentence completion type of strategy in which students fill in the blanks for such statements as: Secretly I wish. . . . My parents are usually. . . . I'd like to tell my best friend. . . . I'm trying to overcome my fear. . . . Another projective strategy, "My House," asks students to draw a picture of their house and its family occupants. Then, students are instructed to write in what the people are saying to each other. Another strategy, "If I Were a Dog," is recommended to teachers as ". . . one way to discover how younger students feel without asking them openly."

Privacy rights should be respected unless

there is a grave social need for their abridgment. In public schools especially, we need to be conscious of persons' rights to privacy because schooling is compulsory, classroom discourse occurs in the presence of many others, and teachers have the authority to set and evaluate student performance. The potential for privacy violations in institutions characterized by coercion, publicity, and power is high. The usual privacy protections of prior informed consent rarely explicitly operate in public schools, so the application of strategies designed to elicit personal information is a genuine threat to the privacy rights of students and their families.

The absence of persuasive research support. The advocates of Values Clarification makes a variety of claims regarding the positive effects of their approach on such variables as school achievement and attitudes, drug usage, reading ability, general self-concept, and classroom behavior. I recently completed an in-depth review of thirteen studies on the effects of Values Clarification and have concluded there is little evidence to support such claims of effectiveness.

For example, one study suggested that reduced drug usage was an outcome of Values Clarification.[4] The suggestion was based on a statistically significant difference between pretest scores and post-test scores on a questionnaire in which students indicated the frequency with which they used various drugs. A closer look at the data and instrumentation is revealing. The largest obtained change was from a pre-test mean of 2.47 (according to the questionnaire this falls between drug usage "almost never" and "every few months") to a post-test mean of 1.96 ("almost never"). Given the questionable validity of self-reporting instruments on drug usage and the dubious distinction between "every few months" and "almost never,"

[4]Reported in Jay Clark, *Operation Future: Third Annual Report* (San Diego, California: Pennant Educational Materials, 1974), pp. 1–24.

one should have little confidence, based on the study, that Values Clarification contributes to reduced drug usage.

Seven studies employed some measure of general self-concept, adjustment or esteem. With the exception of one study, the research on these variables was flawed by unwarranted statistical manipulations or interpretations. Space does not permit an analysis of these studies, but it is fair to conclude that even when well-designed and interpreted studies have found a statistically significant change, that change is very small numerically and, as a result, of questionable education significance.[5] Given these small changes and the difficulty of measuring elusive, affective variables, one should be extraordinarily cautious in claiming that research supports the effectiveness of Values Clarification.

---

[5]A. Lockwood, "The Effects of Values Clarification and Moral Development Curricula on School-Age Subjects: A Critical Review of Recent Research," *Review of Educational Research* 48 (Summer 1978): 325–364.

Final Comments

Values Clarification is admirable for the simplicity and specificity of its recommended classroom strategies, as well as for the clarity of its general rationale. To this extent, hard-working, busy teachers may find it easy to incorporate into their instructional plans. There can be no question that Values Clarification has caught on. The rate of acceptance of Values Clarification appears to have outdistanced that of most recent educational fads. It is now time for a careful critical assessment of the approach. My criticisms are offered in that spirit with the hope that the advocates of Values Clarification will take them seriously and that teachers will be more selective in their usage of this approach to values education.

DISCUSSION QUESTIONS AND ACTIVITIES

1. Does the widespread use of values clarification in many different subjects and educational settings definitively demonstrate its worth and soundness?

2. Will values clarification likely get people "to live life at a deeper intensity and help them to reach the fullest of their potential?"

3. How is values clarification related to humanistic psychology and to certain therapies?

4. Does values clarification conflict with back to basics, or can it help students learn the basics?

5. Is values clarification amoral and atheistic?

6. Is it necessary for values clarification to adopt an ethical relativist stance in order to avoid indoctrination?

7. Why is it unsuitable for teachers to use therapeutic approaches? Are Lockwood's criticisms on the matter well founded?

8. Examine the literature to determine what research studies support the values clarification approach.

9. Investigate the type of classroom materials available for use with values clarification.

10. Invite to class for a presentation a teacher who has successfully used a values clarification approach.

SUGGESTED READINGS

Proponents

Burton, Grace M. "Values Education for Pre-Service Teachers: A Basic." *Contemporary Education* 53 (Fall 1981): 39–42.

Havens, Robert and Kenneth Morrison. "Values Counseling: A Clarifying Approach." *Counseling and Values* 27 (October 1982): 36–39.

Howe, Leland W. and Hart, Gordon. "Counseling with a Focus on Values." *Education* 97 (Spring 1977): 237–41.

Kautz, Carol. "Encouraging the Development of Value Clarification and Life-Coping Skills in Any Classroom Setting." *Illinois Teacher of Home-Economics* 21 (March-April 1978): 177–8.

Kinsler, Karen Taber and Sinatra, Richard. "Promoting Language Arts through Values Clarification." *Reading Teacher* 31 (November 1977): 173–8.

Kirschenbaum, Howard. *Advanced Values Clarification.* Minneapolis: Winston Press, 1973.

Knapp, Clifford E. "The Values of Values Clarification: A Reaction to Critics." *Journal of Environmental Education* 13 (Winter 1981-82): 1–4.

Logan, Donald et al. "The Impact of Classroom Values Clarification Program." *Counseling and Values* 21 (February 1977): 129–135.

McEniry, Robert. "Values Clarification: An Aid to Adolescent Religious Education." *Counseling and Values* 27 (October 1982): 40–51.

McGinnis, Mary D. "Values Clarification." *Volta Review* 83 (December 1981): 466–74.

Martin, Roberta P., ed. "Values Clarification: State of the Art." *Counseling and Values* 26 (July 1982): 220–74. Eight articles about values clarification: its history, issues, application, and future.

Piercey, Fred and Schultz, Kay. "Values Clarifi-cation Strategies for Couples' Enrichment." *Family Coordinator* 27 (April 1978): 175–8.

Raths, Louis, et al. *Values and Teaching,* 2nd ed. Columbus, Ohio: Merrill, 1978.

Schwarberg, Helene. "Let's Develop Survival Skills." *School Shop* 37 (September 1977): 33–34, 66.

Simon, Sidney B. and Clark, Jay. *Beginning Values Clarification: A Guide for the Use of Values Clarification in the Classroom.* La Mesa, Ca.: Pennant Press, 1975.

Simon, Sidney, et al. *Values Clarification: A Handbook of Practical Strategies for Teachers and Students.* New York: Hart, 1972.

Stanely, Toll. "An Implementation Strategy for 'Values Clarification.' " *Clearing House* 50 (May 1977): 385–89.

Thompson, David G. and George R. Hudson. "Values Clarification and Behavioral Group Counseling with Ninth Grade Boys in a Residential School." *Journal of Counseling Psychology* 29 (July 1982): 394–99.

Turner, Thomas N. "Critical Reading as a Values Clarification Process." *Language Arts* 54 (November/December 1977): 909–12.

Warnick, Barbara. "Arguing Value Propositions." *Journal of the American Forensic Association* 18 (Fall 1981): 109–19.

Critics

Baer, Richard A., Jr. "Clarifying My Objections to Values Clarification: A Response to Clifford E. Knapp." *Journal of Environmental Education* (Winter 1981-82): 5–11.

Bennett, William J. and Delattre, Edwin J. "Moral Education in the Schools." *The Public Interest* 50 (Winter 1978): 81–98.

Feldmesser, Robert A. and Hugh F. Cline. "To Be or Not to Be: Moral Education in the

Schools." *New York University Education Quarterly* 13 (Spring 1982): 11–20.

Gluck, Phyllis Gold. " 'Values Clarification': The Engineering of Consensus." *Teachers College Record* 79 (December 1977): 267–74.

Kazepides, A. "The Logic of Values Clarification." *Journal of Educational Thought* 11 (August 1977): 99–111.

Lockwood, Alan L. "The Effects of Values Clarification and Moral Development Curricula on School Age Subjects: A Critical Review of the Literature." *Review of Educational Research* 48 (Summer 1978): 325–64.

Loggins, Dennis. "Clarifying What and How Well?" *Health Education* 7 (March/April 1976): 2–5.

McGough, Kris. "Values Clarification: Your Job or Mine?" *Social Education* 41 (March 1977): 404, 406.

Smith, John K. "Values Clarification and Moral Nonexistence." *Journal of Thought* 12 (January 1977): 4–9.

Suttle, Bruce B. "Moral Education versus Values Clarification." *The Journal of Educational Thought* 16 (April 1982): 35–41.

Wagner, Paul A. "Simon, Indoctrination and Ethical Relativism." *The Journal of Educational Thought* 15 (December 1981): 187–94.

Bibliographical Sources

Harvey, Karen and Horton, Lowell. "Moral/Values Education: An Annotated Bibliography." *Illinois Schools Journal* 58 (Spring 1978): 31–45.

Hill, Russell A.; Klafter, Marcia, and Wallace, Joan. *A Bibliography on Moral/Values Education.* Philadelphia: Research for Better Schools, 1977.

Superka, Douglas P., et al. *Values Education Sourcebook.* Boulder, Colo.: Social Science Education Consortium, 1976.

17
Experiential Education and Learning

As an organized movement, experiential education emerged in the middle and late 1970s and has continued to grow rapidly during the 1980s. As an idea, its roots go back to Aristotle and Buddha, both of whom advocated activities that today would be considered experiential education. In more recent times, John Dewey and his followers have been proponents of experiential education. Experiential learning was first introduced at Rensselaer Polytechnic Institute in Troy, New York, in the 1820s; other colleges followed suit.

Experiential learning occurs whenever the learner is in direct contact with the materials and realities being studied (as opposed to reading, hearing, writing, or talking about referents with which he or she does not come into direct contact). Some writers also make a distinction between experiential education and experiential learning, but others use the terms more or less synonymously, and some substitute other terms such as "action learning" for experiential education. Distinctions can be made between experiential education and learning. Experiential learning has no specific educational objectives, no supervision by the faculty, and may be presented for credit after the experiences are undergone. In contrast, experiential education is carefully planned, employs faculty supervision, specific objectives, and is an integral part of academic studies.

Experiential education and learning begin with action; the action is then observed with the expectation that the same action in similar circumstances would have a similar effect; this may, in turn, lead to grasping a general principle that can be employed in situations in anticipation of predicted results. This process, according to James Coleman, contrasts sharply with information assimilation where the learner receives the information, tries to assimilate a general principle, infers applications of it, and then finally applies it.

Several types of programs will help to illustrate experiential education. One type consists of various work-education programs: cooperative education (alternating classroom learning with work experiences throughout the college years); internships; observer role (as in classrooms, hospitals, etc.); and industry organized programs for credit. A second type (largely experiential learning) provides academic credit for prior learning, either by providing credit for successfully passing standardized examinations or by evaluating credit for experiential learning on the basis of documentations supplied. Service education programs are a third type wherein activities would emphasize services to the public (as a sociology major may work with a public welfare agency). Cross-cultural experiences, a fourth type, would consist of foreign-study programs and intracultural programs (where the student becomes a participant-observer in a sub-culture). Finally, there are individual growth experiences that test one's skills and survival ability in the wilderness.

Are Experiential Learning Programs Effective?

Dan Conrad
Diane Hedin

Dan Conrad and Diane Hedin are coordinators of action learning programs for the Hopkins, Minnesota, public schools and the Minneapolis public schools. They are also on the staff of the Center for Youth Development and Research at the University of Minnesota.

Where can one learn to get things done and to work with others, to solve problems, to accept the consequences of one's actions, to gather and analyze information, to become more open to new experiences, to feel and act like a useful member of the community, to develop greater self-esteem, to become more self-motivated, and to be more concerned about others?

Where are these taught or learned in the secondary school curriculum? According to 4,000 students in some 20 public, private, and parochial school systems across the country, they are taught and learned in experiential programs.

This report of early research is one of several by the Evaluation of Experiential Learning Project, a major effort co-sponsored by the National Association of Secondary School Principals, National Association of Independent Schools, and the National Catholic Education Association with funds from the Rockefeller Family Fund and the Spencer and General Mills Foundations.

The purpose of this article is to describe the evaluation effort, to describe its early evaluation results, and to describe the educational practice being studied.

At the heart of the project is its "Panel of Practitioners," teachers and administrators from 20 diverse school systems from Beverly Hills. California, to Newark, New Jersey[1] With the assistance of seasoned educational evaluators like Ralph Tyler, they are responsible for defining the issues to be studied, for helping select and develop instruments, for implementing

From Dan Conrad and Diane Hedin, "Are Experiential Learning Programs Effective?" NASSP Bulletin 62 (November 1978) pp. 102–7. Used by permission.

[1]Schools included in the Project are: *Independent:* Dana Hall School, Wellesley, Mass.: Francis W. Parker School, Chicago, Ill.; Carolina Friends School, Durham, N.C.; Duluth Cathedral High School, Duluth, Minn.; *Parochial:* St. Benedict's Preparatory School, Newark, N.J.; Bellarmine High School, Tacoma, Wash.; Ward High School, Kansas City, Kans.; *Public:* Eisenhower High School, Hopkins, Minn.; Mitchell High School, Colorado Springs, Colo.; Minneapolis Public Schools, Minn.; Allegheny Intermediate Unit, Pittsburgh; St. Paul Minn. Open School, Minn.; South Brunswick High School, Monmouth Junction, N.J.; Rochester, Minnesota Public Schools; Bartram School of Human Services, Philadelphia, Pa.; Beverly Hills High School, California.; Ridgewood High School, Norridge, Ill.; Kirkwood High School, Kirkwood, Mo.; North Central High School, Indianapolis, Ind.

the design, for helping interpret the data collected — and for keeping the whole study practical, understandable, and applicable to everyday life in schools.

In June 1978, at the Spring Hill Conference Center in Wayzata, Minnesota, the panel examined the data collected during the study's pilot phase. They admit to being surprised, even overwhelmed, by what they found. The biggest surprises were how very positively both teachers and students rate their experiential programs, the significance of the things they report being learned in them, and the extraordinary level of agreement between students and teachers about these program outcomes.

Furthermore, the findings held constant across the broad range of programs represented in the study (internships, volunteer service, political action, outdoor adventure, etc.)[2] and for extremely diverse schools and student populations throughout the country.

EARLY EVALUATION PROCEDURES
AND RESULTS

The first evaluation of the project was to survey people who direct experiential programs. In January 1978, they were asked what they could most confidently claim to be the actual effects of experiential programs on students. They were asked not what they believed *should* happen, but what they had *directly* experienced, seen, and heard. The result represents an important study in itself, being a report of "concerned observers" looking critically, if not disinterestedly, at experiential education.

Among the vast array of observed effects were 24 which appeared with amazing regularity. Together, they comprise an imposing list of

[2]The study encompasses virtually all forms of what is termed experiential education with the notable exception of work-related or vocational programs.

outcomes which schools everywhere hope to achieve, but less often do (or even dare to claim): improved self-esteem, learning responsibility, learning to solve real-life problems, etc. (see Table 1). Given the current level of pessimism in American education, it is encouraging, even startling, to see such confidence about the effects which at least one educational practice seems to be having.

This original survey set the stage for the next and more critical step in the evaluation process. Believing that the consumers of a "product" are usually more reliable judges of its value than its producers or salespersons, we presented in the spring of 1978 this list of observed effects to all the students in each of the programs. The students who were informed that the list represented what some people had said might be the effects of experiential programs were asked: "Which, if any, of these things have you personally learned or gained from the activities in your own experiential program?"

The researchers knew from previous studies and their own experience that students' perceptions of the purposes of a course are often considerably different from and their evaluations less effusive than those of their teachers. Therefore, they expected not more than a 50 percent level of agreement between teachers and students on the effects of the programs. In fact, however, only one item, "to become a more effective consumer," (46%) failed to meet the criteria, but it was a deliberate emphasis in only two of the programs surveyed.

More than half (14) of the items achieved an average agreement level of over 80 percent across all programs. These items are the ones listed in the opening paragraph of this article, plus "learning responsibility to the group or class." "learning responsibility for my own life," "gaining more realistic attitudes toward other people," "increased knowledge of community organizations," and "risk-taking — openness to new experiences." (See Table 1.)

TABLE 1
What Students Learn in Experiential Learning
Composite Profile of 20 Experiential Programs (N = 4,000)

Item (in rank order)	Percentage of Responses		
	Agree*	Disagree*	Don't Know
1. Concern for fellow human beings	93%	4%	3%
2. Ability to get things done and to work smoothly with others	93	4	3
3. Realistic attitudes toward other people such as the elderly, handicapped, or government officials	88	4	8
4. Self-motivation to learn, participate, achieve	88	7	5
5. Self-concept (sense of confidence, sense of competence, self-awareness)	88	7	5
6. Responsibility to the group or class	86	3	11
7. Risk-taking — openness to new experiences	86	7	8
8. Sense of usefulness in relation to the community	86	8	6
9. Problem-solving	86	9	5
10. Risk-taking — being assertive and independent	86	9	5
11. Accept consequences of my own actions	85	9	6
12. Gathering and analyzing information, observation, reflecting on experience	84	8	7
13. Knowledge of community organizations	82	7	11
14. Responsibility for my own life	80	10	9
15. Awareness of community problems	78	13	9
16. Assume new, important tasks in community and school	78	14	8
17. Communication skills (listening, speaking, presenting ideas through variety of media)	77	11	7
18. Awareness of community resources	71	13	16
19. Realistic ideas about the world of work	71	18	11
20. Learning about a variety of careers	70	22	8
21. Use of leisure time	60	26	14
22. Narrowing career choices	54	34	12
23. To become an effective parent	52	29	19
24. To become an effective consumer	46	32	22

*Strongly agree and agree are combined and disagree and strongly disagree are combined.

Each of the other items, such as learning communication skills, learning about community problems and resources, learning about careers, etc., received 80 to 100 percent agreement in those programs where they were a deliberate emphasis. Apparently with good reason, the participants in these experiential programs think they are pursuing something worthwhile in education.

Not only is there substantial agreement between students and teachers about what is learned in experience-based programs, but community people who supervise the students, ranging from free clinic counselors to television network executives, also reported that they observed student progress toward these 24 outcomes. In one school's program (Beverly Hills High School), the students' supervisors were asked to respond to the same questionnaire as the students. The only difference between the student and supervisor rating was that the latter ratings were more positive, with a much higher incidence of "strongly agree" appearing in their responses.

THE NEXT STEP

As interesting and significant as the above results might be, they represent only the beginning of the work of the Evaluation of Experiential Learning Project. The next step will be to subject these observations to more rigorous examination. In their June meeting, the project's staff and Panel of Practitioners gave final form to the formal research design, focusing their investigation on seven issues suggested by the preliminary study: self-concept, responsibility, problem solving, attitudes toward others, learning about the community, communication skills, and career development.

These issues will be examined through standardized tests, project-designed instruments, systematic observations (by teachers, su-

pervisors, parents, and outside observers), case studies, and a myriad of unobtrusive measures. Testing will begin in the fall of 1978 and continue throughout the school year. The aim will be to confirm, qualify, or refute the direct reports of teachers and students.

In addition, they hope to determine what kinds of programs produce what results, what classroom and community activities best help assure their being attained, and what kinds of evaluative techniques are most appropriate to these practices. Among the products of the project will be its research report, a portrait of individual programs and students, a compilation of ideas for program and class activities, and a handbook of evaluative tools which individual schools can use to assess the effectiveness of their own experiential programs.

THE EDUCATIONAL PROGRAMS STUDIED

The early findings of this project suggest that direct community experiences may be an important means for nurturing certain kinds of growth and development in students. That similar findings came from such a diverse range of programs is especially interesting. What the programs have in common is that they all engage students in new and challenging roles outside the school. That they all should report similar results suggests that the researchers may be uncovering effects that are generic to experiential education. If that is the case, not everyone should be surprised.

The notion that *people learn some things best by doing them* (and that adolescents need significant and challenging tasks) is as old as John Dewey, if not Plato. That secondary schools should include experiential learning programs in their general curricula has been an important recommendation of every major commission on youth, education, and citizenship of the last decade. Yet, until now, no one has systematically investigated the assumptions underlying the recommendations, tested the claims made for the programs, or tried to spell out just what is learned through them. This lack of systematic investigation may explain why, for many educators, such programs remain in the category of things that sound good but may turn out to be more troublesome than worthy.

More exhaustive research is needed, and it is forthcoming. In the meantime, the early accounts of what students (and their teachers, administrators, and community supervisors) report to be the effects of experiential learning programs are certainly encouraging. If these results persist through subsequent research, experiential education will have to be viewed as an effective means for achieving some of the highest goals in education.

Experiential Education and Learning: An Assessment

John Martin Rich _____

Experiential education and learning is a growing movement that has been well received by students and most faculty participants. It has a number of desirable features: it gives students experiences with actual problems; students are usually highly motivated; the recall of what is learned is generally better than with formal instruction; student success with experiential education results in increased confidence and self-assurance in learning; and experiential education can produce college-equivalent learning. Despite these and other achievements, certain theoretical weaknesses have frequently been

overlooked and some practical problems have yet to be fully rectified.

CONCEPTUAL AND THEORETICAL WEAKNESSES

Conceptual Weaknesses

Some writers refer to experiential learning as that learning that is acquired outside the classroom.[1] Another group of writers reports that it is confusing to equate experiential learning with learning off-campus or in non-

Written expressly for Innovations in Education: Reformers and Their Critics.

[1]Arthur Levine, *Handbook on Undergraduate Curriculum* (San Francisco: Jossey-Bass 1978), pp. 523–24.

classroom settings.[2] Still others claim that experiential learning can be of both types: non-sponsored life experiences and sponsored institutional activities.[3] Moreover, some studies use the terms "experiential education" and "experiential learning" interchangeably[4] and other studies do not.[5] Thus what is to count as paradigmatic activities is unclear. In addition, those who view experiential learning as learning acquired outside the classroom, would seem to open themselves up to millions of specific learning acts in an individual's life from infancy through old age. Do all of these acts have educational value? Some standards will need to be imposed to sort them out and to keep the term from being so broad as to be virtually meaningless. Though conceptual confusion and ambiguity is not unique to experiential education and learning, if the field is to progress, researchers will need to clear up these confusions and reach greater consensus.

Theoretical Weaknesses

If experiential education and learning is used exclusively as the educational program, it may lead to a one-sided education, because it is based on concrete experiences. Information assimilation, in contrast, is based on having the learner receive information, try to assimilate a general principle, infer applications of it, and then finally apply it. Experiential education rules out theories of verbal learning. The two most important ideas of Ausubel's verbal learning theory are that what a person knows and how this knowledge is structured are most important variables in learning and instruction.[6] The person must already know the relevant ideas contained in the new material. Meaningful learning is brought about by recombining new and known material into new structures and relationships. Thus experiential education and learning, with its emphasis upon action and inductive processes and problem-solving, neglects Ausubel's verbal learning, which has long played a significant role in much classroom learning.

It could only be convincingly argued that experiential learning is in keeping with the way young children learn, rather than with the way students of all ages learn. Thus to use experiential education for older youth would need to be supported for reasons other than those of human development. According to Piaget, the child in the preoperational period from age two to six or seven begins to manipulate symbols and later develops structural frameworks to order external events.[7] In the formal operations period from ages eleven or twelve to fifteen, the adolescent develops complex techniques for dealing with the symbolic world of abstraction and possibility. Thus, since pupils have the capacity to deal with abstractions and are not limited to concrete objects and experiences, reasons are needed other than an alleged congruence of experiential education and human learning.

As Kant has shown, one's conceptual framework makes experience possible.[8] It is necessary to have concepts of space and time in order for experience to be possible; these concepts are *a priori*. (An example of *a priori* knowledge is that if a = b and b = c, then a = c.) One can recognize, as Lewis has done, that what is *a priori* can be maintained in the

[2]Morris T. Keaton, "Experiential Education," *Encyclopedia of Educational Research*, Fifth Education (New York: The Free Press, 1982), 2618-24.

[3]Edward L. Dejnozka and David E. Kapel, *American Educators' Encyclopedia* (Wesport, Conn.: Greenwood Press, 1982), p. 295.

[4]Keaton, "Experiential Education," pp. 618-24.

[5]John Martin Rich, "A Rationale for the Liberal Education of Educators," *Journal of Teacher Education* XXI (May-June 1980): 27-30.

6. D. P. Ausubel, *Educational Psychology: A Cognitive View* (New York: Holt, Rinehart & Winston, 1968).

[7]J. Piaget and B. Inhelder, *The Psychology of the Child* (New York: Basic Books, 1969).

[8]Immanuel Kant, *Critique of Pure Reason*, trans. Norman Kemp Smith (New York: St. Martin's Press, 1965).

face of all experience, and the *a priori* provides us with concepts that can be tested pragmatically.[9] In other words, we test our concepts of space and time by acting on them. The point of all this is that experiential learning, which *begins* with action and induction, is naïve about how one gains knowledge.

Even the bedrock on which experiential education and learning rests—induction—has been seriously questioned by Popper.[10] Theories are not developed by inductive procedures; they begin as imaginative conjectures. Knowledge, then, is not a structure built up by inductive inference from passively received sensation. The process is conjectural and theoretical, a way of putting imaginative questions to the world to see if they can be falsified or disputed.

Thus in this section several related conceptual problems were indicated. The theoretical problems arise out of conflict with other theories of learning (Ausubel), knowledge of human development (Piaget), the way the mind works (Kant and Lewis), and the fallacy of induction (Popper). Now we turn to some practical problems.

WEAKNESSES IN PRACTICE

Although the practical problems are more widely recognized than the conceptual and theoretical ones, they merit review because in some programs the weaknesses can still be found. It is commonly observed that experiential education is popular with students and generally well supported by faculty participants. Although this feature means that motivation problems will be reduced, popularity does not in itself demonstrate the value of a program. Junk food, coffee, and gooey pastries are enjoyed by millions of people, but the nutritional value of these foods and beverages is virtually nil. Some popular programs have little educational value and other popular programs may have considerable value. But which ones have value cannot be known just by majority tastes.

Part of experiential education and learning involves students setting realistic goals for themselves; it is embodied in the meaning of these programs, in contrast to more traditional instruction, that students play a significant role in shaping their own education. The literature indicates that students have difficulty in setting realistic goals for themselves. A basic problem arises in matching the individual to an assignment on the basis of his development needs.[11] The desires of the student are not always compatible with the agency. The school supervisor needs to help in setting realistic objectives.

Placing adolescents in the community for different periods of time means that they will be separated from their peers in school during a period in their lives when peer acceptance is of utmost importance. This separation may lead to a breakdown of their ability to communicate with one another effectively and a growth of insecurity and loneliness. Thus supervising teachers will need to show participants how to forge closer and more meaningful links in their social world.

Experiential education involves the development of new programs, teachers with special abilities, and the cooperation of administrators and community representatives. The more people involved in any program, the more numerous the points at which breakdowns can occur. Thus greater skills, more careful supervision, and large-scale cooperation are needed before such programs can achieve their goals.

Another problem with experiential educa-

[9]Clarence Irving Lewis, *Mind and the World-Order* (New York: Dover Publications, 1929), Chaps. 7 and 8.
[10]Karl R. Popper, *Conjectures and Refutations* (New York: Harper Torchbooks, 1963).

[11]Richard Graham, "Youth and Experiential Learning," In *Youth*, eds. Robert J. Havighurst and Philip H. Dreyer (Chicago: University of Chicago Press, 1975), p. 168.

tion is its bias in favor of activity. Because traditional education places the learner in a passive role, it is assumed that activity will produce greater learning. Although it is true that more learning is likely to occur when students are active (other things being equal), not all activity results in learning. Moreover, not all of the learning that does take place is desirable (bad habits are learned as well as good habits). Additionally, experiential education, according to Coleman, is more time consuming and less efficient than traditional methods of instruction.[12]

In summary, experiential education and learning can be improved by attention to conceptual, theoretical, and practical problems. Conceptual confusions need to be overcome and a working consensus should be gained. The theoretical problems can be handled by recognizing that experiential education cannot be used exclusively but must be supplemented by other forms of education to have a balanced program. The practical problems will require better prepared teachers, closer supervision of students in the field, and forging cooperative relations with business and industry.

---

[12]James S. Coleman, "Differences Between Experiential and Classroom Learning," *Experiential Learning: Rationale,* *Characteristics, and Assessment*, eds. M. T. Keeton and Associates (San Francisco: Jossey-Bass, 1976).

DISCUSSION QUESTIONS AND ACTIVITIES

1. Describe the Evaluation of Experiential Learning Project and how it was conducted.
2. What were the overall students' reaction to the twenty-four items in the survey?
3. What follow-up steps are proposed to subject the findings to more rigorous examination? Are these additional procedures warranted?
4. In what ways does learning in the community differ from school learning?
5. What are the conceptual and theoretical problems in experiential education and learning? Are these problems largely spurious, or do they pose serious, unanswered questions?
6. State the practical problems. How can they most likely be overcome?
7. Organize a class discussion with students who have been involved in experiential education or experiential learning. Have them describe the characteristics of the program and evaluate its overall effectiveness.
8. Investigate the various types of experiential education and learning. Choose a type that is of greatest interest to you and write a report as to its effectiveness.
9. Survey the provisions for experiential education in your local school district. Do the same for the college or university you presently attend.
10. Survey local businesses and industries to determine their cooperative education plans with local secondary schools and colleges.

SUGGESTED READINGS

Brooks, S. and Althof, S. *Enriching the Liberal Arts through Experiential Learning.* San Francisco: Jossey-Bass, 1979.

Conrad, Dan and Hedin, Diane. "National Assessment of Experiential Education: Summary and Implications." *Journal of Experiential Education* 4 (Fall 1981): 6–20.

Crosby, April. "A Critical Look: The Philosophical Foundations of Experiential Education." *Journal of Experiential Education* 4 (Spring 1981): 9–15.

Dewey, John. *Experience and Education.* New York: Collier Books, 1963. (Originally published, 1938).

Hamilton, Stephen F. "Experiential Learning Programs for Youth." *American Journal of Education* 88 (February 1980): 179–215.

Joiner, Bill. "Dilemmas in Experiential Learning Programs: Toward a Holistic Approach." *New Directions for Experiential Learning* No. 8 (1980): 79–95.

Joplin, Laura. "On Defining Experiential Learning." *Journal of Experiential Education* 4 (Spring 1981): 17–20.

Keeton, Morris T. *Experiential Learning: Rationale, Characteristics, Assessment.* San Francisco: Jossey-Bass, 1977.

Knapp, Joan. "Assessment of Prior Learning: As a Model and in Practice." *New Directions for Experiential Learning* 14 (December 1981): 7–31.

Sam, Norman H. "Life Experience—An Academic Con Game?" *Change* 11 (February 1979): 7, 62.

"Youth Participation and Experiential Education." *Child and Youth Services* 4, Nos. 3/4 (1982): 1–156. This issue is devoted to experiential education, featuring a wide variety of articles.

18
Tuition Tax Credits

Tuition tax credits are based on the belief that parents should have a greater voice in their child's education and therefore these provisions seek to re-establish the central role of parental rights and responsibilities. These credits attempt to promote parental choice and greater diversity in education.

Although tuition tax credits were first proposed in the 1950s, the most significant recent bill (which failed to pass) was the Packwood-Moynihan bill (in 1978), which included tax credits for college and university costs and allowed a refund from the treasury for those claiming tuition tax credits in excess of their tax liability. The Reagan administration's proposed Educational Opportunity and Equity Act of 1982 would not contain these provisions.

In the Reagan proposal, families would have been able to recover up to 50 percent of each child's tuition to private or parochial schools. Maximum credit, which would have been phased in over three years in progressive stages, would have provided $500 per child. An income cap attempted to ensure benefits go to working families, and a nondiscriminatory provision precluded credits to those who sent their children to schools that discriminate on the basis of race. Thus the credits, according to proponents, would have been an aid not to nonpublic schools but to taxpaying citizens.

Proponents also believe that public schools constitute a monopoly not only over the poor but over all who cannot afford to pay property taxes for public schools and pay private school tuition. Tax credits are in the national interest, it is claimed, because it frees children of lower and middle classes to seek a more challenging educational environment. With a larger private sector, parents would no longer have to lobby for prayer in schools and other provisions.

Former Attorney General Griffin Bell concluded in 1978 that the Packwood-Moynihan bill was unconstitutional because it violates First Amendment guarantees against the establishment of religion. It would lead to divisive church-state entanglements and benefit sectarian schools more than nonsectarian ones.

The argument that parents whose children are enrolled in nonpublic schools have greater expenses and are thereby entitled to relief under a theory of basic fairness was rejected in 1979 by the U.S. Third Circuit Court of Appeals. Private schools already enjoy tax exempt status and receive considerable benefits under federal aid programs.

The credit of $500 per child in nonpublic schools contrasts sharply with direct federal aid of $145 per pupil in public schools.

The Supreme Court ruled, 5 to 4, that states may give tax benefits to parents to offset some of the costs of their children's school expenses. The justices upheld a Minnesota law granting parents a tax deduction of up to $700 per child for their costs on elementary or secondary education, whether public or private. The Minnesota law differs from the Reagan administration proposal, which provides tax benefits only for those paying private school tuition.

Tuition Tax Credits: Other Benefits

Walter E. Williams

Walter E. Williams (b. 1936) is Professor of Economics at George Mason University, Fairfax, Virginia.

"Tuition Tax Credit Proposals," by Professor E. G. West, which appeared in *Policy Review* (winter 1978) is an insightful discussion of several important educational problems that could be solved in part by the passage of the Tuition Tax Credit bill sponsored by Senators Packwood and Moynihan. In this note I would like to comment briefly on some other educational issues, not raised by Professor West, upon which the Packwood-Moynihan bill could have a favorable effect.

DIVERSITY IN EDUCATION

People exhibit different preferences for a host of goods and services produced in the United States, preferences influenced by factors such as culture, religion, education, and income. In order to resolve or minimize conflict there must be cooperation without conformity; that is, to the extent possible, there must be a variety of goods and services so that people can choose freely in the manner dictated by their preferences. A large, robust private sector increases the likelihood that there will be cooperation without conformity, through the natural evolution of producers of goods and services

who specialize in catering to different tastes. In other words, my purchase of an automobile with a rotary engine does not require that I coerce my neighbors to purchase such an automobile.

A state monopoly in the production of a good or service enhances the potential for conflict, through requiring uniformity; that is, its production requires a *collective* decision on many attributes of the product, and once produced, everybody has to consume the identical product whether he agrees with all the attributes or not. State monopolies in the production of education enhance the potential for conflict by requiring conformity on issues of importance to many people. For example, prayers in school, ethnic history, saluting the flag, and educational tracking are highly controversial issues which have received considerable court attention and have resulted in street fighting and heightened racial tensions. With a larger nonpublic education sector and hence more diversity in education, parents who, for example, wanted prayer reading could realize this preference by simply enrolling their child in such a school. They would not be required either to lobby for laws requiring all schools to present prayers or to pay a tariff to opt out of the public school system.[1]

From Walter E. Williams, "Tuition Tax Credits: Other Benefits." Reprinted from American Education, *Washington D.C.: U.S. Dept. of Education, July 1982. Used by permission.*

[1]Tariff is an appropriate word here because parents who choose to send their children to nonpublic schools must pay tuition *plus* continue to pay for public schools. This has disincentive effects similar to international tariffs which protect and preserve relatively inefficient producers from competitive forces.

RACIAL DESEGREGATION

One criticism of the Tuition Tax Credit bill is that it will promote racial homogeneity in our school systems. In fact, for the most part, schools across the country are already racially homogeneous and, according to the U.S. Civil Rights Commission, they are becoming more so. Contrary to the statements made by its critics, the Tuition Tax Credit may *reverse* this trend not only in education but in other areas of life as well. This result will be achieved through higher quality education in cities which will follow from market competition encouraged through the Tuition Tax Credit. With higher quality education available in cities, middle-class, predominantly white families will have reduced incentives to flee to the suburbs as a way of insuring good education for their children. It is noteworthy to recognize that the flight to suburbia in search of better schooling is becoming less of an exclusively white phenomenon. Blacks are fleeing the cities in unprecedented numbers.[2]

The Tuition Tax Credit bill would create the possibility of school integration in a way that school integration decrees do not—through people *voluntarily* pursuing what they believe to be in their own best interests. The use of the courts to promote racial heterogeneity and cooperation in our school systems can be called nothing less than a dismal failure.

MORE EDUCATIONAL OPPORTUNITY FOR MINORITIES

Clearer than its impact on school desegregation is the Tuition Tax Credit bill's effect on the quality of education. The fact that a grossly inferior education is received by most black children has been chronicled in the news media, professional publications, and elsewhere. Test performance scores show that the great majority of black children are three to five years behind the national norm. These facts make meaningless the argument advanced by the critics of the Tuition Tax Credit, that if it were enacted there would be a ground swell of fly-by-night, poor quality schools which would exploit the poor.

Black parents, educated or not, can discern high and low quality education. This is evidenced by the fact that many black (as well as white) parents have given false addresses so that their children could attend better schools outside of their districts. The recent surge in the number of non-Catholic black parents sending their children to Catholic schools and the increased number of community and Islamic schools in black ghettos all point to the fact that black parents who want higher quality education for their children *and* have the financial resources seize the opportunity to opt out of the public school system. What the Tuition Tax Credit will do is enable more parents, black and white, who are dissatisfied with public education to obtain a better and more productive life for their children.

COSTS

Professor West and others have evaluated the costs of the proposed Tuition Tax Credit in terms of its impact on the federal budget—a particularly narrow view of costs and benefits of the proposed legislation. The social cost of education is the amount of resources that the society gives up. The cost is seriously understated if,

---

[2]The number of blacks living in suburbs between 1970 and 1974 has increased by 550,000, over 11 percent of the net (4,600,000) migration to the suburbs. See: U.S. Department of Commerce, Bureau of the Census, *Current Population*

Reports, Series P-23, No. 55, "Social and Economic Characteristics of the Metropolitan and Non-Metropolitan Population: 1970-1974. (Washington, D.C.: U.S. Government Printing Office, 1975), p. 1.

in our general view, we exclude state and local expenditures. This everyone knows. However, the social cost has not so far entered the debate on the Tuition Tax Credit.

Many nonpublic schools educate youngsters at costs that are only a small fraction of the cost of public schools. Many parochial schools charge an annual tuition of $600 and there are Islamic and community schools which charge similar tuition. On the other hand, the per-child cost of education in some metropolitan school systems approaches $3,000. Old or new mathematics tell us that if we *reduce* the number of children receiving a $3,000 per year, poor-quality education and *increase* the number of children receiving a $600 higher-quality education, the nation as a whole will benefit by reduced educational expenditures and better education.[3]

Therefore, a broader assessment of costs would consider the likely reduction of educational expenditures at the state and local levels—the ultimate result of fewer children attending public schools. Tax credits will provide freer choice and as Professor West comments, " . . . insofar as choice promotes competition the result will be education that is more effective and less costly."

THE PROSPECTS FOR PUBLIC SCHOOLS

The prediction that Tuition Tax Credits would lower the number of children attending public school has given rise to the argument that this tax measure would contribute to the destruction of public schools. This perhaps is the most revealing confession of the opponents of the Packwood-Moynihan bill, who are mostly members of the public education establishment. This position does not differ from one which

says that, if parents were given freedom of choice, many would opt out of the public school system. In other words, the public education establishment is saying that, if their state-granted monopoly powers are reduced, the schools run by them will be destroyed.

Destroyed is obviously too strong a word, because many, many public schools are doing an excellent job of educating America's youth. These are schools which satisfy parents and would not be threatened by increased competition. The schools that *would* be threatened by the reduction of monopoly powers are those public schools failing to do a job at least as good as their nearby competitors. These schools, for the most part, are those in inner cities that produce a product *grossly* inferior to their nonpublic counterparts. If such schools go out of business (become unattended), such an outcome is consistent with market efficiency and enhanced social welfare: The inefficient producers are weeded out and replaced by efficient producers.

CONCLUSION

At the heart of the problem in public education is a system of educational delivery which creates a perverse set of incentives for all parties involved. At the core of the perverse incentives is the fact that teachers get paid and receive raises whether or not children can read and write; administrators receive their pay whether or not children can read or write. Children (particularly minority children) receive grade promotions and diplomas whether or not they can read and write.

The individual parent who is poor is helpless in such a setting. It is quite difficult for the individual parent or group of parents to effectively force the public school system to produce a higher-quality education. The benefit of the Tuition Tax Credit is that it enhances the possi-

---

[3]For an important study of "islands" of black academic excellence, see Thomas Sowell, "Patterns of Black Excellence," *The Public Interest* (spring 1976), pp. 26–58.

bility for the individual parent to *fire* the school providing poor services and to enroll his child in some other school providing better services. The Packwood-Moynihan bill promises to give low-income parents at least some of the powers that their higher-income counterparts have, namely a greater role in determining educational alternatives for their children.

Tuition Tax Credits Revisited

Ed Keller _____

Ed Keller is deputy executive director of the National Association of Elementary School Principals and director of the Association's Federal Relations Division.

In 1978, NAESP and other education associations formed a coalition to defeat the Packwood-Moynihan tuition tax credit proposal, which would have provided tax credits for nonpublic school tuition. Working closely with the coalition, Senator Ernest Hollings (D-S.C.) played a significant role in rallying Senate opposition to the measure.

In 1981 we face the same situation once again, but this time under a Republican administration, whose platform encourages tuition tax credits. Senator Hollings's rationale three year ago is just as valid in 1981 as it was in 1978. Reprinted here are excerpts from an August 1978 letter from Senator Hollings that clearly explicates his, and NAESP's position.

"The Senator from New York [Patrick Moynihan, Democrat] proposes tax credits for private elementary and secondary education from the assumption that the government has an equal duty to both public and private schools, and he charges that 'The federal government has systematically organized its activities in ways that contribute to the decay of nonpublic education.'

"Let us be clear at the outset that the duty is not equal. The government's duty to the public is to provide public schools. The duty of the government toward private or church schools is to leave them alone. This is fundamental. Now comes the Packwood-Moynihan plan, and the duty to leave the private alone is suddenly inverted to the duty to provide for them.

"And provide it would! Today the average federal subsidy to the individual public school pupil is $128. The private school student is helped, too, through federal assistance in providing instruction materials, library resources, guidance and testing programs and so on, at an average per-pupil expenditure of $40. Packwood-Moynihan would completely upend this by providing up to $500 for the private school student—over four times what is given for the public school child. Can

it really be in the public interest to provide quadruple the aid to those attending private schools?
. . .

"We hear a lot of talk nowadays about cost containment and budget cutting. Clearly Senators Packwood and Moynihan are worried about neither. . . . [Current estimates place the cost of the tuition tax credit proposal at over $4 billion.]

"Our educational system cannot afford the kind of infighting that the tuition tax credit would inevitably bring between the supporters of our public and private schools. Each year at appropriations time, they will square off in competition for the limited federal funds available. Once the tuition tax credit has its foot in the door, educational civil war will be an annual affair. And because so many of the private schools are religious, the debates will devolve into religious wars as well.

"I believe that Packwood-Moynihan should be defeated on policy grounds. It is an outlandish proposal which could only wreak havoc on our educational system. But the tuition tax credit is not only bad policy; it is patently unconstitutional, flying in the face of the establishment clause of the First Amendment and therefore violative of the Fourteenth Amendment also. The attorney general of the United States has written a formal opinion which concludes that a tuition tax credit for families with children in private elementary and secondary schools is unconstitutional. That position is supported by most constitutional scholars."

Senator Hollings emphasizes that "this proposal would turn our nation's education policy on its head, benefit the few at the expense of the many, proliferate substandard segregation academies, add a sea of red ink to the federal deficit, violate the clear meaning of the First Amendment to the Constitution, and destroy the diversity and genius of our system of public education."

It should also be noted that:

- Tuition tax credits do not appear as an expenditure item in the federal budget. Instead, they are buried in the budget as reduced income, which means that the federal government's contribution to private schools doesn't show up as the entitlement it is.

- Ample provisions for private school students are already available through existing programs. Recent higher education enactments, for example, substantially increase federal funding to post-secondary education, private as well as public, and the strengthening of the bypass provisions protects both elementary and secondary school private education.

- Tuition tax credits could lead to increased federal regulation of private schools through the Internal Revenue Service or through indirect accreditation controls.

- Tuition tax credits could also lead to a proliferation of splinter group schools.

Although backing off from any commitment to balance the fiscal year 1981 budget, the Reagan administration is reluctant to add to the deficit by its own action. Circulating a hit list of over 140 budget cuts is hardly congruent with the deficit increase of $4 billion that tuition tax credits would cause.

As NAESP and NASSP stated in a recent letter to Mr. Reagan. "The strength of America arises from citizens' commitment to an effective system of public education." Tuition tax credits, if enacted, would destroy this cornerstone of American democracy. They must be opposed.

DISCUSSION QUESTIONS AND ACTIVITIES

1. By reducing the state monopoly of public education, asserts Walter E. Williams, the extent of conflict in society is reduced? Why? Has he demonstrated that a public school monopoly exists?

2. How will tuition tax credits likely reduce racial homogeneity in schools? Evaluate this claim.

3. Why is it misleading to consider only the federal costs in comparing nonpublic and public schools?

4. What public schools will likely be hurt by tuition tax credits? Why should such damages not be lamented.

5. Are parents, even those who organize for concerted action, seriously hamstrung in getting public schools to improve their quality?

6. According to Senator Hollings, what are the respective duties of government toward public and private schools?

7. Sen. Hollings cites the unconstitutionality of tuition tax credits as violative of the First and Fourteenth Amendments. Specifically, how do these violations occur? Examine these two amendments carefully.

8. Would tuition tax credits benefit "the few at the expense of the many" or would the benefits accrue more equitably?

9. Would tuition tax credits likely lead to greater federal regulation of nonpublic schools? What groups would likely support such regulation? Oppose it?

SUGGESTED READINGS

Background Information and Analysis

Catterall, James S. and Henry M. Levin. "Public and Private Schools: Evidence on Tuition Tax Credits." *Sociology of Education* 55 (April-July 1982): 144–51.

Coleman, James. "Public Schools, Private Schools, and the Public Interest." *The Public Interest* 64 (Summer 1981): 19–30.

Erekson, O. H. "Equity Targets in School Finance, Tuition Tax Credits, and the Public Private Choice." *Journal of Educational Finance* 7 (Spring 1982): 436–49.

"Government Neutrality and Separation of Church and State: Tuition Tax Credits." *Harvard Law Review* 52 (January 1979): 696–717.

James, Thomas. "Tuition Tax Credits and the Pains of Democracy." *Phi Delta Kappan* 63 (May 1982): 606–09.

Proponents

Barrett, F. X. "Tuition Tax Credits—the American Way." *Momentum* 13 (October 1982): 2–3.

Coons, John E. and Stephen D. Sugarman. *Education by Choice: The Case for Family Control.* Berkeley, Ca.: University of California Press, 1978.

Freeman, Roger A. "Educational Tax Credits." In *The Public School Monopoly,* ed. Robert B. Everhart. Cambridge, Mass.: Ballinger Publishing Co., 1982, pp. 471–502.

Graham, Anne. "Joining the Discussion: Tuition Tax Credits." *American Education* 18 (July 1982): 13–15.

Moynihan, Daniel Patrick. "The Case for Tuition Tax Credits." *Phi Delta Kappan* 60 (December 1978): 274–76.

Reagan, Ronald. "Tuition Tax Credits: The President's Proposal." *American Education* 18 (May 1982): 16–19.

Sowell, Thomas. "Tuition Tax Credits: A Social Revolution." *American* Education 18 (July 1982): 18–19.

Packwood, Bob and Ernest Hollings. "Tuition Tax Credit Debate. The Case for Tuition Tax Credits. The Case Against Tuition Tax Credits." NASSP *Bulletin* 65 (October 1981): 76–83.

Williams, Walter E. "Tuition Tax Credits: Other Benefits." *American Education* 18 (July 1982): 15–18.

Critics

Anderson, B. "Public Schools Are Under Fire, But We Have Just Begun to Fight." *American School Board Journal* 168 (September 1981): 19–33.

Goldman, Norman. "The Threat of Tuition Tax Credits." NJEA *Review* 54 (May 1981): 18–21.

Jacobs, Martha J. "Tuition Tax Credits for Elementary and Secondary Education: Some New Evidence on Who Would Benefit." *Journal of Education Finance* 5 (Winter 1980): 233–45.

Hollings, Ernest F. "The Case Against Tuition Tax Credits." *Phi Delta Kappan* 60 (December 1978): 277–79.

Keller, E. "Tuition Tax Credits Revisted." *Principal* 60 (January 1981): 44.

Rich, John Martin. "The Libertarian Challenge to Public Education." *The Educational Forum* 46 (Summer 1982): 421–29. Condensed in *The Education Digest* 48 (December 1982): 16–19.

"Shanker Assails Tuition Tax Credits at School Finance Experts' Meeting." *American Teacher* 63 (February 1979): 4.

Shannon, T. A. "Case Against Tuition Tax Credits." *The Education Digest* 48 (October 1982): 21–3.

19
Private Schools

More and more parents are removing their children from public schools and placing them in private and parochial schools. Some do so on academic grounds; others do so for religious reasons; and still others wish to avoid integration. Those who favor aid to private schools generally believe private schools offer a better education than public schools.

Public high schools enroll over 90 percent of the total high school population and have an average of 750 students. Catholic schools enroll about 6 percent and average 500 students, whereas other private schools enroll between 3 and 4 percent and average only 150 students. Pupil-teacher ratios in public and Catholic schools are similar, but the ratio is only about half as large as public schools in other types of private schools.

A study by James S. Coleman compares public schools with Catholic and other private schools in terms of discipline, problems of students, homework, achievement test scores, academic demands made on students, and aspirations for higher education. The study also evaluates the degree of religious segregation and economic segregation in American secondary schools. It concludes that Catholic schools have higher quality on the average and greater equality than public schools.

The public schools, Coleman has said elsewhere, are no longer a "common" institution because residential mobility has brought about a high degree of racial segregation in education, as well as segregation by income. He does not believe that the public interest in common institutions is an overriding public interest. Rather, it is relatively weak compared to interest in helping all children, especially the disadvantaged, receive a better education. Others disagree (see the selections by Butts and Rich in the *Suggested Readings*), citing the vital role that a public educational system can play in a democratic society.

In terms of policy, he opposes the practice of assigning students on the basis of residence because it harms the nonaffluent and increases inequalities in opportunity. Coleman prefers communities based on interests, values, and educational preferences. To support these plans, he would expand the different types of education supported by public funds.

Public and Private Schools

James S. Coleman, Sally B. Kilgore, and Thomas Hoffer

James S. Coleman (b. 1926) took his Ph.D. at Columbia University, taught at Johns Hopkins University, and is now professor of sociology at the University of Chicago. He has been a Fellow at Center for Advanced Studies in Behavioral Sciences. Professor Coleman is a member of the National Academy of Education, American Academy of Arts and Sciences, National Academy of Sciences, and the American Philosophical Association. He is the author of The Adolescent Society, *and co-author of* Youth: Transition to Adulthood, *and the landmark USOE study,* Equality of Educational Opportunity.*

Sally B. Kilgore is special project assistant to James Coleman and the National Opinion Research Center for a longitudinal study of high-school students and book review co-editor for the American Journal of Sociology.

Thomas Hoffer is a doctoral candidate in the Department of Education, University of Chicago and is associated with the National Opinion Research Center.

American elementary and secondary education has overwhelmingly been education in public schools, supported by taxes and governed by local school boards. There have recently been changes in the structure of support and control, with state and federal governments playing increasingly important roles in both respects. But the overwhelmingly public-school character of elementary and secondary education has remained largely unchanged. For many years, the percentage of American children in private schools has been in the neighborhood of 10 percent, as it is currently.

The role of private schools in American education, however, has emerged as an important policy question in recent years. Although any answer to this question depends in part on values, it also depends on facts—facts that address such questions as: How well do public and private schools work for children? Do they work differentially well for different types of children? Are private schools divisive, and, if so, along what lines? Are private schools more efficiently managed than public schools, and, if so, why?

Recent policy discussions concerning private schools in the United States have included proposals that would both increase and decrease their role in American education. On the increase side, there have been proposals for tuition tax credits for private schools, and a bill to provide such credits was narrowly defeated in Congress. At the state level, proposals for educational vouchers have been discussed, and in California there was a recent attempt to get such a proposal on the ballot for referendum. On the decrease side, the Internal Revenue Service proposed that a racial composition requirement, more restrictive than that imposed on most public schools, be a criterion for maintaining tax-exempt status. This is one of a series of attempted policy interventions to constrain the use of private schools by whites escaping a program of mandatory integration in the public schools.

These conflicting policy efforts are all based on certain assumptions about the role of private and public schools in the United States. Examining the assumptions, and showing their truth or falsity, will not in itself resolve the policy questions concerning the roles of public and private education in America. Those policy questions include certain value premises as well, such as the relative roles of the state and the family in controlling a child's education. This examination will, however, strengthen the factual base on which the policy conflicts are fought.

Some of these premises underlying school policies are held by policy makers whose decisions affect the relative roles of private and public schools in America, and some are held by parents who choose between private and public schools for their children. Thus information on the correctness of these premises is useful not only for educational policy making in a nation, state, or city, but also for parental choice.

A word is necessary on the classification of schools used. For much of the analysis, schools are classified not into two sectors, but into three—public, Catholic, and other private schools. This is done because Catholic schools constitute by far the largest single group of private schools, and constitute a less diverse array of schools than all private schools taken together. Three special samples of schools were, however, drawn: Catholic schools that had high proportions (30 percent or more) of black students in them, selected in addition to the representative sample of Catholic schools; a special sample of "high-performance" private

schools—the 11 private schools with the highest proportions of their graduating student bodies listed as semi-finalists in the 1978 National Merit Scholarship competition; and a set of 12 high-performance public schools, selected in the same way as were the high-performance private schools. The high-performance schools are included to provide extremes that can better illuminate some of the research questions that were posed. Because of the way they were drawn, these schools do not represent anything other than themselves; thus they are not "sectors" like the public, Catholic, and other private sectors. Further, the results reported for these high-performance private and public schools cannot be generalized to a larger population of schools or students, but they do suggest something about the character of schools that produce high-achieving students.

EDUCATIONAL ACHIEVEMENT

Two of the most widely held premises underlying policy recommendations that would increase the role of private schools have to do with educational results. The first premise is that private schools produce better cognitive outcomes than do public schools with comparable students; the second, that private schools encourage interest in higher education and lead more of their students to attend college than do public schools with comparable students. This study examined both of these outcomes. Standardized test scores in reading, vocabulary, and mathematics were used to measure cognitive outcomes. Several questions about post-high-school plans, including "As things stand now, how far in school do you think you will get?", were asked of the tested students to determine their interest in higher education.

Three primary questions were brought to the data. The first, a simple and straightforward question, is just how the sectors differed in these respects. It is useful for purely descriptive purposes, to see just what the products of public and private schools in this country are like, how they are similar and how they are different. The answer is that achievement is somewhat higher, in both the sophomore and senior years, in Catholic schools and in other private schools than it is in public schools. Achievement in the high-performance private schools is considerably higher than that in the high-performance public schools, but both are higher than in either of the private (Catholic or other) sectors.

The differences between sectors in educational expectations and aspirations are similar to the differences in achievement. The sectors are ordered in the same way, with public-school students having the lowest educational aspirations and those in the high-performance private schools having the highest aspirations. For the other post-secondary activity — work — the order is reversed. Among seniors who planned to work full time after graduation, a higher proportion in the public schools already had a job lined up. This suggests that the greater vocational resources and opportunities in the public schools lead to a better connection with the world of work for those students who are going into the full-time labor force.

The second question is whether being in a private school made any difference in cognitive achievement or educational aspiration, or whether the greater achievement and aspirations in the private sector were wholly due to selectivity. It is a question that is central for parents and central to policy arguments about the relative merits of public and private schools. Here, measures of the outcome variable for sophomores and seniors in the same schools were used. Only three major sectors (public, Catholic, and other private) were examined; the two high-performance groups were left aside.

In the examination of effects on achievement, statistical controls on family background are introduced, in order to control on those background characteristics that are most related to achievement. A large number of background characteristics are introduced, to insure that the selectivity-related differences are controlled for. The achievement differences between the private sectors and the public sector are reduced (more for other private schools than for Catholic schools), but differences remain. Then there is an examination of imputed growth from the sophomore to the senior year. In a first examination of differential growth, the Catholic schools appear to show about the same growth rates for students comparable to the average public-school sophomore; and the other private schools, about a 25 percent higher growth rate. This, however, is subject to the serious problem of differential dropout in different sectors. The high rate of dropouts in the public sector, which, if present, would expand the senior class by 31 percent, indicates that the sophomore-senior growth rate in the public schools is considerably overestimated. The dropout rates in Catholic and other private schools are less than half as great, indicating much less bias in the estimates of their growth rates. When the dropout bias is taken into account, with an assumed distribution of achievement among the dropouts, the estimated learning rate is considerably higher in both private sectors than in the public sector. Thus the indication is that Catholic and other private schools have a non-trivial effect in bringing about higher cognitive achievement, wholly apart from their selectivity.

In addition, there is a major difference in homogeneity of achievement between Catholic schools on the one hand and public and other private schools on the other. Students of parents with different educational backgrounds achieve at more nearly comparable levels in the Catholic than in the public schools, while the achievement levels are even more divergent in other private schools than in the public schools. And comparison of blacks and Hispanics in Catholic and public schools (controlling on parental income and education) reveals that as sophomores these minority students achieve at a level closer to that of non-Hispanic whites in Catholic schools than in public schools; the achievement gap between minorities and non-Hispanic whites as seniors decreases slightly in Catholic schools, while it increases slightly in public schools. Altogether, the evidence is strong that the Catholic schools function much closer to the American ideal of the "common school," educating children from different backgrounds alike, than do the public schools.

Thus, the evidence is that private schools do produce better cognitive outcomes than public schools. When family background factors that predict achievement are controlled, students in both Catholic and other private schools are shown to achieve at a higher level than students in public schools. The difference at the sophomore level, which was greater for Catholic schools than for other private schools, ranged from about a fifth of the sophomore-senior gain to about two-thirds the size of that gain (i.e., from a little less than half a year's difference to something more than one year's difference). This evidence is subject to a caveat: despite extensive statistical controls on parental background, there may very well be other unmeasured factors in the self-selection into the private sector that are associated with higher achievement.

When we examined gains from the sophomore to the senior year in the three sectors, the first evidence was that students from comparable backgrounds make greater gains in other private schools than in public schools, but that students in Catholic schools do not. However, the much greater sophomore-senior dropout in public schools than in either the Catholic or other private schools shows that the apparent public school gains have a considerable upward bias, leading to the conclusion than greater cognitive growth occurs between the sophomore and senior years in both private sectors than in the public sector.

A caveat to all these results is shown by the high-performance public and private schools. Performance was much higher in both of these sets of schools than in any of the three sectors, although these schools could not be separately studied in the extended sophomore-senior analysis because of ceiling effects in achievement scores.

Turning to educational aspirations, the question arises whether the private-public difference is wholly due to selection or is in part due to effects of the sector. Statistical controls on family background leave a difference, with students in Catholic schools showing especially high aspirations. No differential sophomore-senior growth is found, except for *lower* growth in Catholic schools. This result is suspect, however, because of a ceiling effect due to the higher level of aspirations among Catholic-school sophomores. Using the same reasoning about dropouts as was used in the case of cognitive achievement, it *appears* that there is a positive effect, non-trivial in size, of being in a Catholic or other private school on educational aspirations. An analysis that uses retrospective reports of seniors and sophomores about expectations of attending college in earlier years confirms this, through evidence that the proportion planning to attend college increases more in the private than in the public sector. Thus, although there is some evidence that students have higher college aspirations and expectations in private schools than do students from comparable backgrounds in public schools, it is not extremely strong and cannot be considered conclusive.

Again, the Catholic schools show much greater homogeneity in the educational aspirations among students from different parental education backgrounds than do other schools. Here the other private schools are intermediate and the public schools are at the extreme, public-school students with low educational backgrounds being furthest from those with high educational backgrounds in their own educational aspirations.

The third question is a question about what differences between public and private schools are responsible for the additional achievement that occurs in the private schools. The answer to this is only partial, because the investigation covered only selected differences. But the partial answer is fairly clear.

There are at least two important ways in which private schools produce higher achievement outcomes than public schools. First, given the same type of student (i.e., with background standardized), private schools create higher rates of engagement in academic activities. School attendance is better, students do more homework, and students generally take more rigorous subjects (i.e., more advanced mathematics). The first two of these factors provide modestly greater achievement in private schools. The third, taking advanced mathematics courses, brings substantially greater achievement. The indication is that more extensive academic demands are made in the private schools, leading to more advanced courses and thus to greater achievement. This is a somewhat obvious conclusion, and the statistical evidence supports it. Second, student behavior in a school has strong and consistent effects on student achievement. Apart from mathematics coursework for seniors, the greatest differences in achievement between private and public schools are accounted for by school-level behavior variables (i.e., the incidence of fights, students threatening teachers, etc.). The disciplinary climate of a school, that is, the effectiveness and fairness of discipline and teacher interest, affect achievement at least in part

through their effect on these school-level behavior variables.

Although these answers are only partial, ir that additional school factors may also explain the different outcomes in the sectors, they strongly suggest that school functioning makes a difference in achievement outcomes for the average student. And private schools of both sectors appear to function better in the areas that contribute to achievement.

SOCIAL DIVISIVENESS

Three of the major premises underlying policy recommendations that would decrease the role of private schools have to do with their being socially divisive—along economic lines, religious lines, and racial lines. These have been the principal arguments against giving aid to private education. There are two wholly different issues of economic, religious, and racial segregation raised by the existence of private schools. The first, and the one to which most attention has been given, is the segregation between the public sector and the private sector. The second is the segregation that exists among schools within each sector.

Although these issues are different, they are related, for the criticism that private schools are divisive along economic, religious, or racial lines is a criticism that points to both forms of segregation. First, the existence of a private-school alternative allows those with financial resources to segregate themselves from the remainder in public school; second, the existence of choice among private schools facilitates segregation along these lines within the private sector itself. If, for example, minorities who do attend private schools are concentrated in schools enrolling a small proportion of whites, then even a large proportion of minority students in the private schools is hardly a rebuttal to the charge that private education functions to increase social divisiveness along racial lines.

Yet matters are not so clear as the criticism would suggest, because choice exists within the public sector as well. Residential mobility, the principal way in which such choice is exercised, has increased over the years, and along with it the potential for families with sufficient resources to segregate their children from others, wholly within the public sector. Thus an examination of these issues is not merely to document the obvious. It is rather to examine segregating tendencies as they are manifested both within and between the sectors of education. For each issue area, then, analysis must move from a comparison of segregation between sectors to a comparison of segregation within sectors.

Issues related to the racial and ethnic compositions of the private schools constitute a major component of the controversy surrounding private education. Opposition to policies designed to facilitate private education is frequently based on the assumption that the private schools function as a means for whites to escape the racial integration that has been imposed in the public sector. As evidence of the segregating role that private education plays, critics assert that private schools on the whole enroll proportionately smaller numbers of minority students, particularly blacks and Hispanics.

Past research supports this claim. Kraushaar's 1972 survey of 251 private secondary schools found that, overall, less than 5 percent of the total enrollment was of racial or ethnic minority status. Nonetheless, supporters of private education assert that serious efforts have been made in recent years throughout a large segment of the private sector to reduce the underenrollment of minorities.

This study was designed to provide accurate representation of the black and Hispanic student population in American secondary educa-tion. The two-stage probability sample that was employed drew schools as the first-stage unit and a random sample of students within the selected schools as the second stage. Oversampling was carried out on seven types of schools, four of which were included to facilitate analyses concerned with black or Hispanic students. The normally sampled public schools included school racial composition as one of the stratification criteria.

In summary, we can say the following. For Hispanics, there is very little difference between the public and private sectors, either with respect to the proportions of Hispanics in each sector, or with respect to the internal distribution of Hispanics within the schools of each sector. The distribution of Hispanics between public and private schools is about the same as that of non-Hispanic whites. Within each sector the degree of segregation between the two groups is not especially high, and it is about the same in the public and private sectors. If the income distribution among Hispanics were the same as that among non-Hispanic whites, there would be somewhat higher proportions of Hispanics in the Catholic schools, and thus in the private sector as a whole, than in the public sector.

The results for black-white segregation are considerably more complex. There is a substantially smaller proportion of blacks in the private sector than in the public sector—less than half as high a proportion in the Catholic schools, and less than a quarter as high in the other private schools. The geographic location of private schools accounts for only a small part of this difference between the public and private sectors, though it accounts for a somewhat larger part of the difference between Catholic and other private schools, which are less often found in areas with high numbers of blacks. The income difference between blacks and whites accounts for a substantial part of the public-Catholic difference in proportion of blacks enrolled, though for little of the difference between public and other private schools.

The effect of religious background on school selection was also examined for the Catholic sector. The percentage of blacks who are Catholic is much smaller than the percentage of whites and Hispanics who are Catholic, and, when this factor is taken into account, the differences between blacks and whites in chances of attending Catholic high schools disappear. Finally, when the effects of income and religious background are considered simultaneously, blacks are generally found to be enrolled at higher rates than whites (and Hispanics)who are similar in income and religious background.

Despite the fact that controlling for the effects of income and religion introduces important qualifications to any discussion about the causes of racial segregation in public and private education, it remains the case that the proportion of black students in private schools is substantially lower than that in public schools. But information on the internal segregation between blacks and whites tells a different story: the public sector has a substantially higher degree of segregation than the private sector (or either of its two components separately). Thus, the integrating impact of the lesser degree of segregation within the private sector counteracts the segregating impact of the lower proportion of blacks in that sector.

What is the end result of these conflicting tendencies, the overall impact of private schooling on black-white segregation? An answer can be obtained by comparing the overall black-white segregation among all high schools, public and private considered together, as it currently stands, to the segregation we would expect if the students currently in private schools were absorbed into the public system. We assume that they would be distributed among schools within the public sector in exactly the way whites and blacks are currently distributed in the public sec-

tor. Any differences found in such a comparison would of course be quite small, since only 10 percent of the student population would change schools; but the direction is important.

It we assumed that no private schools existed, and that blacks and whites currently in private schools were absorbed into the public schools with exactly the same distribution among schools as is currently found in the public schools, the degree of segregation for the total U.S. student population would be that given by the segregation index for the public sector, .49. Comparing this to the current segregation index for all U.S. students, also .49, suggest that the two tendencies exactly cancel each other out. But, carried to three decimals, these indices are .493 and .489, which means that the private schools have a small effect in the direction of *less* segregation.

Although much attention has been directed to the possible divisiveness of private schools along racial lines in recent years, the first such concern was the economic divisiveness. This is the most natural form that public-private stratification would take, since private schools are costly to the user, and public schools are free to the user. And it is the stratification that naturally comes to mind when the elite private schools are discussed.

We know, however, that a large number of private schools do not fit this image. The Catholic schools were not designed for an upper-class elite, and many of the other private schools are also based on religious rather than social-class homogeneity. Consequently, despite the fact that sending a child to a private school costs parents money, while sending a child to a public school does not, the diverse origins and affiliations of private schools suggest that private schools as a whole may serve students with economic backgrounds not greatly different from those of student served by public schools.

But even if this is true, it addresses only the question of economic segregation between the public and private sectors, not economic segregation *within* the private sector. And, if there are elite schools and nonelite schools in the private sector, there must be a considerable degree of economic segregation among schools within that sector.

Yet the questions of economic segregation between the private and public school sectors and within the private sector do not exist in a vacuum. They exist, rather, with the framework of some degree of economic stratification among schools in the public sector itself. The geographic mobility by residence that facilitates a degree of racial homogeneity in public schools also facilitates a degree of economic homogeneity. Thus the tendencies of private schools to lead to economic stratification between the private and public sectors or within the private sector must be seen in a context of economic stratification within the public-school sector.

The evidence on the premise that private schools are socially divisive along income lines works in two directions. First, among the three major sectors, the other private schools contain students from somewhat higher income backgrounds and the Catholic schools contain students from slightly higher income backgrounds than the public schools. The differences are primarily at the highest income levels, with all three sectors having a majority of students in a broad middle-income category ranging from $12,000 to $38,000 a year, and similar proportions at different levels within this range. Second, the *internal* segregation by income within each sector goes in the opposite direction, with the public sector showing slightly higher income segregation than either the Catholic or other private sectors. However, income segregation is not high within any sector. The end result of these two forces acting in opposite directions is that U.S. schools as a whole show slightly greater segregation by income than would be the case if private-school students of differing income levels were absorbed into the public schools in the

same way that public-school students of differing income levels are currently distributed among schools.

Historically, issues of religious divisiveness have been central to debates concerning private education. Although economic differences are an important factor in private-school enrollment, religious concerns have been, and continue to be, probably the strongest motivating force in parents' decisions to send their children to private schools. This motivation can be seen better, perhaps, in other countries. For a number of countries have state-supported schools operated by religious groups, along with secular schools; and, in some countries, the major sectors of publicly supported education are those operated by different religious denominations.

About 80 percent of private-sector students in this country are enrolled in schools affiliated with some specific religious denomination, and it is probably safe to assume that an interest in affirming basic religious values within the context of formal education is a major determinant of private-school enrollment. This choice usually presents no problem. But when the question of public aid to private education is raised many see a conflict with the commitment of the United States to the separation of church and state. In addition to the constitutional question, there is a social issue in the potential divisiveness of the orientations of religiously affiliated schools. Specifically, it is sometimes argued that the existence of religiously affiliated schools isolates youth of different faiths and generates intolerance of other religious perspectives. Traditionally, this argument has been applied primarily to Catholic schools, and, because only the numbers of Catholic schools in the sample are sufficient to allow analysis in this area, we examined the extent to which Catholic and non-Catholic students are segregated from each other as a result of private education.

The evidence is strong that private schools are divisive along religious lines. Besides the 30 percent of private schools that are Catholic, enrolling 66 percent of all private-school students, 25 percent of private schools, enrolling 12 percent of private-school students, are affiliated with other religious denominations Examining religious segregation solely in the Catholic/non-Catholic dimension, we found that the great majority of Catholics are in public schools, but that over 90 percent of the students in Catholic schools are Catholic. *Within* each sector, the Catholic/non-Catholic segregation is least in the Catholic schools themselves, greatest in the other private schools. The overall impact of the between-sector segregation and the differing segregation within sectors is, as might be expected, that schools in the United States are more segregated along Catholic/non-Catholic lines than they would be if private-school students were absorbed into the public schools.

POLICY CHANGES AND SCHOOL ENROLLMENT

There has been much discussion recently about the effects of reducing the financial burden of private education. One proposal, which came near passage in Congress, was to provide tax credits for a portion of school tuition. Another widely discussed proposal urged the use of educational vouchers to allow all children to choose freely among private and public schools.

Some have argued that changes such as this would differentially benefit the white upper-middle class, who use private schools more. Such changes would, in this view, extend still further the creaming process which leaves the poor and minorities in the public schools. Others argue that such measures would place private schooling in the reach of those who cannot now afford it, and thus differentially benefit minorities and those less well off financially.

As examination of the predicted effect of a $1,000 increase in income for all income groups shows that this would increase the proportion of blacks and Hispanics in the private sector, as well as the proportion of students from lower-income families. Because a tuition tax credit or a school voucher would even more greatly facilitate private-school enrollment for students from lower-income families relative to students from higher-income families, we can expect that either of those policies would even more greatly increase the proportion of blacks or students from low-income backgrounds in the private sector (primarily in the Catholic sector). If either of these policies failed to increase the proportions of blacks or students from low-income families in private schools relative to that in the public schools, then, overall, either of these policies would provide greater financial benefit to whites than to blacks, or to higher-income than to lower-income families, because of the tuition reductions for parents of those students currently enrolled in the private sector. If one considers only new entrants into the private sector, the fact that a tuition tax credit or voucher plan would likely be more progressive in its effect than a $1,000 increase in income indicates that blacks, Hispanics, and low-income families would differentially benefit. To consider the educational rather than the financial benefits means to consider only the new entrants into the private sector, for it is only their education that would be changed; thus blacks and Hispanics would differentially benefit educationally.

The evidence indicates that facilitating use of private schools through such policies would not increase segregation along racial or economic lines but would decrease it (though the evidence indicates that religious segregation would increase). Such policies would bring more blacks, Hispanics, and students from lower-income backgrounds into the private schools, thus reducing the between-sector segregation, and these students would be moving from a sector of high racial segregation to a sector of low racial segregation, as well as from a sector slightly higher in economic segregation to one slightly lower.

It is hard to avoid the overall conclusion

that the factual premises underlying policies that would facilitate use of private schools are much better supported on the whole than those underlying policies that would constrain their use. Or, to put it another way, the constraints imposed on schools in the public sector (and there is no evidence that those constraints are financial, compared with the private sector) seem to impair their functioning as educational institutions, without providing the more egalitarian outcome that is one of the goals of public schooling.

Neither Direction Nor Alternatives

Gail E. Thomas _____

Gail E. Thomas (b. 1950) is a research scientist ana project director at the Johns Hopkins University's Center for Social Organization of Schools. Her areas of specialization are race and sex differences in educational attainment, black students in higher education, and social and educational research methodology. She is the author of the recently published Black Studies in Higher Education in the 1970s.

James Coleman's recent document, *Public and Private Schools*, has received national attention. However, unlike his 1966 *Equality of Educational Opportunity* (EEO) study, it is doubtful that the conclusion from this document will have a major policy impact. Coleman examines and presents findings regarding arguments for and against increasing the role of private schools. He concludes that his evidence supports policies to increase the role of private schools and shows that private schools are more effective than public schools in educating students.

The bases from which Coleman derived his main conclusions have been widely criticized. Most criticisms concern the methodological weaknesses of the study, including: (1) the problems of self-selection among private-school students (this factor, which could not be adequately controlled, seriously biased Coleman's comparison of public-and private-school students); (2) the failure to disaggregate school data in a manner that permitted a more detailed stratification and comparison of public and private schools; and (3) the biased interpretation of the segregation index which did not take into consideration the massive underrepresentation of minorities in private schools. Because of

From Gail E. Thomas, "Neither Directions Nor Alternatives." Published by permission by Transaction, Inc. from SOCIETY, Vol. 19 #2. Copyright © 1982 by Transaction, Inc.

these and other methodological limitations, most critics, myself included, have concluded that the findings derived from the study were not adequately justifiable. However, rather than dwelling on the methodological limitations of the study, this article will raise questions about its policy implications and the relevancy of its findings for educational and social policy.

POLICY IMPLICATIONS

It is important to view the Coleman document with the present political context and conservative climate of U.S. society. The timely release of the study coincided with the initiation and continuation of congressional debates on tuition tax credit for parents of children attending private schools. Whether intended or unintended, Coleman's findings were presented in policy terms that supported a tuition tax credit. The evidence presented, however, was quite misleading. More importantly, if taken seriously, Coleman's observation could prove detrimental to U.S. public education.

The first finding with questionable policy implications is that a $1,000 income incentive to all parents with children in public school would greatly increase black and Hispanic student enrollment in private schools. Coleman based his claim on hypothetical calculations which showed the frequencies at which whites, blacks, and Hispanics currently enrolled in public schools would be expected to shift to the private-school sector given an income increment of $1,000. Based on these calculations, Coleman concluded that black and Hispanic families would respond to this financial incentive to an equal or greater extent than whites, thereby increasing their enrollment in private schools.

This economic incentive argument is based on a number of faulty assumptions. For example, he assumes that given a $1,000 increase in income, families with children in public schools

will respond uniformly by enrolling them in private schools. This is highly unlikely for several reasons. First, parents who favor the diverse education and broader curriculum offered by public schools may not wish to send their children to private schools. Second, the narrow academic curriculum and disciplinary environment of private schools may not suit all students, especially those with special needs: only 2.7 percent of the present sectarian schools provide programs for the handicapped, 3.0 percent of all nonpublic schools provide vocational education, and approximately 4.4 percent provide compensatory education. Third, it is unlikely that a $1,000 increment will have an appreciable effect on the ability of low-income families to enroll their children in private schools. Only 4.8 percent of families with incomes below $5,000 and only 11.7 percent of families with an income of $5,000-$9,999 have children enrolled in private elementary schools. Transportation costs, depending upon the residential location of low-income families, coupled with incidental fees required for private-school attendance and the increasing cost of private education would offset the potential value of a $1,000 income increment for allowing low-income families to switch their children from public to private schools.

Coleman's economic argument also assumes that money is the only requirement for private-school enrollment. However, students seeking entry to these schools must meet admissions requirements as well. In *The Private High School Today*, Susan Abramowitz *et al.* noted that the disproportionate representation of middle- and upper-class students in private schools is partly due to the selectivity of the admissions process. Seventy-five percent of the private schools in their study used achievement-test data for entry, 87 percent relied on past school records, 58 percent used IQ scores, and 67 percent employed personal references. Forty-three percent of the schools surveyed used all four methods, while an additional quarter used three of the four. It is very likely that private schools will become more selective in the admissions process given an increase in the demand for private schooling.

Coleman's economic argument assumes that if there were an appreciable increase in the enrollment of blacks and Hispanics in private Catholic schools, white parents would not withdraw their children from these schools and enroll them in the non-Catholic private schools. However, past and present racial distribution patterns in housing, education, and employment suggest the contrary. More specifically, studies show that where black concentration is high, white concentration is disproportionately low and vice versa. In some instances, this has been interpreted to mean that most whites are not inclined to remain in environments where blacks are numerically equal or constitute a majority. To the extent that this is true, it seems more reasonable to expect that a sizable increase of blacks and Hispanics in Catholic schools would motivate white parents to withdraw their children from these schools and enroll them in the rapidly growing fundamentalist schools and segregated academies in the private sector. Should this occur, the Catholic schools may take on the predominantly minority character of many of the present inner-city public schools. Also, given these circumstances, the race/class inequality that presently exists within American schools would be maintained or even escalated.

A final misleading assumption in Coleman's economic argument is that private schools would be willing and able to accommodate an increase in minority-student enrollment. However, existing evidence suggests the contrary. Martha Jacobs reported, for example, in "Tuition Tax Credits for Elementary and Secondary Education," that private schools are not very responsive to changes in tuition levels and family-income increments and that such changes would have a limited effect on private-school enrollments. Jacobs also noted that an increase in the

demand for private schooling would encourage private schools to raise their tuition. Private schools would also require a considerable amount of time and money to accommodate a substantial increase in student enrollment. Finally, it is unlikely that private-school administrators would be willing to change their curricula and disciplinary procedures to meet the needs of public-school urban youth.

The second observation by Coleman having grave and misleading policy implications is that a tuition tax credit for parents of private-school students would benefit low-income and minority parents, and increase the enrollment of minority students in Catholic schools. Contrary to this claim, the weight of existing evidence shows that the vast majority of tuition tax credits at the elementary- and secondary-school level will go to white families with children already enrolled in private schools. Thus, minority and low-income families who presently represent a low percentage of private-school enrollment would receive only a small percentage of tax credits. Also, Jacobs presented data which show that minorities pay more for private school attendance but at the same time gain far less than whites in the forms of tax credit. Under a plan that would permit a tax credit for 35 percent of tuition up to $100 per student, blacks would receive only 6 percent of the total benefits at the elementary level, while whites would receive 92 percent of the total benefits at this level. Simultaneously, black families would pay a median tuition of $477 dollars at these levels, as compared to $342 for white families. Data reported elsewhere also show that in the South, where many of the segregated academies exist and where median tuition for private-school attendance is highest, private-school students would account for 41 percent of the total amount of tax credit. This share is largely disproportionate to the 25 percent representation of these students in southern private schools.

Additional data, from the *Current Popula-*

tion Report "Cost and Distribution of Tuition Tax Credit," challenge Coleman's claim that a private-school tuition tax credit will benefit low-income families. These data show that families of public-school children with incomes of $5,000 or less (3.2 percent) would not receive a tax credit, thus receiving nothing from the federal government. Families in the $5,000-$15,000 income bracket (16.4 percent) would receive an estimated credit of $125, thus receiving about $103 million from the federal government. Families with incomes of $15,000 and over (80.4 percent) would receive an average tax credit of $250, thus receiving $1005 million from the federal government. These estimates clearly indicate that the well-to-do have more to gain from a tuition tax credit than the less affluent, and at a greater cost to the federal government.

RELEVANCE AND USEFULNESS

In addition to the underlying methodological weakness and highly questionable policy value of Coleman's findings, a final issue concerns their relevancy and usefulness for current educational and social policy. To begin with, it should be noted that Coleman's document did renew interest in our nation's public schools. In addition, it provided a rich array of data for raising questions about U.S. secondary schools. However, despite these attractive features of the report, the findings as presented are not very informative for educational and social policy. The reason is that the document does not address or provide useful information for improving the nation's public schools, which currently enroll 90 percent of all elementary and secondary students. In addition, many of the public schools are faced with the dilemma of increasing educational equity and, simultaneously, improving educational quality. Given these factors, the recent Coleman document may have proven more

valuable had it offered some alternatives for improving U.S. public education.

Coleman's major finding, that private schools are more effective than public schools, is not very profound. One reason is because (whether real or imagined) most Americans already believe that U.S. private schools provide a better education for their children than public schools. However, despite this belief, there is no reason why private schools should have an advantage over public schools in educating students. The ability of public schools to compete more effectively with private schools and provide a high-quality and equitable education for the majority of American youth will largely depend on at least two factors. The first is the greater responsibility that public-school officials themselves must assume in better educating students. The second factor is increased commitment by the federal government to support and assure the effectiveness of U.S. public schools.

Both school officials and the local, state, and federal governments must give immediate attention to the special problems in inner-city schools. Many of these schools are poor, and predominantly minority. In addition, these schools are confronted with disciplinary problems, declining enrollments, and low student achievement. Teacher quality is also a problem in many of these schools. For example, M. Smith and C. D. Dziuban reported, in "The Gap between Desegregation Research and Remedy," that during initial school desegregation, a disproportionate number of less-experienced teachers were assigned to poor and predominantly black urban schools. In addition, studies show that the academic achievement and retention of black and Hispanic students in public schools of low socioeconomic status is lower than the achievement of their minority peers in schools of high socioeconomic status. These conditions should be given serious consideration in future school desegregation attempts and other efforts designed to increase the equality of educational opportunity for minorities and the quality of education that these students receive.

Coleman reported that the highly focused academic curricula in private schools encouraged greater student interest in higher education and greater subsequent college attendance. This observation implies that the nation's public schools might benefit by increasing the proportion of public-school students in academic programs. Diana Ravitch has reported that only 34 percent of public-school students are in academic curricula, as compared to 70 percent of private-school students. Also, Smith and Dziuban and others have noted that net of (controlling for) ability, minority students are disproportionately enrolled in non-academic programs. Thus, additional efforts are needed to increase the representation of minority public-school students in academic curricula

Paralleling the crisis in urban schools are problems in rural public schools. Approximately two-thirds of U.S. school districts are located in rural areas, and nearly one-third of all public-school students are rural. Research and policy on the problems and issues of rural public education are limited: the various problems of staff recruitment, curriculum development,

transportation costs, and fluctuating enrollments in these schools have not been adequately addressed by federal and state administrators. The impact of declining student enrollments, the potential increase in private-school attendance by middle-class students, and the decrease in federal and state aid for public educational programs (especially those designed for the disadvantaged) are factors that seriously threaten the future of rural and urban public education. Thus the specific impact of each of these factors on American rural and urban public education must be determined.

The preceding issues highlight the irrelevancy of the recent Coleman report. It provides neither direction nor alternatives for dealing with some of the major problems in American public education. The implied assumption of the report is that if more students escape to the nation's private schools, the problems of public education will be solved. However, based on the limited student population that private schools have served in the past and are very likely to serve in the future, this is not a promising alternative. The more realistic challenge is to redirect our public schools to assure a greater quality and a more equitable education for all students. Future investments in educational research and policy activities should address these issues.

DISCUSSION QUESTIONS AND ACTIVITIES

1. In what respects do the policy questions raised by Coleman, Kilgore, and Hoffer rest upon a value decision about the relative role of the state and family in controlling a child's education?

2. What differences were found in cognitive achievement and educational aspiration in comparisons of public and private schools?

3. Can the differences be largely explained by the selectivity of private schools?

4. What specific differences in school characteristics and activities were cited that enable private school students to produce greater achievement?

5. Is the charge valid that private schools increase segregation? For Hispanics? For Blacks?

6. To what extent is there economic segregation between the public and private sectors and within the private sector?

7. Are private schools divisive along religious lines?

8. What are some of the methodological weaknesses of the Coleman study?

9. Why would the income increment of $1,000 not cause much higher enrollment of Black and Hispanic students in private schools?

10. To what extent do private schools provide programs for the handicapped, compensatory education, and vocational education? What is the significance of these figures?

11. What income groups would likely benefit the most from tuition tax credits? Why?

12. What measures, according to Thomas, can be taken to improve the public schools?

13. Organize a class discussion involving three groups of students: those who attended a parochial school, a secular private school, and a public school. Have them compare the characteristics of the schools and evaluate the quality of their educational experiences.

14. Visit nonpublic schools in your local community and prepare a class report on the following characteristics: per pupil expenditures, teacher-pupil ratios, school library holdings, range of curricular offerings, and racial and ethnic compositions of the student body.

SUGGESTED READINGS

Proponents

Coleman, James S. "Public Schools, Private Schools, and the Public Interest." *The Public Interest* 64 (Summer 1981): 19–30.

———. "Response to Page and Keith." *Educational Researcher* 10 (August-September 1981): 18–20.

Coleman, James S. and Others. "Achievement and Segregation in Secondary Schools: A Further Look at Public and Private School Differences." *Sociology of Education* 55 (April-July 1982): 162–82.

———. "Cognitive Outcomes in Public and Private Schools." *Sociology of Education* 55 (April-July 1982): 65–76.

Coleman, James, S., Thomas Hoffer, and Sally Kilgore. *High School Achievement: Public, Private, and Catholic Schools Compared.* New York: Basic Books, 1982.

"Reflections on the 1981 Coleman Study." *Momentum* 12 (October 1981): 4–13. Three articles generally favorable to the Coleman study.

Critics

Breneman, David W. "Coleman II and the Credibility of Social Science Research." *Change* 13 (September 1981): 13.

Colucei, Nicholas. "Should Public Schools Be Judged by Criteria which Symbolize the 'Private School'?" *Capstone Journal of Education* 2 (Winter 1981-82): 18–28.

Crain, Robert L. and Willis D. Hawley. "Standards of Research." *Society* 19 (January-February 1982): 14–21.

Goldberger, Arthur S. and Glen G. Cain. "The Casual Analysis of Cognitive Outcomes in the Coleman, Hoffer and Kilgore Report." *Sociology of Education* 55 (April-July 1982): 103–22.

McPartland, James M. and Edward L. McDill. "Control and Differentiation in the Structure of American Education." *Sociology of Education* 55 (April-July 1982): 77–88.

Page, Ellis B. and Timothy Z. Keith. "Effects of U.S. Private Schools: A Technical Analysis of Two Recent Claims." *Educational Researcher*

10 (August-September 1981): 7–17.

Ravitch, Diane. "The Meaning of the New Coleman· Report." *Phi Delta Kappan* 62 (June 1981): 718–20.

"Report Analysis: Public and Private Schools." *Harvard Educational Review* 51 (November 1981): 481–545. This colloquium presents seven analyses of the report, *Public and Private Schools,* together with responses by the report's authors.

Policy Issues

Butts, R. Freeman. "The Public Schools: Assaults on a Great Idea." *The Nation* (April 30, 1973): 553–60.

Coons, John E. and Stephen D. Sugarman. *Education by Choice: The Case for Family Control.* Berkeley, Ca.: University of California Press, 1978.

Edmonds, E. L. "In Defense of the Private School." *Education Canada* 21 (Fall 1981): 21–23, 48.

Everhart, Robert B., ed. *The Public School Monopoly.* Cambridge, Mass.: Ballinger Publishing Co., 1982.

NASSP *Bulletin* 66 (March 1982): 1–95. A special issue devoted to nonpublic schools.

Phi Delta Kappan 63 (November 1981): 159–168. Five articles—one by Coleman, the other four mostly critical—about the Coleman study, and the policy issues it raises.

Rich, John Martin. "The Libertarian Challenge to Public Education " *The Educational Forum* 46 (Summer 1982): 421–29. Condensed in *The Education Digest* 48 (December 1982): 16–19

20
Back-to-Basics Alternative

Back-to basics is a movement that began in the early 1970s and has grown rapidly in the United States and Canada. In the United States there are more than 5000 fundamental schools (the title given schools that emphasize basics) and their numbers are still growing. In contrast to most other innovations, this type of school was initiated by parents and local citizens who were alarmed over low scores of students on standardized tests, the devaluation of the high school diploma, and what they claimed to be an overly permissive atmosphere in regular public schools. The seventh annual Gallop poll of public opinion about education indicated that 57 percent of all parents would, if given the option, send their children to public schools that emphasize strict discipline, the 3Rs, and dress codes for students and teachers.

Fundamental schools stress the fundamentals or basics, strict discipline (which may include corporal punishment and detention), competition, letter grades, standarized testing, ability grouping, homework, and dress codes. Such schools also place emphasis upon moral standards, courtesy, respect for adults, and patriotism. Other characteristics include teaching logical reasoning, one's history, heritage, and government structure. In keeping with the emphasis on competition and in contrast to some other alternative schools, students are rewarded for achievement but not for effort. Some proponents of fundamental schools see their work as a struggle against "permissive education" in order to preserve values and transmit vital knowledge of the heritage. Others view declining test scores as a principal motivation for establishing fundamental schools.

The back-to-basics alternative is, in a sense, a move by laypeople at the grassroots level for greater accountability in public education. Whether or not well founded, many citizens believe that schools are not teaching the basics effectively and are overly permissive. Fundamental schools have been recognized, though perhaps somewhat reluctantly, by leaders in the alternatives movement as a legitimate alternative to the prevailing model, even though the underlying ideas are not entirely new. If alternative schools are based on freedom of choice, the interests and desires of many citizens cannot be satisfied without the establishment of fundamental schools.

S. B. Neill takes us behind the scenes to view Pasadena's fundamental school and to examine the ideas on which it is based; it is then compared with a remarkably different alternative school within the same school district. In Rich's essay, he outlines a number of social, cultural, and educational factors that precipitated the basics movement; he then attempts to show that only a tenuous connection can be established between fundamental school practices and the teaching of the 3Rs; and finally, he argues that the 3Rs are not basic.

Pasadena's Approach to
the Classic School Debate

Shirley Boes Neill _____

Shirley Boes Neill is a freelance writer in Carmichael, California.

What kind of school is best: traditional, informal, or old style fundamental? From Plato to Piaget and beyond, the controversy persists; even today, American school boards, educators, and citizens are divided in the debate. Pasadena, California, is approaching the classic question in a special way by having students and their parents choose for themselves the kind of school they want.

Eric, a loquacious 12-year-old, justifies his preference for the informal Alternative School in this manner: "I left boredom because I enjoy learning, and I can do it better in bedlam." Eric selected a school in which he chooses his own courses, has a voice in who teaches him, varies his class schedule to personal interests, and helps shape the rules of conduct.

If the school sounds far out—and it does to many educators and parents—there is a second option available to Pasadena Unified School District residents: the currently voguish Fundamental Schools that hark back to the days of the hickory stick and learning by rote. The "bedlam" that Eric ascribes to the Alternative School has no part in the Fundamental Schools. There, formal structure and rigid rules and authoritarian discipline prevail.

Should neither of these special schools grab them, Pasadena students and parents can elect to stay with the regular or traditional schools.

Both the Alternative and Fundamental Schools have attracted considerable public interest, not only in Pasadena but across the country. More than 1,000 requests for information about the Fundamental Schools alone have come from 45 States and several foreign countries. And the press has not overlooked the coexistence of two diverse educational philosophies which set the schools eons apart from each other and from the regular schools in the district. Yet, both types of special schools are reasonably sure of continuation by the district because each has the strong backing of its own determined group of teachers, administrators, parents, and other interested citizens.

The Fundamental Schools were started in 1973 after some 7,000 white students fled the Pasadena public schools in the wake of a 1970 Supreme Court desegregation decision. As a result of this loss the public schools' test scores for 1973 dropped below the 25th percentile, in contrast to the 1969 scores which were near the national norm of 50 percent, according to Henry S. Myers, Jr., president of the unanimously conservative board of education. "At the same time," says Mr. Myers, "entering first-grade students continued to test at 11 points above the national norm, indicating to the board that the problem was attributable to our school system rather than to any decline in student capability."

The board, under Mr. Myers's leadership,

From American Education *12 (April 1976) pp. 6–10. Use by permission.*

took steps to reverse the flight of white students to nearby districts or area private schools. By copying liberally from the highly structured and what Mr. Myers calls the "simple, uncluttered academics" of Catholic and other nonpublic schools, the board offered parents the option of enrolling their children in a public school that stresses the fundamental approach found in many private ones.

Pasadena's special schools offer another advantage. Enrollment in them means that students can stay in the same school until graduation, so long as the school is satisfactory to them and they do not give the school grounds for expulsion. In the regular schools, under Pasadena's desegregation plan, students still face possible transfer whenever any ethnic minority becomes a majority of the school population. The special schools maintain a racial balance about the same as the district's: 42 percent black, 41 percent Anglo-Caucasian, 13 percent Spanish-surnamed, and four percent others. But, since admissions are controlled at the special school through the application process, there is little chance that a school will be allowed to become racially unbalanced.

John Marshall Fundamental, first such school in the district, is also the best known. By the time the school opened in September 1973, the board had received more than 3,000 applications from parents who were interested in having their children fill its 1,000 vacancies in grades K-8. The following year, the school was expanded to 12th grade and 1,850 students were enrolled. Also in 1974, Sierra Mesa Fundamental was opened with 410 students, joined a year later by McKinley Fundamental and Audubon Fundamental Kindergarten. By October 1975, more than 2,600 Pasadena students — ten percent of the district — were enrolled in Fundamental Schools, with more than 1,000 on a waiting list.

At the Fundamental Schools, reading and math are in, and so are homework, spanking, a dress code, and character education. In fact, the schools seem to epitomize what George Gallup had in mind when, in his Seventh Annual Poll, he asked parents if they would send their children "to a special public school that has strict discipline, including a dress code, and that puts emphasis on the three R's" (fifty-seven percent of those polled said yes; 33 percent said no).

The principal of John Marshall is crewcut, fiftyish J. M. (Mike) Kellner. A firm believer in teaching the basics during all of his 25 years as an educator, Mr. Kellner was handpicked by the board to head the school. Now, three years later, he sees the school as offering a legitimate option to many caught in the ferment of a changing, diverse school district.

Mr. Kellner's staff is all volunteer but, in his words, "carefully picked" so that teachers and administrators — individually and collectively — stress the same basics of reading, writing, arithmetic, and discipline. He emphasizes that the stress on basics is not just his or the board's idea but that it stems as well from the parents. When John Marshall was in the planning stages, he notes, "much time was spent in listening to parents and then building a curriculum based on their requests and demands."

Consequently, students must devote a lot of time to all forms of language arts and math and then, according to Mr. Kellner, "move out to geography, history, and the full curriculum." He believes that "we have got to get back on this track, away from the permissiveness of recent years and the fact that schools have had too much curriculum, too many activities, and too broad a base of operation. We are concerned, too, that youngsters show educational achievement at the end of the school year." Board President Myers puts the case more strongly. The future of the country, he contends, may depend on reversing "some of the educational fads that have caused test scores to slide and that show huge deficiencies in student learning."

At John Marshall, structure is paramount

and, in Mr. Kellner's words, "nothing is left to chance." The school uses ability grouping (above average, average, and below average) and A-to-F letter grades. Teachers get help in maintaining a "proper learning environment" in the classroom through the promulgation and enforcement of strict rules of conduct. In one elementary classroom, a handwritten list of Ten Commandment-like reminders for students includes these rules: Talk only when called on; never talk back; and put trash in trash cans.

The reading coordinator's interpretation of reading policy is simple and to the point: "All of the teaching staff stress reading for all students." At seventh- and eighth-grade levels, students must take both reading and arithmetic fundamentals and may take additional courses in reading development and English. Students in grades 9 through 12 are required to take four years of English and at least two years of math. Strongly recommended are two years of foreign language for all students.

The school seems to inspire quietness even from visitors. The building, more than 50 years old and showing its age, establishes a stern, business-like atmosphere that discourages noise. The halls are drab, but inside an elementary classroom, artwork posters, and student-made projects give color and cheer. Almost every hand is raised and every pair of eyes looks to the front of the room when the teacher asks for the spelling of "hover." Next, a student defines without hesitation the word "proofread," and then the entire class performs a proofreading exercise.

In another part of the school, a visitor leaving a junior high classroom where he has just witnessed a debate on gun control expresses amazement: "Those kids were really prepared and organized, and can you believe, they addressed each other as 'Miss' and 'Mister.'"

Mr. Kellner points out that many of the back-to-basic practices stressed by the Fundamental Schools have been either cast out or con-

siderably modified in recent years by most public schools. For example, all students in Fundamental Schools—kindergarten through 12th grade—must have homework assigned to them four nights a week, with the assignments tied to what is being taught in class rather than being just busywork. Homework is corrected by the teacher or another student in class the following day and then sent home so parents can see it. Finally, students must return the homework to the school, where it is filed and retained for future reference. Mr. Kellner deplores the current policy of some schools which allows students to spend the last 15 minutes of a class period doing homework. Parents never see the homework, and the only gauge they have of their youngster's progress in school comes at the end of the grading period.

A dress code for teachers specifies dresses for women and ties and coats for men. "This is the way student advisory groups told us they wanted teachers to appear," says the principal. A student dress code now under consideration would require girls to wear dresses and boys to wear ties in school. The effect of such a dress code on other schools in the district, according to Mr. Kellner, would be revolutionary. "Our kids have to wear shoes to school while at a nearby school the students don't necessarily have to do even that. When we start our youngsters out to work at McDonald's or Bullock's (a large department store), they have to look the part. If they show up dressed like hippies and bums, they won't be able to work at either place."

School policy on discipline is tight, with Mr. Kellner personally supervising the disciplinary measures. The result is noteworthy, according to the principal, because the small amount of "naughty behavior" that took place in the school's first year has tapered off considerably. Paddling is permitted, points out Mr. Kellner—even paddling of junior and senior high school students, although, at that level, a behavior adjustment class is favored. "I will paddle any child at the parent's request, but the best paddlings have taken place in my office by the parents themselves," he notes. In behavior adjustment class—which can last from one to three days—students are required to continue their regular school work. At the end of the student's stay, a school counselor tries to get the youngster back on a positive course before re-enrollment in regular classes.

To reinforce discipline and to teach manners, courtesy, and patriotism, the school requires a 15-minute daily period for all students in character education. Each day, a different topic is chosen from among those submitted by parents, teachers, and students. Every class is expected to explain and dramatize what it thinks the topic means. On a typical day, the blackboard in each classroom contains the character education message: "Self-discipline is essential in a democracy."

Character education is particularly important today, says Mr. Kellner, because "moral and spiritual values are no longer taught in school. Bible reading has disappeared from our classrooms; and, more and more, we lack support from the character-building agencies and youth organizations that used to play a large role in raising and shaping a child." Other public schools in the district apparently agree with him because they too, are integrating character education into their curriculums.

Which students thrive best in a Fundamental School? According to Mr. Kellner, those who prefer a formally structured school will fit well into the Fundamental School. Even students who transfer from schools with a more liberal environment, he says, quickly adjust and seem to like the tighter structure. It is important to remember, he adds, that attending a Fundamental School is a privilege and students who do not want to abide by its rules can leave. But not many do since only six to ten students per year ask for a transfer.

Just two miles away from John Marshall Fundamental is its antithesis, the Alternative School. Housed in Washington Center, which also includes an evening high school, the Alternative School is the only one of its type in the district. It was started in 1972 by incumbent liberal board members who are no longer in office. Initially the University of Massachusetts lent professional and financial support to the school but now the school is on its own. The first 100 students were selected from 1,200 applicants. Today, 750 students attend the Alternative School's grades K-12, and the waiting list numbers more than 500. Expansion of the school is unlikely, at least not while the current board members are in power. "If I had my way, I'd get rid of it," says Board President Myers. "It's ridiculous."

To a visitor, the Alternative School appears casual and loose. From an upstairs window, open to the warm weather, comes the distinguishable but not blaring sound of rock music. Like the Fundamental School, the Alternative School is housed in an older school building where the interior walls are a nondescript green, paint on the radiators is chipped, and the woodwork is nicked.

Students help visitors feel at home "because Paul likes us to do it." Paul is Paul Finot, the principal, and all the students call him by his first name. Bearded, bespectacled, and wearing a corduroy suit, Mr. Finot outlines his ideas on developing self-responsibility and self-learning in students—the school's main objectives.

Basically, his strategy is to start early in giving students responsibility for their own learning, adding more and more as they go up the grade scale. Beginning with grades K-3, students are given some choices within their self-contained classrooms. In grades 4-6, after spending three periods a day in self-contained classrooms, students can decide what they want to learn during the remaining two periods. Seventh and eighth graders spend their mornings working on core curriculum courses, leaving afternoons for subjects they want to take. By the time students reach the ninth grade, "we treat them very much like adults," says Mr. Finot.

School starts at 9:30 a.m. and ends at 8 p.m. The attendance policy must satisfy State and district requirements, but it also allows students credit for extra in-class study, work experience, independent study, "and any other activity that is under the direction of a staff member." The school year is divided into five periods, usually of 10 or 11 weeks but flexible to accommodate different types of courses and activities. Under the schedule students can earn up to 80 academic units per year.

A special intensive module allows students six hours a day for two weeks to study a subject in greater detail, either in class or on a field trip. One group of students decided to go to nearby Catalina Island for seven to nine days of concentrated study of marine biology—and fun. The expedition, planned by students and staff, also offered students the chance to do research with staff members from the University of Southern California. Another group went on a mountain-climbing expedition, led by a teacher and an expert mountain climber. The students finance their expeditions through all sorts of money-raising projects.

The school encourages success literally by never allowing a student to fail a course. Grades follow an A, B, C, D schedule, no F's being given. A student who does not earn one of the four possible letter grades simply forfeits the credit he or she would have earned for the course. In this way, says Mr. Finot, no failure mark appears on any permanent record to plague the student for a lifetime.

Curriculum is left up to the students, but they are made aware that the State requires certain courses for graduation and others for entrance into California's colleges and universities. "The outcome is not what many educators would expect to happen when the decision-mak-

ing is turned over to students," says Mr. Finot. "We could, of course, offer 'underwater basket weaving' or 'howling at the moon' if these were what the kids wanted and we could find the teachers for such courses. But the courses chosen by the kids are surprisingly traditional; our school curriculum resembles the courses given in an English prep school."

Another thing about the Alternative School that probably throws many educators into a tailspin is the principal's assertion that students "can hire and fire teachers." He actually means that students have the option of bringing to him their objections about a teacher. When this does occur, Mr. Finot closely observes and evaluates the teacher; if it becomes necessary, he will eventually try to transfer the teacher. But transfer is no easy matter. "Tenure is still an important consideration and no one can immediately get rid of a teacher the students don't like," he explains. The principal and students also have an agreement about hiring teachers. While Mr. Finot does the actual hiring, students can interview prospective teachers and give him their impressions.

The school's behavior code—shaped by students, parents, and staff—include eight brief rules which disallow on the campus (as the school grounds are called) smoking, drugs or alcoholic beverages, violence, vandalism, stealing, littering, pets, or "actions which interfere with a teaching, learning, or administrative process."

Mr. Finot does not appear to use anything that smacks of threats, an iron hand, or even a heavy grip. Instead, he explains to the students the possible consequences they must consider before taking unpropitious actions. Rather than forbidding them, for example, to print four-letter words in student publications, he tells students that "if you defy board of education policies and guidelines on student publications, I may come under attack and be fired for not censoring you. If I lose my job you may not get another principal who is as flexible and lenient as I am."

Some of the rules of conduct have caused heated discussions on the Alternative School campus before the student body voted to accept them. When students had to decide whether or not to use, share, or allow drugs on campus, the argument ran two days. The students finally outlawed drugs because they feared the school would be abolished if they did not take the action. A rule prohibiting the use of skateboards in the hallway, came about when a board member happened to be visiting the Alternative School just when a student was demonstrating his skateboard expertise in the hallway. The incident helped the board member conclude that the school "is too free-wheeling and absurd."

One student labels decrees like the skateboard ban "rules for survival." Students and teachers at the school "wouldn't have minded the skateboards in the hall," he says, "but since the board members objected, the rule became necessary for survival's sake."

Whereas quiet is the rule at the Fundamental Schools, it is the exception at the Alternative School. One student sitting alone in a classroom explains that it was the only quiet place that he could find to read. In a sixth-grade social studies class, students working individually at round tables manage to make their voices heard above the general hubbub. "It's always this noisy in here but you get used to it," says one youngster. "Besides," adds another, "the teacher can quiet down the room anytime by giving us the silent treatment. He just stops talking to any of us and pretty soon we realize he wants us to be quiet."

In an algebra class of students from grades 7 through 12, the instructor explains to the visitor that he tries to "casualize" everything because "algebra is scary to kids." Dressed in hooded gym outfit and tennis shoes, he blends in with his students. The room is informally arranged, with chairs set in circular rows, wagon-train style. The teacher "throws out a concept" and

then lets the students try to understand it by any means they can. Students are encouraged to look at each other's papers and ask how to do a particular problem. A sixth grader—"officially too young for the class but a whiz at algebra"—sits in a group with two other under-aged students who want to get a head start on higher math. Students are allowed to audit the class without enrolling, says the algebra teacher, "because when kids see that their friends, who are no smarter than they, can succeed in this class, they will enroll."

As with the Fundamental Schools, the question must be asked: Which students succeed best in the Alternative School's environment? The Alternative School, according to Mr. Finot, is for the student who already has the basics and "who can do research and thrive by learning on his own." Upon questioning, students give their own reasons for being in the Alternative School: Thirteen-year-old Vincent Allen likes calling teachers by their first names. Jesus Quintero says he is learning more in his eighth-grade classes than he did in four earlier schools. "Besides," he adds, "I may be able to graduate early if I work hard." Another student, one year from graduating, enjoys the opportunity to pick her own courses. Nevertheless, she adds that she does not have enough credits in math and that she dropped a course in "computation" because the other students in the class were much younger. "I'll have to find another course," she says.

As far as achievement is concerned, the records of both special schools are impressive. Mr. Finot says most of the students in the Alternative School graduate early. Board members credit the Fundamental Schools with playing a key part in the better achievement tests scores, districtwide, by bringing a new sense of "competition" among all the schools.

Board President Myers says: "After the first year of operation, the improvement in the test scores at the [John Marshall] Fundamental School was dramatic but the effect of the competition of the Fundamental School on all of the regular schools was even more spectacular." The three percent decline in reading scores that district schools experienced each year between 1969 and 1973 ended: improvement was again noted. In 1969, district students were scoring at the 45th percentile in reading: by 1973, they had dropped to the 33rd percentile. Spring 1975 testing yielded scores near the 1969 level. The districtwide average for reading by first- and second-grade students was at the 44th percentile and for third graders, at the 39th percentile. First graders at John Marshall scored at the 74th percentile in reading and second graders reached the 67th percentile.

An additional benefit brought by the Fundamental Schools, says Mr. Myers, is the general upsurge in school district enrollment, coming after five successive years of decline. From October 1973 to October 1974, the district gained 600 students and only half of the increase directly resulted from private school closings. Enrollment increased by 150 students in 1975. Myers credits the gains to the Fundamental Schools, adding that test scores are up and young families with children are once again settling in the district and sending their children to public schools.

Giving students and parents a choice of schools answers the frequent call for educational diversity but it also raises problems and controversy of its own. There are lots of questions and concerns about special schools—particularly the Fundamental Schools—voiced by individuals and groups in the community. The board, at the same time, is forging ahead in trying to convert the entire district to the fundamental approach. Superintendent Ramon Cortines admits to "walking a tightrope" most of the time. Some parents resent both types of special schools, Mr. Cortines says, because they

realize that he and the board members are not always in agreement about how they should be run. In addition, one citizens' group is concerned that the Fundamental Schools are too militaristic and regimented and that, in such schools, students will never learn to discipline themselves. There also have been complaints that the Alternative School is "too free-wheeling" and that it gives students "a false sense of security about how much they can control the world."

Some would like to concentrate on the regular schools. One parent, Naomi Kurn, says that, rather than have special schools emphasized, she would prefer that all schools in the district be improved. She adds that more discipline is especially needed in the regular schools.

Educators in the district seem to be just as divided as the parents and community over the special schools. One administrator in the regular school says, for example, that he would like to be able to take the best from each of the special schools by incorporating some of the Alternative School practices while still emphasizing the basics. An administrator in one of the special schools argues that they must remain "special" in order to retain the particular emphasis that parents want for their children. Mr. Cortines believes that practices that have been found successful in Pasadena's special schools should be replicated in the district's regular public school classrooms.

At present, the situation resembles more the noise of the Alternative School class than the quiet of its Fundamental counterpart. One point, though, is clear. Pasadena has turn the corner in discovering how diverse approaches can be used to meet the various needs expressed by students and parents. The problem now, it seems, is how to capitalize on the diversity for all students in the district.

Back-To-Basics: A Reappraisal

John Martin Rich _____

Public education is no stranger to fads and panaceas and transient innovations. Just within the past 10 or 15 years a dozen or so new innovations have been tried and only a few are still in widespread use. One of the latest innovations is a return-to-basics.

In the United States, there are more than 5000 fundamental schools (the title given schools that emphasize basics), and their numbers are still growing. This type of school, in contrast to most innovations, was initiated by parents and local citizens.

As examples, Myers Park Optional School in Charlotte, North Carolina, teaches good manners and patriotism, arithmetic and penmanship, and emphasizes grades, report cards, and rules of deportment.[1] At the John Marshall Fundamental School in Pasadena, stress is placed on the 3Rs, teacher dress codes, ability grouping, strict rules of conduct, corporal punishment, homework, and character education.[2]

The seventh annual Gallup poll of public opinion about eduction indicated that 57 percent of all parents would, if given the option, send their children to public schools that emphasize strict discipline, the 3Rs, and dress codes for students and teachers. This is much more than a reactionary trend. The usual divisions of opinion along racial, religious, economic, and political lines do not seem to fit; persons of different classes, religions, races, and politics have joined in an unlikely combination in support of the basics.[3] The reactions of educators and psychologists have varied: Kenneth Clark strongly supports the basics;[4] some people attempt to explain the push for basics;[5] other warn of the undesirable features of some programs or practices;[6] and still others show how schools can resist the back-to-basics trend.[7]

The return-to-basics movement should come as no great surprise to most educators. In retrospect, numerous signs have portended this development. Let us take a moment to look at these signs in terms of the social-cultural factors and then the educational factors:

Written expressly for Innovations in Education: Reformers and Their Critics.

---

[1]J. S. Shaw, "New Conservative Alternative: Fundamental Schools," *Nation's Schools and Colleges* 2 (February 1975): 31–4 + .

[2]Shirley Boes Neill, "Pasadena's Approach to the Classic School Debate," *American Education* 12 (April 1976): 6–10.

[3]John Egerton, "Back to Basics," *The Progressive* (September 1976): 21–4.

[4]Discussed in "Back to Basics in the School," *Newsweek* 84 (October 21, 1974): 91.

[5]William Van Til, William E. Brownson, and Russell L. Hamm, "Back to Basics—With a Difference," *Educational Leadership* 33 (October 1975): 8–10, 12–13.

[6]Fred M. Hechinger, "All-New Law and Order Classroom," *Saturday Review* (May 3, 1975): 40–1.

[7]"How to Talk to the Back-to-Basics Tiger," *Education USA* 18 No. 148 (July 26, 1976): 273.

SOCIAL AND CULTURAL FACTORS

Vietnam. The exhausting Vietnam war left many Americans bewildered and disconcerted. As more Americans began to oppose the war, some found it necessary to face up to their own inconsistent beliefs and conflicting values. The upshot of the Vietnam debacle was to ruthlessly expose the lack of widespread consensus on a common set of values and the limits of strain the social fabric could endure, short of destruction. Thus the return-to-basics seeks, among other things, to gain value consensus by reestablishing order, discipline, patriotism, and character education.

Watergate. The disillusionment with political life and the conduct of politicians has resulted in some reforms and greater recognition of a need for accountability of public officials. That such events could occur in America has precipitated a renewed interest in teaching basic virtues and sound character traits, which constitute one of the hallmarks of fundamental schools.

Rapid Change. Periods of rapid change generally tend to increase confusion, disequilibrium, and stress. Those unable to cope successfully revert to earlier forms of behavior and seek grasp fleeting ties with the past in order to recover some sense of stability and purpose in a disquieting world. Such periods may place a moratorium on further experimentation and innovation, ushering in a revival of traditions, orthodox values, and schooling practices reminiscent of the best of one's own childhood.

Value Conflict. Numerous value conflicts have flared during the past decade: intergenerational, racial, ethnic, class, and others. Once consensus breaks down and unless workable procedures are available for mediating conflict and reaching a new modus operandi, a period of social and political instability is precipitated. Thus one proposed solution to these periodic upheavals is to reinstitute the teaching of codes of behavior, traditional values, and character traits, and to emphasize greater school discipline.

EDUCATIONAL FACTORS

Failure of Innovations. Many innovations were introduced during the 1960s — nongraded schools, educational television, team teaching, the new math and science, and others — which did not always live up to their promise. Reasons varied for their failure to have a more lasting impact. Even more serious was the disappointment over social science interventionist strategies to change the schools. Additionally, innovations and experiments have been curtailed lately because of financial retrenchment.

Low Test Scores. Evidence is mixed but largely there has been a drop in standardized test scores in recent years. ACT and SAT scores have fallen since 1964; in science, according to the National Assessment of Education Progress (NAEP), a decrease was registered between 1970 and 1973; and the NAEP reports that 13- and 17-year-old students in 1974 wrote in a more "primer-like" style than did the same age group in 1970.

But there was some evidence to support a different view. An NAEP study, part of the Right to Read effort, which is restricted to 17-year-old students covering basic reading skills needed to function in everyday life, indicated that they were two percentage points higher in 1974 than 17-year-olds in 1971. And the NAEP showed that 9-year-olds were better writers than their counterparts of four years ago.

Various reasons have been given for the apparent decline, but no definitive conclusions have as yet been reached. Despite alarm in some quarters, there is no massive slide in test scores; at best, scores have declined somewhat from the crest of the middle sixties. Nevertheless, many citizens urge a return-to-basics as a solution to the problem. Irrespective of the validity of the scores, the perception is that students are not doing as well.

Employment Opportunities. With a recession and a straitened job market, prospective graduates are becoming increasingly concerned over their employment prospects. Employers complain that some of the new graduates lack basic skills and that a high school diploma is no longer an assurance of minimum competencies. Pressures are being placed on some public schools to reinstate the value of a diploma by eliminating social promotions and tightening standards for basic skills.

Accountability Movement. The move toward greater accountability in education has been one of the hallmarks of the 1970s. Accountability is generally conceived as a demand to judge schools by their outputs and to demonstrate a positive relationship between expenditures and desired results obtained. Schools are expected to make wise use of public resources not only by efficient cost accounting procedures but also by raising test scores and overcoming students' lack of discipline and good habits. It is likely that the accountability movement will remain strong through the 1970s.

Alternative Schools. Alternatives arose within public schools as options to the prevailing model in order to provide greater choices. Alternatives have tended to individualize instruction and be based upon neo-progressive lines; but some dissatisfied citizens also recognized that it was perfectly consistent with the ideology of alternatives to demand fundamental schools. Though this may not have been what many alternative proponents originally envisioned, the availability to alternatives offered a policy for the growth of fundamental schools; at the same time, the movement itself has probably reduced conflict during a period of unrest by providing options for most everyone.

THE 3Rs AND FUNDAMENTAL SCHOOL PRACTICES

Fundamental schools, as noted earlier, have a wide range of practices from dress codes to corporal punishment. These practices are supposed to have some integral relationship with learning the 3Rs; however the precise nature of this relationship has yet to be made clear. Is the connection between these practices and the 3Rs logically necessary, casual, complementary, contributory, or one of historical association? Necessary statements do not have to be tested, for they hold for all cases indefinitely (for example: Black cats are black; one cannot be both standing and sitting). Thus the relationship between fundamental school practices and the 3Rs must be contingent (rather than necessary) insofar as empirical evidence is needed. Our problem, however, is that definitive evidence is lacking to show a casual, complementary, or contributory relationship. In fact, there are a number of successful teachers, such as Herbert Kohl,[8] who teach the 3Rs effectively not only by eschewing the above practices but also employing a permissive classroom environment, which most proponents of fundamental schools deplore. Moreover, one can still advocate teaching the 3Rs and traditional subjects without endorsing fundamental school practices.[9] In other words, advocacy of a particular educational theory such as essentialism does not in itself entail a commitment to such practices.

More likely an historical association exists between the practices and the 3Rs in the sense

---

[8]Herbert Kohl, *Reading, How To.* New York: Dutton, 1973.
[9]See Mortimer Smith, "Educational Innovations: Treasure and Dross," *The American Scholar* 43 (Winter 1973–74): 113–39.

that whenever some people think about the 3Rs they associate the practices with them because that was the way they were taught. But such an historical conjunction neither establishes the efficiency of the 3Rs nor any sense of historical inevitability. A potentially large number of other combinations could have occurred—in fact, the historical record indicates several such combinations.

WHAT IS BASIC?

Few educators who have objected to fundamental schools are against teaching the 3Rs more effectively, but they do tend to disagree with the reinstatement of the practices previously mentioned; some also object to using drill and rote learning methods for teaching basic skills. And some go further to recognize that what is basic is considerably broader and more inclusive than what proponents of fundamental schools advocate.[10]

The usual argument for teaching the 3Rs is that they are essential for living successfully in today's world; that is, they are needed in order to handle other school subjects, to score well on tests, to graduate, get a job, perform basic consumer functions in the larger society, and the like. These claims may very well be true or at least partly true; but our interest at this point is to raise even more essential questions about the 3Rs. Whenever the 3Rs are identified as the heart of education, are the claims made in their behalf on extrinsic or intrinsic grounds? Usually the 3Rs are urged, as noted above, on extrinsic grounds; they are considered desirable because they are a means to other desirable outcomes. In contrast, the 3Rs are not usually considered intrinsic values (things that are worthwhile in

themselves apart from any extrinsic value they may have). But if that which is extrinsically valuable is worthwhile only in terms of outcome, and the particular outcome, in turn, is worthwhile only in relation to a still further outcome, we then are caught in an infinite regress unless somewhere along the chain of derivatively valuable things appeal could be made to an intrinsic value. Could it be, then, that what is basic is intrinsically valuable, and since the 3Rs are advanced on extrinsic grounds, then they are not actually basic? Thus we may need to seek what is valuable in itself, for once that is found we need not ask for further justification; yet it can provide justification for studying that which is extrinsically valuable.

That which is basic are educative experiences. Educative experiences, we contend, are intrinsic worthwhile and need no justification. To deny this is to communicate one's insincerity in engaging in educational discourse, because to gain an education one must have or undergo educative experiences and to refuse to acknowledge the fundamental character of educative experiences terminates further discourse and inquiry about education.

To have an educational experience rests upon an ability to make certain elemental distinctions, otherwise everything would seem, as William James characterized the world of the newborn infant, "a blooming buzzing confusion." In any experience or series of experiences one must be able to distinguish contradictory judgments and thereby avoid confused and disordered acts. As the truth of some judgments are determined, general principles can be derived to apply to other judgments whose truth or falsity has yet to be determined. By the ability to make such distinctions experiences can be distinguished and their interconnections ascertained. Experience itself, however, assumes causality. The raw data of experience could be different from the way we find it to be, but the law of causality is necessary because it is a pre-

---

[10]W. R. Wees, "What's Basic," *Orbit* 24, vol. 5, no. 4 (October 1974): 20–1; and D. Hawkins "Balancing Basics: The Three R's Revisited," *Childhood Education* 50 (February 1974): 186–91.

suppositon of experience: it makes experience possible and intelligible.

The criteria of an experience may be a priori, but the application of the criteria are tested by their ability to order experience by making meaningful distinctions. For instance, the initial experience of grasping the concept of division will enable the child (with usually some assistance from the teacher) to distinguish division from addition or subtraction. Or take an experience where a student is learning to apply the scientific method to a problem. In order to understand the scientific method, one would have to distinguish experiences in applying the scientific method from numerous previous experiences in using a common sense approach.

Since experiences occur within a world with others, it is necessary to employ a form of public discourse in order for education as we know it to take place. This discourse, among other things, requires sufficient consideration of others in order that ideas can be exchanged and experiences can be promoted. Thus a minimal degree of mutual concern and willingness to share experiences is presupposed in education.

To fall into the customary practice of using "the basics" as a synonym for the 3Rs is begging the question. In contrast to other educators who have accepted the 3Rs as basic but attempted to make basics more inclusive,[11] we have attempted to show that the 3Rs are not basic. Instead, we have argued that educative experiences constitute a necessary condition for the 3Rs and for other studies and obviates the problem of an infinite regress. The ultimate reason for studying the 3Rs is that they may assist in having educative experiences; yet there are other studies—science, literature, art, philosophy, and so on—that also may enable one to have educative experiences.

In summary, social and educational factors were examined for the rise of fundamental schools, the connection between fundamental school practices and the teaching of the 3Rs was held to be tenuous, and it was argued that educative experiences, not the 3Rs, are basic and that the ultimate reason for studying the 3Rs lies in the extent to which they can promote such experiences. And finally, though citizens have the right to establish fundamental schools, they should be forewarned of some of the weaknesses previously indicated.

------

[11]*Ibid.*

DISCUSSION QUESTIONS AND ACTIVITIES

1. State the underlying philosophy of the John Marshall Fundamental School.
2. What is the connection, if any, between teaching the fundamentals and enforcing a dress code and corporal punishment?
3. Do you agree with the Pasadena's school board president who believes the nation's future depends upon reversing "some of the educational fads that have caused test scores to slide and that show huge deficiencies in student learning"? Consider three factors in answering the question: (1) whether test scores have declined; (2) the actual threat, if such is the case, to the nation's future; (3) whether fundamental schools will likely reverse the decline.
4. What is known about the use of homework and ability groupings on learning?
5. Should schools teach character education? Is the approach used at the John Marshall Fundamental School a desirable way to do so?

6. What is the underlying philosophy of the Alternative School and how would it compare to the John Marshall Fundamental School?

7. Visit fundamental schools in your local community and report to the class on your findings.

8. Rich has cited numerous factors which he believes contribute to a return to basics. Would it have been more accurate for him to state bluntly that declining test scores and lack of rudimentary academic skills are the reasons for the return?

9. What is the connection between fundamental school practices and the 3R's?

10. In Rich's attempt to show that the 3R's are not basic, has he at best only shown that educative experiences are a necessary rather than a sufficient condition? Or, on the other hand, is his argument circular? Vacuous?

SUGGESTED READINGS

Proponents of Back to Basics

Altman, Howard B. "Individualized Instruction and 'Back to Basics': Reconciling Paradoxes." *Journal of College Science Teaching* 11 (September 1981): 20–24.

Brisbin, Dan. "Whad'ya Mean, BACK to Basics?" *Thrust for Educational Leadership* 8 (November 1978): 20–21.

Cooke, David. "Lessons from the Basics." *English Quarterly* 14 (Summer 1981): 27–37.

Cusick, Philip A. "Secondary School Structure: The Critical Dilemma." NASSP *Bulletin* 65 (December 1981): 40–50.

Down, A. Graham. "Why Basic Education?" *National Elementary Principal* 57 (October 1977): 28–32.

Fischer, John Keller. "Life Skills: What Are They?" *Social Science Record* 16 (Fall 1978): 6–8.

Postman, Neil. "Order in the Classroom!" *The Atlantic* 244 (September 1979): 35–38.

Reed, Edna. "A Nostalgic Look at Why Johnny Can't." *Contemporary Education* 50 (Fall 1978): 29–32.

Wellington, James K. "American Education: Its Failure and Its Future." *Phi Delta Kappan* 58 (March 1977): 527–30.

Wolf, Robert E. "Who Should Return to the Basics in Education?" *Contemporary Education* 50 (Fall 1978): 33–35.

Critics

Aronwitz, Stanley. "Toward Redefining Literacy." *Social Policy* 12 (September-October 1981): 53–55.

Burk, James M. "Back to Basics." *Art Education* 32 (October 1979): 4–7.

Farrell, Edmund J. "The Basics: Random Reflections on a Movement." *English Education* 9 (Summer 1978): 199–211.

Pinkey, H. B. "Public Education: Let's Not Oversimplify the Basics Through Rhetoric." *Peabody Journal of Education* 55 (July 1978): 346–50.

Rich, John Martin. "Improving the Quality of Education." *Educational Leadership* 36 (February 1979): 338–40.

Shane, Harold G. "America's Educational Futures." *1999: The World of Tomorrow,* ed. Edward Cornish. Washington, D. C.: World Future Society, 1978, pp. 105–110.

Skean, Susan. "Junior High/Middle School Back to Basics: A Personal Response." *English Journal* 69 (September 1980): 81–82.

Washburn, S. L. "Beyond the Basics: Some Future Uses of the Past." *National Elementary Principal* 57 (October 1977): 33–8.

Further Observations about Innovations and Alternatives

Those who develop an innovation may use various thought processes and procedures. Participants in school settings may have a sense of uneasiness, a feeling of frustration, or a disequilibrium that signals something is amiss. They may then formulate the problem, set up hypotheses, test the hypotheses, and then either accept or reject them. But if the innovative process is examined from the point of view of the school system, the following steps are likely: (1) establishing goals and priorities; (2) determining where changes need to be made; (3) developing a model for an innovative program or practice; (4) testing the model in a pilot program; (5) making modifications of the innovation in light of testing; (6) introducing the innovation in appropriate settings and continue to determine what further changes may be needed; (7) once the innovation has been proven successful, disseminating it to other interested parties and educational systems.

Take the case of the back-to-basics alternative. Disgruntled parents get together because of dissatisfaction over their children's academic achievement and the "pemissiveness" in schools. They formulate the problem more precisely as how to bring about greater achievement, discipline, respect for authority, and the like. And they form two hypotheses: (1) if changes are introduced in the present programs, desired outcomes are likely to result; (2) only by having a alternative program are the desired outcomes to be attained. Perhaps because of previous failures in introducing changes in existing programs, the parents select an alternative school as the most likely avenue of success. They formulate their goals and priorities more carefully by stating them in terms of greater academic achievement, character education, more disciplined behavior, and related goals. In cooperation with the school administration, a pilot program is initiated and, in light of evaluating findings, a decision is made whether the alternative should be continued in its present form, altered significantly, or discontinued altogether.

TYPES OF INNOVATIONS

The innovations presented in Part II fall into different categories. Competency testing follows a behavioral technological model. Emphasis is placed on means-end relationships and the best techniques for achieving ends. Also stressed is the study of observable behaviors that can be quantified and measured scientifically. That which cannot be studied in this fashion is either ignored, discarded, or regarded as of little importance. This model tends to examine external behavior for regularities and uniformities characteristic of a whole class rather than unique factors of the person.

Experiential education employs an inductive model in which students learn by examining particulars before arriving at generalizations. They use their senses in learning, confront the material or actual objects, learn in natural settings in the community and in the workplace, and learn by reflective activity.

Bilingual education and mainstreaming stress individual differences and a compensatory model. Certain groups of students, it is believed, have previously been neglected or the education provided has been inadequate; therefore, new provisions should be offered them in a more integrated setting.

Cognitive moral development and values clarifications use a secular rational approach in contrast to a religious approach based on faith or the authority of the church and/or sacred scriptures, or a secular approach that employs indoctrination. Cognitive moral development uses a developmental model of moral reasoning and a moral hierarchy, whereas values clarification employ exercises to get students to choose values, prize them, and act on them.

Back-to-basics, although it may be part of an alternative school plan, rests on the educational theory known as essentialism. Essentialist educators opposed progressive education practices during the 1930s and 1950s; however, today's back-to-basics movement is more of a reaction by laypersons to declining standardized test scores, insufficient achievement in the 3Rs, and a desire for greater discipline. Essentialism holds that students should learn prescribed subject matter as contained in the subject curriculum, learning should be teacher-directed, and learning involves hard work and discipline.

ASSESSING INNOVATIONS

It is important to determine the significance of an innovation, its appropriate use, and its likelihood of success. Several factors should be considered in making a full assessment of an innovation.

1. Initiator of the innovation. Was the innovation introduced by an individual, group, or organization? For instance, is a national, regional, or local organization sponsoring the innovation and how influential is the organization within the school systems in which the innovation will be introduced? As for groups, are the groups involved central or marginal to the educational system, and how open and effective are their lines of communications? If an individual, is the person part of the establishment or outside of it? For instance, look at the reformers in Part I. How would you classify them in relation to the establishment? Would it be more difficult to get their reform proposals accepted if they were not part of the establishment? But whether one is within or outside the establishment is only one factor; some of the others include the incisiveness of one's argument in favor of the innovation or alternative, one's speaking ability, access to and effectiveness in using the media, and backing by powerful public and private organizations.

2. Scope of the innovation. How many people are directly affected by the innovation? Does it affect part or all of an educational system? Does the innovation affect only schools locally or affect schools throughout the nation? For instance, tuition tax credits potentially could affect more people than programs for educating the gifted.

3. Necessity of retraining. The greater amount of retraining needed before an innovation can be used effectively, the less likelihood the innovation will be successful (other things being equal). Some may resist an innovation from fear of change or lack of confidence in their ability to acquire the newly demanded skills or serious doubts whether the innovation will actually mark an improvement over present practice. Innovations that demand little or no retraining and are easy to understand, use, and evaluate are more likely to prove successful. This is true not only for teaching but business and industry as well.

4. Testing of an innovation. The innovation needs first to be tried out to determine its likelihood of success when adapted to a wider educational setting. Some innovations may not prove viable and will have to be discontinued or modified considerably before they can be broadly accepted. A Rand Corporation study of federal education programs found that a school district's accepting funding for a project did not mean that the project would be implemented the way the federal government intended. Many projects were not implemented and the few that were did not continue the innovations after the funding ended. Moreover, innovations were not usually disseminated to other school districts. Obviously greater supervision by the Department of Education and cooperation with local districts are needed to ameliorate these conditions.

5. Support. Both adequate financial support and support from influential organizations and key individuals are needed for innovations to have the greatest likelihood of success. Some earlier innovations, such as computer-assisted instruction in the early 1970s, were quite costly; other innovations, such as programmed materials, were much less expensive. Large-scale funding alone, however, cannot assure the success of innovations, as was found in the case of certain compensatory education programs of the sixties and the curriculum reform movement that led to the new science and mathematics. Thus adequate funding is a necessary condition but not a necessary and sufficient condition.

Organizational support may be needed before an innovation may be widely accepted. In the United States, for instance, the backing of the National Education Association may mean the difference between success and failure for an innovation. Also to have an innovation supported by an influential educator provides a boost for the innovation's chances of acceptance. A boost was given to such innovations as programmed materials (from B. F. Skinner), the discovery method (Jerome S. Bruner), innovations in teacher education programs (James B. Conant), and career education (Sidney Marland).

6. Likelihood of long-term success. Education leaders are reluctant to invest funds, time, and energy in an innovation without considerable probability of success. There is no sure-fire way to ascertain the chances of long-term success; however, the factors enumerated above may prove helpful in doing so. Thus before adopting an innovation the following factors should be considered: the initiator of the innovation, scope of the innovation, the need for retraining, the testing of the innovation, and the support available.

Appendix

SOURCES FOR RESEARCH PAPERS

Encyclopedias and Research Summaries

Encyclopedia of Education. 10 vols. New York: Macmillan, 1971. Covers all aspects and levels of education in signed articles with bibliographies, including descriptions of educational systems in more than 100 countries.

Encyclopedia of Educational Research. 5th ed., 4 vols. New York: Macmillan, 1982. This considerably expanded edition features 256 signed entries and 317 contributors. Intended for professional educators and interested nonprofessionals, the entries are classified under 18 broad headings beginning with Agencies and Institutions and ending with Teachers and Teaching. Each article is followed by extensive research references.

Second Handbook of Research on Teaching, ed. by Robert M. W. Travers. Chicago: Rand McNally, 1973. Includes 42 chapters on such areas as theories and models of teaching, methods and techniques of research and development, research on special problems of teaching, and research on the teaching of school subjects.

The International Encyclopedia of Higher Education. 10 vols. San Francisco: Jossey-Bass Publishers, 1977. Includes individual articles on educational systems in 198 countries and territories, 282 articles on contemporary topics in higher education, entries about 142 fields of study, information about education associations, acronyms, and a glossary.

American Educators' Encyclopedia, ed. by Edward L. Dejnozka and David E. Kapel. Westport, Conn.: Greenwood Press, 1982. Features nearly 2,000 entries pertaining to all levels of education;

each entry averages 100–200 words, followed by a short list of references. An appendix lists federal legislation, award winners, education association presidents, and other data.

Dictionaries

Dictionary of Education, comp. Carter Good. 3rd ed. New York: McGraw-Hill, 1973. Includes 33,000 entries for English language terms and a separate section covers Canadian and British usage.

International Dictionary of Education, comps. G. Terry Page and J. B. Thomas, London: Kogan Page Limited, 1977. International in scope, the 10,000-plus entries range from the fine points of curriculum development and educational research to the colloquialisms of the classroom.

Acronyms in Education and the Behavioral Sciences, comp. Toyo Kawakami. Chicago: American Library Association, 1971. Defines acronyms from organizations, tests, periodicals, and technical terms.

Abstracts and Indexes

Education Index. New York: Wilson, v. 1-, 1929-. A monthly subject/author index in the English language that indexes over 200 journals, as well as yearbooks, proceedings, bulletins, and government documents. Its uneven coverage lists no author index from 1961–69.

Current Index to Journals in Education (CIJE). New York: Macmillan, v. 1-, 1969-. A publication in the ERIC system to cover periodical literature. It selectively indexes over 700 journals and provides separate subject and author indexes that refer readers to the annotated main entry section.

Resources in Education (RIE). Washington, D.C.: Educational Resources Information Center, v. 1–, 1966–. RIE, which is part of the ERIC system and a companion volume to CIJE, covers unpublished or limited distribution literature. It includes books, documents, reports, proceedings, papers, and curriculum material by subject, author, and sponsoring institution, and it includes abstracts of all articles listed. Many of the articles are available on microfiche.

Historical Sources

Biographical Dictionary of American Educators, ed. John F. Ohles. 3 vols. Westport, Conn.: Greenwood Press, 1978. Provides biographical information about those who have shaped American education from colonial times to 1976. Included are over 680 biographical sketches of eminent educators who had reached the age of sixty, retired, or had died by January 1, 1975.

Education in the United States: A Documentary History, ed. Sol Cohen. 5 vols. New York: Random House, 1974. Brings together significant documents extending from the 16th and 17th century European background to the earliest colonial beginnings to the present. Each volume is prefaced with an historical overview.

Statistical Sources

Digest of Educational Statistics. Washington, D.C.: U.S. Government Printing Office, 1962–. A compendium of statistics on all levels of education. It has a subject index and lists successive years of data to give historical perspective.

Standard Education Almanac. Chicago: Marquis Academic Media, 1968–. An annual almanac that provides statistical data and essays on all levels of education; it features personnel, geographic, and subject indexes and is arranged topically.

U. S. National Center for Educational Statistics. *The Condition of Education: A Statistical Report on the Condition of Education in the United States.* Washington, D.C.: U.S. Government Printing Office, 1975–. An annual compilation of text and statistics on education in relation to political, social, and demographic factors in the U.S.

World Survey of Education V: Educational Policy, Legislation, and Administration. Paris: UNESCO, 1971. Provides basic information about the educational systems of most UNESCO member countries in terms of aims and policies, administration, and the legal basis of the educational system.

Book Reviews

Education Index. New York: Wilson, v. 1–, 1929–. Book reviews drawn from over 200 journals are listed alphabetically by author in the back of each volume.

Book Review Index. Gale Research Co., 1965–. Indexes 422 periodicals in quarterly and annual cumulative editions. Periodicals indexed are primarily in social sciences and the humanities, with some in education.

Index